Systems Education for a Sustainable Planet

Special Issue Editors

Ockie Bosch
Robert Y. Cavana

MDPI • Basel • Beijing • Wuhan • Barcelona • Belgrade

MDPI

Special Issue Editors
Ockie Bosch
Keio University
Japan

Robert Y. Cavana
Victoria University of Wellington
New Zealand

Editorial Office
MDPI AG
St. Alban-Anlage 66
Basel, Switzerland

This edition is a reprint of the Special Issue published online in the open access journal *Systems* (ISSN 2079-8954) from 2014–2018 (available at: http://www.mdpi.com/journal/systems/special_issues/education_for_sustainable_planet).

For citation purposes, cite each article independently as indicated on the article page online and as indicated below:

Lastname, F.M.; Lastname, F.M. Article title. *Journal Name* **Year**, *Article number, page range.*

First Edition 2018

ISBN 978-3-03842-789-6 (Pbk)
ISBN 978-3-03842-790-2 (PDF)

Cover photo courtesy of Prof. Dr. Ockie Bosch

Although we as humans are often very small in the systems we manage, we play an enormous role on how these systems are affected and how to sustainably manage them for generations to come. Who would have thought that removing the bush for farming in Australia would lead to salinisation of very large parts of the country!
Hence the need for comprehensive systems education to help ensure the sustainability of the planet for future generations!

Table of Contents

About the Special Issue Editors

Ockie Bosch B.Sc M.Sc D.Sc Professor—Following Headship of the School of Integrative Systems for ten years at The University of Queensland, Ockie has been Leader of the internationally linked Systems Design and Complexity Management Alliance in the University of Adelaide Business School. His high international reputation is evidenced by his Vice Presidency since 2009 of the International Society for the Systems Sciences (ISSS), President of the ISSS for 2016/17 and Vice-President of the prestigious International Academy for Cybernetics and Systems Sciences. He was honoured in 2015 by Keio University in Japan as a Distinguished Guest Professor of Systems Design and Management. He has been Editor-in-Chief of Systems since April 2016, and serves on the Editorial Boards of several international journals. Professor Bosch's current activities in systemically dealing with complex issues cut across a wide range of disciplines and themes such as management, governance, environmental management, economic development, poverty alleviation and systems education. His more than 80 publications, three book chapters and a book on Systems Thinking for Everyone are evidence of his strong focus and passion to make systems sciences relevant in practice.

Robert Y. Cavana, MCom (Econ), PhD (System Dynamics), is a Reader in Systems Science with Victoria Business School, Victoria University of Wellington, New Zealand. Previously he was Corporate Economist with NZ Railways Corporation. Bob is a past President of NZ Operational Research Society, a past Vice-President of International System Dynamics Society and a former Managing Editor of System Dynamics Review. He was a NZ representative and Company Secretary on the Executive Board of Australia & New Zealand Academy of Management and is currently a Fellow of ANZAM. He received the Hellenic Society for Systemic Studies Honorary Award as "Distinguished Scientist in the Scientific area of Systems Approach" in 2009. He has published in a wide range of international journals, and is a co-author of Systems Thinking, System Dynamics: Managing Change and Complexity 2nd ed (Pearson Education, Auckland, 2007) and Applied Business Research: Qualitative and Quantitative Methods (Wiley, Brisbane, 2001; Chinese edition 2004).

Preface to "Systems Education for a Sustainable Planet"

Because the world is so highly interconnected, complexity characterises all human endeavours. The issues facing us have become increasingly complex due to the fact that they are embedded in a global web of ecological, economic, social, cultural and political processes with dynamic interactions. Such complex problems and challenges cannot be addressed and solved in isolation, or, by applying the single dimensional mindsets and tools of the past. One of the most challenging conceptual and practical issues today, for our society and economy, is to craft innovative approaches that allow us to thrive in the new world we live in. The capacity to conceptualise and redesign, in systems and sustainability terms, will increasingly be what society and employers require. This "requirement" is globally one of the biggest challenges for education. Educators have to ensure they meet the growing need for graduates, from all areas of interest, who not only have an understanding of how they fit into societal and global systems, but also know how to operate in an environment where humanity is exceeding planetary limits. Systems thinking and dynamic approaches offer a holistic and integrative way to assess the major dimensions of complex problems. Together, they contribute needed skills and knowledge to help achieve the attributes industry wants from future graduates. The demand for people that can operate within a systems-based framework and across disciplinary areas is very rapidly increasing in global society. However, it creates a significant pedagogical challenge in that the current university institutional structure tends to be focused on discipline-specific teaching, with limited scope for wider systems approaches. Didactic autonomous discipline-based courses fail to foster the social networking culture that has been proven to enhance the process of deep learning, nor do they promote interactions with other students in other disciplines. To address this problem, we need innovative curriculum designs and learning environments that address academic paradigms as well as industry requirements. This Special Issue highlights key developments in the area of systems education and how some of the many challenges are currently being addressed. The 15 articles published fall into five parts:

- The first article provides an overview and insights from this book;
- Part I includes two articles discussing the design of learning systems for systems thinking and sustainability education;
- Part II contains three articles that provide insights into various systems education programs that are available internationally at tertiary institutions;
- Part III includes three articles outlining diverse approaches to teaching systems thinking and sustainability on tertiary education courses;
- Part IV provides three articles of how systems education can be tailored to meet diverse student needs, and finally
- Part V covers three further associated topics including possible pathways for systems education for a sustainable planet.

The contributions to this issue provide an overview of both formal and informal approaches to systems education for a sustainable planet. The range and magnitude of contributions to this book illustrate the diversity of systems education practices and programs (learning systems) in the global systems community, and the relevance of systems thinking and practice to examining issues related to the long-term sustainability of the planet. As always, the quality of these articles has been greatly improved by the generous and helpful comments of a number of anonymous referees. We would like to thank all the authors and referees for these articles. We would also like to thank the staff at MDPI for their encouragement and support in producing this Special Issue volume.

Ockie Bosch and Robert Y. Cavana
Special Issue Editors

systems

MDPI

Editorial

Overview and Insights from 'Systems Education for a Sustainable Planet'

Robert Y. Cavana [1,*] and Vicky E. Forgie [2]

[1] Victoria Business School, Victoria University of Wellington, Wellington 6140, New Zealand
[2] InterlinkedThinking, Palmerston North 4140, New Zealand; vicky.forgie@gmail.com
* Correspondence: bob.cavana@vuw.ac.nz; Tel.: +64-44-635-137

Received: 25 January 2018; Accepted: 12 February 2018; Published: 13 February 2018

Abstract: An announcement by Bosch and Cavana, in Systems, called for new papers to provide updated perspectives about and fresh insights into developments that influence 'systems education for a sustainable planet'. This paper's objective is to provide an overview of the 14 papers that were published in the special issue, and present some insights and findings from their content. It does this by classifying the papers into five distinct themes, then analysing their content and the linkages between the themes. This process revealed that: (1) Specialised systems education at a tertiary level is predominantly at graduate level, using a diverse range of approaches; and (2) Delivering specialised systems education remains a challenge for programs that endeavour to provide an integrated and interdisciplinary learning experience. Barriers include current institutional structures and the need for students to be both big picture thinkers and detail-oriented technocrats; (3) Teaching systems approaches outside of specialised programs for students (both young and mature) help to expose systems thinking to a wider demographic; (4) The strong links that exist between systems approaches and sustainability goals are increasingly being recognised. Systems education can help transition towards a sustainable planet, as it helps people appreciate that individual actions are not isolated events but contribute to an interconnected system that determines both the well-being of humans and the planet.

Keywords: systems education; sustainability; learning; design; systems thinking; system dynamics; system sciences; sustainable planet

1. Introduction

The special issue of Systems—'Systems education for a sustainable planet'—provides a wealth of material on current initiatives to provide people across all age groups with systems understanding and practical knowledge. Different learning approaches are used, but the message is the same—we need to educate people to work with complexity and uncertainty if we are to progress the goal of a sustainable planet [1–15].

How things are interconnected needs to be better understood when working with sustainability goals, and, increasingly, such links are being forged. As Gregory and Miller [3] point out that sustainability and systems thinking are so intimately entwined that it is impractical to focus on one and not the other. Unravelling complex problems and searching for solutions requires understanding of pressures, drivers, causes, and the functional dynamics of the underlying systems. Wells and McLean [14] also highlight the strong link between systems and sustainability. As they say: "It is no coincidence that the contemporary champions and exponents of systems thinking have been drawn inexorably, and seamlessly, to these challenges of sustainability. Nowhere do the qualities of connectedness and complexity come more naturally to the fore than in attempts to nourish those complex living systems that both encompass human community and in which human life on earth is embedded" [14] (p. 71).

The latest Living Planet Report, which is directed at sustainability, observes: "System thinking can help us ask the right questions by examining complex problems layer by layer and then analysing the connections between these layers" [16] (p. 89). Instead of focusing on the size of a nation's Ecological Footprint, this Living Planet Report publication hones in on root causes and how solving problems in a complex world requires knowledge of the hierarchical relationship between events or symptoms, patterns or behaviours, systemic structures, and mental models. Citing the work of Cavana and Maani [17], Maani and Cavana [18], and Nguyen and Bosch [19], the report discusses the need to consider and analyse the relationships in a system to be better positioned to bring about positive change. "To understand where each of us has the greatest leverage to lead toward a systemic transition in favour of sustainable development, it is important to recognise what elements we are working on within the complex system, and that we need to adjust our mental models for problem-solving. Only then can we effect genuine and lasting change" [16] (p. 91).

The range and magnitude of the contributions to this special issue illustrate the diversity of systems education practices and programs (learning systems) in the global systems community, and the relevance of systems thinking and practice to examining issues related to the long-term sustainability of the planet. Many of the widely recognised learning approaches and methodologies applied by the systems community are referred to throughout this special issue, including, for example, the systemic inquiry approaches of C. West Churchman [20] and Peter Checkland [21]; Etienne Wenger's social theory of learning [22]; Stafford Beer's Viable System Model [23]; the Critical Systems Heuristics process of Werner Ulrich [24]; Robert Flood and Michael Jackson's System of Systems Methodologies [25]; and the system dynamics related work by Jay Forrester [26], Peter Senge [27], Dennis and Donella Meadows [28], and John Sterman [29].

Figure 1 provides a word diagram that was created from the keywords from each of the 14 special issue papers. The size of the word reflects the frequency of that word in the lists of keywords. For example, the central importance of the word 'systems' can be clearly seen, together with the other high frequency words such as education, learning, system, dynamics, thinking, design, systemic, management, sustainability, etc.

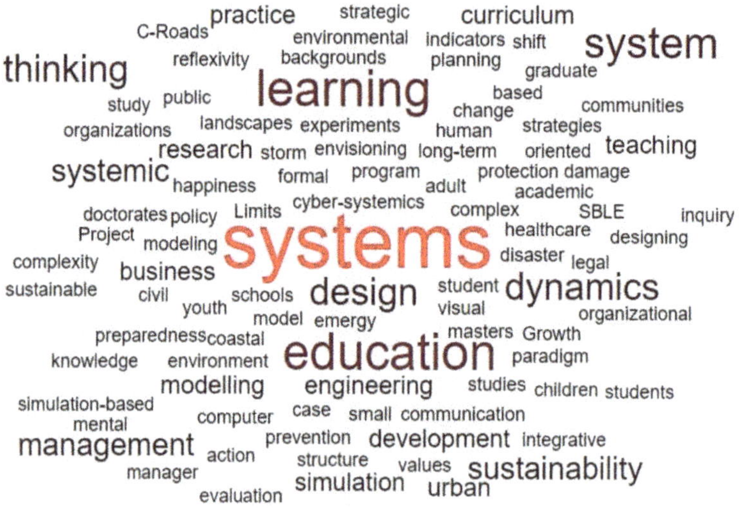

Figure 1. A Word diagram of the keywords from the 14 special issue papers.

The material provided by the authors for the special issue [2–15] discusses the current status of systems education and the extent to which the systems community is delivering on the ambition to provide a systems education for a sustainable planet. For the purposes of this paper, the 14 special issue papers have been classified into five distinct themes, as illustrated in Figure 2. While some of the papers could be classified into two or more themes, each paper has been allocated to the theme it is most closely aligned to. These themes have been identified following similar principles to content analysis as outlined in Cavana et al. [30].

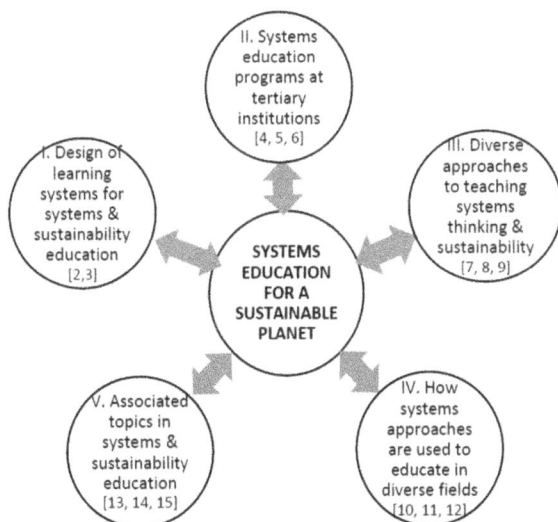

Figure 2. Theme classification of the 14 special issue papers.

In the ensuing sections, the papers within each theme are briefly discussed along with some of the main insights that emerge. Next, there is a section outlining further integrating insights and issues, followed by some concluding remarks.

2. Design of Learning Systems for Systems and Sustainability Education

The following two papers are on these themes:

Ison & Blackmore [2]—*Designing and Developing a Reflexive Learning System for Managing Systemic Change.*
Gregory & Miller [3]—*Using Systems Thinking to Educate for Sustainability in a Business School.*

Greater recognition that the problems that arise when dealing with sustainability are highly interrelated has not necessarily been accompanied by acknowledgement that managers (in health, social, environmental, cultural, business, etc., areas) need to be educated to work with complexity, as opposed to drawing tight boundaries and applying simplistic, linear solutions. As Ison and Blackmore reflect [2], in most western societies, thinking systematically remains more 'mainstream' than thinking systemically or holistically. This is despite the fact the field of cybernetics and systems has been operational for more than 50 years and systems education has been offered in higher education for over 40 years. Responding to the growing number of significant "wicked problems" and "super-wicked problems" requires an education that teaches systems thinking and practice skills [2]. Super-wicked problems according to Levin et al. [31] are greater than "wicked problems", because they have the following additional characteristics: (i) Time is running out; (ii) Those seeking to end the problem are also causing it; (iii) There is no central authority; and (iv) Policies discount the future irrationally. It is the view of Ison and Blackmore that despite the increased urgency to respond to "super-wicked" problems, higher education institutions are becoming less able to organise the inter and trans-disciplinary ways of working that are required to make progress [2].

Gregory and Miller [3] push the boundaries by challenging faculty to be critical of their own academic paradigm and associated practices. If a systems approach to teaching is to be adopted, the dominant modes of thought and practice (i.e., the existing mental models) have to be questioned. They propose that business schools embed sustainability and systems thinking theory and practice into all modules taught, because just noting the connected nature of management knowledge is not sufficient. Gregory and Miller also advocate a need to equip students to better recognise the more complex and pluralistic views of the world and expose them to the tools to address such complexities [3]. Their view that most programs include systems thinking and sustainability as 'bolt-ons' as opposed to embedding systems thinking and sustainability in an integrated way throughout the curriculum extends to most educational institutions. However, to deeply embed such concepts in a curriculum is no easy challenge. While systems thinking can provide a theoretical basis for discussions about sustainability, both systems thinking and sustainability are conceptually problematic [3]. Another major issue is the current paradigm that we operate, which has a focus on economic growth rather than sustainability. The systems thinker who guides rather than controls and employs a more systemic version of management (as per Senge [27,32]) remains less visible than the transformational, achievement-oriented individualistic leader [3].

Teaching systems thinking and system dynamics is challenging. The human mind struggles to assess the (especially unintended) consequences associated with complex, interrelated components within a system [33–35]. An evaluation of a systems theory and methodology course for graduate students undertaken by Salner [36] found that mature and intelligent students, even when instructed, could not readily grasp and apply systems concepts [2]. Expertise in systems cannot be acquired through rote learning, and the learning process is not linear [3]. A dynamic epistemic learning experience occurs, which, according to Ison and Blackmore, requires a student to progress through periods of chaos, confusion, and being overwhelmed by complexity before reaching a point at which a new conceptual understanding enables a change in their mental models. Without this change it is not possible to move to a higher level of complexity and elucidate previously unclear concepts [2].

There are other papers in the special issue that also provide examples of how different systems educators have developed courses to cement the link between working with complexity and sustainability. The Systems Science Graduate Program taught at Portland State University in Oregon, USA has four courses explicitly on sustainability, as well as others that teach the tools methods, models, and concepts that are relevant to working with sustainability [6]. At the Technische Universität München thinking systemically and applying a holistic discipline/sector-crossing assessment approach is taught as a prerequisite to developing strategies for a sustainable built environment [8]. In Sydney, Australia, Gray et al. describe a tertiary level bid to operationalise trans-disciplinary learning that propels students from learning about sustainability to active involvement in formulating solutions [9].

3. Systems Education Programs at Tertiary Institutions

Courses in system dynamics have been offered at tertiary level since the early 1970s. The Open University systems program started in 1971 [2]. Internationally, the majority of formal qualifications provided in the systems field are at the Masters or graduate level. Different learning systems have evolved to meet the requirements of a diverse cross section of students. The following papers provide an insight into the present-day benefits and challenges associated with delivering systems education programs:

Davidsen, Kopainsky, Moxnes, Pedercini, and Wheat [4]—*Systems Education at Bergen.*
Pavlov, Doyle, Saeed, Lyneis, and Radzicki [5]—*The Design of Educational Programs in System Dynamics at Worcester Polytechnic Institute (WPI).*
Wakeland [6]—*Four Decades of Systems Science Teaching and Research in the USA at Portland State University.*

The University of Bergen in Norway has been a progressive leader in building system dynamics skills and capacity across the world, teaching students from many different countries. This has been done with the establishment of an International Masters Program in System Dynamics in 1995 and a PhD program a few years later. Since 2010, an on-campus European Master Program in System Dynamics has been provided (along with 3 other European universities). System dynamics educators at the University of Bergen also run concentrated short-term courses tailored for government officials from developing countries, teach in different countries, provide on-line courses, and undertake project work that involves applying system dynamics in practice [4].

The Worcester Polytechnic Institute (WPI) is unique in that it provides a complete systems education program. This includes the B.S. in System Dynamics, Graduate Certificate, M.S., and PhD degrees in System Dynamics. There are also courses taught in system dynamics that are open to all students in the university [5]. This allows students to get an exposure to systems approaches but not a formal qualification. WPI also has a distance learning program that attracts primarily mid-career professionals who enrol in courses part-time. More than half are above the age of 35 [5].

Wakeland [6] introduces the Systems Science Graduate Program at Portland State University in Oregon, USA. This was launched in 1970 to cater for PhDs, and in the 1980s it extended to Masters and undergraduate courses. Wakeland notes that only a few of the many systems science programs created during the 1960s and 1970s still remain. Of the programs that remain in the USA, and the degree programs in Europe and Australasia, there is a strong connection with the engineering, computer science, and mathematics disciplines. There is also a practitioner focus. At Portland State University, student numbers peaked over a decade ago. While the students currently undertaking graduate study earned their bachelor's degrees in over 27 different fields, computer science, mathematics, and physics were the foremost. In the view of the systems faculty staff at the university, successful degree completion is more likely when the student has a technical background [6].

The location of systems courses within tertiary institutions influences the educational link between systems thinking and sustainability. Traditionally, many master programs in systems have been based in technical departments because, as noted by Wakeland [6], a technical background aids degree completion. There are efforts underway to change this. The Systems Science Program at Portland State University has recently been relocated in the School of the Environment within the College of Liberal Arts and Sciences, a move that will enhance the scope for students to shift in the direction of environmental concerns and sustainability-related topics [6]. The home of the European Master Program in System Dynamics at the University of Bergen is the Department of Geography [4]. At the Worcester Polytechnic Institute, the systems program is housed in the Department of Social Science and Policy Studies [5]. At the University at Albany, system dynamics is taught by the Rockefeller College of Public Affairs and Policy [7].

4. Diverse Approaches to Teaching Systems and Sustainability

Systems courses and how they are taught is a dynamic problem in itself. As Davidsen et al. [4] comment, there is a need to adapt teaching methods to meet the dynamic and increasing complexity of educational challenges. One response is to use hands-on teaching approaches. The following three papers provide examples of this:

Deegan, Stave, MacDonald, Andersen, Ku, and Rich [7]—*Simulation-Based Learning Environments to Teach Complexity: The Missing Link in Teaching Sustainable Public Management.*
Geyer, Stopper, Lang, and Thumfart [8]—*A Systems Engineering Methodology for Designing and Planning the Built Environment—Results from the Urban Research Laboratory Nuremberg and Their Integration in Education.*
Gray, Williams, Hagare, Mellick Lopes, and Sankaran [9]—*Lessons Learnt from Educating University Students through a Trans-Disciplinary Project for Sustainable Sanitation Using a Systems Approach and Problem-Based Learning.*

Deegan et al. [7] in their paper write about how a Simulation-Based Learning Environment (SBLE) was implemented in a first class on modelling methods. This class is part of the core Masters in Public Administration (MPA) program taught by the Rockefeller College of Public Affairs and Policy at the

University at Albany, New York. The authors note that SBLEs have been widely used in business education but are relatively new to public management education programs. The advantage of using a SBLE is that it compresses "the time it takes to 'experience' long-term effects of policy options and allow learners to experiment with different assumptions. Cases can be crafted to ensure that diverse stakeholders' positions are patent and visible, while simulation tools can give students the opportunity to test the effects of diverse alternative interventions" [7] (p. 220).

As part of the Energy-Efficient and Sustainable Building Masters course program at the Technische Universität München, students are taught systems analysis and how to run partial simulations. This program allows students to work with a systems model that supports decision processes. The model was constructed as part of a research project aimed at determining what makes a 'livable city', and it is used to teach students an integrative way to plan a sustainable built environment that will allow them to develop strategies for complex situations [8]. The students, who have Bachelors' degrees in either architecture or civil/environmental engineering, work together in interdisciplinary groups. A lecture series in another module (Sustainable Architecture, City, and Landscape Planning) provides sectoral views, and follow-on seminars are specifically aimed at teaching students how to bridge the sectoral views and take an integrative approach.

Gray et al. [9] describe a practical student learning experience that combines systems thinking approaches with Problem-Based Learning (PBL) interventions. PBL "is a format that encourages active participation by plunging students into a situation requiring them to define their own learning needs within broad goals set by the faculty" [9] (p. 245). As part of their course, students joined a team of researchers working on a trans-disciplinary research project. The participants were undergraduate and postgraduate students who were studying courses in a range of disciplines, and at three different universities in Sydney, Australia. PBL interventions were applied via learning platforms across pertinent aspects of (1) regulation and institutions, (2) visual communication, and (3) technology. Operationalising this applied learning experiment was not without its own PBL for both students and faculty involved [9]. It is argued that this teaching method provides an authentic learning experience bringing together a range of elements considered relevant to educating students about environmental sustainability through a systems thinking approach [9].

5. How Systems Approaches are Used to Educate in Diverse Fields

To embed systems thinking more widely in society and generate the paradigm shift to move towards the goal of a sustainable planet, new initiatives are required. The following papers provide examples of teaching and research initiatives to extend systems education into new or non-traditional areas:

Sun, Hyland and Cui [10]—*A Designed Framework for Delivering Systems Thinking Skills to Small Business Managers.*
Ronan and Towers [11]—*Systems Education for a Sustainable Planet: Preparing Children for Natural Disasters.*
Ratnapalan and Uleryk [12]—*Organizational Learning in Health Care Organizations.*

The Sun et al. paper discusses how many small business managers lack the systems thinking skills required to be sustainable in the long term. To address this short-coming, and extend systems education, the authors developed a dedicated framework for teaching students who are mostly adult learners. The course content aims to provide practical knowledge and encourages considering sustainability more broadly than purely for monetary measures [10]. Developing the framework involved a systems analysis of the needs of small business managers and applying adult learning and teaching theory. Systems skills were taught with the aid of scenarios that encapsulate situations that small business managers regularly experience.

There are known benefits associated with introducing systems education at a young age—a significant one being that the skills learned can be transferred to many future life situations. Ronan and Tower [11] investigate how hazards and disaster preparedness education programs can be taught as part of a systems-based inter-connected curricula across various ages at primary level. The authors argue that systems education has the scope to make children more resilient and reduce vulnerability by increasing physical and emotional preparedness. In addition, there is the added potential to harness the enthusiasm and motivation of children to mobilise households and communities to become more prepared [11].

The Ratnapalan and Uleryk paper discusses organisational learning in health care establishments. Organisational learning is defined as the "process of collective education in an organization that has the capacity to impact an organization's operations, performance and outcomes" [12] (p. 24). In the health sector, the use of systems approaches allows on-going education and fosters formal and informal learning across teams of people who have occupations that range from cleaners to surgeons. According to Ratnapalan and Uleryk, organisational learning is essential for managing complex interconnected systems where common background knowledge is critical for each staff member to execute their assigned functions and communicate the pertinent information needed for patient safety.

6. Associated Topics in Systems and Sustainability Education

The final three papers introduce novel ideas:

Campbell and Lu [13]—*Emergy Evaluation of Formal Education in the United States: 1870 to 2011.*
Wells and McLean [14]—*One Way Forward to Beat the Newtonian Habit with a Complexity Perspective on Organisational Change.*
Richardson [15]—*Taking on the Big Issues and Climbing the Mountains Ahead: Challenges and Opportunities in Asia.*

The concept of 'embodied energy', i.e., 'emergy', is used by Campbell and Lu to measure the inputs into education subsystems (elementary, secondary, and college/university) between 1870 and 2011 in the USA. Derived by Odum [37] emergy is an equivalence measure (quantified in one kind of available energy, e.g., solar joules) that estimates the units of energy used-up in the process of making a product or service. Campbell and Lu use emergy data to calculate the stock of knowledge in the USA based on the assumptions that (1) the emergy required for much of the information stored in human knowledge can be evaluated through an analysis of the formal education system of a nation; (2) the work performed by individuals in carrying out economic and social activities is primarily a function of their levels of education and experience; and (3) human knowledge does not diminish with use and therefore stays with an individual over their lifetime [13]. The hypothesis is that accumulated knowledge ultimately determines the kinds of economic and social activities that can be carried out within a country [13].

How systems sciences can become more persuasive in bringing about a paradigm change is covered from different angles by the final two papers in the special issue.

Wells and McLean [14] present their 'One Way Forward' model as a way to catalyse the transformational change needed for sustainability. They argue that the poor success rates achieved by current change initiatives make finding new ways of doing things an imperative. Using the 'One Way Forward' model involves unlearning previous knowledge, embracing ambiguity, and adopting an adaptive attitude that allows experimentation with what works and what does not. The One Way Forward model is a facilitated process (likened to Open Space Technology, Appreciative Inquiry, and World Café) that can be used to allow groups to work towards sustainability challenges by operationalising a whole of systems approach. The model is structured with three distinct phases that continually feedback on each other as new learning evolves. These are Envisioning (what we really want), selecting and monitoring Indicators of Progress (what we will see), and Strategic Experiments (iterative cycle of action and reflection to learn what works) [14].

Richardson [15] first describes his experience with system dynamics modelling and education in Singapore and then goes on to name three people who, in his view, respond to the call of Jay Forrester [38] to use systems approaches to "address the big issues" and get the message out:

Dennis Meadows, Junko Edahiro, and John Sterman. Each of these individuals has successfully advocated the use of systems approaches, created new knowledge, and built a public profile for the systems community [15]. Richardson then moves on to work that still needs to be done "to climb the mountains ahead". For him this work includes promoting economic dynamics, providing the visionary leadership required to capture public attention to engage with climate change (through projects such as Sterman et al.'s C-Roads [39]), and actively using system dynamics modelling to provide pathways forward for creating economies and societies that seek to maximise human well-being. This will continue the battle for political break-through that started with the "Limits to Growth" message [28].

7. Further Issues and Insights

As the focus of the special issue is 'systems education for a sustainable planet', we now move on to discuss some of the key issues observed by the different authors and new initiatives to better align systems education with current needs.

7.1. Teaching Approaches

The use of case studies that involve simulation is increasing in popularity as a teaching mode for systems education. Using integrated system dynamics models is an effective teaching tool to show how policy problems cannot be dealt with in small solvable chunks that are unconnected to broader policy and management [7]. Simulation runs can also demonstrate that multiple pathways can be taken with large and complex policy problems, and unexpected consequences can result from actions.

One of the strengths of the case study/simulation teaching method is, if well structured, it allows links to be made to material presented in other courses that students study and thereby builds a more integrated learning experience. At Rockefeller College, readings are assigned from different core classes to encourage students to cross-connect content [7]. Likewise, at the Technische Universität München the course material from another class provides the background information needed to evaluate the modelling simulation runs [8].

The use of simulation-based learning environments (SBLE) and case studies that cross different core classes can, however, be problematic for student learning. Deegan et al. [7] noted that students can struggle with too many moving pieces and keeping track of information and material provided at different time intervals and in different contexts. Deegan et al. concluded: "Overall, our impression was that the inclusion of this suite of exercises around the Pointe Claire Coastal Protection scenario considerably increased the overall complexity of, and perhaps the workload of, the class. This had the effect of bifurcating student reactions to the class with some students liking the additional sense of challenge, while others just wanted to be done with what, in the end, was just another core class they had to complete" [7] (p. 234).

Large-scale model building approaches are routinely criticised for being unmanageable and not providing outcomes able to be clearly explained. Use of SBLE and case studies for learning does place more importance on interpreting model outcomes but does not necessarily result in better understanding of the model structure and dynamics. Many of the students at Rockfeller College, despite being provided with the model equations and being required to build a simple version of the simulator as an assignment, treated the results as 'black box' [7]. To overcome the 'black box' issue, the Technische Universität München uses problem-specific partial models that the students can more readily understand and interpret. The partial model simulation is used to test alternative scenarios, answer specific questions occurring in the planning process, and provide quantified support for decision-making [8].

The combination of systems thinking and problem-based independent learning described by Gray et al. [9] had diverse learning outcomes for students. The students most happy in the cross disciplinary research project were those working within their known discipline (visual communication) and those who were seeing how this linked to the wider project goals. These students worked in teams, with students doing the same course. The students studying law who were required to move from learning about existing legislation to drafting new legislation found this step too big. The requirement to work independently with just teacher guidance was a challenging learning experience [9].

Different teaching methods are used to broaden the reach of systems education and cater for students with distinct needs. Distance learning poses a unique set of issues. On the positive side, distance learning provides educational opportunities that would not be available if class attendance was required. However, not having face-to-face personal contact can be an impediment to learning for students who enjoy interaction. A considerable amount of effort is required to overcome the disadvantages associated with lack of face-to-face personal contact. At WPI, technology is used for on-line lectures, discussion boards, releasing new material in modules, and providing virtual office hours to emulate the classroom experience. However, this requires additional resources and these need to be budgeted for [5].

7.2. Institutional Issues

"To become systems thinkers requires students to not only understand the commitments but also to be able to practice them when studying other disciplines and also in their own contexts" [3] (p. 321). When students, such as those enrolled in the Open University, study on-line, come from a wide range of backgrounds, are mature, and mostly study while working full time, it is difficult to design learning systems that connect student learning with their own context/lifeworld [2].

Embedding learning systems requires extensive changes to the usual silo student learning experience. Curricular need to be highly integrated so that material introduced at the start of tertiary education is compulsory to apply in later classes. As noted by Gregory and Miller [3], while there are now more programs with systems thinking components, very few programs infuse systems thinking throughout the curriculum. For systems thinking to occupy such an elevated position in the curriculum, a systems approach would need to be adopted at the departmental and ideally institutional levels. As most formal and non-formal education and training settings militate against emergence and self-organisation, this will require different structures and organisation than is currently found [2]. Also as Gregory and Miller highlight, to authentically engage with the challenge of embedding systems thinking and sustainability in teaching programs, both theory and practice need to be implemented in their own operations [3].

While increasing graduate expertise to use a simulation-based learning environment has the potential to extend the scope for systems approaches by, for example, engaging the public in decision making using system dynamics simulation models, there are still bridges to cross. Resources need to be made available. Teaching using SBLE requires access to faculty who are well trained in complex modelling and have access to up-to-date relevant case studies [7]. There is also a need for both the simulator and the supporting material to be thoroughly developed and tested before use [7].

7.3. Specific Demand for Students with Systems Qualifications

As noted by many authors, systems approaches still do not infiltrate most decision-making processes. Consequently, the demand for graduates with systems skills and capabilities is not strong. Ison and Blackmore [2] note the lack of institutionalised demand-pull for systems thinking expertise illustrated by the lack of advertised positions with this skill specification. Many of the students engaged in distance learning are already employed and undertake study, because they see it as an option to improve their career opportunities.

The situation appears to be different in Singapore. Richardson's explanation is: systems thinking was used by the founding political leaders to shape the political-social economy, and this has been continued by successors [15]. In Singapore, a country that is highly planned and regulated, systems thinking has become institutionalised. This has been aided by having top leaders, especially those in government, with degrees that combine science, technology, and engineering, augmented by graduate work in public administration and management. As a consequence, when system dynamics models are effectively presented, management can see their usefulness for aiding public policy and decision-making. The strong emphasis on science and technology in Singapore's secondary schools also means that students are well equipped for the technical requirements of systems modelling [15].

Despite the established need for more systems approaches to the wicked problems that society faces, there is still no strong body of empirical evidence for how to design learning experiences that equip systems thinkers for diverse roles [2], and no consensus on what the core skill set should be [5].

8. Concluding Comments

A possible explanation for the difficulties that arise with systems learning may be that educators do not teach in a way that allows a cross disciplinary team approach. There is an internal inconsistency in expecting big picture issue thinkers to be the same people as detailed technocrats. Not a lot of people have this ability. Sterman [39], in his later career, has moved in this direction, but the discipline is expecting these diverse skills in students learning at tertiary levels.

Maybe the best way to teach 'systems education for a sustainable planet' is in 'teams' as described in the PBL paper of Gray et al. [9]. Everyone in the team can work to their strength, as long as they are taught and understand the same common shared 'systems language, structure and methods' as a vehicle for working together towards shared values and objectives. For example, the social and environmental scientists can bring their understanding of the impact cause by social and environmental issues, and the engineers and mathematicians can work to their strengths building intricate models. We cannot expect the same tertiary student to be an expert in all these areas, but we can expect students to be educated to the same level of 'systems understanding' and then appreciate their strengths and limitations in working on multi-disciplinary projects with other team members.

Looking ahead, if simulation-based learning environments are as useful as the papers here suggest, building up a library of generic models that can be used for teaching across tertiary programs is an option. These can be tweaked for specific case study situations. The availability of such models will allow more time and effort to go into understanding and explaining the outcomes from a systems model. If a modeller cannot do this to a high standard, the not insignificant amount of resources and effort that go into constructing a customised model will be wasted.

This paper has drawn on the papers published in the special issue of Systems on 'systems education for a sustainable planet' for its insights and findings. There are many other sources of information and programs that teach systems education. Information on these can be found, for example, at the following websites:

International Society for Systems Sciences (ISSS)—http://isss.org/world/
System Dynamics Society (SDS)—https://www.systemdynamics.org/

Nevertheless, we highly recommend the papers in this special issue as an excellent resource for students evaluating their options for systems study or, alternatively, for any teachers/instructors wanting to establish new courses or extend existing programs. The papers collectively provide some very useful insights into how to design and deliver comprehensive systems education to better achieve a more sustainable future for the planet Earth!

Conflicts of Interest: The authors declare no conflict of interest.

References

1. Bosch, O.; Cavana, R.Y. Special Issue: Systems Education for a Sustainable Planet. *Systems* **2013**, *1*, 27–28. [CrossRef]
2. Ison, R.; Blackmore, C. Designing and Developing a Reflexive Learning System for Managing Systemic Change. *Systems* **2014**, *2*, 119–136. [CrossRef]
3. Gregory, A.; Miller, S. Using Systems Thinking to Educate for Sustainability in a Business School. *Systems* **2014**, *2*, 313–327. [CrossRef]
4. Davidsen, P.I.; Kopainsky, B.; Moxnes, E.; Pedercini, M.; Wheat, D. Systems Education at Bergen. *Systems* **2014**, *2*, 159–167. [CrossRef]

5. Pavlov, O.V.; Doyle, J.K.; Saeed, K.; Lyneis, J.M.; Radzicki, M.J. The Design of Educational Programs in System Dynamics at Worcester Polytechnic Institute (WPI). *Systems* **2014**, *2*, 54–76. [CrossRef]
6. Wakeland, W. Four Decades of Systems Science Teaching and Research in the USA at Portland State University. *Systems* **2014**, *2*, 77–88. [CrossRef]
7. Deegan, M.; Stave, K.; MacDonald, R.; Andersen, D.; Minyoung, K.; Rich, E. Simulation-Based Learning Environments to Teach Complexity: The Missing Link in Teaching Sustainable Public Management. *Systems* **2014**, *2*, 217–236. [CrossRef]
8. Geyer, P.; Stopper, J.; Lang, W.; Thumfart, M. A Systems Engineering Methodology for Designing and Planning the Built Environment—Results from the Urban Research Laboratory Nuremberg and Their Integration in Education. *Systems* **2014**, *2*, 137–158. [CrossRef]
9. Gray, J.; Williams, J.; Hagare, P.; Mellick Lopes, A.; Sankaran, S. Lessons Learnt from Educating University Students through a Trans-Disciplinary Project for Sustainable Sanitation Using a Systems Approach and Problem-Based Learning. *Systems* **2014**, *2*, 243–272. [CrossRef]
10. Sun, D.; Hyland, P.; Cui, H. A Designed Framework for Delivering Systems Thinking Skills to Small Business Managers. *Systems* **2014**, *2*, 297–312. [CrossRef]
11. Ronan, K.R.; Towers, B. Systems Education for a Sustainable Planet: Preparing Children for Natural Disasters. *Systems* **2014**, *2*, 1–23. [CrossRef]
12. Ratnapalan, S.; Uleryk, E. Organizational Learning in Health Care Organizations. *Systems* **2014**, *2*, 24–33. [CrossRef]
13. Campbell, D.E.; Lu, H. Emergy Evaluation of Formal Education in the United States: 1870 to 2011. *Systems* **2014**, *2*, 328–365. [CrossRef]
14. Wells, S.; McLean, J. One Way Forward to Beat the Newtonian Habit with a Complexity Perspective on Organisational Change. *Systems* **2013**, *1*, 66–84. [CrossRef]
15. Richardson, J. Taking on the Big Issues and Climbing the Mountains Ahead: Challenges and Opportunities in Asia. *Systems* **2014**, *2*, 366–378. [CrossRef]
16. WWF. *Living Planet Report: Risk and Resilience in a New Era*; WWF International: Gland, Switzerland, 2016.
17. Cavana, R.Y.; Maani, K.E. A Methodological Framework for Integrating. Systems Thinking and System Dynamics. In Proceedings of the ICSTM2000: International Conference on Systems Thinking in Management, Geelong, Australia, 8–10 November 2000.
18. Maani, K.E.; Cavana, R.Y. *Systems Thinking, System Dynamics: Managing Change and Complexity*, 2nd ed.; Pearson Education: Auckland, New Zealand, 2007.
19. Nguyen, N.C.; Bosch, O.J.H. A Systems Thinking Approach to identify Leverage Points for Sustainability: A Case Study in the Cat Ba Biosphere Reserve, Vietnam. *Syst. Res. Behav. Sci.* **2013**, *30*, 104–115. [CrossRef]
20. Churchman, C.W. *The Systems Approach*; Delta Books: New York, NY, USA, 1968.
21. Checkland, P.B. *Systems Thinking, Systems Practice*; Wiley: Chichester, UK, 1981.
22. Wenger, E. Communities of Practice and Social Learning Systems: The Career of a Concept. In *Social Learning Systems and Communities of Practice*; Blackmore, C., Ed.; Springer: London, UK, 2010; pp. 179–198.
23. Beer, S. *Diagnosing the System for Organizations*; Wiley: Chichester, UK, 1985.
24. Ulrich, W. *Critical Heuristics of Social Planning*; Haupt: Bern, Switzerland, 1983.
25. Flood, R.L.; Jackson, M.C. *Creative Problem Solving: Total Systems Intervention*; Wiley: Chichester, UK, 1991.
26. Forrester, J.W. *Industrial Dynamics*; Pegasus: Waltham, MA, USA, 1961.
27. Senge, P.M. *The Fifth Discipline. The Art and Practice of the Learning Organization*; Century Business: London, UK, 1990.
28. Meadows, D.H.; Meadows, D.L.; Randers, J.; Behrens, W.W., III. *The Limits to Growth*; Universe Books: New York, NY, USA, 1972.
29. Sterman, J.D. *Business Dynamics: Systems Thinking and Modeling for a Complex World*; Irwin McGraw Hill: Boston, MA, USA, 2000.
30. Cavana, R.Y.; Delahaye, B.L.; Sekaran, U. *Applied Business Research: Qualitative and Quantitative Methods*; Wiley: Brisbane, Australia, 2001.
31. Levin, K.; Cashore, B.; Bernstein, S.; Auld, G. Overcoming the tragedy of super wicked problems: Constraining our future selves to ameliorate global climate change. *Policy Sci.* **2012**, *45*, 123–152. [CrossRef]
32. Senge, P.M.; Roberts, C.; Ross, R.; Smith, B.; Kleiner, A. *The Fifth Discipline Fieldbook: Strategies and Tools for Building a Learning Organization*; Currency, Doubleday: New York, NY, USA, 1994.

33. Forrester, J.W. System dynamics, systems thinking, and soft OR. *Syst. Dyn. Rev.* **1994**, *10*, 245–256. [CrossRef]
34. Sterman, J.D. All models are wrong: Reflections on becoming a systems scientist. *Syst. Dyn. Rev.* **2002**, *18*, 501–531. [CrossRef]
35. Simon, H. Theories of Bounded Rationality. In *Decision and Organization*; McGuire, C., Radner, R., Eds.; North-Holland Publishing Company: Amsterdam, The Netherlands, 1972.
36. Salner, M. The Role of the Systems Analyst in Educational Planning. Ph.D. Thesis, University of California, Berkeley, CA, USA, 1975.
37. Odum, H.T. *Environmental Accounting: Emergy and Environmental Decision Making*; John Wiley and Sons: New York, NY, USA, 1996.
38. Forrester, J.W. System dynamics -The next fifty years. *Syst. Dyn. Rev.* **2007**, *23*, 359–370. [CrossRef]
39. Sterman, J.D.; Fiddaman, T.; Franck, T.; Jones, A.; McCauley, S.; Rice, P.; Sawin, E.; Siegel, L. Climate interactive: The C-ROADS climate policy model. *Syst. Dyn. Rev.* **2012**, *28*, 295–305. [CrossRef]

systems

MDPI

Communication

Designing and Developing a Reflexive Learning System for Managing Systemic Change [†]

Ray Ison * and Chris Blackmore

Applied Systems Thinking in Practice Research Network, Engineering & Innovation Department, MCT Faculty, The Open University (UK), Walton Hall, MK7 6AA, UK; c.p.blackmore@open.ac.uk

* Author to whom correspondence should be addressed; ray.ison@open.ac.uk; Tel.: +61-4-0430-8180.

† This paper builds on an earlier chapter "Blackmore, C.P.; Ison, R.L. Designing and Developing Learning Systems for Managing Systemic Change in a Climate Change World. In *Learning for Sustainability in Times of Accelerating Change*; Wals, A., Corcoran, P.B., Eds.; Wageningen Academic Publishers: Wageningen, The Netherlands, 2012; pp. 347–364" and a conference paper "Ison, R.; Blackmore, C. Designing and Developing a Reflexive Learning System for Managing Systemic Change in a Climate-Change World Based on Cyber-Systemic Understandings. In Proceedings of European Meeting on Cybernetics and Systems Research (EMCSR 2012), Vienna, Austria, 9–13 April 2012".

Received: 24 January 2014; in revised form: 25 March 2014; Accepted: 3 April 2014; Published: 15 April 2014

Abstract: We offer a reflection on our own praxis as designers and developers of a learning system for mature-age students through the Open University (OU) UK's internationally recognised supported-open learning approach. The learning system (or course or module), which required an investment in the range of £0.25–0.5 million to develop, thus reflects our own history (traditions of understanding), the history of the context and the history of cyber-systemic thought and praxis including our own engagement with particular cyber-systemic lineages. This module, "Managing systemic change: inquiry, action and interaction" was first studied by around 100 students in 2010 as part of a new OU Masters Program on Systems Thinking in Practice (STiP) and is now in its fourth presentation to around 100 students. Understanding and skills in systemic inquiry, action and interaction are intended learning outcomes. Through their engagement with the module and each other's perspectives, students develop critical appreciation of systems practice and social learning systems, drawing on their own experiences of change. Students are practitioners from a wide range of domains. Through activities such as online discussions and blogging, they ground the ideas introduced in the module in their own circumstances and develop their own community by pursuing two related systemic inquiries. In this process, they challenge themselves, each other and the authors as learning system designers. We reflect on what was learnt by whom and how and for what purposes.

Keywords: cyber-systemics; communities of practice; systemic inquiry; reflexivity; designing learning systems; landscapes of practice

---

1. Managing Systemic Change

Contemporary news media often refer to systemic failure as a description of a context where seemingly little can be done or as synonymous with "no one person is at fault". It would appear that there is limited appreciation that thinking based on the different traditions of systems scholarship [1,2] can be used to systemically address issues associated with change, strategy or failure. Rarely also do contemporary media accounts distinguish between systemic (relational, joined up) and systematic (linear, step-by-step) understandings and practices. In this paper, and the case we report, systems thinking/practice is conceptualized as comprising both systemic and systematic thinking/practice *i.e.*, together they comprise a whole, or duality [1]. Thinking systemically or holistically, in comparison to systematically, appears far from the "mainstream" in most western societies. This paper reports on the authors' praxis as designers of a learning system that aims to address this deficiency. It tells the story of a learning system design within the Systems Thinking in Practice (STiP) post-graduate program at the Open University, UK (OU) developed to build praxis capability in relation to the systemic issues mature students confront in their professional and personal lives. The paper is a response to the editors' invitation to contribute to this special issue; it is not a report of research designed systematically to evaluate our module and program because the resources to do so were not available to us.

The STiP program has two main foci: managing systemic change and thinking and acting strategically which are manifest as two core compulsory courses or modules. This paper primarily considers managing systemic change (OU module code TU812) but keeps in mind the strategic context. The underlying premise on which the notion of "managing systemic change" is built is that by using systems thinking in practice, it is possible to appreciate potential changes in a situation of concern that are systemically desirable and, if managed appropriately, become culturally feasible (see [3] where these ideas are explicated further). The strategic opportunity offered by TU812 is that through this combination of processes, it is possible to alter the trajectory of change.

In this paper, we will elucidate further what we mean by "managing systemic change" and why and how we have designed a learning system to develop capability to do it. Two design features are highlighted (i) systemic inquiry, action and interaction and (ii) landscapes of practices and systems praxis. A limited set of evaluative data are presented to address the question: has our learning system design been fit for purpose? To conclude we reflect on the challenges for reflexive learning system design raised by our experiences as designers. Firstly, though we explore the history of our situation and the cybersystemic understandings upon which we build.

2. Building on Cyber-Systemic Understandings

Systems education began at the OU in 1971 when John Beishon was appointed as the first Professor of Systems in the new Faculty of Technology. Beishon, leading the Systems discipline, thus faced the challenge of creating a new program of study in a form he and his colleagues were inventing as they went along, as well as drawing together conceptual and methodological material from the cybernetic and systems fields—which were then still in their infancy. From these beginnings, internationally recognised cyber-systemic teaching materials, scholarship and research and transformative learning have been produced for over 40 years. Cybersystemics is a neologism that has been coined and is useful, we argue, for breaking out of the dualism, manifest in social and organizational separations (such as different professional societies), associated with the use of systems and cybernetics concepts [4]. The 'OU provides an excellent case study of how the intellectual lineages of cybernetics and systems have been mutually influencing in the pedagogy that has been undertaken since 1971.

Beishon set the essential directions for systems teaching. Under his chairmanship, the course T241, Systems Behaviour, the first systems course, ran for 18 years from 1972–1990 with several other systems courses running in parallel and following on. In appreciating the OU context, it is important to know that a course (now called a module) currently involves an investment anywhere between 0.25 and 1 million pounds. Historically, OU courses generally settled into a 60 or 30 credit structure where one credit equates to about 10 h of study. The design praxis reported here concerns "Managing Systemic Change: Inquiry, Action and Interaction", (TU812), a 30 credit module which is one of two core modules in the STiP program. At a conservative estimate, over 30,000 students have studied Systems courses at the OU. A "student" in the Open University today has the median age of 32 and is probably in full-time employment whilst studying—students may also come from anywhere in the world though a greater percentage come from the UK and Ireland, followed by continental Western Europe. The OU is recognized internationally for its model of supported open learning; it is the largest academic institution in the UK, in terms of student numbers with "more than 240,000 students, close to 7,000 tutors, more than 1100 full-time academic staff and more than 3,500 support staff" (see [5]). A M.Sc. in the OU comprises 180 credits with the option of a 30 or 60 credit research project component.

It is possible also to obtain a PG Certificate (60 credits) or PG Diploma (120 credits) on the way to gaining a M.Sc. or as awards in their own right.

The founding rationale for the OU Technology Faculty, of combining disciplines of synthesis (systems, design) with disciplines of analysis, remains relevant today in fields such as sustainable development [6,7], innovation studies, health, engineering and organizational change and viability (e.g., [8]). Systems thinking and practice skills are in demand for addressing consistent public policy failure in response to a range of "wicked problems" [9,10] including human-induced climate change, what Levin *et al.* [11] call a "super wicked" problem. These authors attribute super-wicked problems with four additional features in addition to the 10 proposed by [12], notably: (i) "time is running out", (ii) "those seeking to end the problem are also causing it", (iii) there is "no central authority", and (iv) "policies discount the future irrationally". Despite the growing sense of urgency to respond to "super-wicked" problems, higher education institutions now seem less able to organize inter and trans-disciplinary modes to deal with the challenges such issues of global significance raise. Examples include the demise of the 17-year initiative at Hawkesbury described in [13] as well as the Systems initiative at the University of Queensland (see [14]). Nor do they seem able or willing to invest in curricula that address the growing need for cybersystemic understandings [7]. For example, complexity "managing" skills are recognized as being deficient among graduates and thus constrain UK international competitiveness [15]. King and Frick [16] describe systems thinking as a difficult skill to acquire and as not commonly taught. There are fortunately some exceptions [17]; the ISSS (International Society for the Systems Sciences) has attempted to maintain an ongoing conversation about systems education (see [18]) as has IFSR (the International Federation for Systems Research) through conversations devoted to the topic [19].

However, despite Systems education being offered in higher education for over 40 years, there is still no strong body of empirical evidence for what is required for good design of learning experiences, whether at a distance, as in the OU, or face-to-face. When faced with the challenge of designing the OU's first Master's level Systems offering in 2007, we had 36 years of accumulated experiential understanding as well as a limited number of research studies to draw upon. We review some of this research in the next section.

2.1. Exploring the Research Base

USA research evaluating a systems theory and methodology course for graduate students has shown that otherwise mature and intelligent students could not grasp and apply systems concepts [20]. This presents the systems educator with a major design challenge. If learning is considered a prerequisite for the emergence and evolution of systems thinking in practice which addresses complexity and is adaptive, then a theory of learning is required which makes sense of our actions in the world. It is also essential to track current on-going efforts to develop and teach concepts about systemic practices able to engage with complexity. This is because it is known [20–22] that personal change in epistemic assumptions is absolutely essential to any major breakthroughs in decision making based on understanding and application of emerging theories to practical problems. If, as Salner found, many people are not able to fully grasp relatively simple systemic concepts (such as non-linear processes, or self-reflexive structures), they will not be able to rethink organizational dynamics in terms of "managing" complexity or systemic change without substantial alteration in worldviews (their "applied" epistemology). Salner [22], drawing on earlier work by Perry [21,23] and Kitchener [24], describes the prevailing theory on epistemic learning as involving the deliberate breaking down and restructuring of mental models that support worldviews. According to Salner [22], Prigogine provides an additional lens on this theory in his discussion of "dissipative structures". This theory provides a model of the dynamics of epistemic learning; each learner goes through a period of chaos, confusion and being overwhelmed by complexity before new conceptual information brings about a spontaneous restructuring of mental models at a higher level of complexity thereby allowing a learner to understand concepts that were formally opaque.

Systems **2014**, *2*, 119–136

There is considerable experience of teaching systems thinking for complexity management in the UK, but it has not been well researched. As a result, it is not known how well it is done, or whether it could be done more effectively for a wider range of learners. Systems, cybernetic and complexity research are historically connected in their concern for understanding communication and control, emergence, self-organization, feedback and interconnectivity, but in learning system design terms, it is important to distinguish at the outset between learning concepts abstracted from their context and use or as part of what we at the OU call an active pedagogy *i.e.*, as part of praxis in the learner's own context/lifeworld. Over the years, we have also become aware of another important pedagogical design issue which has triggered increasing ethical concern. Developing new courses or ways of teaching may be insufficient to develop STiP competencies which are sustained if the institutional structures (e.g., promotions procedures, *etc.*) and the key relationships (the organization) of a firm where a learner is employed are inimical to the further development and testing of their mental models. Thus, we hypothesize, there is a need to consider what characteristics are most likely to be needed for the design of "learning systems" (a system where there is a high degree of connection between learner, tutor, course, work context, and academic management of the curriculum). It is possible that a learning system capable of sustaining life-long STiP competencies will require different structures and organization than is currently found in most formal and non-formal education and training settings which often militate against emergence and self-organization.

2.2. Learning System Design and Facilitation of Learning—Some General Principles

It can be argued that OU academics are designers and developers of "learning systems" rather than simply producers of courses [25,26]. Our praxis has evolved over 40 years under joint pressures of competition from other providers and new technologies for design and delivery of material and mediation of learning [27]. How we have come to understand the concept of a "learning system" and its design is outlined in Figure 1.

Following Wenger [28], we contend that learning of itself cannot be designed but social infrastructure that fosters learning can be and that there are few more urgent tasks in today's societies [29]. Ison *et al.* [26] distinguish between first- and second-order design of learning systems by applying *cybernetic* frameworks of understanding (Figure 1). First-order design is characterised by blueprints, goal-seeking behaviour and an assumption that control is possible. Second-order design contextualises whatever is designed and occurs when designers show awareness that the design setting includes themselves and their history.

In keeping with a second-order design approach, the authors/designers of TU812 began by considering their own histories and their own understandings of the system of interest of which TU812 was a part. The notion of a "trajectory" was used—a past, present and future pathway—developed by Wenger [28] to help people understand their identities in relation to a community of practice. The example of the authors' trajectories was also used to guide students to explore, and share with each other in their online forum, their own trajectories as points of entry to the module. They also concluded the module by reflecting on a particular aspect of their trajectory and how they might make changes—this concerned the extent to which they interacted with other people in their practices related to managing systemic change and the extent they might want to in future. Wenger [28] (p. 155) claims that "a sense of trajectory gives us ways of sorting out what matters and what does not, what contributes to our identity and what remains marginal" and in his later work he connects the idea of learning as a trajectory with "The concept of learning citizenship which refers to the ethics of how we invest our identities as we travel through the landscape." Thus, learning of individuals is still very much within a social context, recognising the potential of an individual to bridge communities and to help connect others to communities that will enhance their learning capability.

"For Blackmore [30] a learning system comprises interconnected subsystems, made up of elements and processes that combine for the purpose of learning. The placement of a boundary around this system depends on both perspective and detailed purpose. From a first-order perspective the design of a learning system might seemingly involve combining elements and processes in some interconnected way as well as specifying some boundary conditions—what is in, what is out—for the purposes of learning. The specification of learning outcomes (often expressed as aims and/or objectives) in the absence of any real contextual understanding about learners predisposes, or restricts, most OU distance-learning course designs to this approach. However, we and others in the OU, have in our design practice made the shift described by Bopry [31] as moving from prescription of instructional methods and means to the development of cognitive tools to provide support for the activity of the learner. With this shift we see a "learning system" as moving from having a clear ontological status (e.g., this course) to becoming an epistemic device, a way of knowing and doing (sensu Maturana—see [32]). This is consistent with Blackmore's [30] claim that appreciative systems (sensu Vickers [33]) are learning systems suggesting a design perspective that is more organic and observer dependent viz: let us consider this situation as if it were a learning system, or, in Vickers' terms. "I have found it useful to think of my life's work in terms of appreciative systems".

Reflecting this turn Russell and Ison [34,35] suggest it is a first-order logic that makes it possible to speak about, and act purposefully to design or model a "learning system". A second-order logic appreciates the limitations of the first-order position and leads to the claim that a "learning system" exists when it has been experienced through participation in the activities in which the thinking and techniques of the design or model are enacted and embodied. An implication of this logic is that a "learning system" can only ever be said to exist after its enactment—that is on reflection. The second-order perspective is not a negation of the first—they can be understood as a duality. This first to second-order shift also enables a more effective engagement with the difficult concept of "learning"."

Figure 1. Understanding a Learning System? (from Ison *et al.* [26] (p. 1344)).

3. Central Learning System Design Elements

Figure 2 is a summary from one of the designer's perspective of the overall module (*i.e.*, learning system) design for TU812 "Managing Systemic Change: inquiry, action and interaction". It is not possible here to go into detail about every feature; the module has the following administrative features: (i) it was co-designed by the authors, in conjunction with other professionals such as editors, graphic designers, specialist consultants, *etc.*, and presented for the first time in 2010 as part of a new STiP MSc; (ii) it is a 30 credit module requiring approximately 300 h of study time by mainly mature age students who study at a distance; (iii) the module is a compulsory component of two named qualifications—a Post Graduate Diploma (STiP) and M.Sc. (STiP) and can be counted towards some other awards. In the STiP qualification context, monitoring and evaluation of learning is a key part of our design principles. Three tutor-marked assignments (TMAs) and one end-of-module project-based assignment (EMA) are used to assess the module.

Figure 2. A conceptual model of a system to study how to manage systemic change using the Open University module TU812. Source: Open University [36] (p. 177).

Iterative use of a "learning contract" in successive TMAs was designed to test if students can make the shift from a systematic to a systemic design. The move from a systematic to a systemic design can be understood through the move from a tabular matrix with independent cells to a systemic diagram, such as an SSM (soft systems methodology) style activity model which encompasses connections and feedback processes. This is more than a shift in representation, though this is also needed. This evolving learning contract forms the foundation for their engagement with the course concepts so that the students' own learning needs and desires for situational transformation can be accommodated within the module context.

In the rest of this section, we address two of the main conceptual elements that were built into the module design, systemic inquiry and landscapes of practice.

3.1. Systemic Inquiry, Action and Interaction

As the module title suggests, inquiry, action and interaction are three key elements of managing systemic change. Inquiry, referred to as "systemic inquiry" in the module, (following [3,37]) is, we argue, a key form of practice for situations that are best understood as interdependent, complex, uncertain and possibly conflictual and in which there are multiple stakeholders each with their own history and perspective. Systemic inquiry, in the sense developed in this module, is also an expansion of traditional practices associated with project and program management because it assumes uncertainty and complexity as a starting point. Systemic inquiry can be seen as an antidote to living in an increasingly "projectified world" [1] and an extension of concerns with inquiry-based approaches evident in the scholarship of C. West Churchman and Peter Checkland (see [38]).

The way "action" is understood in the module is straightforward—it is about putting thinking into action to effect change, change that is systemically desirable and culturally feasible *i.e.*, it is change that is more than being just desirable or feasible. As all action is achieved through some form of practice, a key element of the module involves the learner critically exploring what systems practice is and how it can be done as well as appreciating what sort of difference it can make (this is S1 in Figure 3). In the module, students undertake two systemic inquiries; as Figure 3 depicts the course is about reflexive practice, which is more than reflective practice *i.e.*, we understand reflexivity to be a second-order practice involving reflection on reflection.

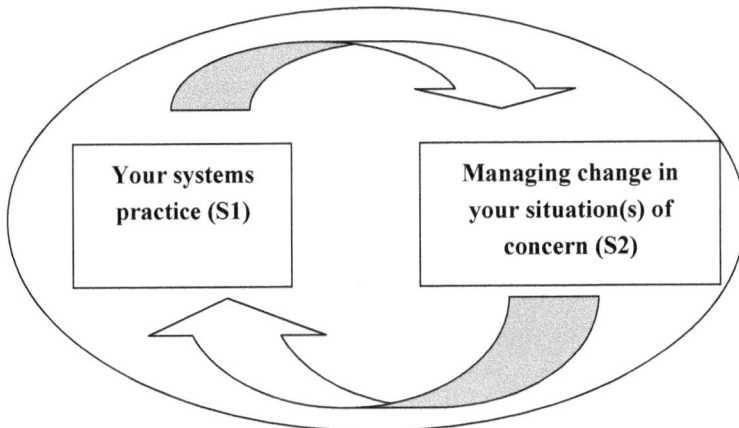

Figure 3. A virtuous cycle of inquiry in which an appreciation of systems practice (S1) when enacted can contribute to managing change in a situation or situations of concern (S2) that is systemic, at the same time as deepening understanding and practice of systems practice (S1) which can be applied in new situations (Sn). Source: Open University [36] (p. 58).

The module design starts with the practitioner and their situation (Part 1), expands to include the dynamics of practitioner, situation, frameworks and methods (Part 2) and then expands to include material that develops skills and understanding and interaction through social learning and communities of practice (Part 3). This design recognises that as more stakeholders become involved the complexity expands as do the demands for practice involving interaction of some form with others (stakeholders, clients, employees, employers *etc.*). Had our situation involved face-to-face teaching or more interactive blended learning, we would probably have started out differently.

3.2. Landscapes of Practices and Systems Praxis

Wenger's social theory of learning, elaborated in his work on Communities of Practice [28], also has interaction at its core. For Wenger, social learning is about learning in a social context and learning can be viewed as a journey through landscapes of practices (LoPs). TU812 students use the ideas of CoPs and LoPs in relation to situations of their own choice. Wenger [39], (p. 140) argues that "As learning gives rise to a multiplicity of interrelated practices, it shapes the human world as a complex landscape of practices. Each community is engaged in the production of its own practice—in relation to the whole system, of course, but also through its own local negotiation of meaning. This process is therefore inherently diverse".

The LoPs concept enables students to review their own future learning trajectories by helping them review their multi-membership of communities, recognise the multiple levels of scale with which they identified and generally providing them with a potential way of considering what they perceive beyond the communities and practices with which they most identified from their own experience. Wilding [40] reflected in her blog on what she had learned as she had taken her journey through landscapes of practices in her Open University studies. For Wilding, it was a range of concepts, methods and techniques that had made her think differently about her connections with communities of practice; "What I have also realised is that my academic studies have put me at the periphery of a number of different communities of practice. In a very formal sense I have accessed the documented know-what and know-how of that community with only incidental access to individuals from that community and then I have moved on".

Students found particularly inspiring Wenger's suggestion that " … we each have a unique trajectory through the landscape of practices. This trajectory has created a unique point of view, a location with specific possibilities for enhancing the learning capability of our sphere of participation. From this perspective, our identity, and the unique perspective it carries is our gift to the world" [41], (p. 197). An example of a TU812 student using this unique trajectory idea in reflecting on her practice comes from Wilding [42] "*I realised I'd been learning all this systems stuff and then feeling disappointed that others around me hadn't—suddenly this became my responsibility—my gift—I'm their bridge into systems practice. This is not an easy role to take on. When you are a change agent working inside an organisation, it's like a game of chess, you have to pick your moves, pick your timing and it seems that I too have to try and temper the theory*".

Blackmore [2] adapted Wenger's concept of a landscape of practices to map a landscape of systems praxis in relation to a range of focuses that authors writing about social learning identified with. Fourteen themes arose from these authors' accounts of their trajectories, multi-membership and working at multi-scale which give some idea of what learning for sustainability in times of accelerating change might look like. These themes were

(1) Institutions, organisations and institutionalising
(2) Ethics, values and morality
(3) Communication
(4) Facilitation
(5) Managing interpersonal relationships and building trust
(6) Communities and networks
(7) Levels and scale
(8) Boundaries and barriers
(9) Conceptual frameworks and tools
(10) Knowledge and knowing
(11) Transformations
(12) Time lag and dynamics of praxis
(13) Design for learning

(14) Stability, sustainability and overall purpose.

The concepts of communities and landscapes of practices have proven to be useful elements in the design of TU812 particularly as ways of conceptualising students' actions and interactions in managing systemic change in their own situations.

3.3. Fit for Purpose?—The Student Experience of TU812

In this section, we first provide evidence of impact, before discussing the evidence for student experience to date in relation to our design considerations. As outlined earlier, evidence has not, unfortunately, been gained through a comprehensive and rigorous systematic evaluation of the module or STiP program (though since beginning this paper, some funding to begin such a study has been obtained). A module at the OU is almost literally a fixed product until the course review date—in the case of TU812 the first opportunity to substantially revise course content is 2017. In the interim, as designers we have to use the feedback to hand to adjust, not substantially alter, each new presentation Evidence comes from four sources: (i) sector wide analysis in the UK; (ii) the OU's internal monitoring and evaluation procedures for all modules, including end of module surveys of students; (iii) comments from the module External Examiner, part of the UK and OU's quality control processes and (iv) qualitative data from surveys, comments within the module on-line Forum (within the OU's standardized Moodle-based virtual learning environment, or VLE) and student and alumni blogs.

3.4. Sector-Wide Positioning

It is not always easy to judge a program's performance in relation to sector wide offerings. Within UK HE data collection, TU811 and TU812 are recorded under the Business and Management subject Innovation, Enterprise and Creativity. Data prepared by Martin Reynolds for internal program review purposes show that the part-time market is small and driven by the OU. In 2006/07, the market was 4 FTEs (Full Time Equivalents) rising to 91 FTEs in 2010/11. The increase was due to the OU's entry in 2007/08. The 2010/11 data shows that the OU had 74 FTEs from a total market of 91 FTEs. The next largest provider was the University of the West of Scotland (4 FTEs). Other institutions record STiP-like qualifications under different subject categories such as Change or Strategic Management. "Systems" content is covered within many Masters in Management qualifications rather than typically as a standalone offer. For example, systems thinking and strategic modeling is a component of LSE's M.Sc. in Management qualifications. The University of Derby is offering a M.Sc. in Business and Systems Thinking (full-time) but the University of Bristol is no longer accepting students on its M.Sc. in Systems Learning and Leadership, and Northumbria has withdrawn its M.Sc. in Complex Systems Thinking and Practice. So, the STiP Award provides a unique HEI offering at PG level in the UK. Whilst some universities including the OU have a record of incorporating Systems thinking within modules associated with established disciplinary areas—typically, business studies, health studies, international development, environmental management—the OU appears to be the provider of the only accredited Masters level program in Systems Thinking.

3.5. OU Monitoring and Evaluation

Data on student registrations on TU812 are shown in Table 1 alongside registrations in the other core module for the STiP program "Thinking strategically: systems tools for managing change" (OU course code TU811). In four presentations, 365 students have registered on TU812; this is at the higher end of student registrations on PG modules offered by the MCT (Mathematics, Computing and Technology) Faculty at the OU. As shown in Table 2, 18–40% of students registering on TU812 came from outside the UK in the first two presentations, the majority being from an EU member state other than UK or Ireland. Student completion rates for TU812 ranged from 79–81% for the first two presentations (2010–11) whilst pass rates were 75–76%. These are typical of supported open learning

Systems **2014**, 2, 119–136

completion rates and may be contrasted with the recent development of MOOCs (Massive open online courses) where completion rates average about 7% and rarely exceed 25% [43].

Table 1. Data on students registering on STiP core module presentations (TU 811 and TU 812) 2010–2013 (N.B. Historically registration at the OU is module, not award based, though this is changing so data applying to each module do not necessarily apply to the same students).

Year	TU811	TU812	Total
2010	91	107	198
2011	134	83	217
2012	111	78	189
2013	110	97	207
Total	446	365	811

Table 2. Core STiP module student origins 2011–12.

Module	Presentation	Non-UK%	EU	Ireland	Outside EU
TU811	2011	31%	18%	3%	9%
TU811	2012	28%	11%	5%	12%
TU812	2011	40%	28%	4%	8%
TU812	2012	18%	15%	n/a	1%

Evidence of STiP impact to date can be seen through citations data and sales figures for the set of co-published books produced for the STiP programme (Table 3) as well as publication, including citation, data for recent scholarly publications by the STiP team and STiP graduates (e.g., [8,40,42,44]).

Table 3. Book sales (includes print sales, MyCopy sales, bulk sales and individual eBook sales—as of April 2013) and chapter downloads 6 June 2010—March 2013 of the four books co-published by the Open University with Springer (UK) for use in the STiP (Systems Thinking in Practice MSc programme).

Title	2010	2011	2012	2013	Total	
	Chapters	Chapters	Chapters	Chapters	Books	Chapters
Systems Thinkers (ST)	3344	2548	3621	574	1437	10,903
Systems Approaches (SA)	1101	1171	1499	424	1022	4195
Systems Practice (SP)	346	439	582	107	477	1474
Social Learning Systems (SLS)	969	1281	1451	406	465	4107
TOTAL					3401	20,679

With respect to annual course surveys following the 2012 presentation (completed by 61 students or 47.5%), there was positive support for the teaching support (96.6%), teaching materials (69%) and learning outcomes (85.5%). Keeping up with the workload at 62.1% did not seem highly problematic nor did study experience (69%).

3.6. External Examiner Comments

As with all HE teaching programs in the UK external examiners from within the HE sector have been appointed to independently monitor and report on quality. In the case of the OU, appointments have historically been at the level of each module. External examiners submit reports annually and module teams are expected to respond to comments as soon as practicable. The first TU812 external examiner in a final report based on four years of experience commented that: *"over* (the four years) *I have seen a steady increase in the quality of the scripts and the maturity of the program. I believe that the course is excellently run. The OU should be commended on its commitment to innovative programs of this kind."* It was said that *"the team has worked well together to build a program of high quality. There is a strong sense that this program is run by a team, unlike some programs I have seen which feel like collections of individuals with all of the disjunctures that then have to be knitted together. Staff are committed and listen to constructive feedback.*

This has led to a maturing of the program, and a high quality of output from the students". The external congratulated the team on producing and developing an excellent course and noted concerns that in limited instances, students may pass without proper engagement with the course and that courses of this nature really need to have time for good face-to-face contact. The examiner claimed that *"if the core competencies learned relate to the ability to recognise, catalyse, facilitate systemic change, then it follows that part of the training should support the facilitation skills required. Facilitation training cannot be done at a distance. So I would request that consideration be given to building this into this* program". This supports our desire where possible to build blended learning opportunities for our students.

3.7. Qualitative Sources

Feedback from qualitative sources ranges from some of the most positive and enthusiastic we have ever received as educators to feedback that is less than enthusiastic. The balancing of systems theory with practice that Wilding (ibid) refers to was also a challenge for us, the authors, in relation to TU812. Our praxis-based approach was not readily appreciated by all our students, many of whom came from quite practical engineering and technology backgrounds because of our faculty base. For some coming from more positivist traditions, having to be self-critical and to explore assumptions underlying one's own thinking and doing was a step too far. Others however felt fundamentally changed by the experience of discovering their own epistemology. TU812 became known within the OU as a "marmite" module, as students who responded to requests for feedback tended to either love it or hate it (mimicking the advertising campaign for the well known yeast extract spread found in many households in the UK). We found that those students whose views on the module were in the mid-range rarely offered us detailed feedback. For example, in the 2012 annual survey, the module did not appear to meet all students' expectations (rated at 46.4% which is below average). This can be explained in part based on the background research in the area of systems/teaching/learning which suggests that a bimodal response amongst students is likely.

Posting to the module VLE (virtual learning environment) on 3 April 2012, a thread exemplifies a very positive response:

" ... ... I took the PFMS model [a conceptual model of practice comprising practitioner, framework of ideas, method and situation] to take a snapshot on what has happened with my framework of ideas, my methods and myself by engaging in the TU812 module. It was nice to take in the shifts I made and to realize how much easier it is to work with this model than the first time I looked at it.

I can only concur with K's statement in his posting ... ... "I can conclude already now that I am not the same person any more than I was before I started this module. And while all people are changing all the time, I experience this module as a catalyst for personal change. Without studying this module, I wouldn't be undergoing such a fundamental, mind-opening change in such a short time. That's a very satisfying experience."

Thank you K, for your well-chosen words (so authentic Description: wink). Thank you TU812 team and fellow students here at the course forum for such a wonderful module ... ... ".

Another posting to the VLE in December 2013 from a "student" recently retired from a mining multi-national exemplifies the potential for personal, systemic transformation offered by TU812. In this instance, the person had studied systems, especially SSM, early in his career:

"Anyway, my thinking is going along these lines now, i.e., that systemic inquiry is "always appropriate", either as the opening gambit and/or as the end game. All my "systems" activities for the last 20–30 (i.e., post "soft"), have taught me that in many cases where a system has "failed", it has been because the "system design" did not address the right problem, or had not explored the problem in sufficient depth. Thus, in my practice (gained from the "virtuous circle" process), I have, as far as possible, tried to ask "is this the right problem" or, "are (we) asking the right question". Asking these questions has to be systemic, as I see it, because of the uncertainty (i.e., we don't

know the answer at this stage). This process is holistic and usually quickly leads you (to) a point where you can say with a lot less uncertainty that this (is) a "difficulty" and can be dealt with systematically or this is messy/wicked/whatever and will require a much more rigorous inquiry. Having given it a bit more thought (maybe even at home), this is the point at which you have to go to your "paymaster" and try to convince him/her that the benefits that will accrue from a properly constituted and resourced inquiry will be cost-effective. Then it's out of your hands".

Our OU experience of systems education points to a range of issues that confront the would-be systems educator. Perhaps the most significant is the lack of institutionalised demand-pull for STiP skills and capabilities e.g., through advertised posts, capability and skills frameworks; professional success narratives and the like.

4. Challenges for Reflexive Learning System Design

If the future of our climate-changing world is unknowable, there is a need to take more responsibility for systemic effects of human actions [6]. This reflection shows how this can be done through designing and participating in learning systems that generate effective systems practice. Our design for a coupled system—student and context—has realised many of its design ambitions—but has also come with certain costs in that it alienates some students and the OU standard evaluation processes are not sensitive to our design ambition. As we go forward we face challenges regarding how far we can go with this design without for instance more face-to-face elements and keeping to a generic form of STiP rather than tying it into one sector or another e.g., health, environmental management, *etc.*

Our module and program raises the challenge of praxis rather than just the theory or practice and this in turn raises questions about the epistemological issues at the heart of systems education, pressures in some quarters to move to more utilitarian methods and tools-based teaching and the nature of evaluation where transformative learning is the ambition. The former Centre for Systemic Development (University of Western Sydney, Hawkesbury) (e.g., [13,45–47]) as well as Systems educators at the OU have tried to incorporate what is known about making epistemic change happen for people, and it has been done in the past with encouraging short term results as far as we know (e.g., [48–50]). What is lacking is any longer term (and longitudinal) check on the degree to which learning that we can "see" is being utilized and further developed in practical situation improvement in organizations. However, the failure to embed STiP in contemporary organizational life can be seen as a form of institutional failure as much as a failure in learning system design [10,51]. There is a strong case to return to the ambition articulated by Erich Jantsch [52] and examine why his vision of the systems-based transdisciplinary university has failed to materialize. This is particularly so as his vision remains relevant today [5,29].

A research program to address these concerns is needed and under development at the OU. Our reflections demonstrate that the purposeful design of a second-order learning system in which reflexivity is an emergent outcome is possible—*i.e.*, students can carry out simultaneously the two inquiries described in Figure 3, and thus think about thinking as well as design their designing. As evidence of the transformative potential of our module and program, readers are invited to read Helen Wilding's reflections on her study of the module TU812 and the other core module in the STiP program (Thinking strategically—TU811) (see [53]). The emergence of a self-organising and enthusiastic LinkedIn on-line community of 394 STiP alumni can be seen as testimony to the impact of our program. In the context of the theme for this special issue of Systems Education for a Sustainable Planet, recent discussion threads by STiP alumni have included: the Circular Economy; Innovation for a complex world; and multiple threads about systems praxis.

In the context of sustainability and transformative education, much still needs to be learnt about the relationship between knowledge, learning and action [54,55] and the institutional settings that are conducive to innovative forms of praxis. Many models and frameworks have been developed that help to conceptualise this relationship (see [17]) including some of those included in TU812. Our experience with TU812 affirms earlier experiences we have had that when engaged with rigorously within an

Systems **2014**, 2, 119–136

appropriately designed learning system, systems thinking and practice can orchestrate effective, reflexive, transdisciplinary praxis. Our experience shows that it is possible to transcend disciplinary background, domain of concern as well as cultural background to facilitate the emergence of profound learning relevant to managing our co-evolutionary futures. In our human circumstances, more investment in learning systems of this nature seems warranted.

Acknowledgments: The authors thanks the editors of this special edition for the invitation to contribute, the comments of reviewers and the Managing Editor for help with manuscript preparation. All TU812 student quotes are used with permission.

Author Contributions: Equal contributions by both authors.

Conflicts of Interest: The authors declare no conflict of interest.

References

1. Ison, R.L. *Systems Practice: How to Act in a Climate—Change World*; Springer: London, UK, 2010.
2. Blackmore, C. *Social Learning Systems and Communities of Practice*; Springer: London, UK, 2010.
3. Checkland, P.B.; Poulter, J. *Learning for Action*; John Wiley & Sons: Chichester, UK, 2006.
4. Ison, R.L. Cybersystemic conviviality: Addressing the conundrum of ecosystems services. *Cybern. Human Knowing* **2011**, *18*, 135–141.
5. The Open University in Facts and Figures. Available online: http://www.open.ac.uk/about/main/the-ou-explained/facts-and-figures (accessed on 24 January 2014).
6. Blackmore, C.P.; Ison, R.L. Designing and Developing Learning Systems for Managing Systemic Change in a Climate Change World. In *Learning for Sustainability in Times of Accelerating Change*; Wals, A., Corcoran, P.B., Eds.; Wageningen Academic Publishers: Wageningen, The Netherlands, 2012; pp. 347–364.
7. Ison, R.L.; Bawden, R.D.; Mackenzie, B.; Packham, R.G.; Sriskandarajah, N.; Armson, R. From Sustainable to Systemic Development: An Inquiry into Transformations in Discourse and Praxis. In *Systemic Development: Local Solutions in a Global Environment*; Sheffield, J., Ed.; ISCE Publishing: Litchfield Park, AZ, USA, 2008; pp. 231–252.
8. Robinson, D.T. Introducing managers to the VSM using a personal VSM. *Kybernetes* **2013**, *42*, 125–139. [CrossRef]
9. *Tackling Wicked Problems: A Public Policy Perspective*; Australian Public Service Commission (APSC): Canberra, Australian, 2007.
10. Seddon, J. *Systems Thinking in the Public Sector*; Triarchy Press: Axminster, UK, 2008.
11. Levin, K.; Cashore, B.; Bernstein, S.; Auld, G. Overcoming the tragedy of super wicked problems: Constraining our future selves to ameliorate global climate change. *Policy Sci.* **2012**, *45*, 123–152. [CrossRef]
12. Rittel, H.W.J.; Webber, M.M. Dilemmas in a general theory of planning. *Policy Sci.* **1973**, *4*, 155–169. [CrossRef]
13. Wals, A.E.J.; Bawden, R.J. *Integrating Sustainability into Agricultural Education. Dealing with Complexity, Uncertainty and Diverging Worldviews*; Interuniversity Conference for Agricultural and Related Sciences in Europe (ICA), Universiteit Gent: Gent, Belgium, 2000.
14. Nguyen, N.C.; Bosch, O.J.H. The art of interconnected thinking—Starting with the young. *Systems* **2014**. submitted for publication.
15. Robertson, D. The emerging political economy of higher education. *Stud. Higher Educ.* **1998**, *23*, 221–228. [CrossRef]
16. King, K.S.; Frick, T. Systems Thinking: The Key to Educational Redesign. Presented at the Annual Meeting of the American Educational Research Association, Montreal, Canada, 19 April 1999; Available online: https://www.indiana.edu/~tedfrick/aera99/transform.html (accessed on 24 January 2014).
17. Bosch, O.J.H.; Nguyen, N.C.; Maeno, T.; Yasui, T. Managing complex issues through evolutionary learning laboratories. *Syst. Res. Behav. Sci.* **2013**, *30*, 116–135. [CrossRef]
18. International Society for the Systems Sciences. Available online: http://isss.org/world/SIG-call-for-papers (accessed on 24 January 2014).

19. Bosch, O.J.H.; Drack, M.; Horiuchi, Y.; Jones, J.; Ramage, M. Informing the Development of Systems-Oriented Curricula at the University Level: The Systems Education Matrix. International Federation for Systems Research. Proceedings of the Fourteenth Fuschl Conversation, Fuschl, Austria, 29 March–3 April 2008; Available online: http://ifsr.ocg.at/world/node/45 (accessed on 24 January 2014).

20. Salner, M. The Role of the Systems Analyst in Educational Planning. Unpublished Doctoral Dissertation, School of Education, University of California, Berkeley, CA, USA, 1975.

21. Perry, W.G. Cognitive and Ethical Growth: The Making of Meaning. In *The Modern American College*; Chickering, A., Ed.; Jossey-Bass: San Fransisco, CA, USA, 1981; pp. 76–116.

22. Salner, M. Adult cognitive and epistemological development in systems education. *Syst. Res.* **1986**, *3*, 225–232. [CrossRef]

23. Perry, W.G. *Forms of Intellectual and Ethical Development in the College Years—A Scheme*; Holt, Rinehart and Winson: New York, NY, USA, 1970.

24. Kitchener, K.S. Cognition, metacognition and epistemic cognition: A three level model of cognitive processing. *Hum. Dev.* **1983**, *26*, 222–232. [CrossRef]

25. Ison, R.L. Supported Open Learning and the Emergence of Learning Communities. The Case of the Open University UK. In *Creating Learning Communities. Models, Resources, and New Ways of Thinking about Teaching and Learning*; Miller, R., Ed.; Solomon Press: Brandon, FL, USA, 2000; pp. 90–96.

26. Ison, R.L.; Blackmore, C.P.; Collins, K.B.; Furniss, P. Systemic environmental decision making: Designing learning systems. *Kybernetes* **2007**, *36*, 1340–1361. [CrossRef]

27. Ison, R.L. The Design of "Learning Systems": Experiences from the Open University, UK. In Proceedings of the Towards an Information Society for All 2—New Pathways to Knowledge Conference, Berlin, Germany, 8–9 March 2002.

28. Wenger, E. *Communities of Practice*; Cambridge University Press: Cambridge, UK, 1998.

29. Bosch, O.J.H.; Nguyen, N.C.; Sun, D. Addressing the critical need for "New Ways of Thinking" in managing complex issues in a socially responsible way. *Bus. Syst. Rev.* **2013**, *2*, 48–70. [CrossRef]

30. Blackmore, C. Learning to appreciate learning systems for environmental decision making—A "Work-in-Progress" perspective. *Syst. Res. Behav. Sci.* **2005**, *22*, 329–341. [CrossRef]

31. Bopry, J. Convergence toward enaction within educational technology: Design for learners and learning. *Cybern. Human Knowing* **2001**, *8*, 47–63.

32. Maturana, H.; Poerkson, B. *From Being to Doing. The Origins of the Biology of Cognition*; Carl-Auer: Heidelberg, Germany, 2004.

33. Vickers, G. *Human Systems are Different*; Harper & Row: London, UK, 1983.

34. Russell, D.B.; Ison, R.L. The Research-Development Relationship in Rural Communities: An Opportunity for Contextual Science. In *Agricultural Extension and Rural Development: Breaking out of Traditions*; Ison, R.L., Russell, D.B., Eds.; Cambridge University Press: Cambridge, UK, 2000; pp. 10–31.

35. Russell, D.B.; Ison, R.L. Designing R&D Systems for Mutual Benefit. In *Agricultural Extension and Rural Development: Breaking out of Traditions*; Ison, R.L., Russell, D.B., Eds.; Cambridge University Press: Cambridge, UK, 2000; pp. 208–219.

36. *TU812 Managing Systemic Change: Inquiry, Action and Interaction*; Study Guide; Open University: Milton Keynes, UK, 2010.

37. Churchman, C.W. *The Design of Inquiring Systems: Basic Concepts of Systems and Organisations*; Basic Books: New York, NY, USA, 1971.

38. Ramage, M.; Shipp, K. *Systems Thinkers*; Springer: London, UK; The Open University: Milton Keynes, UK, 2009.

39. Wenger, E. Conceptual Tools for CoPs as Social Learning Systems: Boundaries, Identity, Trajectories and Participation. In *Social Learning Systems and Communities of Practice*; Blackmore, C., Ed.; Springer: London, UK, 2010; pp. 125–144.

40. Wilding, H. My Journey through a Landscape of Practices. Just Practising: My Trials and Tribulations as a Systems Practitioner. 2011. Available online: http://helen.wilding.name/2011/03/07/my-journey-through-a-landscape-of-practices/ (accessed on 24 January 2014).

41. Wenger, E. Communities of Practice and Social Learning Systems: The Career of a Concept. In *Social Learning Systems and Communities of Practice*; Blackmore, C., Ed.; Springer: London, UK, 2010; pp. 179–198.

42. Wilding, H. The Launch. Just Practising: My Trials and Tribulations as a Systems Practitioner. 2011. Available online: http://helen.wilding.name/2011/06/01/the-launch/ (accessed on 24 January 2014).

43. Parr, C. Mooc Completion Rates "Below 7%" Times Higher Education 9 May, 2013. Available online: http://www.timeshighereducation.co.uk/news/mooc-completion-rates-below-7/2003710.article (accessed on 24 January 2014).

44. Bailey, A. Once the capacity development initiative is over: Using communities of practice theory to transform individual into social learning. *J. Agr. Educ. Ext.* **2013**. [CrossRef]

45. Macadam, R.; Packham, R. A case study in the use of soft-systems methodology: Restructuring an academic organisation to facilitate the education of systems agriculturists. *Agr. Syst.* **1989**, *30*, 351–367. [CrossRef]

46. Bawden, R. Creating Learning Systems: A Metaphor for Institutional Reform for Development. In *Beyond Farmer First: Rural People's Knowledge, Agricultural Research and Extension Practice*; Scoones, I., Thompson, J., Chambers, R., Eds.; Intermediate Technology: London, UK, 1994; pp. 258–263.

47. Bawden, R.J. *Systemic Development: A Learning Approach to Change*; Occasional Paper #1; Centre for Systemic Development, University of Western Sydney: Hawkesbury, Australia, 1995.

48. Peters, G. On Systems Methodology. In *Improving the Human Condition: Quality and Stability of Social Systems*; Ericson, R., Ed.; Springer: New York, NY, USA, 1979.

49. Clarke, A.; Costello, M.; Wright, T. *The Role and Tasks of Tutors in Open Learning Systems*; Industrial Training Research Unit, Lloyds Bank: Cambridge, UK, 1985.

50. Blackmore, C.; Carr, S.; Corrigan, R.; Furniss, P.; Ison, R.L.; Morris, R.M. Environmental Decision Making—A Systems Approach. In Proceedings of the Second Australasian Systems Conference, University of Western Sydney, Hawkesbury, Australia; 1998.

51. Caulkin, S. Kittens are Evil': Heresies in Public Policy. 2013. Available online: http://www.simoncaulkin.com/article/406/ (accessed on 24 January 2014).

52. Jantsch, E. Inter- and transdisciplinary university: A systems approach to education and innovation. *Policy Sci.* **1970**, *1*, 403–428. [CrossRef]

53. Discovering a Landscape of Research Practice. Available online: http://helen.wilding.name (accessed on 24 January 2014).

54. *Knowledge, Learning and Societal Change*; Final Draft—Science Plan for a Cross-Cutting Core Project of the International Human Dimensions Programme on Global Environmental Change; International Human Dimensions Programme (IHDP): Bonn, Germany, 2011.

55. Blackmore, C. What kinds of knowledge, knowing and learning are required for addressing resource dilemmas? A theoretical overview. *Environ. Sci. Pol.* **2007**, *10*, 512–525. [CrossRef]

systems

MDPI

Article

Using Systems Thinking to Educate for Sustainability in a Business School

Amanda Gregory [1],* and Susan Miller [2]

[1] Business School, University of Hull, Hull, HU6 7RX, UK
[2] Business School, Durham University, Durham City, DH1 3LB, UK; s.j.miller@durham.ac.uk
*   Author to whom correspondence should be addressed; a.j.gregory@hull.ac.uk.

Received: 26 March 2014; in revised form: 18 June 2014; Accepted: 20 June 2014; Published: 11 July 2014

Abstract: This paper explores what it means for a business school to embed systems thinking and sustainability into the curriculum by looking at both the application of systems thinking to the design of sustainable programmes and the teaching of system thinking to support understanding of sustainability. Although programmes that include systems thinking and sustainability as "bolt ons" are becoming more common, how these may best be integrated throughout the curriculum is still largely unexplored. In this paper, curriculum design is viewed through the lens of Stafford Beer's Viable System Model; viewing the management curriculum in this way emphasises the essential interconnectedness of the subject matter rather than its reduction into blocks of knowledge that are containable within standard size teaching modules. Merely recognising the interconnected nature of management knowledge does not go far enough, though, and there is a complementary need to equip students with approaches for describing more complex and pluralistic views of the world and to address such complexities. In this paper, the specification of a module, underpinned by Flood and Jackson's System of Systems Methodologies, that might serve to achieve these ends by introducing business students to a range of systems approaches is discussed. The challenges that realizing such an undertaking in practice might involve are also reflected on.

Keywords: systems thinking; sustainability; education; curriculum design; business schools

1. Introduction

The debate about the role of business schools (used throughout this paper as a catch all term for deliverers of management education in the higher education sector) in society is a recurring one (see, for example [1,2]) and the recent financial crisis brought a new dimension to the debate [3,4]. As business schools educate the CEOs and managers of organizations that, through their operations, have effects that fundamentally impact on ecological, economic and social sustainability, it seems logical that the role of business schools should reflect a concern for sustainability in its broadest sense. Indeed, it has been suggested that ethics and sustainability should become core threads running through the curriculum in business schools [5] but there are "genuine concerns about business schools and their inability to come to terms with the sustainability agenda, despite different initiatives to nudge them towards that direction; society and social issues mean little or nothing in mainstream business education, which is unashamedly steeped in the narrow pursuit of economic performance" [6]. Cross-cultural theories of management might suggest that such an orientation is a consequence of the top ranking business journals all being published in the US and dominated by scholars based in the same country, and research into textbooks used in business schools also shows an Anglo-American dominance [7–9]. Consequently, notions of the transformational, achievement-oriented and personally rewarded leader abound while more systemic versions of management are scarcer; a popular, early exception being the work of Senge [10] on the learning organization. In the last five or so years, much work has been undertaken in the areas of responsible management education [11–14] and critical management education [15–19] although both are still largely represented in the curriculum as an alternative perspective or a beyond the mainstream view.

With relatively few exceptions, e.g., [20–24], systems thinking does not seem to have impacted on higher education in general and business schools and graduate schools of management in particular, despite it being well established [25–32] that systems thinking has much to contribute to sustainability discourses and applications. Increasingly, though, there is recognition that systems thinking provides a theoretical basis for discussions about sustainability and that both should command a place in the business school curriculum. Barter and Russell [33] analyse two key United Nations publications, Our Common Future [34] and the 25 year update of Resilient People: Resilient Planet [35], which, they argue, bring forward understanding of systemic thinking and responsible leadership. In highlighting "the key protagonists for enabling sustainable outcomes as business leaders and corporate strategists" who should "accept new responsibilities, as are congruent with an expanded understanding of the impact of organizational actions on a systemically interconnected world" [33], Barter and Russell place systems thinking prominently in the management education curriculum. In similar vein, Zsolnai *et al.* [36] redefine the roles and duties of management and management education to include, amongst other priorities, sustainability and holistic problem solving.

In light of the above, it may be surmised that, if business schools are to come to terms with the sustainability agenda, they need to embrace a more systemic perspective. Such a change would require a holistic understanding of the concept itself (there are many ways of being systemic) and also the questioning of what sustainability means from different perspectives. Indeed, Wals and Jickling [37] suggest that sustainability as a concept is "flawed" and that recognizing this is important since "Students must be in the position to examine critiques of scientism and technical rationality, and related life styles. If our universities and colleges do not facilitate this, then they basically fail to involve them in one of the biggest political challenges of our time" (p. 223). Hence, it is important to recognize that systems thinking and sustainability are both conceptually problematic and, consequently, to deeply embed such concepts in a business school curriculum is no easy challenge. If business schools are to really engage with this challenge then they need to understand systems thinking and sustainability in theory and practice by not only teaching about both but also applying the theory to their own operations.

This paper initiates an exploration of what it means for a business school to embed systems thinking and sustainability into the curriculum in a dynamic environment that is currently exploring what both mean. The focus is primarily on using systems thinking to understand and, if deemed desirable, achieve sustainability as it is assumed that the former is a necessary prerequisite for the latter. It is recognised that there are many aspects of "being systemic" that a business school might address but, given that the scope of this paper is already broad, some of these are, for pragmatic reasons, being regarded as beyond its scope. For example, it is recognized that the question of how business schools deliver is an important issue that impacts on sustainability but it falls outside the scope of this paper; although the work of Bawden *et al.* [38] on pedagogy is acknowledged as being particularly relevant. It is realized that this paper could be criticized for being too partial in focus while, at the same time, being criticized for being too ambitious in seeking to look at both the application of systems thinking to the design of programmes and the teaching of system thinking to support understanding of sustainability. It is believed that the two are too intimately entwined to focus on one and not the other and this should be evident if these concerns are summarily discussed:

- The design challenge

It is increasingly acknowledged that it is not sufficient to adopt a reductionist rationale to programme design and merely "bolt on" subjects in response to unfolding events [39]. This is particularly the case with respect to the teaching of ethics and sustainability where there is a need to inculcate a capacity in students to look holistically at business and ask questions about whether business is "doing the right things". Paul Danos, dean of Dartmouth College's Tuck School of Business, refers, in recognition of such a need, to the development of "deep courses where students are forced into that skeptical mindset of truly questioning … " [3]. Although programmes that infuse such thinking skills throughout the entire curriculum are becoming more common, how such integration may be achieved is still a largely underexplored area. In this paper, this issue is primarily viewed through a design lens although alternative lenses, such as the political, are considered highly relevant.

Business schools bring together academics from different disciplinary backgrounds ranging from the so-called "hard" disciplines [40] which seek to build knowledge cumulatively based on the scientific method, to the "soft" which are more focused on critiquing existing knowledge and paradigm plurality [41]. Non-specialist undergraduate business management programmes, postgraduate programmes such as the MBA, and masters in management which cover multiple functional areas of business are where such disciplines collide often resulting in a theoretical and political minefield which students, very often confused by the variety of different paradigm perspectives, are expected to negotiate. To be clear though, it is not merely a superficial truce, involving the artificial integration of different subject areas, that is required for the sake of simplicity; rather, the need to expose contrasting, even conflicting, perspectives, to recognise that even what counts as valid knowledge may be contested, and to do this in a way that is meaningful for both students and staff. Systems thinking has the potential to bring such understanding about but acceptance that systems thinking should have such an elevated position, some might argue, when space in the curriculum is hard won, not only with academic colleagues but also with students [42,43], is not easy to establish. Atwater *et al.* [21] reflect on this in terms of the systems archetype, the tragedy of the commons, with the limited resource being credit hours and recommend that systems be introduced in a required class early in the curriculum and students should then be encouraged or required to apply them in subsequent modules in other functional disciplines. A similar approach to Atwater *et al.* is suggested in this paper and this leads to the second issue of this paper, what to include in a module on systems thinking and how to embed learning from such a module throughout the curriculum.

- The curriculum content challenge

It has been argued that the nature of the business and management curriculum masks the essential interconnectedness of the subject matter [44], overemphasising the analysis of individual parts of firms at the expense of an appreciation of the integrative nature of organizational systems as a whole [45]. As a consequence of such a silo-based approach, there is a danger of the partial and narrow analyses of complex problems [46], amenable to simplistic solution-seeking. However it can be argued that simply recognising the messy systemic nature of problems [47] does not go far enough and it also needs to be acknowledged that such problems are open to multiple interpretations about their causes, consequences and possible solutions. The inclusion of systems thinking in the curriculum should enable students to move beyond questioning unitary interpretations and describing more complex and pluralistic views of the world, to enabling them to express their own personal concerns rooted in their local contexts and equip them with approaches to address such complexities.

Atwater *et al.* argue that " … people must be trained in the principles, concepts, and tools of systemic thinking in order to understand and work effectively with and within complex social systems." [21] (p. 13) and focus on causal loop mapping [48], a process whereby a visual representation is produced of how the variables in a system are connected, as an important approach in enabling understanding of how structure drives behavior. Such an approach is a particularly relevant technique when it comes to environmental management and sustainability but there is a wider range of systems approaches which are concerned with forms of complexity other than structural, such as economic, political and social complexity. Indeed, this wider range of approaches demand attention if Atwater *et al.*'s own ambition is to be realized and, in this paper, a module that serves to introduce business students to a range of systems approaches is described.

It should be clear from the above, that this is an exploratory paper and it is intended that the concerns that are raised will be the subject of further work. In the next section, discussion will be made of the use of viable system theory [49–51] for the design and management of curriculum content and an overview provided of a module on systems approaches.

2. Utilizing Systems Thinking in Curriculum Design

If the potential for systems thinking in the business school context is to be realized its practical utility needs to be demonstrated; curriculum design represents an opportunity to do this. Stafford Beer's [49–51] Viable System Model (VSM) is presented as a "thorough working out of ideas from the science of organisation, or cybernetics" [52] (p. 87) but can the VSM be meaningfully applied to programme design? Can programmes be designed to be sustainable learning systems in themselves, capable of responding to changes in their environments that could not be foreseen at the point of creation?

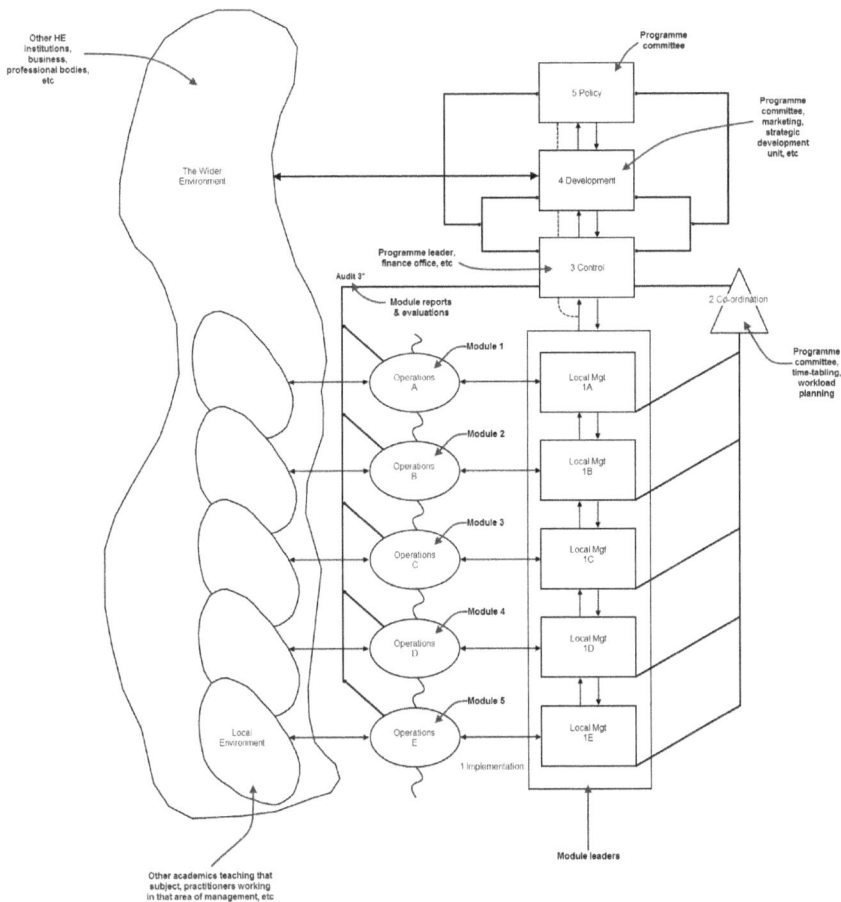

Figure 1. A programme portrayed as a viable system.

Programmes are multi-dimensional in nature and should be viewed holistically (as an emergent whole—the programme) rather than simply being seen as the sum of the parts (a collection of modules). A systems perspective acknowledges that one module will be limited in terms of what it enables

Systems **2014**, 2, 313–327

students to see, but a programme that is informed by systems thinking should facilitate, through its design, students' ability to learn by reflecting on the links between the parts (modules) in order to better understand multi-dimensional issues, such as how to balance development with sustainability, that are beset with multiple interpretations. The conceptualization of a programme in this way focuses attention on how learning "spaces" [53] can be created in which both students and staff are encouraged to focus on the differences and links between modules.

The need for integrating mechanisms is not the only concern in programme design. The sustainability of programmes and their ability to remain relevant and current suggests a concern for content management particularly given the dynamic and changing nature of management knowledge. The logic of the VSM suggests that a programme should be viewed as a structure of unfolding complexity: with different levels of recursion, for example, from the university to the module level and each level absorbs variety from its local environment accordingly. This is important because the VSM is fundamentally based on the notion of maximum autonomy of the parts within the cohesive whole which in such an application is accommodating of dynamic and flexible approaches to content and teaching reflecting the different paradigmatic assumptions and approaches within subject areas.

Focussing at the programme level, the "system in focus", Figure 1 sets out the necessary functions (Systems 1 to 5 which are Operations, Co-ordination, Control, Development, and Policy) and communication flow/feedback loops between these:

- System 1, Operations, activities directly relate to the system's reason for being. In Figure 1 the Operations are the modules that make up the programme. Each of these has its own localized management or module leaders and own localized relations with the outside world (for example the accounting and finance module leader is expected to interact with practitioners and academics in that profession). The only restriction to the autonomy of System 1 (the module) is the requirement that it function as part of the whole (the programme) and the module leader would receive confirmation of their goals and objectives from System 5 (the programme committee), refined into targets (learning objectives), to ensure that they are complementary to the objectives of the wider systems (the programme and beyond) of which they are a part.
- To ensure that the modules are not destabilized by the others acting in a silo way (for example, duplication of content and balance of assessment methods) the modules are Co-ordinated by System 2 (multiple co-ordinating mechanisms including the informal, e.g., coffee shop chats between module leaders, and formal, e.g., programme committee meetings).
- The modules are intermittently subject to audit by System 3* (the programme leader) and routinely report on performance to System 3, Control, which is also responsible for reviewing budget proposals and allocating resources in accord with current policies and priorities.
- System 4, Development, brings together the programme leader, the marketing team and strategic development unit to synthesise internal information with information about the wider environment of the programme such as benchmarking against other institutions' offerings. System 4 must have a good grasp of what is going on internally if it is to capture relevant external information. If a rapid change or response is required then information is channeled to the Control function (programme leader) or if there is information that is longer term in nature then this goes to System 5, Policy (the programme committee).
- System 5 formulates policy on the basis of information received from System 4 and communicates this downward through System 3 for implementation. System 5 (the programme leader representing the programme committee) must also articulate the identity and purposes of the programme to the wider system (the programme portfolio) of which it is a part.

It may be deduced from the above summary that the VSM balances a variety of competing pulls on any system; not only top-down *versus* bottom-up but also the internal demand for balance, System 3, with the outward and future oriented pulls expressed through System 4.

The above example demonstrates that it is possible to use the VSM as a heuristic device; to encourage critical thinking about how programmes and modules are designed and managed, especially:

- ensuring the appropriate engineering of variety [54] e.g., that the programme leader focus on information relevant to the whole and does not get overwhelmed by detail at the module level while giving autonomy to the parts (modules and their leaders) to ensure that decisions are taken at the most appropriate level;
- considering necessary co-ordination mechanisms, integrative spaces and information flows;
- establishing the distinctiveness of the programme through a strong awareness of the identity of the whole.

It is also worth noting that if a university has multiple campuses where it offers its programmes, perhaps at home and overseas, then it may also be useful to see System 1 parts as different locations in which the programme is offered as this ensures that attention is paid to local conditions/cultures.

3. Systems Thinking as Curriculum Content

In this section a module will be described which aims to educate business school students in the concepts, methodologies and commitments of systems thinkers in order that they might better understand and work effectively for sustainability with and within complex social systems themselves.

The content and form of such a module is driven by the definition of appropriate learning outcomes, such as to:

- promote the need for a systems approach through their reflection on important complex issues such as sustainability not only in theoretical terms but also their own experiences of "messes" [47];
- apply different systems methodologies and to be aware of their acceptability and utility in different contexts of application;
- appreciate the partiality of any approach.

In delivering such a module, attention would have to be given to providing a map of the systems terrain which enlightens rather than confuses; to this end, Jackson's [55] extended version of Jackson and Keys' [56] "system of systems methodologies" (SoSM) (see Figure 2) can be usefully employed. Such a simplified "map" is a useful teaching device at the start of such a module but once students get deeper into systems thinking its limitations become increasingly evident and they may be encouraged to critique it. The framework illustrates that problems cannot all be typified in the same terms and whilst it may be viewed as being able to contribute to real life problem solving it does not represent real life.

PARTICIPANTS

	Unitary	Pluralist	Coercive
Simple	FUNCTIONALIST Systems Analysis; Systems Engineering; Operational Research	INTERPRETIVIST Strategic Assumption Surfacing and Testing	EMANCIPATORY Critical System Heuristics
Complex	STRUCTURALIST Lean Systems Thinking, Socio-Technical Systems, System Dynamics, and Organizational Cybernetics	INTERPRETIVIST Soft Systems Methodology	POSTMODERN SYSTEMS APPROACHES Participatory Appraisal of Needs and the Development of Action

(left margin vertical label: S Y S T E M S)

Figure 2. A version of the system of systems methodologies with example approaches.

The SoSM enables the range of systems approaches, reflecting different paradigmatic underpinnings, to be appreciated and these are summarised here:

- The first attempts to apply systems ideas to problem solving began about the time of the Second World War, with approaches such as operational research, systems analysis and systems engineering (collectively referred to as the "hard systems approaches" reflecting their positivist underpinnings). These approaches may be useful in contexts where optimizing the effectiveness and efficiency in achieving agreed goals is paramount [55].
- Drawing heavily on Forrester's work on System Dynamics [57], Senge [10] presented Systems Thinking as an approach for enabling managers to understand how structure can drive system behaviour thus enabling managers to understand how a system comes to be in its present state (such an approach has been used to significant effect in public policy work, see for example, [58,59]).
- Lean Systems Thinking (LST), for example [60], focuses on eradicating failure demand and improving the ability of the system as a whole to enhance the customer experience. LST emphasises the need to create an evidence base and impetus for change by working through the stages of "check" (understand the organization as a system), "plan" (identify levers for change), and "do" (take direct action on the system).
- Strategic Assumption Surfacting and Testing (SAST) [61] relinquishes the functionalism of hard systems thinking for a more interpretivist orientation and the ill-structured nature of problem situation is explicitly recognised. SAST is concerned with "wicked problems" (characterised by interconnectivity, conflict, and uncertainty) debated from opposing perspectives and culminating in their resolution through a higher level of understanding.
- Critical Systems Heuristics (CSH) [62], following the work of Churchman [63], is concerned with identifying and addressing organizational and societal inequities brought about through the exclusion of certain stakeholders from decision making processes. The value assumptions which lead to such exclusionary behaviour are often presented as given hence CSH seeks to expose them to question. Thus, this approach offers a more critical and potentially emancipatory perspective.
- Participatory Appraisal of Needs and the Development of Action (PANDA), Taket and White [64] established the nature of intervention in postmodern form. This approach emphasises multiple

Systems **2014**, 2, 313–327

interpretations of the world, being tolerant of difference and the importance of being responsive to what is achievable at the local level.

Merely having a good understanding of the systems methodologies is necessary but not sufficient for good systems practice as developing a deep appreciation of the underpinning philosophy, encapsulated in three commitments [55], is equally, perhaps more, important:

- critical awareness relates to the critique of the different systems methodologies and social awareness of the societal and organizational context;
- improvement relates to the achievement of "something beneficial" reflecting a circumspect aspiration in the light of the postmodernist challenge to the notion of universal liberation;
- pluralism recognizes the need to work with multiple paradigms without recourse to some artificial "unifying" metatheory; the ability to use methods disconnected from the paradigm of their genesis but with an awareness of the paradigm that they are being used to serve, and the existence of other ways of being pluralistic, for example Mingers and Brocklesby's multi-methodology [65].

To become systems thinkers requires students to not only understand the commitments but also to be able to practise them when studying other disciplines and also in their own contexts. Such a requirement is similar to that addressed by Giving Voice to Values (GVV) pedagogy [66–73] and learning may be derived from this. The focus of GVV is essentially systemic with faculty members "guiding a discussion of feasible applications of the core principles of their respective disciplines and on knowing how to act in a responsible way in a given context" [73] (p. 59). Such a focus is similar to that of Grey, Knights and Willmott [74] (p. 100) who argue that a critical approach should start with the students' own lived experience and this might be regarded as fundamental to the design of the assessment on any systems-based module or programme. Schwandt's work on integrating learning with sensemaking [75] (p. 189) may be drawn on in requiring students to describe their own problem situations, which forces them to reflect on their experience of complexity. Given the multicultural nature of the student body of many business schools, much may be learnt through this process of reflection about the practical applicability of systems methodologies in different contexts. For example, a group might question whether rich pictures, a technique used in Soft Systems Methodology [76,77], would be acceptable in religions that declare that there should be no portrayal of a person's image.

In describing their own situations, students are required to think about what they are prioritising and what they are down-playing in order to justify their choice of methodology (of course, theoretically this might be done through the SoSM). Although such a form of module assessment may focus on the application in detail of one systems methodology, it also gives students the opportunity to recognize that once they have used a methodology there may be a need to shift to another; enabling understanding of the demands of complexity and pluralism to be demonstrated. Systems thinking sees value in all the different developed and emerging systems approaches, viewing them as a complementary set, capable of being used in combination to address the real world complexity, heterogeneity, ambiguity and paradox that means that no one approach alone is sufficient to address. A multi-methodogical approach is advocated to cope with complexity that is inevitable when addressing grand challenge issues such as sustainability. Such an approach therefore utilizes a variety of developed and emerging systems approaches and methodologies that are based on opposing paradigms. The contradictory nature of their underlying philosophical assumptions means that they cannot simply be integrated so the approach seeks to manage paradigm diversity by encouraging them to confront one another on the basis of "reflective conversation" [78,79]. No methodology is allowed to escape unquestioned because it is continually confronted by the alternative rationales offered by others. The preferred way of working [80] is to observe a continuous commitment to methodological pluralism by working with "dominant" and "dependent" methodologies in creative combination. For example, CSH and SSM might be used in a complementary and iterative way to decide, firstly, who ought to be involved in a particular intervention and to bring that group together to explore the problem situation

Systems **2014**, *2*, 313–327

and, secondly, this might then involve further boundary critique and questioning of who ought be involved as SSM supports stakeholders in seeing different parts of the problem situation. Pollack [81] calls this a "parallel" approach to multi-methodology as opposed to a "serial" approach. Working with seemingly incommensurable methodologies in this way (CSH having emancipatory underpinnings which contrast to the interpretivist underpinnings of SSM) goes some way towards mirroring the challenges of paradox and contradiction inherent in the messy and multi-faceted problems of the real world and using a range of theoretical perspectives to reflect on practice. There is a rich stream of literature that provides useful instruction on the challenges that such a critical form of systems thinking and practice brings (see for example, [82,83]).

4. Reflections

> *"A significant obstacle to sustainability becoming more embedded into the business school ethos is that a major mind-shift away from academic traditions is required for this to become a reality".* [6]

The idea that accepted dominant modes of thought and practice should be challenged is central to a systems approach. Embedding a systemic approach in the curriculum represents an opportunity to not only challenge students to be critical but also for faculty to challenge themselves to be critical about being critical (following [84,85]). How far are faculty prepared to be critical of their own academic paradigm and associated practices? The process of questioning what is acceptable may lead to far greater awareness of where the boundaries lie, what is amenable to change and what is not, which highlights the relevance of the political lens. Such considerations extend beyond the local faculty context to, in the UK, the external examiner (an academic at another institution who is responsible for assuring the academic quality of a module or programme) and professional accrediting bodies who can be either a major facilitator of or impediment to change. It is intended that further work will look through a political lens at the issue of how negotiations are managed about what is regarded as relevant knowledge for inclusion in the business school curriculum and the consequent inclusion, or not, of sustainability and systems thinking.

5. Conclusions

In this paper, the argument was advanced that sustainability and systems thinking must be regarded to be a complementary set; concern for one without the other is necessary but not sufficient. Systems theory provides the theoretical basis for discussions about sustainability and sustainability provides an important concern of practical relevance for systems thinking. To understand the implications of embedding either in the curriculum is no small feat and it is necessary to not merely seek to "bolt on" these subjects to the curriculum but rather to apply the logic of both to our own endeavors. This paper initiated such an undertaking by exploring what it means for a business school to promote a concern for the sustainability of programmes through the application of systems thinking to their design. In this paper, curriculum design was viewed through the lens of the VSM. Viewing the management curriculum in this way, emphasises the essential interconnectedness of the subject matter rather than the reduction of the curriculum into blocks of knowledge that are containable within standardized teaching modules. Merely recognising the messy systemic nature of management knowledge does not go far enough, though, and it was recognized that there is an associated need to equip students with approaches for describing more complex and pluralistic views of the world, and enable them to address such complexities. In this paper, the specification of a module that serves to introduce business students to a range of systems approaches was described. Learning from such a systems module might feasibly be enthused throughout an entire programme as it is carried through to other modules by requiring students to view the functional areas of management in holistic terms. It is recognized that the recommendation for systems thinking to occupy such an elevated position in the curriculum heralds a mind-shift, and although programmes that include systems thinking in the curriculum are becoming more common, programmes that infuse systems thinking throughout the curriculum are still rare and how this might best be achieved is still largely unexplored. Finally, it was proposed that, if a more holistic and searching approach to business and management issues is to be achieved, it is necessary that the negotiation between faculty, students and other stakeholders, such as those responsible for ensuring the quality of management education programmes, be viewed through a political lens as such negotiations focus on the question of what is regarded as valuable knowledge and what is not. In conclusion, this paper takes up the challenge of addressing what is required for a concern for systems thinking and sustainability to be embedded in business schools; as a result of this exploration it should be recognized that this is a grand challenge that needs to be pursued, to quote Churchman [63], in a collective "heroic mood".

Acknowledgments: The authors would like to express their gratitude to the guest editors of this special issue of Systems and the reviewers who provided very helpful constructive feedback on earlier drafts of this paper. We would also like to thank Grace Lu for her patience and support.

Author Contributions: Both authors contributed equally to the initial development of ideas and thinking in relation to the paper. Amanda Gregory then worked on the development of the paper with Sue Miller commenting on drafts which gave led to the further elaboration of key arguments expressed in the paper.

Conflicts of Interest: The authors declare no conflict of interest.

References

1. Mintzberg, H. *Managers not MBAs*; Berrett-Koehler Publishers: San Francisco, CA, USA, 2004.
2. Cornuel, E. The role of business schools in society. *J. Manag. Dev.* **2005**, *24*, 819–829. [CrossRef]
3. The Economist. How do Business Schools Remain Relevant in Today's Changing World? 1 December 2009. Available online: http://www.economist.com/node/15006681 (accessed on 26th June 2014).
4. Podolny, J.M. The buck stops (and starts) at business school. *Harv. Bus. Rev.* **2009**, *87*, 62–67.
5. Rayment, J.; Smith, J. The current and future role of business schools. *Education + Training* **2013**, *55*, 478–494.
6. The Guardian. Business Schools: "The Silent but Fatal Barrier to the Sustainability Agenda". 13 March 2014. Available online: http://www.theguardian.com/sustainable-business/business-schools-deadly-sustainability-agenda (accessed on 15th May 2014).
7. Engwall, L. The anatomy of management education. *Scand. J. Manag.* **2007**, *23*, 4–35. [CrossRef]
8. Fougère, M.; Moulettes, A. Disclaimers, dichotomies and disappearances in international business textbooks: A postcolonial deconstruction. *Manag. Learn.* **2012**, *43*, 5–24. [CrossRef]
9. Engwall, L. Foreign role models and standardisation in Nordic business education. *Scand. J. Manag.* **2000**, *15*, 1–24. [CrossRef]
10. Senge, P.M. *The Fifth Discipline. The Art and Practice of the Learning Organization*; Century Business: London, UK, 1990.
11. UN Global Compact. The Principles for Responsible Management Education. 2007. Available online: http://www.unprme.org/resource-docs/prme.pdf (accessed on 26 March 2014).
12. Rabasso, C.A.; Rabasso, J. A Chomskyan approach to responsible critical management education. *J. Global Responsib.* **2010**, *1*, 66–84.
13. Kaul, M.; Smith, J. Exploring the nature of responsibility in higher education. *J. Global Responsib.* **2012**, *3*, 134–150. [CrossRef]
14. Wilcox, T.; Sheldon, P.; Wardrop., J. A capabilities approach to curriculum design: Developing responsible business professionalism. *Int. Rev. Bus. Res.* **2012**, *8*, 107–117.
15. Alvesson, M.; Willmott, H. *Critical Management Studies*; Sage: London, UK, 1992.
16. Clegg, S.; Kornberger, M.; Carter, C.; Rhodes, C. For management? *Manag. Learn.* **2006**, *37*, 7–27. [CrossRef]
17. Spicer, A.; Alvesson, M.; Kärreman, D. Critical performativity: The unfinished business of critical management studies. *Hum. Relat.* **2009**, *62*, 537–560. [CrossRef]
18. Clegg, S.; Dany, F.; Grey, C. Special issue critical management studies and managerial education: New contexts? New agenda? *Management* **2011**, *14*, 271–279.
19. Alvesson, M.; Spicer, A. Critical leadership studies: The case for critical performativity. *Hum. Relat.* **2012**, *65*, 367–390. [CrossRef]
20. Bui, H.T.M.; Baruch, Y. Learning organizations in higher education: An empirical evaluation within an international context. *Manag. Learn.* **2012**, *43*, 515–544.

21. Atwater, B.J.; Kannan, V.R.; Stephen, A.A. Cultivating systemic thinking in the next generation of business leaders. *Acad. Manag. Learn. Educ.* **2008**, *7*, 9–25. [CrossRef]

22. Atwater, B.J.; Pittman, P.H. Facilitating systemic thinking in business classes. *Decis. Sci. J. Innovat. Educ.* **2006**, *4*, 273–292.

23. Waddock, S. Finding wisdom within: The role of seeing and reflective practice in developing moral imagination, aesthetic sensibility, and systems understanding. *J. Bus. Ethics Educ.* **2011**, *7*, 177–196.

24. Werhane, P.H. Mental models, moral imagination and system thinking in the age of globalization. *J. Bus. Ethics.* **2008**, *78*, 463–474. [CrossRef]

25. Capra, F. *The Web of Life—A New Synthesis of Mind and Matter*; Harper Collins: London, UK, 1996.

26. Capra, F. *The Hidden Connections: A Science for Sustainable Living*; Harper Collins: London, UK, 2003.

27. Gregory, A.J.; Atkins, J.; Burdon, D.; Elliott, M. A problem structuring Method for eco-system based management: The DPSIR framework. *Eur. J. Oper. Res.* **2013**, *227*, 558–569. [CrossRef]

28. Ison, R. *Systems Practice: How to Act in a Climate Change World*; Springer: London, UK, 2010.

29. Midgley, G.; Reynolds, M. Systems/operational research and sustainable development: Towards a new agenda. *Sustain. Dev.* **2004**, *12*, 56–64. [CrossRef]

30. Nguyen, N.C.; Graham, D.; Ross, H.; Maani, K.; Bosch, O. Educating systems thinking for sustainability: Experience with a developing country. *Syst. Res. Behav. Sci.* **2012**, *29*, 14–29. [CrossRef]

31. Nguyen, N.C.; Bosch, O.J.H. A systems thinking approach to identify leverage points for sustainability: A case study in the Cat Ba Biosphere Reserve, Vietnam. *Syst. Res. Behav. Sci.* **2013**, *30*, 104–115.

32. Paucar-Caceres, A.; Espinosa, A. Management science methodologies in environmental management and sustainability: Discourses and applications. *J. Oper. Res.Soc.* **2011**, *62*, 1601–1620. [CrossRef]

33. Barter, N.; Russell, S. Two snapshots reinforcing systemic thinking and responsibility. *J. Global Responsib.* **2014**, *5*, 45–54. [CrossRef]

34. World Commission on Environment and Development. *Our Common Future*; Oxford University Press: Oxford, UK, 1987.

35. United Nations Secretary—General's High Level Panel on Global Sustainability. *Resilient People, Resilient Planet: A Future Worth Choosing*; United Nations: New York, NY, USA, 2012.

36. Zsolnai, L.; Junghagen, S.; Tencati, A. Redefining the roles and duties of management. *J. Global Responsib.* **2012**, *3*, 121–133. [CrossRef]

37. Wals, A.E.J.; Jickling, B. "Sustainability" in higher education: From doublethink and newspeak to critical thinking and managingful learning. *Int. J. Sustain. High. Educ.* **2002**, *3*, 221–232. [CrossRef]

38. Bawden, R.; McKenzie, B.; Packham, R. Moving beyond the academy: A commentary on extra-mural initiatives in systemic development. *Syst. Res. Behav. Sci.* **2007**, *24*, 129–141. [CrossRef]

39. Arkin, A. School for Scandal. In *People Management*; CIPD: London, UK, 2013.

40. Neumann, R.; Parry, S.; Becher, T. Teaching and learning in their disciplinary contexts: A conceptual analysis. *Stud. High. Educ.* **2002**, *27*, 406–417.

41. Lattuca, L.; Stark, J. Will disciplinary perspectives impede curricular reform? *J. High. Educ.* **1994**, *65*, 401–426. [CrossRef]

42. Thompson, T.A.; Purdy, J.M. When a good idea isn't enough. Curricular innovation as a political process. *Acad. Manag. Learn. Educ.* **2009**, *8*, 188–207. [CrossRef]

43. Rubin, R.S.; Dierdorff, E.C. On the road to abilene: Time to manage agreement about MBA curricular relevance. *Acad. Manag. Learn. Educ.* **2011**, *10*, 148–161. [CrossRef]

44. Pfeffer, J.; Fong, C.T. The end of business schools? Less success than meets the eye. *Acad. Manag. Learn. Educ.* **2002**, *1*, 78–95. [CrossRef]

45. Zald, M.N. Spinning disciplines: Critical management studies in the context of the transformation of management education. *Organization* **2002**, *9*, 365–385. [CrossRef]

46. Ghoshal, S. Bad management theories are destroying good management practice. *Acad. Manag. Learn. Educ.* **2005**, *4*, 75–91. [CrossRef]

47. Ackoff, R.L. The art and science of mess management. *Interfaces* **1981**, *11*, 20–26. [CrossRef]

48. Maani, K.E.; Cavana, R.Y. *Systems Thinking, System Dynamics: Managing Change and Complexity*, 2nd ed.; Pearson Education NZ: Auckland, New Zealand, 2007.

49. Beer, S. *Heart of Enterprise*; Wiley: Chichester, UK, 1979.

50. Beer, S. *Brain of the Firm*, 2nd ed.; Wiley: Chichester, UK, 1981.

51. Beer, S. *Diagnosing the System for Organizations*; Wiley: Chichester, UK, 1985.
52. Flood, R.L.; Jackson, M.C. *Creative Problem Solving: Total Systems Intervention*; Wiley: Chichester, UK, 1991.
53. Beyes, T.; Michels, C. The production of educational space: Heterotopia and the business school. *Manag. Learn.* **2011**, *42*, 521–536. [CrossRef]
54. Ashby, W.R. *An Introduction to Cybernetics*; Methuen: London, UK, 1956.
55. Jackson, M.C. *Systems Approaches to Management*; Kluwer/Plenum: London, UK, 2000.
56. Jackson, M.C.; Keys, P. Towards a system of systems methodologies. *J. Oper. Res. Soc.* **1984**, *35*, 473–486. [CrossRef]
57. Forrester, J.W. *Industrial Dynamics*; MIT Press: Cambridge, MA, USA, 1961.
58. Cavana, R.Y.; Clifford, L.V. Demonstrating the utility of system dynamics for public policy analysis in New Zealand: The case of excise tax policy on tobacco. *Syst. Dynam. Rev.* **2006**, *22*, 321–348. [CrossRef]
59. *Munro Review of Child Protection Part One: A Systems Analysis*; Department for Education: London, UK, 2010.
60. Seddon, J. *Freedom from Command and Control: A Better Way to Make the Work Work*; Vanguard Education Ltd.: Buckingham, UK, 2003.
61. Mason, R.O.; Mitroff, I.I. *Challenging Strategic Planning Assumptions*; John Wiley and Sons: Chichester, UK, 1981.
62. Ulrich, W. *Critical Heuristics of Social Planning*; Haupt: Bern, Switzerland, 1983.
63. Churchman, C.W. *The Systems Approach*; Delta Books: New York, NY, USA, 1968; (reprinted 1979).
64. Taket, A.; White, L. *Partnership and Participation: Decision-Making in the Multiagency Setting*; Wiley: Chichester, UK, 2000.
65. Mingers, J.; Brocklesby, J. Multimethodology: Towards a framework for mixing methodologies. *Omega* **1997**, *25*, 489–509. [CrossRef]
66. Gentile, M.C. A faculty forum on giving voice to values: Faculty perspectives on the uses of this pedagogy and curriculum for values-driven leadership. *J. Bus. Ethics Educ.* **2011**, *8*, 305–307.
67. Chappell, S.; Webb, D.; Edwards, M. A required GVV ethics course: Conscripting ethical conversations. *J. Bus. Ethics Educ.* **2011**, *8*, 308–319.
68. Warnell, J. "Ask more" of business education: Giving voice to values for emerging leaders. *J. Bus. Ethics Educ.* **2011**, *8*, 320–325.
69. Trefalt, S. Integrating giving voice to values across the MBA curriculum: The case of Simmons School of Management. *J. Bus. Ethics Educ.* **2011**, *8*, 326–331.
70. Stumpf, S.A. Engaging MBAs in voicing values through peer coaching. *J. Bus. Ethics Educ.* **2011**, *8*, 332–336.
71. Arce, D.G. Giving voice to values in economics and finance. *J. Bus. Ethics Educ.* **2011**, *8*, 343–347.
72. Adkins, C.P. A pathway for educating moral intuition: Experiential learning within the giving voice to values curriculum. *J. Bus. Ethics Educ.* **2011**, *8*, 383–391.
73. Gentile, M. The holy grail: Educating for values-driven leadership across the curriculum and giving voice to values. *Global Focus.* **2014**, *8*, 56–59.
74. Grey, C.; Knights, D.; Willmott, H. Is a Critical Pedagogy of Management Possible? In *Rethinking Management Education*; French, R., Grey, C., Eds.; Sage: London, UK, 1996.
75. Schwandt, D.R. When managers become philosophers: Integrating learning with sensemaking. *Acad. Manag. Learn. Educ.* **2005**, *4*, 176–192. [CrossRef]
76. Checkland, P.B. *Systems Thinking, Systems Practice*; Wiley: Chichester, UK, 1981.
77. Checkland, P.; Poulter, J. *Learning for Action: A Short Definitive Account of Soft Systems Methodology and its Use, for Practitioners, Teachers and Students*; John Wiley and Sons: Chichester, UK, 2006.
78. Gregory, W.J. Discordant pluralism: A new strategy for critical systems thinking? *Syst. Pract.* **1996**, *9*, 605–625.
79. Jackson, M.C. *Systems Thinking: Creative Holism for Managers*; Wiley: Chichester, UK, 2003.
80. Jackson, M.C. Towards coherent pluralism in management science. *J. Oper. Res. Soc.* **1999**, *50*, 12–23. [CrossRef]
81. Pollack, J. Multimethodology in series and parallel: Strategic planning using hard and soft OR. *J. Oper. Res. Soc.* **2009**, *60*, 156–167. [CrossRef]
82. Brocklesby, J. Becoming Multi-Methodology Literate: An Assessment of the CognitiveDifficulties of Working Across Paradigms. In *MultiMethodology—The Theory and Practice of Combining Management Science Methodologies*; Mingers., J., Gill, A., Eds.; Wiley: Chichester, UK, 1997; pp. 189–216.

Systems **2014**, *2*, 313–327

83. Midgley, G. *Systemic Intervention: Philosophy, Methodology, and Practice*; Kluwer/Plenum: New York, NY, USA, 2000.
84. Mingers, J. What is it to be critical? Teaching a critical approach to management undergraduates. *Manag. Learn.* **2000**, *31*, 219–237.
85. Reynolds, M. Reflection and critical reflection in management learning. *Manag. Learn.* **1998**, *29*, 183–200.

systems

MDPI

Communication

Systems Education at Bergen

Pål I. Davidsen [1], **Birgit Kopainsky** [1], **Erling Moxnes** [1], **Matteo Pedercini** [2] **and I. David Wheat** [1,*]

[1]   System Dynamics Group, Department of Geography, University of Bergen, Post Box 7800, 5020 Bergen, Norway; pal.davidsen@geog.uib.no (P.I.D.); birgit.kopainsky@geog.uib.no (B.K.); erling.moxnes@geog.uib.no (E.M.)

[2]   Millennium Institute, 1634 Eye Street, NW Suite 300, Washington, DC 20006, USA; mp@millennium-institute.org

*   Author to whom correspondence should be addressed; david.wheat@geog.uib.no; Tel.: +47-555-83-081; Fax: +47-555-83-099.

Received: 12 February 2014; in revised form: 28 March 2014; Accepted: 11 April 2014; Published: 16 April 2014

Abstract: At the University of Bergen in Norway, educating students to use computer models and to think systemically about social and economic problems began in the 1970s. The International Masters Program in System Dynamics was established in 1995, and a Ph.D. program began a few years later. Student enrolment doubled in 2010 with the establishment of the European Master Program in System Dynamics. International diversity has been a hallmark of the Bergen program; each year, students come from about 30 different countries and more than 95% of the degrees have been awarded to students from outside of Norway. However, a Bergen systems education is not confined to a classroom in Norway. Projects in developing countries, emerging economies, and developed countries have taken the systems perspective and modeling tools on the road and, increasingly, online. Whatever the delivery mode, the goal is the same: capacity building among international students, planners and managers, and local stakeholders. This paper describes the Bergen program and its impact on systems thinking and modeling throughout the world.

Keywords: education; policy design; simulation; system dynamics; systems thinking

---

1. Introduction

At the University of Bergen in Norway, graduate education in computer modeling of social and economic problems began more than forty years ago. After several years of offering various modeling courses, the university established the International Master Program in System Dynamics in 1995, and a Ph.D. program began a few years later. International diversity is a hallmark of the Bergen program, and this paper describes its approach to systems education and its impact on systems thinking and modeling throughout the world.

2. Background

The Bergen program grew out of an interdisciplinary information science program established in 1971 and chaired by Svein Nordbotten, now professor emeritus at the University of Bergen [1]. As former head of computing at the Norwegian Census Bureau, he was intrigued by the work of the American computer pioneer and MIT professor Jay W. Forrester, the founder of the modeling discipline now known as system dynamics (SD) [2]. At Bergen, Nordbotten taught a course called *Cybernetics and System Dynamics* and collaborated with other scientists at the Christian Michelsen Institute. That motivated several graduate students to write theses using the SD methodology, and software ("SIMPAS") was developed for the modeling, simulation, and visualization of complex, dynamic systems.

Years later, one former student—Bergen professor Pål Davidsen—went to MIT as a Visiting Scholar and worked with Forrester and other prominent system dynamicists on several SD projects,

Systems **2014**, 2, 159–167

including *Road Maps*, an extensive set of instructional lessons aimed at developing systems thinking intuition and formal modeling skills [3]. Not long after returning to Bergen, Davidsen was asked by the university president to establish an international master's degree program in system dynamics, and the first students enrolled in the fall semester of 1995. Initially located in the Department of Information Sciences, the Bergen System Dynamics Group is now part of the Department of Geography within the Faculty of Social Sciences [4].

The number of new students each year was small during the formative period, but grew to 20 by 2009 and doubled in 2010 with the expansion of scholarships and degree options. In the fall semester of 2013, nearly 60 students took SD modeling courses in Bergen.

A constant since the beginning has been the international mix of students. In 1997, the first master's degree was awarded to a student from Ghana, and an Egyptian student earned the first Ph.D. in 2001 (Mohamed Saleh, the first Ph.D., is an associate professor at the Faculty of Computers and Information at Cairo University). In recent years, as many as 30 different countries have been represented among new enrolments, and more than 95% of the degrees since 1997 have been awarded to students from outside of Norway.

The expansion in 2010 resulted from Bergen's participation in founding the European Master Program in System Dynamics (EMSD), a joint study program with European Commission scholarship funding for both European and non-European students [5]. Bergen's founding partners include Radboud University in Nijmegen in the Netherlands, the University of Palermo in Italy, and the New University of Lisbon in Portugal. The EMSD students begin their studies in Bergen, where they take the foundation SD modeling courses during the fall semester. They move on to either Palermo or Lisbon in the spring, with the choice depending on their preference for public management [6] or sustainability issues [7]. The second fall semester reunites all EMSD students in Nijmegen, where they develop *group model-building* and organization intervention skills in issue settings that involve interaction with diverse stakeholders [8]. During the last semester of the two-year program, EMSD students write their theses at one of the four universities and receive degrees from the specific universities they attend.

The original vision, including the international perspective, still guides the Bergen program. The goal is to educate future planners and managers so they will be able to: (1) use computer-based modeling, simulation and visualization in the identification and analysis of complex, dynamic problems that span social sectors and scientific disciplines; (2) identify solutions to such problems in the form of strategy development, policy design, and decision making; and (3) help stakeholders understand relationships between the structure and dynamics of social systems. This computer-based modeling approach utilizes a systems thinking perspective and, in turn, enhances that perspective. The synergistic value emerges from the iterative process of thinking systemically about the world around us, formulating equations to specify our thoughts, observing simulation results, analyzing a model's structure in light of its behavior, and then refining that computer model *and our mental model* to reflect new insights and their policy implications.

Opportunities to learn about SD are available worldwide, and the International System Dynamics Society maintains a list of universities offering courses on every continent ([9]). However, as noted by other authors in this issue, the "programs that offer substantial coursework in system dynamics and a degree titled 'System Dynamics' can be counted on one hand" [10]. The University of Bergen is on that short list.

3. Curriculum

The masters curriculum in Bergen consists of six SD modeling courses during the first year and a thesis during the second year. In addition, special topics courses are offered each semester. Each course consists of 36 lecture hours and 18 computer lab hours, and most projects require an independent student modeling project.

During the fall semester, first-year students take three foundation courses sequentially. The first, *Principles of Dynamic Social Systems* [11] is taught by Erling Moxnes and gives an introduction to the SD method. Students learn to recognize typical problematic behaviors of dynamic systems, exemplified by global warming, overgrazing, unemployment, epidemics, and price fluctuations. They learn how to represent hypotheses for social problems, and how to use simulation to understand ways that systemic structures produce problematic behavior. Students experience how easily dynamic systems can be misperceived, and they witness examples of well-intended but malfunctioning policies [12]. The course also gives students training in applying the scientific method to socioeconomic problems, and it provides a common language for interdisciplinary research.

Davidsen, the founder, teaches the second course, *Model-based Analysis and Policy Design* [13]. Students gain extended knowledge about the SD method, with particular emphasis on model-based problem identification and analysis as well as hypothesis formulation and analysis for policy design. They gain knowledge about the intimate relationship that exists between structure and behavior (dynamics) and the shifts in causal loop governance that may take place in non-linear systems. They learn to recognize the significance of a robust strategy development and the associated policy design and decision-making. Students apply their knowledge in a series of comprehensive case studies. The compact learning content of these case studies allows the students to recognize and investigate the dynamic properties of generic system structures, as they appear in a variety of domains. The case studies are presented in class and the students are challenged to address each of them using modeling and simulation, addressing problem identification and validation on the one hand and policy design and impact assessment on the other. Each exercise is followed by an extensive de-briefing session. Particular emphasis is placed on student recognition of dynamic patterns of problematic behavior and the corresponding underlying structures, as well as student ability to formulate and assess the impact of policies designed to address such problems. Students are trained to distil the essence of their insights and present it in the form of compact causal loop diagrams to facilitate effective communication with potential stakeholders.

The third course, *System Dynamics Modeling Process* [14] is taught by David Wheat. This project-based course is devoted to developing skills needed to build *explanatory* models of dynamic problems that emerge from real-world complex social and economic systems. Each student has an intense six-week assignment to build an SD simulation model that represents a plausible, operational, and systemic explanation of a specific dynamic problem. With as many as 50 students in the course, the supervisory work is also intense, and three teaching assistants are employed to help the instructor provide timely guidance to each student modeler.

In 2010, Wheat developed a new course—*Policy Design and Implementation* [15]—which is now fourth in the curriculum sequence. Student learn to build feasible (instead of wishful-thinking) policy models and communicate effectively with policy makers and staff about policy options, drawing on both the SD and public policy and management literature. The individual policy modeling project requires each student to (1) restructure a pre-existing explanatory model of a dynamic problem with a feasible policy for alleviating problematic behavior cost-effectively, (2) develop an interactive simulator to help policy makers and staff improve their mental models of the issue and their assessment of the cost-effectiveness and feasibility of particular policy options, and (3) write a short report that identifies policy implementation obstacles and suggests strategies for dealing with those challenges. The course utilizes a framework to help SD modelers envision operational requirements of their simulation-based policies and build more useful models [16–18].

Experimental Methods in Social Systems [19] is the fifth course, and it provides theory and methods for the design, programming, and analysis of laboratory experiments. Building on previous instruction in simulator development, this course includes optimization to establish performance benchmarks and statistics for hypothesis testing. Students design and carry out their own pilot laboratory experiments with a focus on purpose, hypotheses, design, and analysis. For their individual projects, students can design experiments to address behavioral theories or learning interventions [20]. The experimental methods course complements the modeling courses by strengthening the link with more traditional scientific methods.

Systems **2014**, *2*, 159–167

Model-based Socioeconomic Planning [21] is the final required course in the first-year curriculum. Conceived by Davidsen and adjunct lecturer Matteo Pedercini (a Bergen Ph.D.), the course is currently organized and taught by Pedercini with assistance from senior research fellow Birgit Kopainsky. It is unique because of its origin as a course designed for planners and managers in developing countries, in conjunction with national planning assistance provided to those countries by Millennium Institute consultants such as Pedercini [22,23]. Now, in addition to the sponsored participants from developing countries, all Bergen degree students take the course and experience immersion in a realistic and problematic development setting.

Students take on roles as strategic planning consultants to "Zambaqui", a hypothetical country facing common developmental issues such as poverty, high mortality, land degradation, and water scarcity. The multiple and diverse issues make the exercise especially challenging and engaging. Early on, the need to adopt an integrated approach becomes evident: changes taking place in one sector cause changes in all other sectors. Using group model building methods [24], instructors lead students through the development of a small, basic integrated SD planning model for Zambaqui's government. The background analysis of the key issues is based on joint exploration of relevant data and multimedia from actual countries, a search of relevant literature, and interactive discussion, all with the aim of developing a shared understanding of the nature of such issues and their importance for development. Students then work in teams that address different issues facing the country and develop issue-specific models to be merged with the integrated model. Students must provide practical answers and policy recommendations to Zambaqui's government, as well as deal with misunderstandings and delays in communication that are introduced with the specific intent of recreating a realistic modeler-client exchange. Such training enables graduate students as well as professionals and researchers in the field of sustainable development planning to use quantitative methods to strengthen their analytical capacities. Post-training surveys indicate a high degree of satisfaction with the course and after several years former students from around the world still recall their trip to Zambaqui as a fundamental step in their SD education journey through Bergen.

4. Beyond the Traditional Classroom

A Bergen systems education is not confined to a Bergen classroom. The authors—three professors and two lecturers—manage active travel schedules and work with students, stakeholders, clients, and colleagues facing pressing issues around the world. Pedercini's work for the Millennium Institute and Kopainsky's research projects funded largely by the Norwegian Research Council build systems thinking and modeling capacity with a wide range of stakeholders in developing countries. Currently, these activities support integrated planning for facilitating transitions towards a green economy, adaptation to climate change, and food security at different institutional levels.

A senior research fellow at Bergen, Kopainsky focuses her efforts on the multitude of ecological, economic and social processes that affect food production and distribution. Specifically, she uses a food systems approach to address policy issues surrounding environmental change and food security in sub-Saharan Africa. She uses SD to foster understanding of leverage points and preconditions for a transition to sustainable, equitable and resilient agri-food systems [25] and diffusion of desired policies among smallholder farmers and other concerned stakeholders [26]. Her current work builds on parallel food systems research in Switzerland, where she and her colleagues built an SD model to prioritize policy options aimed at closing an ever widening gap between food demand and domestic food supply in the context of rising pressure on the natural resources used for food provision [27]. Her systems education challenge involves food producers, processors, distributors, retailers, and consumers [28]. Using SD-based experiments to evaluate alternative instructional strategies for transferring knowledge, she concludes that performance and understanding can be improved when stakeholders interact with a simulation in an exploratory but stringently guided way [29,30].

Davidsen, Moxnes, and Wheat have exported SD to the Baltic region. In Latvia, they worked with colleagues at Riga Technical University to develop systems thinking and modeling skills

Systems **2014**, *2*, 159–167

among graduate students and faculty, and then assisted on a major energy conservation project [31]. In Lithuania, Wheat's initial guest lectures at ISM University of Management and Economics evolved into three SD-based courses in applied microeconomics, in monetary policy, and in public finance. With funding from the Department of Geography at Bergen, his research on the systemic interaction of economics and demographics was extended to the problems associated with a declining and aging population in the small Baltic state. The methodological approach is relatively unknown there and has caught the attention of demographers, economists, and policy analysts [32–35].

Wheat's use of SD to teach economics [36–39] was instrumental in gaining support from the Norwegian Centre for International Cooperation in Education so he could work with Ukrainian colleagues to develop SD modelling capacity within the finance department at the National University at Kiev-Mohyla Academy [40,41]. The three-year project funded four workshops in Kiev and enabled twelve graduate students and two assistant professors to spend a semester in Bergen. In addition to taking three basic modeling courses, they participated in Wheat's macroeconomics seminar to develop an SD model of the still-struggling economy in Ukraine. To sustain the collaboration beyond the three-year funding period, he is developing an online curriculum that builds on a dozen years' of experience teaching online SD-based economics courses to students in the United States [42]. The reaction from students has been encouraging; for example:

> Female Ph.D. student: *System dynamics was a completely new tool for me. I had never heard about it before. The same with Norway—I didn't know anything about the country. Both were the best experiences ever—system dynamics as a useful and interactive modeling tool and Norway as an extremely beautiful country with tolerant and welcoming people.*

> Male Ph.D. student: *System dynamics serves as a bridge between modeler and client, which increases the usefulness of mathematical modeling. The structural approach—the core feature of system dynamics—develops operational thinking and increases understanding of socio-economic problems in the real world.*

Moxnes also uses technology to teach across the globe. He has developed an interactive online distance-learning course in *Natural Resources Management* [43] that convenes a worldwide virtual classroom. The course aims to build intuitive understanding of the theories and principles underlying the utilization and management of natural resources, which are often mismanaged with dramatic consequences for stakeholders. A second objective is to help course participants develop skills and competencies needed for proper management of resources such as water reservoirs, fisheries, forests, animal herds, non-renewable resources, and climate. The course makes use of online animations and simulators to give students practice in decision-making and develop their intuition about the dynamics of natural resource management. Students are challenged by increasingly complex tasks to construct knowledge themselves. Online suggested solutions and videos give immediate feedback and encourage generalization of insights.

5. Going Forward

The systemic nature of social and economic problems is increasingly evident to observant citizens around the world. Developing international capacity to address such problems has been the hallmark of a systems education at Bergen. Yet, designing and delivering a systems education is a dynamic problem in itself. We know that, as educators, we must adapt our methods to meet the dynamic and increasingly complex educational challenges ahead. Our confidence going forward is rooted in the ideals, enthusiasm, and encouragement of our students, whether they are in a classroom in Norway, on a computer screen in Kiev, or on the road to Zambaqui.

Acknowledgments: The authors wish to thank the editors of the special issue and four anonymous reviewers for their comments and suggestions.

Author Contributions: All authors contributed equally to this work.

Systems **2014**, *2*, 159–167

Conflicts of Interest: The authors declare no conflict of interest.

References

1. Svein Nordbotten's Homepage. Available online: http://www.uib.no/personer/Svein.Nordbotten# (accessed on 12 February 2014).
2. Forrester, J.W. *Collected Papers of Jay W. Forrester*; Pegasus: Waltham, MA, USA, 1975.
3. Road Maps. Available online: http://www.clexchange.org/curriculum/roadmaps/ (accessed on 12 February 2014).
4. International Master Programme in System Dynamics. Available online: http://www.uib.no/en/rg/dynamics (accessed on 12 February 2014).
5. European Master Programme in System Dynamics. Available online: http://www.europeansystemdynamics.eu (accessed on 12 February 2014).
6. Bianchi, C. Enhancing strategy design and planning in public utilities through "dynamic" balanced scorecards: Insights from a project in a city. *Syst. Dynam. Rev.* **2008**, *24*, 175–213. [CrossRef]
7. Antunes, P.; Santos, R.; Videira, N. Participatory decision making for sustainable development—The use of mediated modelling techniques. *Land Use Pol.* **2006**, *23*, 44–52. [CrossRef]
8. Vennix, J.A.M. *Group Model Building: Facilitating Team Learning Using System Dynamics*; John Wiley & Sons: New York, NY, USA, 1996.
9. Courses in System Dynamics. Available online: http://www.systemdynamics.org/courses/ (accessed on 12 February 2014).
10. Pavlov, O.V.; Doyle, J.K.; Saeed, K.; Lyneis, J.M.; Radzicki, M.J. The design of educational programs in system dynamics at Worcester Polytechnic Institute (WPI). *Systems* **2014**, *2*, 54–76. [CrossRef]
11. Principles of Dynamic Social Systems, GEO SD302. Available online: http://www.uib.no/emne/GEO-SD302 (accessed on 12 February 2014).
12. Moxnes, E. Not only the tragedy of the commons: Misperceptions of feedback and policies for sustainable development. *Syst. Dynam. Rev.* **2000**, *16*, 325–348. [CrossRef]
13. Model-Based Analysis and Policy Design, GEO SD303. Available online: http://www.uib.no/emne/GEO-SD303 (accessed on 12 February 2014).
14. System Dynamics Modelling Process, GEO SD304. Available online: http://www.uib.no/emne/GEO-SD304 (accessed on 12 February 2014).
15. Policy Design and Implementation, GEO SD308. Available online: http://www.uib.no/emne/GEO-SD308 (accessed on 12 February 2014).
16. Wheat, I.D. Model-Based Policy Design that Takes Implementation Seriously. In *Policy Informatics Handbook*; Desouza, K., Johnston, E., Eds.; MIT Press: Cambridge, MA, USA, in press.
17. Wheat, I.D. Teaching Policy Design: Using a Case Study of Unintended Consequences When the EU Regulates Hospital Doctors' Hours. In Proceedings of the 31st International Conference of the System Dynamics Society, Cambridge, MA, USA, 21–25 July 2013.
18. Wheat, I.D. What can system dynamics learn from the public policy implementation literature? *Syst. Res. Behav. Sci.* **2010**, *27*, 425–442. [CrossRef]
19. Experimental Methods in Social Systems, GEO SD306. Available online: http://www.uib.no/emne/GEO-SD306 (accessed on 12 February 2014).
20. Moxnes, E.; Jensen, L. Drunker than intended: Misperceptions and information treatments. *Drug Alcohol Depend.* **2009**, *105*, 63–70. [CrossRef]
21. Model-Based Socioeconomic Planning, GEO SD321. Available online: http://www.uib.no/emne/GEO-SD321 (accessed on 12 February 2014).
22. Barney, G.O. The global 2000 report to the president and the Threshold 21 model: Influences of Dana Meadows and system dynamics. *Syst. Dynam. Rev.* **2002**, *18*, 123–136. [CrossRef]
23. Pedercini, M.; Barney, G. Dynamic analysis of interventions designed to achieve millennium development goals (MDG): The case of Ghana. *Socio-Econ. Plan. Sci.* **2010**, *44*, 89–99. [CrossRef]
24. Andersen, D.F.; Richardson, G.P. Scripts for group model building. *Syst. Dynam. Rev.* **1997**, *13*, 107–129. [CrossRef]

25. Kopainsky, B.; Huber, R.; Pedercini, M. Exploring synergies between system dynamics and a social-ecological systems framework. The case of the Swiss agri-food system between production, environmental and public health goals. *Syst. Res. Behav. Sci.* **2014**. submitted for publication.

26. Kopainsky, B.; Tröger, K.; Derwisch, S.; Ulli-Beer, S. Designing sustainable food security policies in sub-Saharan African countries: How social dynamics over-ride utility evaluations for good and bad. *Syst. Res. Behav. Sci.* **2012**, *29*, 575–589. [CrossRef]

27. Kopainsky, B.; Tribaldos, T.; Flury, C.; Pedercini, M.; Lehmann, H.J. Synergien und Zielkonflikte zwischen Ernährungssicherheit und Ressourceneffizienz in der Schweiz. *Agrarforschung Schweiz* **2014**, in press.

28. Saldarriaga, M.; Kopainsky, B.; Alessi, S.M. Knowledge Analysis in Coupled Social-Ecological Systems. What Do Stakeholders in Sub Saharan Africa Know about the Dynamic Complexity of Climate Change, Agriculture and Food Security? In Proceedings of the 31st International Conference of the System Dynamics Society, Cambridge, MA, USA, 21–25 July 2013.

29. Kopainsky, B.; Sawicka, A. Simulator-supported descriptions of complex dynamic problems: Experimental results on task performance and system understanding. *Syst. Dynam. Rev.* **2011**, *27*, 142–172. [CrossRef]

30. Kopainsky, B.; Alessi, S.M.; Pedercini, M.; Davidsen, P.I. The effect of prior exploration as a learning strategy in system dynamics learning environments. *Simulat. Gaming* **2014**. [CrossRef]

31. Blumberga, A.; Blumberga, D.; Bažbauers, G.; Davidsen, P.; Moxnes, E.; Dzene, I.; Barisa, A.; Žogla, G.; Dāce, E.; Bērzina, A. *Sistēmdinamika Vides Inženierzinātnu Studentiem*; RTU Vides aizsrdzības un siltuma sistēmu institūts: Riga, Latvia, 2010.

32. Wheat, I.D. A Simulation Model of Demography & Economy in Lithuania. In Proceedings of 25th European Conference on Operational Research (EURO XXV), Vilnius, Lithuania, 8–11 July 2012.

33. Wheat, I.D. Modeling Fertility in Lithuania: A Preliminary Report. In Proceedings of the 30th International Conference of the System Dynamics Society, St. Gallen, Switzerland, 22–26 July 2012.

34. Wheat, I.D. Modeling Mortality in Lithuania. In Proceedings of the 6th European System Dynamics Workshop, Istanbul, Turkey, April 2013.

35. Činčytė, R.; Wheat, I.D. Diagramming a Feedback Model of Emigration. In Proceedings of 25th European Conference on Operational Research (EURO XXV), Vilnius, Lithuania, 8–11 July 2012.

36. Wheat, I.D. The feedback method of teaching macroeconomics: Is it effective? *Syst. Dynam. Rev.* **2007**, *23*, 391–413. [CrossRef]

37. Wheat, I.D. Empowering students to compare ways economists think: The case of the housing bubble. *Int. J. Pluralism Econ. Educ.* **2009**, *1*, 65–86. [CrossRef]

38. Wheat, I.D. Teaching Economics as if Time Mattered. In *Handbook of Pluralist Economics Education*; Reardon, J., Ed.; Routledge: London, UK, 2009.

39. Wheat, I.D. Do stock-and-flow feedback diagrams promote learning in macroeconomics? *Int. J. Pluralism Econ. Educ.* **2010**, *1*, 343–355. [CrossRef]

40. Wheat, I.D.; Lukianenko, I. Learning Economics with Dynamic Modeling: An International Collaboration. In Proceedings of the International Developments in Economics Education Conference, Exeter, UK, September 2013.

41. Myrhol, F.K. ionerer i Ukraina. SIU-Magasinet. Available online: http://www.siu.no/Globalmeny/Publikasjoner/Alle-publikasjoner/SIU-magasinet-nr.-1-2014 (accessed on 12 February 2014).

42. A Virtual Economics System Teaches Students about the Real Economy: Distance Learning with iThink. Available online: http://www.iseesystems.com/community/connector/Zine/2013_Spring/index.aspx (accessed on 12 February 2014).

43. Natural Resources Management, GEO SD660. Available online: http://www.uib.no/kurs/GEO-SD660-V. 2014 (accessed on 12 February 2014).

systems

MDPI

Communication

The Design of Educational Programs in System Dynamics at Worcester Polytechnic Institute (WPI) †

Oleg V. Pavlov *, James K. Doyle, Khalid Saeed, James M. Lyneis and Michael J. Radzicki

Department of Social Science and Policy Studies, Worcester Polytechnic Institute, 100 Institute Rd., Worcester, MA 01609, USA; doyle@wpi.edu (J.K.D.); saeed@wpi.edu (K.S.); jmlyneis@myfairpoint.net (J.M.L.); mjradz@wpi.edu (M.J.R.)

* Author to whom correspondence should be addressed; opavlov@wpi.edu.

† Based on "Doyle, J.K.; Eberlein, B.; Ford, A.; Hines, J.; Lyneis, J.M.; Parsons, K.; Pavlov, O.; Radzicki, M.J.; Saeed, K.; Warren, K. Design of a Master of Science Degree Program in System Dynamics at WPI. In Proceedings of the 27th International Conference of the System Dynamics Society, Albuquerque, NM, USA, 26–30 July 2009".

Received: 11 February 2014; in revised form: 12 March 2014; Accepted: 19 March 2014; Published: 21 March 2014

Abstract: Educational programs leading to degrees in system dynamics are rare and thus of critical importance to the future of the field of system dynamics. However, to a large extent such programs have not yet been made transparent to the system dynamics community as a whole. The present article describes the design and rationale for undergraduate and graduate programs at Worcester Polytechnic Institute (WPI). The goal of the article is to invite feedback from the system dynamics community about our specific programs as well as to facilitate wider discussion about the appropriate content, design, and pedagogy of degree programs and courses in system dynamics.

Keywords: system dynamics education; computer modeling; curriculum design; academic program management

1. Introduction

System dynamics (SD) courses are taught at dozens of universities throughout the world. However, only a small number of institutions offer enough courses for complete degrees in system dynamics. In most cases, the system dynamics curriculum is part of a larger curriculum in a school of, for example, Business or Public Policy, and the primary means of educational delivery beyond a few introductory courses is research mentorship with individual system dynamics faculty. In a few cases, the system dynamics curriculum is part of a larger "system sciences" program that covers a wide variety of different modeling approaches. Those programs that offer substantial coursework in system dynamics (say, five courses or more) and a degree titled "System Dynamics" can be counted on one hand.

At the same time, there has long been interest within the system dynamics community in examining and understanding the nature and quality of university curricula in system dynamics. Certainly, the growth and well being of the field depends on the availability of high-quality education in system dynamics. Nearly twenty years ago, Barlas [1] argued that for system dynamics to be a successful discipline there need to be university educational programs that provide formal training. Not only such programs would teach the foundations of the system dynamics method, they would also ensure consistency in the interpretation of the skills and act as conduits for the latest developments in the field to be passed on to students.

However, various efforts over the years to develop curriculum guidelines have thus far not been successful. An alternative approach may be to encourage programs to voluntarily make available to others the design and rationale behind their programs, which would open them up to scrutiny and

Systems **2014**, *2*, 54–76

constructive criticism from peers. Thus far there has been little published literature in the system dynamics field describing the actual or recommended design, content, and pedagogy of system dynamics courses and programs (although, see, e.g., [1–6]).

The present authors believe that, given their rarity, university programs in system dynamics have a special responsibility to the field to make the content and design of their programs transparent. Thus, the purpose of the present article is to describe the development and design of degree programs in System Dynamics at Worcester Polytechnic Institute (WPI), as a way of encouraging the discussion of general issues of curriculum design. For example, how should programs in System Dynamics be structured and taught? What topics and in what sequence should be covered? What pedagogies should be emphasized? Is there a place for an undergraduate program or are graduate programs in system dynamics more appropriate? What topics beyond the field should a system dynamics student be familiar with (e.g., business, economics, psychology, mathematics)? This article does not answer all these questions, but we hope that the discussion will continue.

2. Attributes of University Courses

Based on the literature review and our own experience, we suggest that system dynamics courses can be characterized by several attributes, as shown in Table 1. These attributes form a convenient framework for course comparisons. We discuss some of the attributes of WPI courses in this article.

The ultimate goal of any system dynamics course—which can be part of a system dynamics program—is to teach students the system dynamics method so they can apply it to various situations. While there are many practitioners of system dynamics and courses have been taught for years, there is still no unequivocal set of skills identified and agreed upon by the system dynamics community as the skill core of the system dynamics method. Andersen and Richardson [2,7], who were two of the early authors to write about system dynamics curricula, emphasized that system dynamics training should methodically teach the seven stages of system dynamics modeling inquiry: problem recognition, system conceptualization, model representation, model behavior, model evaluation, policy analysis and model use. Richmond [8] groups various skills into the following sets: dynamic thinking, closed-loop thinking, generic thinking, structural thinking, operational thinking, continuum thinking and scientific thinking. Based on their experience at Delft University, Meyers *et al.* [5] add that communication and reporting, team and project work and academic reflection are also important skills for system dynamicists. As model development and use is an iterative process, there is a great deal of overlap and interaction between the modeling stages. The necessary skills of system dynamics can also be deduced from the content of textbooks on the subject, and there are several of them on the market.

Table 1. Attributes of a System Dynamics Course.

Skills Taught. What is exactly covered?
Target Audience. Is the course graduate, undergraduate or both? Or is it part of an executive education program?
Type Of Course. Is it a stand-alone course or is it part of a program?
Registration Requirement. Is it a mandatory or elective course?
Faculty. Do tenured/tenure-track, full time or part-time faculty teach it?
Difficulty Level. Is the course introductory or advanced?
Course Organization. Is it a dedicated system dynamics course or does the course include a system dynamics module?
Purpose. Is the purpose of the course to teach SD, or to teach something else using SD?
Course Design. Is it project based, lecture, laboratory, case-studies, simulation games?
Delivery Method. Is it online, class-based or hybrid?
Length. Is it a semester, term, short workshop, or self-paced online course?
Academic Credit, full academic credit, continuing education credit, or none
Tuition, free to high

What is an appropriate audience for a system dynamics course or a program? Barlas [1] concludes that an "undergraduate stand-alone course dedicated exclusively to system dynamics … is least common, yet most important for the growth of the field". He notes that only very few universities offer undergraduate courses in system dynamics and calls for more undergraduate education in system dynamics. A review of system dynamics courses in the U.S. reveals that most courses in system dynamics are still at the graduate level (see Appendix A). Massachusetts Institute of Technology (MIT) also offers system dynamics workshops as part of its executive education program.

The majority of available courses are stand-alone courses or they are part of a non-system dynamics program. For example, the Delft University of Technology lists two courses—Introduction to System Dynamics and Advanced System Dynamics—that are mandatory courses for one undergraduate program and one Master's program, though these programs do not grant system dynamics degrees [5]. At Portland State University, system dynamics is taught as part of the graduate program in system science. System dynamics can also be incorporated into various application or modeling courses as a module. For example, Barlas [1] integrated a system dynamics module in a mathematical modeling course.

Unless a system dynamics course or program receives external funding, to be sustainable a university has to charge tuition to recover the course delivery cost. Thanks to government funding of the educational system, the University of Bergen in Norway offers a free online course on resource management. On the other hand, WPI currently charges $3,843 for a three-credit-hour graduate course, which is a typical tuition charge at a private American university. For anyone who does not require academic credit, WPI offers an audit registration option, which is half the regular tuition rate. A non-credit two-day class-based system dynamics course by isee systems costs $1200–1500 (see [9]). A five-day online workshop by Strategy Dynamics Ltd., a U.K. company, is £250, or about $400. A five-day executive education course at MIT is $8,100 (see [10]).

3. System Dynamics at WPI

System dynamics was established at WPI by Michael Radzicki, who began teaching a two-course undergraduate sequence in system dynamics in 1990. James Doyle was recruited in 1992 to teach group model building and judgment and decision making. By 1996 Khalid Saeed had joined WPI as Head of the Department of Social Science and Policy Studies, the department that administers WPI's system dynamics programs. Soon thereafter, in 1998, Saeed, Doyle, and Radzicki established the world's first Bachelor of Science degree program in System Dynamics at WPI [11]. Professor of Practice James M. Lyneis and Elise Axelrad joined the WPI system dynamics faculty in 2001, followed by Oleg Pavlov in 2002. In 2003 WPI began offering its first graduate courses in system dynamics. Some of these courses had previously been taught as distance learning courses at MIT, and several of the faculty involved in that program (Bob Eberlein, Andy Ford, Jim Hines, and Kim Warren) were brought in as adjunct faculty to keep the courses going. By 2004 nine graduate courses as well as a five-course graduate certificate program in system dynamics had been established. The first Ph.D. student in the interdisciplinary doctorate program in system dynamics, Shelly Friedman, graduated in 2005. In 2006 the M.S. program in System Dynamics was approved by the WPI Faculty and Trustees. The first four graduates of the M.S. program were awarded their degrees in May of 2007. Table 2 summarizes the development of system dynamics programs at WPI.

Systems **2014**, *2*, 54–76

Table 2. History of System Dynamics at Worcester Polytechnic Institute (WPI).

1990	First SD courses
1998	B.S. degree program in SD
2003	First graduate SD courses
2004	Graduate certificate in SD
2005	First Ph.D. graduate
2006	M.S. degree program in SD
2007	First M.S. graduates

4. Program Goals

The WPI System Dynamics teaching faculty has adopted the following mission statement for the university's programs in system dynamics:

- System dynamics is a method for understanding and changing the behavior of systems. It centers around the development and use of *formal computer models* that:

   (1) Apply the accepted system dynamics theory of structure (endogenous behavior, positive and negative feedback loops, accumulations and delays, and representation of decision-making);

   (2) Are constructed following the scientific method (problem defined in terms of a reference mode of problem behavior, dynamic hypothesis as a theory of that behavior, formal computer model of the hypothesis, testing of the model/hypothesis against data, extensive analysis, and policy design); and

   (3) Use best practice tools and techniques (system dynamics software, units checking, standard formulations, generic models and building blocks, graphical functions, *etc.*).

- These three components collectively define rigorous system dynamics. Further, in real world applications:

   (4) Models should be developed so as to achieve client confidence and acceptance (using various approaches including "group model building")

   (5) Model development must be taught in the context of the application field.

5. Program Design

WPI is the only institution in the U.S. that offers complete educational programs that lead to the B.S. in System Dynamics, Graduate Certificate, M.S., and Ph.D. degrees in System Dynamics (Figure 1). WPI currently offers 11 online semester-long graduate system dynamics courses (see [12]) that are also open to advanced undergraduate students. For the benefit of the undergraduate program, there are also two undergraduate class-based system dynamics courses and two project-based courses. System dynamics courses can be taken as an elective by WPI Economics majors. Additionally, system dynamics has been incorporated into various undergraduate economics courses.

The online program also acts as a hub that connects professionals and scientists with system dynamics experts, thus forming a community of practice. The interaction, which is important for building such a community of practice, is facilitated through WPI-sponsored online discussion boards, online sessions with instructors, and an active online group in LinkedIn called "WPI System Dynamics" which was established several years ago. The online LinkedIn group currently has 214 members at different levels of SD expertise.

The academic component of the online program is overseen by the Department of Social Science and Policy Studies. However, the administrative elements (enrollment, marketing, and online delivery) are managed by the Corporate and Professional Education (CPE) division at WPI, which has been an integral part of this university for nearly 30 years. All existing CPE programs are financially self-sufficient.

Below we provide more information on WPI programs. It should be noted that WPI follows separate academic schedules and uses different academic credit systems for its undergraduate and graduate programs. Undergraduate programs follow a term calendar, while graduate programs follow a semester calendar. Also, an undergraduate course is worth 1/3 unit. So the system dynamics requirement of 5/3 units means five undergraduate courses in system dynamics. A graduate course is counted as 3 credit hours. The Masters degree in SD requires 30 credit hours, or 10 graduate-level courses.

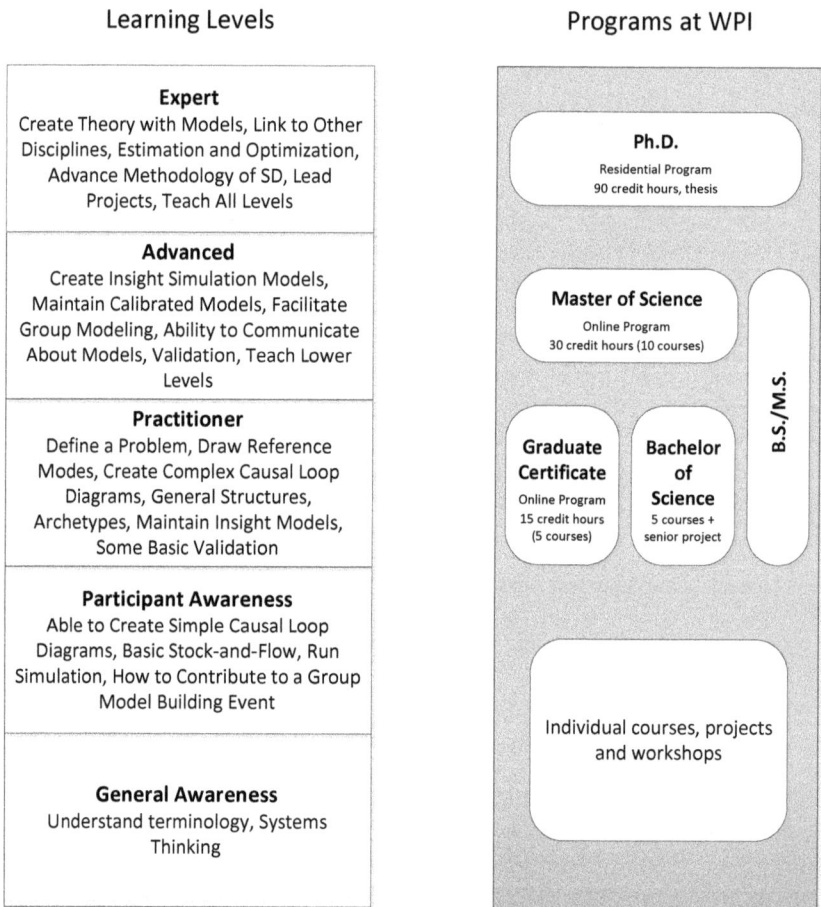

Learning Levels   Programs at WPI

Expert
Create Theory with Models, Link to Other Disciplines, Estimation and Optimization, Advance Methodology of SD, Lead Projects, Teach All Levels

Advanced
Create Insight Simulation Models, Maintain Calibrated Models, Facilitate Group Modeling, Ability to Communicate About Models, Validation, Teach Lower Levels

Practitioner
Define a Problem, Draw Reference Modes, Create Complex Causal Loop Diagrams, General Structures, Archetypes, Maintain Insight Models, Some Basic Validation

Participant Awareness
Able to Create Simple Causal Loop Diagrams, Basic Stock-and-Flow, Run Simulation, How to Contribute to a Group Model Building Event

General Awareness
Understand terminology, Systems Thinking

Ph.D.
Residential Program
90 credit hours, thesis

Master of Science
Online Program
30 credit hours (10 courses)

Graduate Certificate
Online Program
15 credit hours
(5 courses)

Bachelor of Science
5 courses + senior project

B.S./M.S.

Individual courses, projects and workshops

Figure 1. A Tiered Learning Levels view of skills and matching education programs in system dynamics at WPI. The courses, workshops and projects that are mentioned in the figure are on system dynamics.

5.1. Bachelor of Science in System Dynamics

Tables 3 and 4 explain the learning outcomes and distribution requirements for the Bachelor of Science in System Dynamics.

5.2. Master of Science Degree in System Dynamics

WPI's M.S. program in system dynamics was the culmination of more than a decade of strategic planning and curriculum development on the part of several faculty. Students are required to complete 30 credit hours (10 courses). At least 21 of these credit hours (7 courses) must be in system dynamics. The remaining 9 credit hours may be taken in mathematics, management, economics, or additional system dynamics courses. Six of these 9 credit hours may also be supervised research. Table 5 shows course requirements for the M.S. in system dynamics (full course descriptions appear in Appendix B).

Table 3. Learning Outcomes of the System Dynamics Major.

1. Ability to recognize the dynamic patterns of behavior in real-world data.	8. An understanding of basic concepts in software programming and management science.
2. Ability to formulate feedback hypotheses representing problems and understand the hypotheses' logic.	9. An understanding of how to apply scientific principles in system dynamics modeling.
3. Ability to translate feedback hypotheses into stock and flow models.	10. Ability to develop, organize, manage, and successfully conduct a significant system dynamics project.
4. Ability to experiment with stock and flow models in order to establish their fidelity.	11. Ability to locate and integrate valid and appropriate information from multiple fields and perspectives for use in systems dynamics models.
5. Ability to design experiments with a stock and flow model, implement them, and interpret their results, in order to arrive at effective solutions that address the defined problems of a system dynamics project.	12. An understanding of the endogenous causes of societal problems.
6. Literacy in the technical aspects of problems in the student's area of application.	13. An appreciation of the inter-connectedness between technology, society, and the environment.
7. Ability to communicate effectively the results of a system dynamics analysis in speech and writing.	14. Ability to form and work effectively in groups involving system dynamics modelers, appropriate domain experts, and stakeholders.

Source: WPI Undergraduate Catalog 2013–14.

Table 4. Program Distribution Requirements for the Bachelor's Degree in System Dynamics.

The normal period of residency at WPI is 16 terms. In addition to the WPI requirements applicable to all students, completion of a minimum of 10 units of study is required in system dynamics, social science, basic science, and mathematics, and computer science as follows:

SYSTEM DYNAMICS REQUIREMENTS	MINIMUM UNITS
1. System Dynamics (Note 1)	5/3
2. Other Social Science (Note 2)	5/3
3. Business (Note 3)	2/3
4. Mathematics/basic sciences/engineering (Note 4)	8/3
5. Computer Science (Note 5)	2/3
6. Application Area (Note 6)	5/3
7. MQP	1

Table 4. *Cont.*

NOTES:
1. Only social science courses with a "5" in the second digit of the course number count toward the system dynamics requirement.
2. Must include microeconomics or macroeconomics, cognitive or social psychology, and public policy.
3. Must include organizational science.
4. Must include differential and integral calculus, differential equations, and numerical or statistical analysis.
5. Courses on computer programming and programming languages are recommended.
6. This requirement is satisfied by a cohesive set of work from the fields of social science, management, science, mathematics, computer science, or engineering as specified in the curriculum the guidelines for system dynamics major.

Source: WPI Undergraduate Catalog 2013–14.

Table 5. Course requirements for the M.S. in system dynamics.

1. **Foundation courses**, required courses (6 credits)	SD 550 System Dynamics Foundation: Managing Complexity SD 551 Modeling and Experimental Analysis of Complex Problems
2. **Methodological courses**, two or three courses (6 to 9 credits) from the following courses:	SD 552 System Dynamics for Insight SD 553 Model Analysis and Evaluation Techniques SD 554 Real World System Dynamics SD 556 Strategic Modeling and Business Dynamics SD 557 Latent Structures, Unintended Consequences, and Public Policy
3. **Application courses**, three or four courses (9 to12 credits) from the following courses:	SD 560 Strategy Dynamics SD 561 Environmental Dynamics SD 562 Project Dynamics SD 565 Macroeconomic Dynamics
4. **Electives**, one to three courses (3 to 9 credits) from the following or additional courses from the previous lists:	SD 590 Special Topics in System Dynamics (credit as specified) Graduate independent study courses in System Dynamics (credit as specified) MA 510/CS522 Numerical Methods MA 512 Numerical Differential Equations Approved graduate coursework in an application area (e.g., economics, psychology, management, engineering, or applied sciences)

Source: WPI Undergraduate Catalog 2013–14.

SD550 serves as our basic introductory modeling course and is a prerequisite to all other courses in the program. SD551 serves as an advanced modeling course—it covers more advanced skills and more challenging and more open-ended modeling assignments. SD550 and SD551 serve as prerequisites for most of the advanced methodology courses.

Methodological courses, as opposed to application courses, develop important basic skills in greater detail than is possible in the introductory courses. SD552 is designed to build students' modeling skills by increasing their ability to identify and adapt generic structures. SD553 covers basic topics in model evaluation and analysis, including use of subscripts, achieving and testing for robustness, use of numerical data, sensitivity analysis, and optimization/calibration of models. SD554 in many ways serves as a "capstone" course for the program. In this course students, under the direction of an experienced system dynamics consultant, work throughout the term on a consulting project in their own organization that they design and implement from start to finish.

Application courses are advanced topical courses that focus on the application of system dynamics in a particular domain of inquiry. Elective courses allow students the flexibility to take more system dynamics courses, explore new topics through one-on-one collaboration with a faculty member, improve their math skills, or develop expertise in an application area of system dynamics. Up to 6 credit hours can be Directed Research. This requirement allows students to undertake an optional Master's Thesis.

5.3. Graduate Certificate in System Dynamics

A Graduate Certificate program requires 15 credit hours of graduate study (5 courses). Students take one or both of our Foundation Courses (SD550 and SD551), and complete the rest of the credits by taking a variety of methodological and application courses in system dynamics.

5.4. B.S./M.S. in System Dynamics

Undergraduate students can pursue a 5-year combined Bachelor's/Master's degree, in which the Bachelor's degree is awarded in any major offered at WPI and the Masters degree is awarded in System Dynamics. For this program, WPI allows the double counting of up to four courses.

5.5. Interdisciplinary Master's Degree in Systems Modeling

The departments of Mathematical Sciences and Social Science and Policy Studies offer an interdisciplinary Master's degree in systems modeling. The program requires 30 credit hours (10 courses) in Mathematics, System Dynamics, and electives taught in engineering, science and management departments. Students entering the program must have a Bachelor's degree, which is typically in science or engineering. Students complete 15 credit hours in system dynamics and 15 credit hours in mathematical modeling and an applications area (e.g., industrial engineering, management, infrastructure planning, telecommunications planning, and power systems). Up to 6 credit hours may be done as a supervised project which allows for an optional Master's Thesis.

5.6. Interdisciplinary Doctorate in System Dynamics

Social Science and Policy Studies collaborates with other departments to offer an interdisciplinary doctoral program in System Dynamics. Each program of study requires at least 60 credit hours of study and is adapted to the interests of the student and the interests of the participating faculty. A typical doctoral committee consists of three or more faculty members from participating departments.

6. Delivery Methods

Undergraduate system dynamics courses are delivered in the traditional classroom-based format. To allow for broader geographic reach, convenience and accessibility than class-based courses, WPI's graduate courses in system dynamics are implemented exclusively in a distance learning format through WPI's Division of Corporate and Professional Education (CPE). There are no classroom sections of the courses. They are delivered in an online asynchronous format through WPI's web-based course delivery system, myWPI, powered by the Blackboard Learning Management System. Teaching courses online reduces the cost to students as they do not incur additional expenses for travel, lodging and meals as would be required for a residential course.

Graduate online courses are taught on the same semester schedule as WPI's graduate classroom courses and students receive regular deadlines for completion of homework assignments and other tasks. The courses are just as challenging as classroom courses at WPI, often requiring 15–20 h per week of effort or more from students. Course lectures (as streaming video files) and supporting materials such as Power Point files are posted to myWPI. As in a classroom course, students receive

Systems **2014**, 2, 54–76

detailed and timely feedback on their work. Faculty-student and student-student interaction takes place primarily via electronic discussion boards and email. WPI's distance learning students are full members of the WPI community and have electronic access to all services available to on-campus students (e.g., library, bookstore, and technical help). Instructors can choose to record the lectures at their individual computers using commonly available video recording software such as Camtasia or tape lectures at the WPI's Academic Technology Center (ATC).

Distance learning poses a unique set of challenges. The absence of face-to-face personal contact among students and faculty can potentially be a serious impediment to learning, especially for students who favor in person interactions. At WPI, we attempt to use technology to emulate the classroom experience. Below are a few solutions that we have adopted and which seem to be working well for us.

(1) *Talking head*: Most of the lectures are recorded and professionally edited in a studio on campus in such a way that videos show not only slides and demonstrations of computer models but also the image of the instructor superimposed on top of the slides as the talking head.

(2) *Discussion board*: Instructors may dedicate a sizable part of the grade to discourse on the discussion board. The discussion board tool is integrated with Blackboard. If the online discussions slow down, instructors may stimulate lackluster exchanges with challenging questions.

(3) *Synching the class*: There is potentially a danger of losing class focus and the relevance of discussions to the syllabus of a course in the asynchronous format that we choose to follow in view of the many time zones involved and the fact that our students often need flexibility due to other commitments. We overcome this problem by not posting lessons all at once but revealing them according to a fixed schedule so students work on the same materials during the week assigned to a lesson. Assigning high penalties for late homework submissions also encourages students to observe the lesson schedule of a course. These measures greatly help create synchronism in our otherwise asynchronous classes.

(4) *Virtual office hours*: Though not every instructor uses them, the option of virtual office hours is available with Adobe Connect, which is a video-conferencing tool integrated with Blackboard. Based on student course evaluations, certain types of students are particularly appreciative of the life interaction.

Since developing online materials is rather time consuming, frequently revising and updating courses remains a challenge. We have discovered that the best strategy for keeping the curricula current is to do revisions gradually rather than revamping an entire course all at once. From the program management perspective, counting time spent on course maintenance towards the faculty load creates strong incentives for the faculty to keep on-line courses vibrant and up-to-date.

7. Students

WPI is a technological university, but it recognizes the importance of the humanities, arts and social sciences in its undergraduate curriculum, and therefore all undergraduate students must complete two social science courses before they graduate. The system dynamics courses are open to all students in the university and since they are housed in the Department of Social Science and Policy Studies, any system dynamics course is counted towards the social science requirement. This helps with the enrollment in the undergraduate system dynamics courses.

The students enrolled in WPI's graduate system dynamics programs are primarily mid-career professionals who enroll in courses part-time. They are not necessarily looking for a brand new career, but for the most part want to do their current job better by incorporating the tools and techniques of system dynamics. More than half of the students are above the age of 35. The students are widely geographically dispersed around the U.S. and the world, with only about 15% residing in WPI's home state of Massachusetts. Our student body as a whole is already highly educated. Many students in graduate system dynamics courses have advanced degrees in other fields (e.g., M.B.A., M.D., M.S. in Engineering, Ph.D.). We also offer graduate SD courses which are taught on-site at various companies around New England as part of a corporate education program leading to the Certificate or the Master's degree in Systems Engineering.

Some students in graduate courses are researchers who see the systems thinking paradigm coupled with the power of system dynamics modeling as the intellectual and methodological foundation of their desire to extend beyond the limited modes of inquiry of traditional disciplines. Established researchers may take a course to acquaint themselves with the system dynamics methodology and its applications. Some of our students are researchers who already have a good understanding of traditional fields of inquiry but might need to acquire only sufficient understanding of system dynamics to draw new ideas and methodology into their work. After taking one or two courses, while maintaining a foothold in their traditional first disciplines, these researches are able to understand system dynamics sufficiently to communicate and collaborate with expert modelers.

Enrollment in system dynamics courses at WPI is shown in Table 6. It should be noted that in addition to our primary population of part-time M.S. students, a small number of B.S./M.S. and interdisciplinary Ph.D. students also register for graduate online courses.

Table 6. Enrollment in System Dynamics Courses at WPI.

Academic year	Undergraduate		Graduate	
	Sections	Enrollment	Sections	Enrollment
1998–99	2	12	N.A.	N.A.
1999–00	5	119	N.A.	N.A.
2000–01	5	141	N.A.	N.A.
2001–02	5	71	N.A.	N.A.
2002–03	3	78	N.A.	N.A.
2003–04	5	95	8	99
2004–05	4	107	10	91
2005–06	4	86	7	97
2006–07	3	93	10	101
2007–08	5	109	8	107
2008–09	3	87	9	91
2009–10	3	65	14	117
2010–11	2	42	12	85
2011–12	3	55	9	70
2012–13	2	64	11	76

8. Faculty

There are currently three full-time tenured faculty in Social Science and Policy Studies at WPI who teach in the system dynamics programs. In addition, there are six adjunct faculty who regularly teach online courses. WPI has been fortunate in being able to draw on the talents of system dynamics experts from around the world for its programs. Collectively, the system dynamics teaching faculty bring a wealth of experience and expertise to the program, and include three winners of the Jay Forrester Award as well as five past Presidents of the International System Dynamics Society. The list of faculty and their research interests appear in Appendix C.

9. Course Design

The System Dynamics courses at WPI emphasize building modeling skills through homework assignments that receive prompt and detailed feedback from the instructor. Variations in approach and emphasis are encouraged in the belief that students benefit from learning why and how diverse faculty may approach a given problem or topic differently. In all of our modeling courses students gain hands-on experience with reference modes, hypothesis formulation using causal and stock-flow diagrams, equation-writing, and model analysis. We believe that lasting, generalizable learning is best obtained by returning to the same topics again and again, with different instructors, in different courses, while studying different problem domains. Our goal is to turn students into experienced modelers who, upon graduation, will be able to manage a modeling project in a real organization from start to finish.

Table 7. System Dynamics skills taught in SD550.

System Dynamics as a theory of behavior	Scientific modeling process	Tools and tricks
• Policy Resistance/Unintended Consequences • Fundamental Behavior Patterns • Causes of dynamic behavior: feedback and accumulation • Basic Archetypes (success to successful, limits, fixes that fail, shifting burden) • First-order positive systems (analytical solution, rate-level graph, doubling time) • First-order negative systems (analytical, rate/level, half-lives) • Draining processes, Goal-gap • Exponential average • First-order system with inflow and outflow (all linear) • S-shaped Growth (carrying capacity) • Overshoot and Collapse (resource depletion) • Growth feedbacks from Sterman Ch. 10 • Product Diffusion Model • Epidemic (SI and SIR) • Stock Management with 3-stock delay • Material Delays (1st, 3rd, 6th, pipeline) • Second-order systems and oscillations (role of minor and major loops)	• System Dynamics "Standard Method": conceptualization (problem definition, dynamic hypothesis), formulation (model construction, testing, validation), use (testing and understanding, policy design) • Conceptualization exercise— Peer-to-Peer • Modeling and policy design exercise—Tragedy of Commons/Fishbanks (formulation including carrying capacity, graphical function, first-order stock control, analysis of each loop's parameter sensitivity, policy design focused on info from system and when action needs to be taken) • Material delays exercise (relative peaks of inflows, outflows, stock; equilibrium; distribution relative to average) • A business case exercise	• Vensim • Causal-loop diagramming (basics and conventions, link/loop polarities, *etc.*) • Problems with CLDs • Stock-flow diagrams (as means of building models) • Graphical integration • Calculating equilibrium and setting up model in equilibrium using equations • Units checking • Graphical Functions (normalization, *etc.*) • First-order stock control • Test inputs (step, pulse, cycle, ramp, exponential, noise) • Sensitivity testing • Loop knockout

Rather than focus on the topics a course covers, when we design (and redesign) courses, we place more emphasis on skill achievement. Each lecture, assignment, or activity is considered in relation to the general "skill" categories described in our mission statement. These "skill grids" help instructors plan their courses and help them keep track of what other instructors are doing. They also allow us a high-level view of the entire program, which helps us assess the amount of overlap and redundancy across courses (while keeping in mind that a certain degree of redundancy is desirable) as well as to identify important omissions in our program.

Table 7 provides an example of a skill grid for our introductory course, SD550. It constitutes a statement of what we think is important to include in an introductory system dynamics course, with an emphasis on skills taught in various goal categories *versus* the traditional linear format of a course syllabus. This list of topics is comparable to the list in an introductory system dynamics course described in Barlas [1].

10. Conclusion

In this article we have tried to give an overview, in some detail, of the design and rationale for our degree programs in system dynamics. We hope that by sharing this information about our program, we will obtain feedback from the system dynamics community about what we are doing wrong and perhaps, occasionally, feedback on what we are doing right. We also hope to encourage the field of system dynamics to more fully and collectively address the question of what a graduate of a system dynamics program should know and be able to do and how best to achieve those goals. In addition, we hope that by sharing our experience, other universities will be encouraged to travel down the long and difficult path of turning a few system dynamics courses into a substantial degree program.

While the usual discussion about online education revolves around the quality of online courses, creating and managing online programs brings forth a host of issues that are typically not of serious concern in class-based instruction. For distance education to work, the university must be able and willing commit significant additional resources besides the instructor's time to such programs.

Systems **2014**, *2*, 54–76

Creating an online program requires facilities and staff for videotaping and editing lectures as well as handling email and phone communication with students. Such a mundane task as registering for a course might suddenly turn into an ordeal and a flurry of frantic emails when students have to figure out the registration process remotely. Therefore, it is essential for an online program to have dedicated, patient and well-trained staff who can provide administrative support to the program on a day-to-day basis.

This article is not a comprehensive review of program design. We did not address resource requirements and the financial side of running a program. We did not cover many agency issues. For example, we did not discuss how to convince university administration of the viability of a program and how to reach an agreement with them about cost and revenue sharing. Also, we did not cover the issues of student and faculty recruitment in the context of managing instructional capacity in the competitive marketplace that higher education has become.

Acknowledgments: The authors would like to thank members of the system dynamics faculty at WPI for their collegiality and support. In addition, the authors would like to acknowledge the important role played by Pam Shelley and Diane Poirier in guiding the development and operations of the system dynamics programs and making sure they meet the needs of our students. Pam Shelley is an Associate Director of Marketing and Diane Poirier is an Associate Operations Manager within the WPI's division of Corporate and Professional Education.

Author Contributions: The article is based on the collective experience of all authors who have developed the system dynamics program at Worcester Polytechnic Institute and have been teaching in it for many years. They contributed and commented on this manuscript at all stages.

Conflicts of Interest: The authors declare no conflict of interest.

References

1. Barlas, Y. Formal System Dynamics Education in Universities. In Proceedings of the 1993 International System Dynamics Conference, Cancun, Mexico, July 1993.
2. Andersen, D.; Richardson, G.P. Toward a pedagogy of system dynamics. *TIMS Stud. Manage. Sci.* **1980**, *14*, 91–106.
3. Barlas, Y. Academics of system dynamics: It's core definition, topics, and terminology. *Int. J. Pol. Model.* **1995**, *7*, 1–15.
4. Hovmand, P.S.; O'Sullivan, J.A. Lessons from an interdisciplinary system dynamics course. *Syst. Dyn. Rev.* **2009**, *24*, 479–488. [CrossRef]
5. Meyers, W.; Slinger, J.; Pruyt, E.; Yucel, G.; van Daalen, C. Essential Skills for System Dynamics Practitioners: A Delft University of Technology Perspective. In Proceedings of the 28th International Conference of the System Dynamics Society, Seoul, Korea, 25–29 July 2010.
6. Clauset, K.H., Jr. Notes on the teaching of system dynamics. *Syst. Dyn. Rev.* **1985**, *1*, 123–125. [CrossRef]
7. Andersen, D.F.; Richardson, G.P. A Core Curriculum in System Dynamics. In *Occasional Papers in Public Affairs*; Graduate School of Public Affairs, SUNY-Albany: Albany, NY, USA, 1978.
8. Richmond, B.M. Systems thinking: Critical thinking skills for the 1990s and beyond. *Syst. Dyn. Rev.* **1993**, *9*, 113–133. [CrossRef]
9. Intermediate Dynamic Modeling with STELLA and iThink. Available online: http://www.iseesystems.com/store/Training/InterDynamicModelingIthink.aspx (accessed on 11 February 2014).
10. Business Dynamics: MIT's Approach to Diagnosing and Solving Complex Business Problems. Available online: http://executive.mit.edu/openenrollment/program/business_dynamics_mits_approach_to_diagnosing_and_solving_complex_business_problems/5 (accessed on 11 February 2014).
11. Doyle, J.K.; Grabowski, M.W.; Kao, A.H.; Radzicki, M.J.; Rissmiller, K.J.; Saeed, K. A Bachelor of Science Degree Program in System Dynamics at WPI. 1998. Available online: http://www.systemdynamics.org/conferences/1998/PROCEED/00005.PDF (accessed on 11 February 2014).
12. Online Master of Science. Available online: http://cpe.wpi.edu/online/sd-master.html (accessed on 11 February 2014).

Appendix A.

Table A1. A Sample of Courses in System Dynamics in the U.S. Universities, WPI Excluded.

University/Courses	Location	Undergraduate	Graduate
California State University, Chico	Chico, CA		
Applied Strategic Decision Making		•	
Business Dynamics		•	•
Seminar in Strategic Management and Administrative Policy			•
Canisius College	Buffalo, NY		
Sustainability & System Dynamics		•	•
Central Connecticut State University	New Britain, CT		
Management Systems		•	
James Madison University	Harrisonburg, VA		
System Dynamics Modeling, Simulation, and Analysis		•	
Introduction to System Dynamics			•
System Dynamics II: Advanced Model Building and Validation			•
Massachusetts Institute of Technology	Cambridge, MA		
Introduction to System Dynamics		•	•
System Dynamics for Business Policy		•	•
Applications of Systems Dynamics			•
Doctoral Seminar in Systems Dynamics			•
System Dynamics II			•
Portland State University	Portland, OR		
System Dynamics			•
Texas A&M University	College Station, TX		
Strategic Construction and Engineering Management			•
University at Albany, Public Administration and Policy Department	Albany, NY		
Introduction to System Dynamics		•	
Data, Models, and Decisions I (contains a module on system dynamics)			•
System Thinking and Strategic Management (contains qualitative system dynamics			•
Business Dynamics: Simulation Modeling for Decision-Making			•
Simulation for Policy Analysis and Design			•
Advanced Topics in System Dynamics			•
University of Houston	Houston, TX		
Systems Thinking			•
University of Southern Maine	Portland, ME		
Special Topics in Management: Introduction to System Dynamics			•
University of Utah	Salt Lake City, UT		
System Dynamics and Environmental Policy			•
Complexity and Systems Thinking			•
University of Washington	Seattle, WA		
Information Dynamics I			•
Virginia Tech	Blacksburg, VA		•
Applied Systems Engineering (Systems Thinking and Modeling)			•
Advanced Dynamic Modeling			
Washington State University	Pullman, WA		
Modeling the Environment		•	
System Dynamic Models of Environmental Systems			•
Washington University in St. Louis	St. Louis, MO		
A system Dynamics Approach to Designing Sustainable Social Policies and Programs			•
Special Topics: Group Model Building	Salem, OR		
Willamette University			•
Business Dynamics: Systems Thinking and Modeling for a Complex World			•

Sources: University websites; System Dynamics Society. Last accessed: 5 November 2013.

Appendix B. WPI Graduate Courses in System Dynamics

SD 550. System Dynamics Foundation: Managing Complexity

Why do some businesses grow while others stagnate or decline? What causes oscillation and amplification—the so called "bullwhip"—in supply chains? Why do large scale projects so commonly over overrun their budgets and schedules? This course explores the counter-intuitive dynamics of complex organizations and how managers can make the difference between success and failure. Students learn how even small changes in organizational structure can produce dramatic changes in organizational behavior. Real cases and computer simulation modeling combine for an in-depth examination of the feedback concept in complex systems. Topics include: supply chain dynamics, project dynamics, commodity cycles, new product diffusion, and business growth and decline. The emphasis throughout is on the unifying concepts of system dynamics.

SD 551. Modeling and Experimental Analysis of Complex Problems

This course deals with the hands on detail related to analysis of complex problems and design of policy for change through building models and experimenting with them. Topics covered include: slicing complex problems and constructing reference modes; going from a dynamic hypothesis to a formal model and organization of complex models; specification of parameters and graphical functions; experimentations for model understanding, confidence building, policy design and policy implementation. Modeling examples will draw largely from public policy agendas. Prerequisites: SD 550 System Dynamics Foundation: Managing Complexity

SD 552. System Dynamics for Insight

The objective of this course is to help students appreciate and master system dynamics' unique way of using of computer simulation models. The course provides tools and approaches for building and learning from models. The course covers the use of molecules of system dynamics structure to increase model building speed and reliability. In addition, the course covers recently developed eigenvalue-based techniques for analyzing models as well as more traditional approaches. Prerequisites: SD 550 System Dynamics Foundation: Managing Complexity and SD 551 Modeling and Experimental Analysis of Complex Problems

SD 553. Model Analysis and Evaluation Techniques

This course focuses on analysis of models rather than conceptualization and model development. It provides techniques for exercising models, improving their quality and gaining added insights into what models have to say about a problem. Five major topics are covered: use of subscripts, achieving and testing for robustness, use of numerical data, sensitivity analysis, and optimization/ calibration of models. The subscripts discussion provides techniques for dealing with detail complexity by changing model equations but not adding additional feedback structure. Robust models are achieved by using good individual equation formulations and making sure that they work together well though automated behavioral experiments. Data, especially time series data, are fundamental to finding and fixing shortcomings in model formulations. Sensitivity simulations expose the full range of behavior that a model can exhibit. Finally, the biggest section, dealing with optimization and calibration of models develops techniques for both testing models against data and developing policies to achieve specified goals. Though a number of statistical issues are touched upon during the course, only a basic knowledge of statistics and statistical hypothesis testing is required. Prerequisites: SD 550 System Dynamics Foundation: Managing Complexity and SD 551 Modeling and Experimental Analysis of Complex Problems, or permission of the instructor.

Systems **2014**, *2*, 54–76

SD 554. Real World System Dynamics

In this course students tackle real-world issues working with real managers on their most pressing concerns. Many students choose to work on issues in their own organizations. Other students have select from a number of proposals put forward by managers from a variety of companies seeking a system dynamics approach to important issues. Students experience the joys (and frustrations) of helping people figure out how to better manage their organizations via system dynamics. Accordingly the course covers two important areas: consulting (*i.e.*, helping managers) and the system dynamics standard method—a sequence of steps leading from a fuzzy "issue area" through increasing clarity and ultimately to solution recommendations. The course provides clear project pacing and lots of support from the instructors and fellow students. It is recommend that students take SD 554 Real World System Dynamics toward the end of their system dynamics coursework as it provides a natural transition from coursework to system dynamics practice. Prerequisites: SD 550 System Dynamics Foundation: Managing Complexity and SD 551 Modeling and Experimental Analysis of Complex Problems

SD 556. Strategic Modeling and Business Dynamics

The performance of firms and industries over time rarely unfolds in the way management teams expect or intend. The purpose of strategic modeling and business dynamics is to investigate dynamic complexity by better understanding how the parts of an enterprise operate, fit together and interact. By modeling and simulating the relationships among the parts we can anticipate potential problems, avoid strategic pitfalls and take steps to improve performance. We study a variety of business applications covering topics such as cyclicality in manufacturing, market growth and capital investment. The models are deliberately small and concise so their structure and formulations can be presented in full and used to illustrate principles of model conceptualization, equation formulation and simulation analysis. We also review some larger models that arose from real-world applications including airlines, the oil industry, the chemicals industry and fast moving consumer goods. Students work with selected business policy problems based on generic structures discussed in the lessons. Prerequisite: SD 550 System Dynamics Foundation: Managing Complexity

SD 557. Latent Structures, Unintended Consequences, and Public Policy

This course addresses policy resilience and unintended consequences arising out of actions that are not cognizant of the latent structure causing the problem. An attempt is made to identify the generic systems describing such latent structures. The latent structures discussed include a selection from capacity constraining and capacity enabling systems, resource allocation, and economic cycles of various periodicities. Problems discussed in lessons include pests, gang violence, terrorism, political instability, professional competence in organizations, urban decay, and economic growth and recessions. Students work with selected public policy problems relevant to the generic latent structures discussed in the course. Pre-requisites: SD 550 System Dynamics Foundation: Managing Complexity, SD 551 Modeling and Experimental Analysis of Complex Problems

SD 558. Introduction to Agent-Based Modeling

The purpose of this course is to provide students with an introduction to the field of agent-based computer simulation modeling in the social sciences. The course begins with an outline of the history of the field, as well as of the similarities and differences between agent-based computer simulation modeling and system dynamics computer simulation modeling. An important goal of the course is to provide students with guidelines for deciding when it is preferable to apply agent-based modeling, and when it is preferable to apply system dynamics modeling, to a particular problem. Through a series of example models and homework exercises students are introduced to the software that is used in the course. Generally speaking, as the course progresses students will be introduced to increasingly complicated agent-based models and exercises so that their modeling skills will grow. The goal is to increase students' modeling skills so that they will eventually be able to create their own agent-based models from scratch. The remainder of the course is devoted to examining models of socioeconomic phenomena that reside within two broad categories of agent-based models: cellular automata models and multi-agent models. Along the way the cross-category, cross-disciplinary, principles of agent-based modeling (micro-level agents following simple rules leading to macro-level complexity, adaptation, evolving structure, emergence, non-ergodicity) are emphasized.

SD 560. Strategy Dynamics

This course provides a rigorous set of frameworks for designing a practical path to improve performance, both in business and non-commercial organizations. The method builds on existing strategy concepts, but moves substantially beyond them, by using the system dynamics method to understand and direct performance through time. Topics covered include: strategy, performance and resources; resources and accumulation; the 'Strategic Architecture'; resource development; rivalry and the dynamics of competition; strategy, policy and information feedback; resource attributes; intangible resources; strategy, capabilities and organization; industry dynamics and scenarios. Case studies and models are assigned to students for analysis. Prerequisite: SD 550 System Dynamics Foundation: Managing Complexity or permission of the instructor.

SD 561. Environmental Dynamics

Environmental Dynamics introduces the system dynamics students to the application in environmental systems. The course materials include the book *Modeling the Environment*, a supporting website, lectures and the corresponding power point files. Students learn system dynamics with examples implemented with the Stella software. The course includes a variety of small models and case applications to watershed management, salmon restoration, and incentives for electric vehicles to reduce urban air pollution The students conclude the course with a class project to improve one of the models from the text. The improvements may be implemented with either the Stella or the Vensim software. Prerequisite: SD 550 System Dynamics Foundation: Managing Complexity.

SD 562. Project Dynamics

This course will introduce students to the fundamental dynamics that drive project performance, including the rework cycle, feedback effects, and inter-phase "knock-on" effects. Topics covered include dynamic project problems and their causes: the rework cycle and feedback effects, knock-on effects between project phases; modeling the dynamics: feedback effects, schedule pressure and staffing, schedule changes, inter-phase dependencies and precedence; strategic project management: project planning, project preparation, risk management, project adaptation and execution cross project learning; multi-project issues. A simple project model will be created, and used in assignments to illustrate the principles of "strategic project management." Case examples of different applications will be discussed. Prerequisite: SD 550 System Dynamics Foundation: Managing Complexity.

SD 563. Health Care Dynamics

Why would people go to the doctor more (or less) tomorrow than today? In this course students will explore and learn to simulate behaviors of health care providers, patients, and payers in the U.S. health care system with the goal of better understanding how macro-level patterns emerge from micro-level behaviors. A suite of system dynamics models is developed to explore problems of controlling health care costs and patient utilization. The smaller system dynamics models merge into a larger policy system model that can be used to explore proposed improvements and policy resistance in this sector of the economy. In addition to developing a policy-level model of the health care system, models will be developed on such topics as the spread and control of contagious diseases including SARS, AIDS, seasonal influenza, and pandemic flu, and the dynamics of medical centers of excellence. The objective of the course is to enable the student to develop a system-wide perspective and a framework for health care problem-solving. Prerequisites: SD 550 System Dynamics Foundation: Managing Complexity.

SD 565. Macroeconomic Dynamics

There are three parts to this course. The first acquaints a student with dynamic macroeconomic data and the stylized facts seen in most macroeconomic systems. Characteristics of the data related to economic growth, economic cycles, and the interactions between economic growth and economic cycles that are seen as particularly important when viewed through the lens of system dynamics will be emphasized. The second acquaints a student with the basics of macroeconomic growth and business cycle theory. This is accomplished by presenting well-known models of economic growth and instability, from both the orthodox and heterodox perspectives, via system dynamics. The third part attempts to enhance a student's ability to build and critique dynamic macroeconomic models by addressing such topics as the translation of difference and differential equation models into their equivalent system dynamics representation, fitting system dynamics models to macroeconomic data, and evaluating (formally and informally) a model's validity for the purpose of theory selection. Prerequisites: SD 550 System Dynamics Foundation: Managing Complexity.

Courses which are no longer offered

SD 555. Psychological Foundations of System Dynamics Modeling

This course examines the cognitive and social processes underlying the theory and practice of system dynamics. The errors and biases in dynamic decision making that provide the primary rationale for the use of system dynamics modeling will be traced to their root causes in cognitive limitations on perception, attention, and memory. Group processes that influence the outcome of modeler-client interactions and appropriate psychological techniques for eliciting and using mental data to support model building will also be addressed. Additional topics will include the reliability of alternate data sources for modeling, techniques for quantifying soft variables, design issues in group model building, the relative advantages of qualitative and quantitative modeling, and client attitudes toward modeling. Prerequisite: SD550 System Dynamics Foundations: Managing Complexity or permission of the Instructor

SD 590. System Dynamics Modeling for Organizational Change

The course is based on the following premise: The goal of most SD modeling is to create results and systemic improvement is caused by fundamental shifts in thinking and actions. In short, the successful SD modeling process is a vehicle for organizational change. However, organizations change only because people change and this has significant implications for SD practitioners. The course has a dual focus. One theme is organizational-understanding how people think, the basis of action and the implications for individual and group change. The other focus is the modeling process and how specific techniques can maximize organizational impact. An important part of the course is a "mini" project, during which students apply course concept for real users. Along the way students assess and improve their own ability to facilitate change. Prerequisites: Students are required to have completed SD550, SD560 or SD561 or permission of the Instructor

Systems **2014**, *2*, 54–76

Appendix C. WPI System Dynamics Teaching Faculty

Current Faculty

James K. Doyle. Associate Professor of Psychology and Department Head at WPI (Ph.D., University of Colorado, Boulder, 1992). Areas of expertise: applied social and cognitive psychology, judgment and decision making, risk perception and communication, psychological foundations of system dynamics, and mental models of complex systems.

Robert Eberlein. Co-President, ISEE systems, Inc. (Ph.D., Massachusetts Institute of Technology). Expertise: system dynamics software design and development, model analysis and evaluation, sensitivity analysis, and model optimization. He has been working in the field of System Dynamics for 30 years and has extensive experience teaching and consulting. He recently spent 18 months working in the Health Services and Systems Research department at Duke NUS Graduate medical school. He has been active in the System Dynamics Society as President (2004), Secretary, VP Meetings and, currently, VP of Electronic Presence.

Karim Chichakly. Co-President of isee systems and practitioner in the isee Systems Innovation Practice. He has nearly 20 years of system dynamics experience building models primarily in the areas of business strategy, business processes, and public policy, including variations of a national health care model and several infectious disease models. He has a Bachelor's and Master's degrees from Skidmore College, Dartmouth College as well as a Master's in system dynamics from WPI, and a Ph.D. in computer science from University of Vermont.

Andrew Ford. Professor of Environmental Science, School of Earth and Environmental Sciences, Washington State University (Ph.D., Dartmouth College). Areas of expertise: energy modeling, environmental dynamics and policy, and regional planning. In his research he focuses on environmental problems and energy in the western USA. He also teaches a class on climate change.

Michael J. Radzicki. Associate Professor of Economics at WPI (Ph.D., University of Notre Dame, 1985). Professor Radzicki is the creator of WPI's program in system dynamics and co-creator of WPI's program in trading system development. He received his Ph.D. in economics from the University of Notre Dame and his training in system dynamics modeling from the Massachusetts Institute of Technology. In addition, he is a certified Rapid-I Predictive Analytics Analyst. Professor Radzicki's research focuses on predictive analytics, simulation science, and the application of techniques from these areas to problems in economics, finance, and management. He has been invited to speak around the world in venues such as the White House, the Royal Society, the New York Stock Exchange, the United States Departments of Energy, Transportation, and Homeland Security, and Sandia National Laboratories. He has also served on the editorial board of several professional journals and as a consultant to numerous Fortune 500 corporations. In addition to his work in data analysis and simulation, Professor Radzicki is an avid long distance runner, martial artist, golfer, and currency trader. In 2006 he served as president of the System Dynamics Society.

Oleg V. Pavlov. Associate Professor of Economics and System Dynamics at WPI (Ph.D., University of Southern California, 2000). Areas of expertise: system dynamics modeling, computational economics, economics of information systems, and complex economics dynamics. He is past President of the Economics Chapter of the System Dynamics Society and now serves on the Executive Board of the Economics Chapter. He is the Coordinator for the WPI graduate system dynamics program.

Khalid Saeed. Professor of Economics and System Dynamics at WPI (Ph.D., Massachusetts Institute of Technology, 1981). Dr. Saeed was a student of Jay Forrester at MIT and has worked on developing system dynamics models of real-world systems. His insight models have been used to test policies for environmental sustenance, replicate psychology experiments, design innovative organizations, implement developmental agendas, and improve performance of governance systems. He has been teaching the art and science of system dynamics for the past several decades. Dr. Saeed also published on methodological issues. As part of a multidisciplinary team he recently studied the

US organ transplant system. This project was supported by HRSA. Dr. Saeed is a former President of the System Dynamics Society (1995) and a recipient of the Jay Forrester Award in System Dynamics.

Jim Thompson. Independent Management Consultant based in Connecticut (Ph.D. University of Strathclyde, Glasgow, Scotland). Dr. Thompson is an experienced system dynamics modeler of health care applications and an enthusiastic instructor with the ample experience of teaching workshops, in-class courses and designing online courses. He developed and periodically teaches a Health Dynamics course in the online graduate system dynamics program at WPI. He works with a wide group of stakeholders to resolve issues in health care systems—new pharmaceuticals introductions, evaluating medical technologies, challenges unique to care for frail elderly, control of infectious diseases, and capacity planning. From 2010 through 2012, Dr. Thompson was Head of the Health Systems Design Laboratory at Duke-NUS Graduate Medical School in Singapore, where he focused on health service delivery of treatment and care for persons with age-associated dementia.

John Morecroft. Senior Fellow at London Business School (Ph.D. Massachusetts Institute of Technology). He is an expert in the use of business modeling and simulation for strategy and scenario analysis. He has been a consultant for international organizations including McKinsey and Co., Royal Dutch/Shell, BBC and Mars. Dr. Morecroft is a founding member of the System Dynamics Society. He was an Associate Dean of the Executive MBA Program at London Business School. He also taught at MIT. He is a past Editor of the System Dynamics Review and a member of the Strategic Management Society and INFORMS.

Kim Warren. Owner and Director of Strategy Dynamics Ltd. He is an experienced strategy consultant and teacher who wrote Competitive Strategy Dynamics (Wiley 2002) and Strategic Management Dynamics (Wiley 2008). These two books focus on the strategy dynamics framework which was designed by Dr. Warren as a tool for improving business performance over time. He was teaching strategy dynamics at London Business School from 1990 to 2012. In 2013, he was President of the International System Dynamics Society. Dr. Warren is a recipient of the Jay Forrester award from the International System Dynamics Society. He holds an MBA and Ph.D. from London Business School.

Former Faculty

Jennifer Kemeny. Independent Consultant. For over 25 years she has pioneered increasingly powerful approaches to create real results—critical insights, renewed motivation and fundamental transformation for her clients. She has worked with Senior Executives in companies of all sizes; from the world's largest institutions to small start-up companies. She has broad for-profit industry experience, but has also devoted considerable time to educational and health care issues. Ms. Kemeny graduated from Dartmouth College in 1975 with a degree in Mathematics/Computer Science. At MIT's Sloan School, from 1980–1986, she pursued doctoral studies in System Dynamics, with a minor in Organization Theory. Ms. Kemeny has an ABD from MIT.

Elise Axelrad, currently a Senior Scientist at HUMPro. Dr. Axelrad was an Assistant Professor at WPI during 2001–2006. Her expertise is in psychology and statistics, with focus on judgment and decision making, problem framing, research design, data analysis, modeling and simulation. She holds degrees from the University of Toronto and she earned a Ph.D. in psychology at Duke University. Prior to WPI, Dr. Axelrad was a Research Associate at University at Albany.

Jim Hines. Consultant at astute SD. Areas of expertise: system dynamics modeling, insight from models, software development, system dynamics consulting methodology. Dr. Hines consulted to public and private-sector organizations in a variety of industries including electronics, software, financial, publishing, shipbuilding, and aerospace. In addition to teaching at WPI, he had taught system dynamics at MIT and at Brown University. He holds a Ph.D. in system dynamics from MIT, an MBA in finance and statistics from the University of Chicago, and a BA in English and Anthropology from Amherst College.

Systems **2014**, *2*, 54–76

James M. Lyneis, currently an Independent Consultant and a Senior Lecturer at MIT, where he teaches System Dynamics and System and Project Management. At WPI, he was a Professor of Practice in System Dynamics. He worked for 25 years in the Business Dynamics Practice of PA Consulting Group (formerly known as Pugh-Roberts Associates). He was General Manager for Pugh-Robert's European office from 1988–1990. At Pugh-Roberts, Dr. Lyneis specialized in the application of system dynamics techniques to business strategy, market analysis, project management, and management training, and worked in the telecommunications, electric utility, aerospace, and financial services industries. Prior to consulting, he was an Assistant Professor at MIT's Sloan School of Management. Dr. Lyneis is the author of the book Corporate Planning and Policy Design: A System Dynamics Approach, as well as numerous journal articles. He has a Ph.D. in Business Administration from the University of Michigan and undergraduate degrees in Electrical Engineering and Industrial Management from MIT.

systems

MDPI

Communication

Four Decades of Systems Science Teaching and Research in the USA at Portland State University

Wayne Wakeland

Systems Science Program, School of the Environment, Portland State University, 1604 S.W. 10th Ave., Portland, OR 97201, USA; wakeland@pdx.edu; Tel.: +1-503-725-4975; Fax: +1-503-725-8489

Received: 8 February 2014; in revised form: 14 March 2014; Accepted: 1 April 2014; Published: 8 April 2014

Abstract: Systems science is defined in general fashion, and a brief background is provided that lists some of the systems science-related societies, conferences, journals, research institutes, and educational programs. The Systems Science Graduate Program at Portland State University in Portland, OR, USA, is described in detail, including its history, curriculum, students, faculty, and degrees granted. Dissertation topics are summarized via word diagrams created from dissertation titles over the years. MS degrees, student placement, and undergraduate courses are also mentioned, and future plans for the program are described including its support for sustainability education.

Keywords: masters; doctorates; graduate students; student backgrounds

1. Introduction

Systems science [1] is the study of general principles that govern systems of widely differing types, and the use of systems ideas and methods in interdisciplinary/transdisciplinary research and socio-technical system design and management. Systems science draws on the natural and social sciences, mathematics, computer science, and engineering to address complex problems in both the public and private sectors.

For historical context, both the International Society for the Systems Sciences [2] and the system dynamics field were founded in 1956. The Hawaii International Conference on Systems Sciences [3] began its annual conference in 1967, and the International Journal of Systems Science [4] began publication in 1970. The first conference on system dynamics was held in 1976.

The need for interdisciplinary approaches to understanding and solving complex problems has received increasing attention in recent years, nationally and globally [5,6], and a focus on complex systems is central both to advances in science and engineering, real-world problem solving, and interdisciplinary research. Table 1 shows a small sample of institutes with a systems and complexity science focus. While the term interdisciplinary is most commonly used to describe systems-oriented endeavors, the terms crossdisciplinary, transdisciplinary, or multidisciplinary may be more apt or descriptive in some cases. Interdisciplinary usually involves an integration or synthesis of more than one discipline, whereas crossdisciplinary tends to refer to importing concepts from a different discipline in order to shift perspective without necessarily effecting an integration or synthesis. Trandisciplinary is often used to connote the idea of transcending specific disciplines and operating at a more holistic level, and multidisciplinary simply means employing multiple disciplines. Systems science is perhaps best described as transdisciplinary, although interdisciplinary is not incorrect.

Table 1. Example Systems-Oriented Research Institutes.

Name	Focus	Founded	Location
International Institute for Applied Systems Analysis [7]	Policy-oriented global problems	1972	Vienna, Austria
Santa Fe Institute [8]	Complex adaptive systems	1984	Santa Fe, NM, USA
New England Complex Systems Institute [9]	Complex systems	1996	Cambridge, MA, USA
Max Plank Institute for Dynamics and Self Organization [10]	Complex, self-organizing systems	2003	Gottingen, Germany
ARC Centre for Complex Systems [11]	Complex systems	2004	Australia

2. Background

The Systems Science Graduate Program [12] (SySc) at Portland State University (PSU) was launched in 1970 as one of the first three doctoral programs offered when PSU became a university. The choice of systems science, along with environmental studies and urban studies, was motivated by a policy in the state of Oregon that prohibited duplication of doctoral programs at state-funded universities. So the initial doctoral programs were interdisciplinary and hoped to be at the cutting edge. The vision for SySc was to serve as a resource and focal point for integrative, systems-oriented teaching and research on the PSU campus and within the broader PSU community. The new doctoral programs initially reported directly to the dean of graduate studies.

In the mid-1980s, in order to strengthen the base of support for the program, SySc began working closely with nine academic units so as to allow students to minor in systems science while pursuing a primarily disciplinary Ph.D. This option was especially popular in Psychology, Engineering and Technology Management, and the Business School. In addition, of course, some students continued to major in systems science. As the state began to relax its policy regarding doctoral program duplication, many of the participating departments established their own Ph.D. programs. Consequently, SySc began transitioning to a stand-alone program. A Master of Science degree was added, and SySc began to offer interdisciplinary undergraduate courses in PSU's University Studies general education program.

Figure 1 shows that SySc is focused near the intersection of systems research and systems practice; it emphasizes systems ideas, methods, and applications (the shaded area within the dotted ellipse). Systems engineering, analysis, and management are not a primary focus, nor are some of the more abstract systems theories such as chaos theory and fractals. This focus allowed the program to complement rather than compete with established departments, such as Electrical and Computer Engineering, Civil and Industrial Engineering, Computer Science, Mathematics, and Management Science. Of course, Figure 1 does not intend to fully represent the many subfields and theories relevant to systems science, as only a small sample of them are included within the "Systems Research" circle. Others not shown include graph theory, network theory, hierarchy theory, fuzzy logic, game theory, catastrophe theory, and control theory, to name a few.

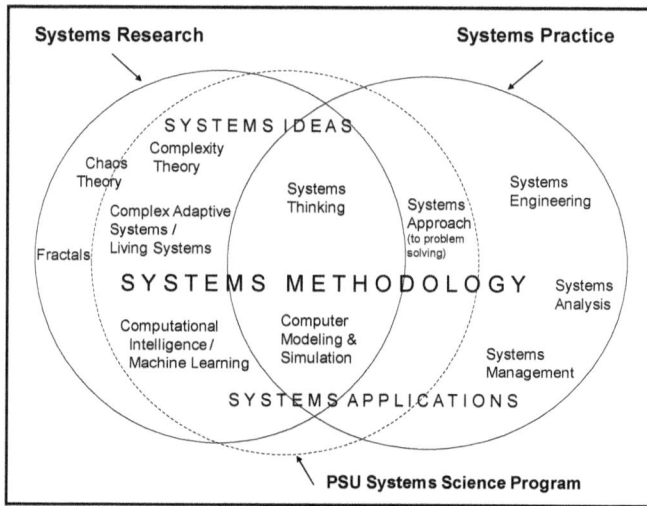

Figure 1. Graphic depiction of the field of Systems Science and the PSU Systems Science Program.

2.1. Program Curriculum

The core SySc program has grown rapidly in recent years, fostering interdisciplinary collaborations within PSU, especially in computer science, electrical and computer engineering, urban studies, business, and public administration and policy; and also with strategic and community partners. Interdisciplinary graduate and undergraduate courses enable PSU students to learn systems ideas, theories, thinking approaches, as well as modeling and data analysis/data-mining methods.

Table 2 provides a brief summary of the courses and their role in the curriculum, by level, with graduate classes listed first. Recently, undergraduate (UG) sections have been proposed for several of the graduate classes in order to bolster their viability, and two new courses were initiated recently with both graduate and UG sections. For graduate courses, the role of each course is noted, including core, core methods, methods, or electives. The six UG classes that were developed in recent years are shown at the bottom of the table. Four of these new UG courses were developed by SySc graduate students. In addition to supporting the degree programs, eight of the graduate courses support graduate certificates, and this is noted in the table. The table also notes that four of the recently developed courses emphasize sustainability. Course frequency is provided as well, either high (annually), medium (bi-annually), or low (less often).

Table 2. Systems Science Curriculum Details.

Level	Name	Role	Grad. Cert. *	Sustainability?	Freq	When Intro	Notes
Grad	Systems Theory	Core			H	70's	
Grad	Systems Approach	Core			H	70's	Renaming to Holistic Strategies for Problem Solving + add UG
Grad	System Dynamics	Core Methods	CM (req'd)		H	80's	
Grad	Game Theory	Elective			L	80's	Adding UG section to bolster
Grad	Artificial Life	Elective			L	80's	
Grad	AI: Neural Networks	Methods	CI (req'd)		L	80's	Instructor retired; some revamping needed
Grad	Discrete System Simulation	Methods	CM (req'd)		H	80's	
Grad	Quantitative Methods of Systems Science	Core Methods	CM & CI		L	90's	Major revision planned to incr. relevance to environ. scientists
Grad	Systems Philosophy	Elective			H	90's	Adding UG section to bolster
Grad	Discrete Multivariate Models	Core Methods	CM & CI		H	90's	
Grad	Business Process Modeling & Simulation	Methods	CM		L	90's	Outreach: business
Grad	Manufacturing System Simulation	Methods	CM		L	90's	Outreach: engineering & technology management
Grad	Agent Based Simulation	Methods	CM		H	2002	Outreach: social science, computer science
Grad	Systems Ideas and Sustainability	Elective		Yes	M	2009	Adding UG section to bolster interest
Grad	System Sustainability and Organizational Resilience	Elective		Yes	M	2011	Outreach: public policy
Both	Systems Thinking for Business	Elective			H	2013	Outreach: business
Both	Data Mining with Information Theory	Elective			H	2013	Outreach: computer science, social science, biomedicine
UG	Models in Science				H	2010	Create UG presence
UG	Indigenous and Systems Perspectives on Sustainability			Yes	H	2011	Ditto
UG	Intro. to Agent Based Modeling				H	2012	Ditto
UG	Modeling Social-ecological Systems			Yes	H	2012	Ditto
UG	Networks in Society				H	2013	Ditto
UG	Decision-Making in Complex Environments				H	2013	Ditto

* CM = computer modeling. CI = computational intelligence.

Although the number of courses that focus explicitly on sustainability is just four, the field of systems science is well positioned to provide tools, methods, concepts, and models for helping to evaluate and foster sustainability, especially with respect to environmental stewardship and economic prosperity. Important principles are discussed in game theory (e.g., prisoner's dilemmas, evolution of cooperation), systems philosophy (e.g., open systems, externalities), and the systems approach (systems archetypes, such as limits to growth and tragedy of the commons).

Figure 2 depicts two frequently employed SySc methods in order to give a flavor of what is taught in SySc. Figure 2A shows the lattice of possible models of four variables as identified by the systems-oriented data analysis method called reconstructability analysis (RA) which is taught in the SySc course entitled Discrete Multivariate Models. RA was developed by Broekstra, Cavallo, Cellier, Conant, Jones, Klir, Krippendorff, and others (*c.f.* [13–15]). Figure 2B depicts an artificial neural network (ANN), a widely used artificial intelligence method taught in the SySc course entitled "AI: Neural Networks" (there are many good texts, *c.f.* [16]). ANNs are "trained" to predict outcomes given a set of inputs.

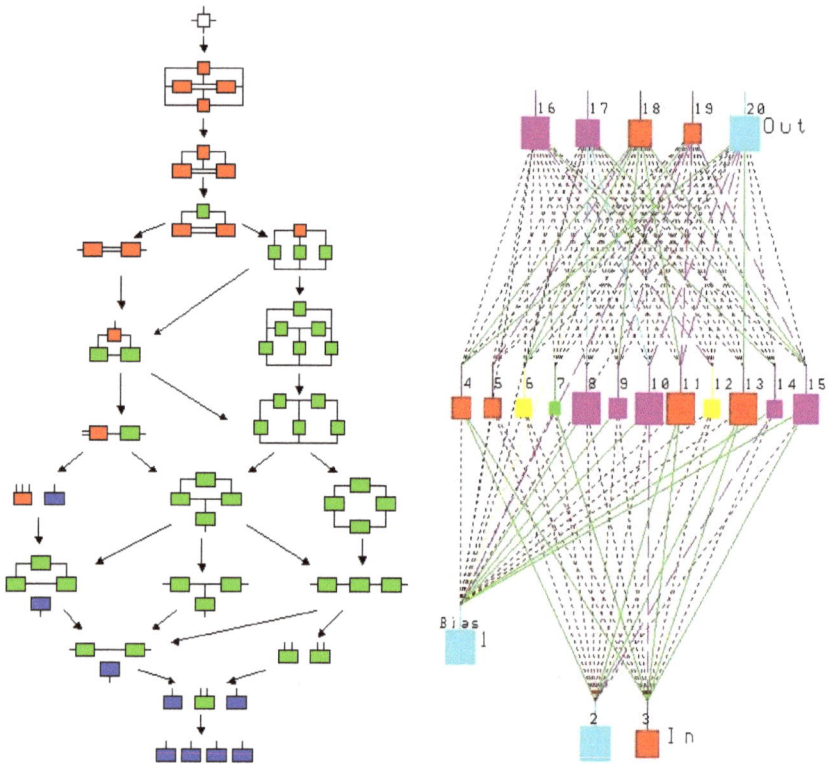

Figure 2. (A) Lattice of models of four variables in reconstructability analysis. A box is a relation; a line, with branches, uninterrupted by a box, is a variable. Arrows indicate decomposition and colors represent the number of variables contained in a relation. **(B)** Artificial Neural Network with a one hidden layer.

The top structure in Figure 2A is ABCD, which is the data itself; and the bottom structure is A:B:C:D, which is the independence model. The symbols in Figure 2A represent the various possible types of interactions amongst the four variables, as determined by considering their covariance structure. Fitness of models is assessed using information theoretic measures. Figure 2B indicates that the network has two inputs, five outputs, and three layers (input, hidden, and output). The weights connecting the nodes are determined through a training process employing input/output data records that seeks to minimize the error in the values at the output layer compared to the actual data, both for the dataset used for training and test data sets not used for training.

2.2. Comparison to other Systems Science Programs in the USA and Globally

Dozens of systems science programs were created during the 1960s and 1970s, but only a few such programs remain today. Two examples in the USA include [17] at Binghamton University (SUNY) which has been closely linked with industrial engineering and automation for the past decade, and [18] at Washington University which is located in the Department of Electrical and Systems Engineering. Another example of a system science MS degree program can be found at the University of Ottawa, Canada [19]. Systems-oriented degree programs in Europe and Australasia tend to focus on systems engineering or complex systems mathematics. The SySc program at PSU shares with these other programs strong connections with engineering, computer science, and mathematics, but also provides a strong practitioner focus that features applications in biomedicine, health policy, and environmental sustainability.

2.3. Student Population

Our student population has varied over the years from two dozen students in the early years, to over 100 students a decade ago when departmental participation was in full bloom. During this time period, the core program also grew from ten to thirty students, and in recent years, the core program has increased to nearly 50 students: 30 doctoral students and 20 master's students. The non-core doctoral programs are being phased out, and there are currently less than 10 departmental students finishing up their research. "Core" SySc students take four to six core SySc courses and four to six elective SySc courses, plus elective courses across campus appropriate to support their research. A multi-disciplinary track was create several years ago in part to accommodate applicants seeking a more traditional interdisciplinary rather than transdisciplinary learning experience. Students in the multi-disciplinary track take three SySc core courses and three SySc electives, plus core sequences in two other field/disciplines such as environmental science, business, economics, computer science, or mathematics.

Our students come from an amazingly diverse collection of backgrounds. A recent review of the backgrounds of 44 core SySc students (27 Ph.D., 17 MS) revealed that they had earned their bachelor's degree in 27 different fields. Figure 3A shows the most common bachelor's degrees. Nearly all of the 27 doctoral students had already earned a Master's degree, as represented in Figure 3B. Two students had previously earned terminal degrees, one in architecture and one in medicine. Based on the subjective impressions of the faculty, having a more technical background tends to be correlated with successful completion, but communication skills, ability to focus, and time management seem to be nearly equally as important.

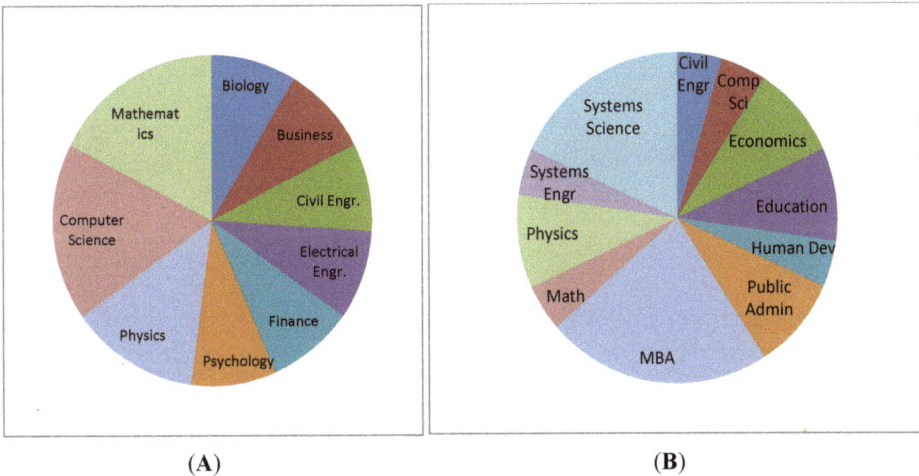

Figure 3. (**A**) Distribution of SySc Student Bachelor's Degrees, (**B**) SySc Student Master's Degrees.

Table 3 provides data regarding the long term trends for annual graduation rates for doctorates and MS degrees, and, more recently annual graduate and undergraduate student credit hour generation rates. Note that most of the UG credit hours are generated by graduate students teaching UG courses, and that several of these courses were developed by the students.

Table 3. Annual Graduation Rate and Annual Student Credit Hour Generation Rate, by Decade.

	1972–79	1980–89	1990–99	2000–09	2010–13
Departmental Ph.D. Graduates	0	0.7	2.7	6.2	3.0
SySc Core Ph.D. Graduates	1.1	2.0	2.6	1.3	1.3
SySc MS Graduates	0	0	0	2.8	6
Graduate Student Credit Hours	n/a	n/a	n/a	900	865
Undergraduate Student Credit Hours	0	0	0	156	480

2.4. Faculty

Until recently, core faculty consisted of 2.67 tenure lines, a 0.75 FTE fixed term faculty member, plus two to three adjunct faculty members who teach one or two courses per year (representing the teaching equivalent of another tenure line). Due to a recent retirement, however, that number has dropped to two tenure lines, plus adjunct faculty who teach one or two classes each. Core faculty members were George Lendaris, who focused on the systems approach and the use of neural networks and reinforcement learning for system control, Harold Linstone, who focused on technological forecasting and assessment, Martin Zwick, who focuses on systems philosophy and theory, game theory, and data mining using discrete mathematical models, Andy Fraser, who emphasized information theory and dynamical systems, and Wayne Wakeland, who focuses on the use of computer modeling and simulation to better understand the behavior of complex systems.

Besides coursework and student dissertation research, SySc faculty members also engage in externally funded research. In recent years, annual research expenditures have often exceeded $100K, which has helped to provide support for many graduate students. Table 4 provides a brief summary of externally funded research.

Table 4. Externally Funded Systems Science Research.

Project Period	Brief Project Description	Researcher	Role	Funding Source	Amount
1999–2002	Adaptive Critics for Controller Design	Lendaris	PI	NSF	$300K
2002–2003	State Space Designs for Aircraft Control	Lendaris	PI	NASA	$57K
2003–2006	Surface Design for Controllers	Lendaris	PI	NSF	$218K
2003–2006	Modeling Intracranial Pressure Dynamics in Pediatric Traumatic Brain Injury	Wakeland	co-PI	Thrasher Research Fund	$320K
2003–2006	Optimizing IV & V Costs and Benefits using Simulation	Wakeland	co-PI	NASA	$624K
2009–2011	SD Model for Reducing Risks of Prescription Drug Abuse and Diversion	Wakeland	PI	Purdue Pharma, L.P.	$198K
2011–2014	System Dynamics of Prescription Opioid Misuse	Wakeland	PI	NIH/NIDA	$360K
2014	Dynamic Model of Concussion Recovery	Wakeland	PI	Brain Trauma Foundation	$91K

Research-active faculty are sometimes able to reduce their teaching load, but due to the small size of the program, all SySc core faculty must teach at least one course per term and must advise many students, necessitating carefully balancing of priorities. The normal teaching load is four 4-credit quarter-long courses per year. It is possible for over half a faculty member's student credit hour generation to be derived from advising students regarding dissertation or thesis research, and supporting individualized readings and conference courses. These additional credit hours, however, do not (cannot) take the place of teaching regular catalog courses.

3. Results

3.1. Doctorates

As summarized in Table 3, nearly 200 Systems Science PhDs have been earned since the program's inception, specifically, 9 in the 1970's, then 27, 54, 79, and 17 in subsequent decades.

Figures 4–6 show Word diagrams that were created from the titles of dissertations awarded in the first two decades, the third decade, and the most recent decade, respectively. Several trends are visible in Figures 4–6. First, the words Systems, Analysis, Model, and Technology are prevalent in each of the figures. Business was featured in Figure 4, but was supplanted by the word Industry over time. The frequency of the words Performance, Organizational, Information, and Decision has increased over time. The word Economic was featured only in Figure 4, and the words Selection and Health were featured only in Figure 5.

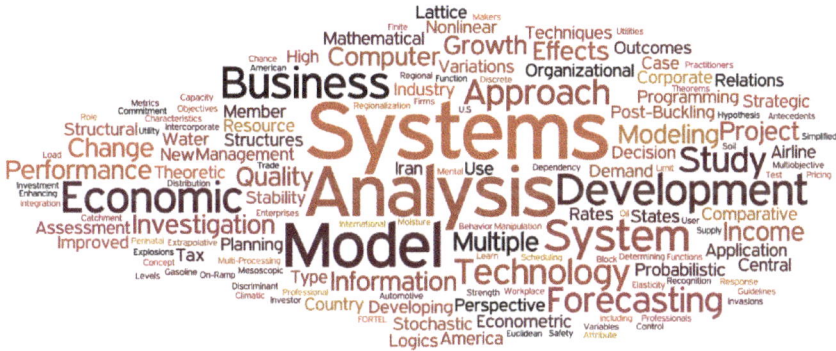

Figure 4. Word Diagram of Dissertation Titles 1972 to 1993.

Figure 5. Word Diagram of Dissertation Titles 1994 to 2003.

Figure 6. Word Diagram of Dissertation Titles 2004 to 2013.

3.2. Masters Degrees

In addition, as summarized in Table 3, since 2002, over 50 MS degrees have been awarded. Most MS students have chosen the exam option, although students have recently been choosing the thesis option, with topics such as renewable energy, operational efficiency, and machine learning.

3.3. Student Placement

SySc develops the students' skills as generalists, which employers value highly as a complement to the specific skills being sought. Some of our graduates are now faculty members at PSU and several other universities, while other graduates have started companies such as consulting firms or software development firms. Many of our graduates work in governmental agencies, such as Bonneville Power, the Veterans Administration, or the National Laboratory System; and others work as researchers at public institutions and private enterprises, including healthcare, high technology, and energy consulting. Others are teaching or serving as administrators at secondary schools or community colleges. Many create their own roles in their organizations, either at the outset or over time.

4. Concluding Remarks

The evolution of PSU's Systems Science Program is continuing—SySc is now part of the PSU's School of the Environment (SoE) within the College of Liberal Arts and Sciences, and it is likely that student research topics will tend to shift towards environmental concerns and sustainability-related topics, although not to the exclusion of core systems subjects such as the development of systems methods, biomedicine, health policy, and urban systems. The move to the SoE occurred because SySc had become the only academic unit at PSU that was not located in a school or college. Several options were explored, including the Maseeh College of Engineering and Computer Science, the College of Urban and Public Affairs, and the Mathematics and Statistics department in CLAS, but the SoE proved to be the best option.

As noted earlier, many systems science programs merged over time with a specific disciplinary department, and this has tended to lead to a significant narrowing of their focus. The same could happen with SySc. However, being located in a highly interdisciplinary environmental school as opposed to a specific department should bode well for SySc, especially because systems science methods can help to strengthen the quantitative analysis capabilities of students interested in environmental science and management. As shown in Table 2, the curriculum has been evolving rapidly in recent years, and that evolution is expected to continue. In addition, despite a high degree

Systems **2014**, *2*, 77–88

of uncertainty in recent years, it seems reasonable to believe that the prospects for SySc remain bright, due in no small part to its ability to respond quickly to needs as they arise.

Conflicts of Interest: The author declares no conflict of interest.

References

1. Wikipedia Entry for Systems Science. Available online: http://en.wikipedia.org/wiki/Systems_science (accessed on 8 February 2014).
2. International Society for the Systems Sciences. Available online: http://isss.org/world/index.php (accessed on 8 February 2014).
3. Hawaii International Conference on Systems Sciences. Available online: http://www.hicss.hawaii.edu/ (accessed on 8 February 2014).
4. International Journal of Systems Science website. Available online: http://www.tandfonline.com/toc/tsys20/current#.UvKCw7QWmbA (accessed on 8 February 2014).
5. Mabry, P.L.; Olster, D.H.; Morgan, G.D.; Abram, D.B. Interdisciplinarity and systems science to improve population health. *Am. J. Prev. Med.* **2008**, *35*, S211–S224. [CrossRef]
6. Sa, C.M. 'Interdisciplinary strategies' in U.S. research universities. *High Educ.* **2008**, *55*, 537–552. [CrossRef]
7. Website for a Long-Standing International Systems Institute Located in Europe: IIASA. Available online: http://en.wikipedia.org/wiki/International_Institute_for_Applied_Systems_Analysis (accessed on 8 February 2014).
8. Sante Fe Institute Website. Available online: http://www.santafe.edu/ (accessed on 8 February 2014).
9. New England Complex Systems Institute Website. Available online: http://necsi.edu/ (accessed on 8 February 2014).
10. Website for the Max Planck Institute for Dynamics and Self-Organization. Available online: http://www.ds.mpg.de/ (accessed on 8 February 2014).
11. Wikipedia Entry for Recently Established Systems Research Center Located in Australia. Available online: http://en.wikipedia.org/wiki/ARC_Centre_for_Complex_Systems (accessed on 8 February 2014).
12. Website for the Portland State University Systems Science Graduate Program. Available online: http://www.pdx.edu/sysc/ (accessed on 8 February 2014).
13. Hai, A.; Klir, G.J. An empirical investigation of reconstructability analysis: Probabilistic systems. *Int. J. Man Mach. Stud.* **1985**, *22*, 163–192. [CrossRef]
14. Klir, G. Reconstructability analysis: An offspring of Ashby's constraint theory. *Syst. Res.* **1986**, *3*, 267–271. [CrossRef]
15. Zwick, M. An overview of reconstructability analysis. *Kybernetes* **2004**, *33*, 877–905. [CrossRef]
16. Haykin, S. *Neural Networks and Learning Machines*, 3rd ed.; Prentice Hall: Upper Saddle River, NJ, USA, 2009.
17. Systems Science and Industrial Engineering Programs at Binghamton University (SUNY). Available online: http://www.binghamton.edu/ssie/grad/ (accessed on 8 February 2014).
18. Ph.D. in Systems Science & Mathematics at Washington University. Available online: http://ese.wustl.edu/graduateprograms/Pages/PhDinSystemsScienceandMathematics-1.aspx (accessed on 8 February 2014).
19. Masters Degree in Systems Science at University of Ottawa. Available online: http://www.grad.uottawa.ca/Default.aspx?tabid=1727&monControl=Programmes&ProgId=607 (accessed on 8 February 2014).

Article

systems

MDPI

Simulation-Based Learning Environments to Teach Complexity: The Missing Link in Teaching Sustainable Public Management

Michael Deegan [1], Krystyna Stave [2], Rod MacDonald [3], David Andersen [4], Minyoung Ku [4] and Eliot Rich [5,*]

1 U.S. Army Corps of Engineers, Institute for Water Resources, 7701 Telegraph Road, Alexandria, VA 22315, USA; Michael.A.Deegan@usace.army.mil
2 School of Environmental and Public Affairs, University of Nevada Las Vegas, 4505 Maryland Parkway, Las Vegas, NV 89154, USA; krystyna.stave@unlv.edu
3 Institute for System Dynamics in the Public Sector, University at Albany, State University of New York, 1400 Washington Avenue, Albany, NY 12222, USA; rmacdonald@albany.edu
4 Department of Public Administration, Rockefeller College of Public Affairs and Policy, University at Albany, State University of New York, 1400 Washington Avenue, Albany, NY 12222, USA; david.andersen@albany.edu (D.A.); mku@albany.edu (M.K.)
5 Department of Information Technology Management, School of Business, University at Albany, State University of New York, 1400 Washington Avenue, Albany, NY 12222, USA
* Author to whom correspondence should be addressed; erich2@albany.edu; Tel.: +1-518-956-8359.

Received: 16 January 2014; in revised form: 27 April 2014; Accepted: 16 May 2014; Published: 22 May 2014

Abstract: While public-sector management problems are steeped in positivistic and socially constructed complexity, public management education in the management of complexity lags behind that of business schools, particularly in the application of simulation-based learning. This paper describes a Simulation-Based Learning Environment for public management education that includes a coupled case study and System Dynamics simulation surrounding flood protection, a domain where stewardship decisions regarding public infrastructure and investment have direct and indirect effects on businesses and the public. The Pointe Claire case and CoastalProtectSIM simulation provide a platform for policy experimentation under conditions of exogenous uncertainty (weather and climate change) as well as endogenous effects generated by structure. We discuss the model in some detail, and present teaching materials developed to date to support the use of our work in public administration curricula. Our experience with this case demonstrates the potential of this approach to motivate sustainable learning about complexity in public management settings and enhance learners' competency to deal with complex dynamic problems.

Keywords: public management; simulation-based learning environment; SBLE; simulation case study; coastal protection; storm damage; system dynamics; complexity

1. Introduction: A Public Management Education Challenge

There is a new challenge facing public management education—to teach public managers to handle a broad range of novel situations characterized by complexity when dealing with an emerging class of problems that we dub "sustainable" public management problems. This paper first gives a quick overview of the current state of public management education, poses a preliminary multi-dimensional concept of complexity that encompasses both positivist and social constructionist view of complexity, and proposes a broad design for simulation-based learning environments (SBLEs) to teach in this complex domain. We next present an example of one such SBLE—the Pointe Claire Coastal Protection Case, a case focusing on the decisions of a fictional Regional Coastal Planning

Systems **2014**, *2*, 217–236

Commission on the Mississippi Coast faced with the dual threat of current storm damage from hurricanes such as those already hitting the coast (e.g., Katrina) as well as the future probable threats of enhanced damage due to global warming. Finally, the paper discusses how this SBLE was implemented in a first class on modeling methods in the core MPA program of the Rockefeller College of Public Affairs and Policy at the University at Albany, SUNY (the Rockefeller College, for short) and presents some instructor reflections on the effectiveness of the Pointe Claire Coastal Protection Case as a teaching method to enhance student competence to deal with dynamic problems in this complex domain. The paper concludes with thoughts about future research needed in this area.

Traditional Public Management Education and Complexity

The Current State of Public Management Education

Public management education relies heavily on traditional classroom learning which assumes that knowledge and skills needed for sustainable public management can be transferred from the instructor to the students through readings and lectures. As noted by Comfort and Wukich [1], the majority of courses on crisis management currently offered in MPA programs are designed and managed based on this traditional teaching and learning approach. However, rapid change in public policy decision making environments, especially the increase in technical and social complexity, has expanded the set of qualities expected of public managers, and the ways to nurture these qualities in MPA programs. The U.S. National Association of Schools of Public Affairs and Administration (NASPAA) suggests higher education and training programs in public management, public policy, and public affairs programs pursue five competencies as the core qualities of successful public managers: the ability (1) to lead and manage in public governance; (2) to participate in and contribute to the policy process; (3) to analyze, synthesize, think critically, solve problems and make decisions; (4) to articulate and apply a public service perspective; and (5) to communicate and interact productively with a diverse and changing workforce and citizenry [2]. However, the details of each competency are left to institutions that run education or training programs to define. Appendix A shows how the Rockefeller College has elaborated the NASPAA's five core competencies. Among the five competencies, our SBLE example model mainly seeks to achieve the third competency, that is, the ability to analyze, synthesize, think critically, solve problems and make decisions.

A Proposal for Thinking about Complexity

Public managers and policy makers in the 21st century are required to manage complex systems whose boundaries spill over agency, jurisdictional, and sector boundaries. Within these systems uncertainty is commonplace. Ever since Lindblom [3] first brought up complexity as a new topic, the literature has reviewed many features of such "wicked problems." Although various approaches to conceptualizing complexity exist (e.g., complex adaptive systems, agent-based, soft-systems methodology, and many others cataloged by [4]), little attention has been paid to methods and approaches for teaching and learning in and about complex systems in public management settings.

Here, we suggest a taxonomy of "complexity in public policy decisions" encompassing positivistic and interpretive features of systems complexity. This taxonomy, shown in Figure 1, classifies the features of complexity in public management settings largely into two dimensions: (1) *positivistic complexity*, which is a bundle of objectively observable and measureable features that make public policy problems difficult to manage (such as decision-making in the face of stochastic uncertainty or feedback complexity within complex systems models); and (2) *socially constructed complexity*, an interpretive perspective which results from the diverse interactions of multiple stakeholders with often competing points of view, leading to intra-group, organizational, or political conflicts. The taxonomy includes suggested analysis methods for different kinds of positivist complexity in parentheses.

Technical goal issues
(Use optimization)

Stochastic Uncertainty
(Use Decision Trees)

Positivist
Complexity
(Model as
Micro-
World)

Dynamic Complexity
(Use difference equations,
System Dynamics)

Thinking Through
Time

Stock-and-Flow
Thinking

Detail Complexity
(Use MAU Models)

Feedback
Complexity

Other...

Complexity in
Public Policy
Decisions

Individual Value
Differences

Electoral Politics

Conflict

Stakeholder Complexity

Organizational
Values and Norms

Socially
Constructed
Complexity
(Model as
Boundary
Object)

Complex, Diverse
and Competing
Policy Goals

Equity vs. Efficiency

Legal and Institutional
constraints

Free Market vs.
Interventionist
Orientation

Other...

Etc.

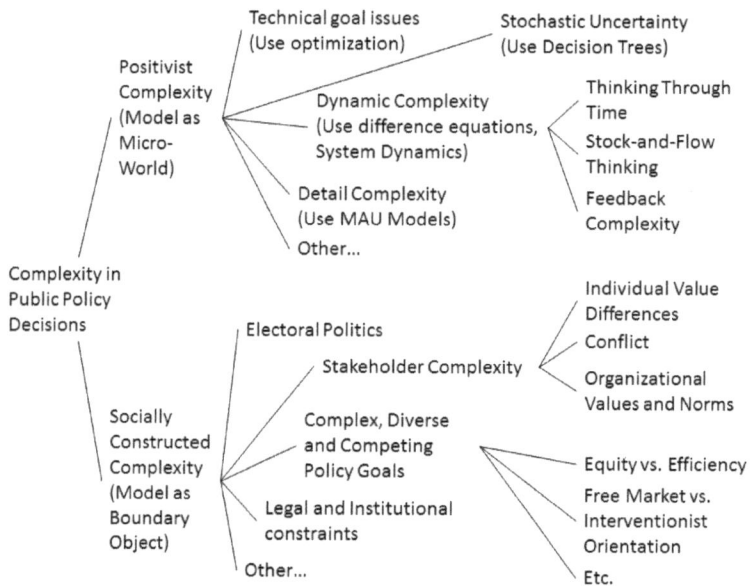

Figure 1. A taxonomy of complexity in public policy decisions.

How This Paper Addresses Complexity in the Public Management Curriculum

In this paper, we address the question of how to teach complexity in public management curriculum by reporting on a curricular innovation—the introduction of a simulation-based learning environment—and reflect on the effectiveness of the approach. Simulation-based cases are widely used in business education, but are relatively new in public management education [5]. We believe they offer significant advantages for public management education and should be more widely used. In particular, simulation-based cases allow the pairing of realistic scenarios with accessible technology for rapid experimentation. Simulations compress the time it takes to "experience" long-term effects of policy options and allow learners to experiment with different assumptions. Cases can be crafted to ensure that diverse stakeholders' positions are patent and visible, while simulation tools can give students the opportunity to test the effects of diverse alternative interventions.

2. Development of the Simulation-Based Learning Environment

With the taxonomy shown in Figure 1 in mind, we designed a simulation-based learning environment (SBLE) to help students understand how to manage multiple dimensions of complexity. A simulation-based learning environment is a package of materials and exercises designed around a simulation model. The goal of the SBLE is to help learners discover concepts in the process of experimenting with the simulation. The environment instantiates the "double-looping learning model" proposed by Sterman [6] for teaching and learning about complexity. Kim *et al.* [7] have previously extended and applied this vision of double loop learning to applied projects in the public sector and Ghaffarzadegan and Andersen [8] have applied similar concepts to developing theory about public safety. The two main branches in Figure 1 reflect two quite different views of what role a model may play in public policy analysis. The top branch suggests that a model can be used as a "micro-world": a representation of a particular policy environment with all its related types of system-level complexity to help managers (and students) explore and understand uncertainty and feedback complexity. The bottom branch of the diagram in Figure 1 suggests that a good model can serve as a "boundary object" or as an artifact that can be used to support active dialogue and learning between involved stakeholders, helping them navigate socially constructed boundaries in the system. Black [9] and Black and Andersen [10] have provided a more complete elaboration of how formal models can serve as boundary objects in the policy process.

Exercises within the environment are typically scaffolded such that initial exercises provide learners with a high degree of guidance, then successive exercises provide progressively less external instruction and require greater learner autonomy [11]. SBLEs can be designed for varying degrees of facilitation, ranging from stand-alone packages that require almost no live facilitation to exercises used in classroom settings with significant instructor involvement [12]. Progressively removing scaffolding in a series of exercises promotes double-loop learning by building learning skills at the same time as it facilitates specific content learning. The exercises in this SBLE guide students to confront and examine different aspects of decision complexity. Following the double-loop model, participants are first guided to experience complexity, then reflect on their experience to make sense of it.

We modified a core Rockefeller College class in Data, Models, and Decisions to include an extended 10 week unit dealing with the efforts of a community on the Gulf Coast of the United States to manage coastal protection planning. The curricular unit was called the Pointe Claire Coastal Protection Planning Exercise and consisted of a variety of models drawn from standard topics in the class (decision trees, difference equations, and multi-attribute utility models), all dealing with coastal protection. All the exercises concerned the Pointe Claire Coastal Protection Case Study. The focus of the Pointe Claire case is community policy-making for protection against storm damage. Although Pointe Claire is a fictitious coastal town set on the US Gulf Coast, its issues are common among many real Gulf Coast communities. It is based on an actual planning project undertaken by the US Army Corps of Engineers on the Mississippi Coast, but is not calibrated to any specific place.

In addition to analytic exercises, students engaged in role-playing assignments where student teams analyzed the positions of various stakeholders within the community. Students wrote policy white papers to the Executive Director of the Coastal Planning Commission from the point of view of a newly hired executive assistant helping the Executive Director deal with the technical complexities of the coastal planning project (the Commission in the case study was working with the US Army Corps of Engineers) as well as differing perspectives of various stakeholders on the planning commission. As one part of the overall 10-week Planning Exercise, students worked with a system dynamics simulation model that depicts complex dynamic interactions involved in coastal protection.

The purpose of the Pointe Claire SBLE was two-fold: (1) In substantive terms, to teach students to use a complex simulation model as a tool to understand a multi-faceted set of interactions and come up with robust policy conclusions; and (2) In terms of the policy process, to teach students how to use complex models to help groups of public policy stakeholders come to agreement around policy goals. The SBLE was designed around the CoastalProtectSIM simulation model, which allows participants to explore the effect of policies under normally variable storm conditions as well as conditions expected under climate change. The complete learning environment consists of a system dynamics simulation model of the impact of storms on a typical coastal community plus a series of exercises that focus on stakeholder complexity and decision making within a community-based governing board tasked with planning for such storms in the face of future-possible global warming threats. The learning environment had three phases: (1) Set up; (2) Guided Use of the Simulator; and (3) Post Simulation Debriefing. The content of each phase and our qualitative assessment of the effectiveness of the exercise are contained in Sections 4.2 and 4.3 below.

The CoastalProtectSim model is the centerpiece of the Pointe Claire Simulation-Based Learning Environment. The model and exercises were developed by a team: The lead modeler currently works for the US Army Corps of Engineers and used his experience working in water resources for the Corps as a basis for much of the model structure. While the model was based on representative characteristics of coastal communities, it is a simplified model for teaching. The biogeophysical science of this coastal region has not been as carefully calibrated as would be the case in an actual model developed by the

Systems **2014**, *2*, 217–236

Corps. Because the simulation model was a keystone to the larger set of activities, it is presented in more detail below.

3. The CoastalProtectSIM Model

CoastalProtectSIM captures elements of complexity within the problem context: (1) delays in constructing coastal protection; (2) cost sharing challenges for construction and annual maintenance; (3) impacts of costal land development on natural barriers; and (4) the timing of benefits and costs in net present value calculations for long range coastal flood risk planning.

The model uses a random number generator based on a seed parameter to create weather scenarios, whereby the probability of any particular storm may generate a surge large enough to exceed natural and man-made protection. The mechanism motivating the seeds is key the use of the model as a test of policy ideas. Each seed corresponds to what we refer to as a different "random world". The model can be simulated in several hundred different simulated worlds that differ in their behavior. Every time the simulation is run with the same seed, the model uses exactly the same set of random numbers to create exogenous storm behaviors. So for a given random seed (random world), students can get identical effects each time they run the model. This makes it easier for students to understand how the model is running under their policy constructs. However, students can also switch to another seed and generate another random world that obeys the same rules by selecting a parameter in the rerun menu, changing the size and timing of the exogenous natural environmental conditions, and again evaluate their plans under a different series of events with different timing.

In addition, an optional global warming scenario is built into the model that allows for the amplification of the storm surges based on severity of storms and sea level rise. Costs associated with mitigation and benefits from damages avoided are calculated in terms of their net present value at the required 7% discount rate for new projects at the US Army Corps of Engineers. CoastalProtectSIM requires the decision maker to determine whether the long term benefits are worth the investment of short and intermediate term mitigation measures. The time span for the model is 40 years to allow for long term and short term tradeoffs to be explored. In this section, we describe the model structure and provide base run behavior for three random "normal" and two climate change scenarios. The section concludes with a description of several policy runs and a discussion of tradeoffs for each strategy.

3.1. Model Description

CoastalProtectSIM (Figure 2) captures the essential elements of coastal storm planning. It has five model sectors: (1) structural mitigation; (2) land development and natural barriers; (3) storm intensity and climate change; (4) costs associated with damages and mitigation measures; and (5) benefits from cumulative tax revenue. Table 1 provides a legend for the causal map to help the reader identify each of the five variable types discussed in this section of the paper.

Table 1. Legend for CoastalProtectSIM causal map, shown in Figure 2.

Causal link color	CoastalProtectSIM Model Structure
Blue	Policies to mitigate damages and minimize recovery costs
Brown	Natural barriers to protect the community
Purple	Storms and climate change
Red	Disaster damages and mitigation costs
Green	Benefits from tax revenue and damages avoided

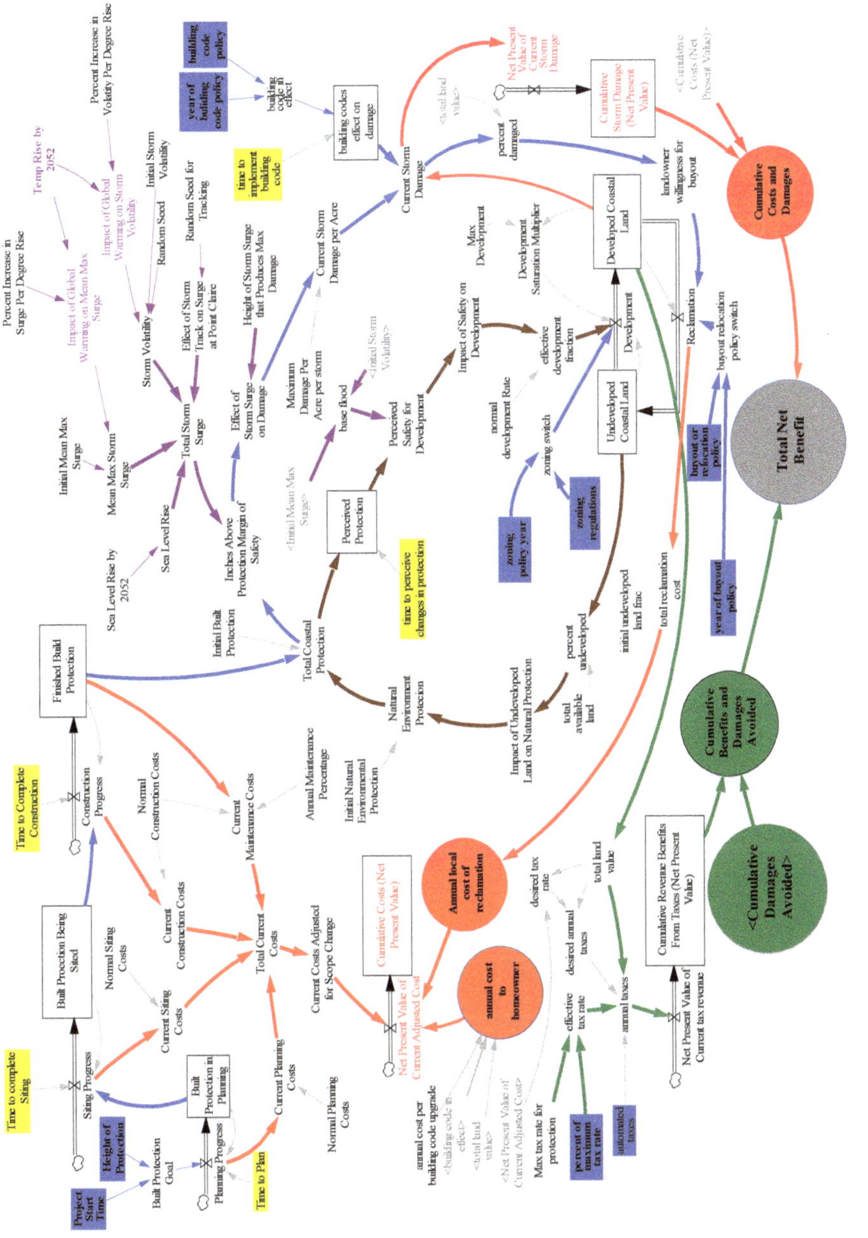

Figure 2. CoastalProtectSIM model structure.

3.1.1. Structural Mitigation (Blue Links in Figure 2)

The structure shown in the upper left corner of the causal map (Figure 2) captures the connection between the planning and implementation of structural coastal barriers, such as constructed levees, dams and beach nourishment projects. Community decision makers identify the desired height of protective structures and the project start time. The time to complete the plan formulation process is not within the control of the local decision maker. The *Built Protection in Planning* accumulation accounts for the time between the decision to construct protective barriers and the time it takes to complete reconnaissance and feasibility studies. In the U.S. Army Corps of Engineers' budgeting process, completed plans lead to *Built Protection Being Sited* through Preconstruction Engineering and Design (PED) investigations, which is an intermediate step before formal construction. The final accumulation, *Finished Build Protection*, is based on the rate of construction for protective structures along the coast. In the default settings of the model, which we term the "base run", the total delay for these three stocks is 10 years, which corresponds to the average delay time in the Corps's planning and construction process.

Projects that have been completed increase the *Total Coastal Protection* which reduce the amount of storm surge the community experiences directly (*Inches Above Protection Margin of Safety*). The model assumes a threshold over which storm surge will produce some degree of property damage. As storm surge rises above the total protection on the coast, the *Effect of Storm Surge on Damage* increases to a potential *Maximum Damage per Acre per Storm*, which has been set for the base run at maximum of \$100K/acre. *Current Storm Damage* is also influenced by the *building codes effect on damage*, which represents a policy whereby floodplain managers are able to successfully implement codes to guarantee lower levels of property damage during the next storm event.

If the *Current Storm Damage* is higher than the protection provided by structural policies or strict building code enforcement, the resulting *percent damages* indicate the extent of damages in the community. If this percent is relatively large, the *landowner willingness for buyout* will increase as well. It is conceivable landowners would be willing to relocate during the recovery period, thus creating open space and increasing the level of *Undeveloped Coastal Land* and reducing *Developed Coastal Land*. The potential balancing feedback loop suggests an opportunity to minimize future damages. Alternatively, a *zoning regulation* can be enforced to restrict *development*, which would help to guarantee the balancing loop maintains its goal seeking behavior. There is a caveat with respect to the link between *percent damaged* and *landowner willingness for buyout*. CoastalProtectSIM has model structure (hidden in this view) that activates federal disaster assistance in very large disasters, which may reduce the willingness to relocate in certain cases.

3.1.2. Natural Barriers (Brown Links)

The level of *Undeveloped Coastal Land* (center of Figure 2) acts as a natural barrier to protect against storm events. As this level increases, its *impact on Natural Protection* increases, which enhances the *natural environment* during major storm events. Communities that maintain large sand dunes between developed property and the ocean, as well as sustainable beaches solutions to import or relocate sand on the shore have more protection during hurricanes and major storm events. The natural barriers combine with structural protection to increase the *Total Coastal Protection*, which as previously discussed minimizes storm surge and flood damages. However, this added protection also increases the *perceived protection* in the community. A high *perceived safety for development* adds pressure on the community to expand and develop on the shore. As the *impact of safety on development* increases, *development* in the community will increase as well. Since this balancing loop contains a relatively long delay between actual and perceived safety in the community, it can lead to oscillations in the level of safety with the system.

Systems **2014**, *2*, 217–236

3.1.3. Storms and Climate Change (Purple Links)

The CoastalProtectSIM model operationalizes storms through two concepts: mean storm surge and volatility. *Total Storm Surge* is a function of *Mean Max Storm Surge, Storm Volatility, Sea Level Rise,* and *the effect of storm track*. The *Mean Max Storm Surge* is set at 108 inches in the base run, with the potential to increase based on the *impact of global warming on mean max surge*. *Storm Volatility* is formulated as a Random Normal variable with a range of −50–400 inches, an *initial storm volatility* of 24 inches (the standard deviation of the variable), with a dynamic *impact of global warming* to amplify the volatility over time. This variable is sampled for each storm based on a *Random Seed* that effectively selects one possible future pattern of storm conditions. To account for climate change, the model uses *Temperature Rise by 2052* to affect volatility through an assumed relationship of *percent increase in volatility per degree rise*. In the base run, the temperature rise is set at zero. *Sea Level* is a third contributing factor to storm surge. It is set at zero in the base run. The fourth and final contributing factor is the *Effect of Storm track on surge*, whose purpose is to add a layer of uncertainty in the model. That is, not every storm is perfectly predicted. In most cases, the storm surge is not as high as the protective barriers, which results in a zero *effect of storm surge on damage*.

3.1.4. Disaster Damages and Mitigation Costs (Red Links)

There are two types of costs recorded in CoastalProtectSIM. The first are costs associated with the implementation of mitigation policies. The model calculates *current planning costs, current siting costs, current construction costs,* and *maintenance costs* at an annual rate which feed into a *Net Present Value of Current Adjusted Costs* (upper left corner of Figure 2). There are major financial challenges for many communities who wish to participate in structural mitigation measures on the coast. Even after project construction has been completed, communities must participate in cost-sharing for the maintenance of these projects. In the model, the costs are recorded and discounted at the U.S. Federal government required rate of 7%.

The second cost in the model is the cost to purchase or reclaim property. Even in cases where the federal government supports a buyout of local property, there is usually some level of cost sharing on the part of the non-federal partner. In addition, there are costs associated with the implementation of strict building code policies, which carry a direct burden to the homeowner. Finally, the cost to recover a community after disaster is recorded as stock of *Cumulative Storm Damages*. Taken together, these costs determine the outcome of a given set of mitigation policies.

3.1.5. Benefits from Tax Revenue and Damages Avoided (Green Links)

The model calculates benefits as shown in the lower left corner of Figure 2. CoastalProtectSIM allows the decision maker to implement a tax policy to offset the community cost-sharing burden. It is assumed that taxes are collected solely to offset the costs of crisis prevention. The model calculates a *desired tax rate* based on the *Net Present Value of Current Adjusted Costs*. The *total land value* is used to determine an appropriate tax rate.

CoastalProtectSIM contains a second, parallel model that runs "behind the scenes" without policy intervention. Both models are subject to the same storms. The resulting damages from the "no intervention" model is compared to the policy runs in the "policy intervention" model. The *Cumulative Damages Avoided* is the difference between *Cumulative Storm Damages* in the two models. *Cumulative Damages Avoided* is added to the revenue generated from taxes for a total *Cumulative Benefits and Damages Avoided*. The difference between this total and the *Cumulative Costs and Damages* is recorded as *Total Net Benefits*.

3.2. Model Behavior

The model generates storms and storm surges over the course of a 40 year period. The storms are randomly generated and a percentage of the storms may exceed the man-made and natural barriers and

Systems **2014**, *2*, 217–236

cause storm damage. The model is used to test strategies under various scenarios and communicate the results. Multiple iterations with variations on strategies expose students to the effects of dynamic complexity on the policy process.

The following selection of model runs highlights different types of uncertainty and tradeoffs unique to this particular policy domain.

3.2.1. Base Run

The base run for each random pattern of storm conditions has the same set of policy and planning assumptions. At the start of the simulation, the Pointe Claire community has minimal flood risk management policies in place. It relies on natural barriers to provide flood protection. The base run for each random seed shows the costs to Pointe Claire from different types of storm "challenges." A policy mix that performs well under one random seed may not achieve the same level of success under another random seed. Figure 3 presents the effects of three different random seeds.

Random Seed 1: The base run in the first example (run with random seed = 48) shows the effect of four storm events beyond the protection of its natural barriers. The first event occurs midway in the run, with a second event 10 years later. The final two events are rather small and occur at the end of the base run.

Random Seed 2: In the second sample base run (with random seed = 10) the community is hit with three events in a row. All events occur late in the run, starting at approximately 2046.

Random Seed 3: In the third example (random seed = 20), the community is hit with an event almost immediately. The next event beyond its natural barriers occurs approximately 25 years later. A third event occurs another 10 years later, with each subsequent event slightly less damaging than the previous.

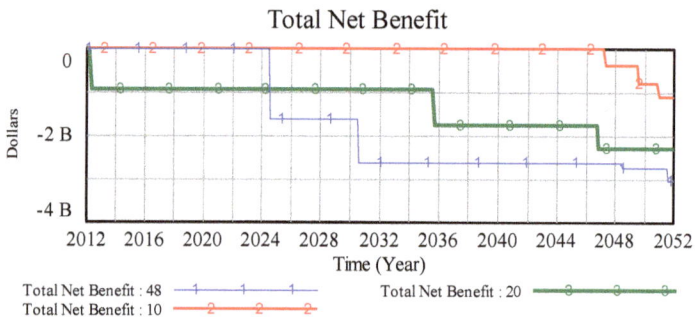

Figure 3. Total Net Benefit in response to three sample random storm patterns.

3.2.2. Climate Change

Three examples of different climate change scenarios under random seed 20 are presented in this paper. The base run with sea level rise at 6 inches has some impacts in the later years of the run. The total cumulative damages are similar to the base run. A second global warming run with parameter change for temperature rise of 3 degrees (5% surge per degree) results in relatively higher damages toward the end of the run. A final global warming run in random seed 20 had a 3 degree temperature rise with a 10% surge per degree. This global warming test results in a change in both frequency and severity of damage, with several more events creating damage in the later years. This final test shows cumulative damages nearly double the size of the base run. Figure 4 presents the base run along with the effects of different climate change scenarios.

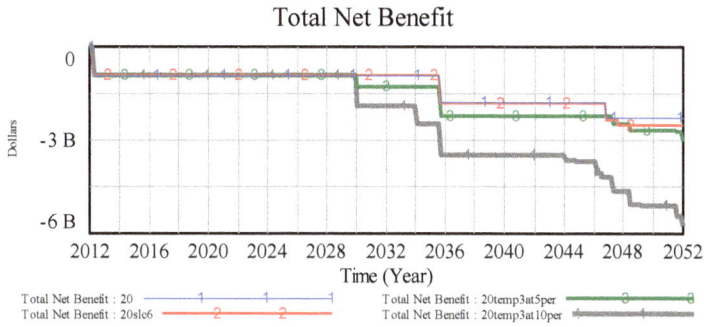

Figure 4. Total Net Benefit in response to three sample random storm patterns, with climate change.

3.2.3. Policy Runs

The CoastalProtectSIM model has several types of policy alternatives available to decision-makers. A description of each policy, with recommended policy values along with default values in the base run is described in Table 2. The recommended values are merely suggestions to decision maker to provide some boundaries and make it easier to keep track of many policy mix combinations. The contents in Table 2 were provided to the decision makers to describe all policy options in CoastalProtectSIM model.

Table 2. CoastalProtectSIM Policy Information Provided in the SBLE.

Policy Parameter	Description	Default/Recommended Policy Values
Height of Protection	Built protection for Pointe Claire includes projects such as seawalls, beach replenishment, and barrier island replenishment. The height of built protection adds to the community's existing natural environment protection. It takes approximately 5 years to complete the initial planning studies and at least another 5 years to complete the construction project. The height of man-made protection will determine the construction and annual maintenance costs. In the real world, cost-sharing requirements make it difficult for some communities to participate in agreements with the Corps. Therefore, both construction and maintenance costs should be considered to determine the appropriate height of protection.	Default: 0 Policy values: 0, 18, 24, or 36 inches
Tax Rate for Protection	There are several costs to consider in the model: costs for planning, construction, and operations and maintenance. Taxes should cover the non-federal share of these costs.	Default: 0 Policy values: tax rate between 0 and 0.002
Automated Tax Rate	You may notice it is difficult to set the tax rate just right. Instead of setting the tax rate for protection, you may opt to use the automated taxes feature. When this feature is activated, you will be guaranteed to collect taxes exactly at the cost of your height of protection	Default: 0 Policy values: 0 or 1
Building Code Enactment and Enforcement Policy	One way to avoid damages without clearing homes from the floodplain is to develop strict building codes for flood proofing and elevating structures above the base flood elevation level. Building codes would not eliminate all of the damage during a storm. Set the building code policy to any number between 0 and 1. This will be the percentage of structures (the goal) you expect to be in compliance with your codes. Also, keep in mind that building codes come at a cost to the property owner. Building codes should be considered as part of a holistic flood risk management strategy. Since costs will be immediate and benefits will potentially occur only after damages are avoided, the year in which the building policy is implemented plays an important role in both cumulative costs and damages.	Default: 0 Policy values: between 0 and 1
Year of Building Code Policy	The enactment and enforcement of building code policies make structures less prone to storm surge damage. These policies reduce damages and save money when storm surges exceed the height of protection. Building codes increase property maintenance costs on homeowners and businesses. Unlike seawalls and large structural mitigation projects, building codes place more financial responsibility on the individual. Floodplain managers are accountable for the implementation of these policies. These policies are rather important, as FEMA Community Rating System (CRS) points and National Flood Insurance Program (NFIP) discounts depend on their successful implementation.	Default: 2020 Policy values: between 2012 and 2052
Buyout or Relocation Policy	Buyouts, relocations, and reclamation policies remove homes from the floodplain. Pointe Claire does not have the resources to remove homes before a disaster strikes. However, if you decide to implement a buyout policy, landowners will be inclined to accept a buyout during major events. They are less likely to accept a buyout during smaller events. Federal programs such as the FEMA Hazard Mitigation Grant Program help minimize reclamation costs on the local community. The buyout policy in Coastal Sim represents the percentage of properties offered a buyout during the next event.	Default: 0 Policy values: 0 to 1
Year of Buyout Policy	Select the year when the buyout policy goes into effect. It is assumed that once the policy goes into effect, buyouts will be offered for every event after that year. Keep in mind, buyouts will not be offered immediately. Buyout offers are only extended to residents after events where Pointe Claire incurs damages. In this model, if no storm occurs after the buyout policy, then no land is reclaimed.	Default: 2020 Policy values: 2012 to 2052
Zoning Regulations	Each community faces a delicate balance between zoning for "open space" and zoning for land development. Zoning regulations prevent new development in flood prone areas. Development in Pointe Claire can change over time based on policy decisions. The value of the zoning policy is the percentage of development prevented. Keep in mind that strict zoning policies lower the tax base in Pointe Claire. A lower tax base lowers the amount of tax revenue that may be collected to offset the cost of structural protection projects. Therefore, zoning regulations could generate costs for remaining homeowners.	Default: 0 Policy values: 0 to 1
Zoning Policy Year	Select the year when zoning policies will go into effect. Zoning policies take effect immediately. Zoning regulations should be considered as part of a holistic flood risk management strategy. The year in which these policies go into effect may not lead to immediate implementation. Therefore, the year the zoning policy is implemented is important policy and determined by the user.	Default: 2020 Policy values: 2012 to 2052

• *Structural Protection*

Figures 5–7 illustrate the effect of some of the policy options on the simulation results. The timing of costs and benefits present a challenge to the decision maker, as some policies only yield a strong net present value due to events in the later years of the model run. Other policies could be hindered by factors beyond the community's control, such as delays in the Corps planning process. Yet, other policies show that no single approach is enough to sustain development in this coastal community. The handful of policies selected for discussion in this paper highlight challenges in policymaking and strategic communication, as each policy mix holds a unique set of tradeoffs. For simplicity, each policy described in this section uses the same random seed (48) in the base run.

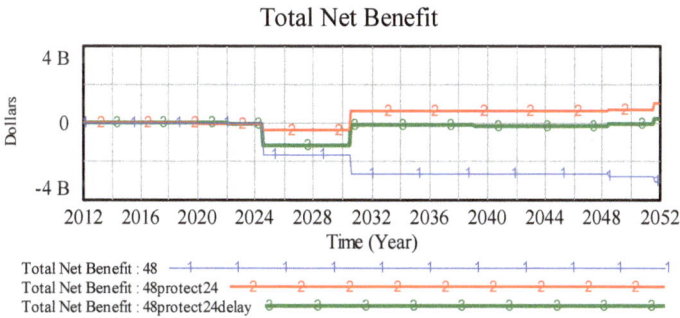

Figure 5. Total Net Benefit in three sample random storm patterns, with structural mitigation Policy run 2 that represents building an additional 24″ height in physical barriers with no planning or implementation delay and policy run 3 represents the same scenario with a delay.

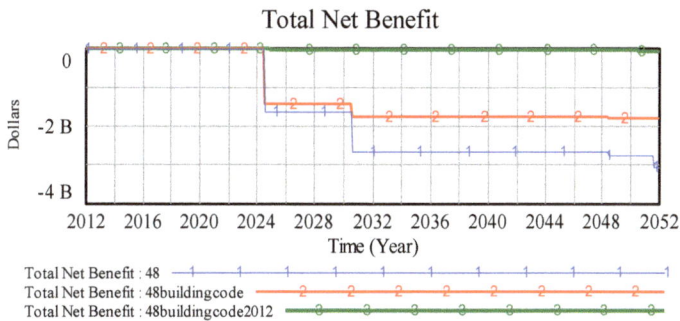

Figure 6. Total Net Benefit in three sample random storm patterns with build code enforcement.

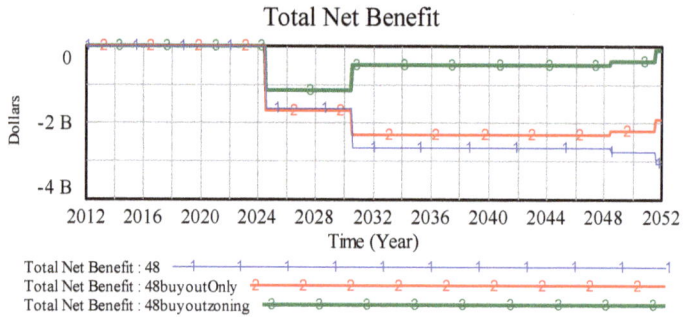

Figure 7. Total Net Benefit in three sample random storm patterns with buyouts and zoning policies.

The policy run for structural mitigation is interesting for two reasons. First, on the surface the policy appears to be rather successful against the base case. Whereas the base run results in final total costs to the community in excess of 3 billion dollars, the coastal protection from engineered solutions yields a net benefit in damages avoided of nearly 2 billion dollars. Recall random seed 48 has four events that exceed the community's natural barrier protection. After the first event, the policy solution does not produce enough benefit to warrant the cost of the project. However, as the model continues to run, it is clear the benefits exceed the costs. Also important to note, the Corps of Engineers uses a 50 year life for most of its planning studies. The second interesting observation on this policy is its sensitivity to delays in the system. The model was run a third time to reflect an additional five year delay in the coastal protection project. This delay results in rather severe damages in during the first event. In fact, total net benefits of the policy just barely rise above zero, which is due to avoided damages in the last year of the run. This example shows two ways CoastalProtectSIM model can help decision makers identify and discuss the uncertainty and timing of costs and benefits in flood prone communities.

- *Building Codes*

While a "building code only" approach does not quite produce robust outcomes in random world 48, the policy highlights an interesting challenge for decision makers. For this policy run, the community sets building codes at a goal of 100% compliance. To reflect the political capital needed to get such level of compliance, the policy goes into effect in 2020. Compared to the base run, the delay in implementation results in damages similar to the base during the first major event. However, with each subsequent event most of the damages are avoided. A third run of the model with an earlier implementation start date (2012) is a vast improvement on the same policy with a slower rollout strategy. In this run, building codes are fully implemented by the first major event and most of the damages are avoided. However, since building codes have a burden on the individual property owner, the result is a net zero benefit to the community.

- *Buyouts and Zoning*

The above sample of runs gives a partial sample of work that students were encouraged to complete in their final papers. In addition to running these and other runs one at a time, all of the student groups wound up presenting policy packages that ran combinations of policy clusters. Perhaps, the most realistic feature of the CoastalProtectSIM model is the fact that no single policy serves as the magic bullet in flood risk management. Flood risk management requires a holistic systems view of the problem. This is certainly true at the Corps today, where a new focus has been placed on coordinating structural and nonstructural measures. The "buyout only" approach barely outperforms the base case in random world 48. There are two inherent challenges with this policy. First, damages must be large enough for property owners to be willing to accept a buyout, but not too large to receive federal assistance to recover status quo *ex ante*. Second, buyout policies alone do not remove the pressure to redevelop on the coast. A third run of the model with buyouts and zoning policies prove to be a more sustainable solution. While net benefits are not quite above zero by the end of the run, these policies show that a holistic approach has more potential benefit. That is, by placing pressure on both the inflow and outflow of the land development sector stocks, the policy mix helps to contain future damages.

4. How the Simulator Was Used in the Class Context

The Pointe Claire SBLE was used as part of a larger 10-week Planning Exercise based on the Pointe Claire Coastal Protection Case Study in an MPA core class on data, models, and decisions. This is the place in the core program at the Rockefeller College where basic principles of modeling and how modeling can be used to support the policy process are taught.

4.1. Relationship to Other Units Taught in the Modeling Class

The first two thirds of this class treats various topics in modeling and the final third is devoted to databases and data management. In the first two thirds of the class, each modeling topic has one or more lecture units and an associated problem set. All problem sets had at least one problem that was set in the Pointe Claire case situation. Pointe Claire appeared as a decision tree in the unit on decision analysis and as a set of running equations in the unit on difference equations. The unit on multi-attribute utility (MAU) modeling came after the SBLE based on the CoastalProtectSIM model and most students drafted a MAU model to represent stakeholder preferences in the Pointe Claire Region. The point was driven home over and over that a single case situation contains many kinds of complexities and can be modeled using different modeling tools.

One of the best points of the class was the demonstrated ability of students to integrate insights from various types of modeling insights in their final group assignments. Most groups provided a synthesis of insights from the simulation model with insights that they had gained in the formal decision analysis units of the course or more frequently in the multi-attribute utility modeling portions of the course. For example, quite frequently students used MAU analysis to characterize differences in stakeholder preferences for various performance measures presented within the CoastalProtectSIM model.

4.2. Components of the Complete Simulation-Based Learning Environment

The actual CoastalProtectSIM simulator described above was linked to numerous in-class exercises as well as individual and group assignments. Those exercises and assignments can be described in three clusters.

4.2.1. Simulator "Set Up" Activities

- Students engaged in an in-class exercise working with the C-LEARN simulation [13], a high fidelity simulation system used to forecast impacts of CO_2 emissions on global warming over a 50 year plus time horizon (See Appendix B-1 in Supplementary file).
- Students drafted a memo detailing a way to use the C-LEARN simulator as part of the coastal protection planning process in the Pointe Claire Region (see Appendix B-2 in Supplementary file).
- Students participated in a group model-building exercise in which the class mapped out a system structure similar to the structure of the CoastalProtectSIM (See Appendix B-3 in Supplementary file).

4.2.2. Guided Use of the Simulation

- Students participated in two computer lab exercises where they formulated portions of the CoastalProtectSIM model to become more familiar with how the model was formulated in detail (See Appendix B-4 in Supplementary file).
- Students participated in role playing exercises in classroom discussions so that they gained a better feel for how key stakeholders took positions on coastal protection.
- Students were given a detailed handout with instructions for running the simulator and given time in the lab to interact with the model working in small groups.

4.2.3. Post-Simulation Debriefing Activities

- Working in small groups, students "solved" the policy problem and drafted a policy memo with a supporting set of PowerPoint slides indicating what they found to be the "best" policy solution and why (See Appendix B-5 in Supplementary file).
- Students did background reading in three related perspectives on public policy formation—(A) readings on stakeholder analysis and management in the policy process, (B) readings in the creation of mini-publics as a way to achieve policy consensus, and (C) readings on organizational learning and systems thinking as goals of networks or organizations working in the public policy field.
- Students drafted individual papers using the three sets pf background readings in public policy plus their work with the simulator (See Appendix B-5 in Supplementary file).

4.3. Qualitative Assessment of What Worked Well (or not)

This core MPA class has had a relatively stable content for the past 15 years and our author team has had substantial experience teaching this class over that whole period. Using that background and experience to reflect on the class, we present below five of the relative successes (and remaining challenges) of using a more fully elaborated learning environment to structure much of the class. These brief reflections serve as our informal attempt to "benchmark" these new innovations against prior offerings of this same class.

(1) The previous versions of the class suffered from the impression that models of policy problems are small solvable chunks with no clear connection to the broader policy and managerial context in which they arise. This impression arises because the course presents multiple small problems organized in problem sets (and repeated on in-class examinations). This approach certainly did a better job of illustrating a single larger problem domain and illustrating that multiple approaches can usefully be applied to a large and complex policy problem.

(2) The Pointe Claire case was easier to relate to readings and other topics taught elsewhere in the core curriculum. The three assigned readings on the policy process, used to help structure the final assignment, were taken directly from another core class. Students immediately cross-connected the content of that other core class on institutions and politics (involving stakeholder analysis and the formation of "mini-publics") with the content of this case. The lesson was easy to see—the stuff that we teach in several core classes is all connected in complex policy domains.

(3) This design probably had too many moving pieces. Portions of the assignments handed out in week 8 of the class referred back to details that were described in a handout that had been discussed in week 2 of the class. Some students lamented that they had a hard time keeping all of the pieces of the assignments straight. Students seeking a more straight-forward "cookbook" approach to modeling were frustrated by much of the open-ended nature of the linked assignments—how much do we need to remember from one place in the class to the next.

(4) The very best students in the class were challenged by all of the moving parts and did extraordinary work on their final group and individual assignments. Compared to past versions

of the class, case assignments were much more developed and students had a nuanced understanding of many topics that went beyond simple model mechanics.

(5)   While several attempts were made to "open up the simulator" (e.g., students were given a version of the simulator that had all of the equations open for manipulation and all students were required to build a simple version of the simulator as one of their difference equation assignments), many students still treated results from the CoastalProtectSIM simulator as "black box" results.

Overall, our impression was that the inclusion of this suite of exercises around the Pointe Claire Coastal Protection scenario considerably increased the overall complexity of and perhaps the workload of the class. This had the effect of bifurcating student reactions to the class with some students liking the additional sense of challenge, while others just wanted to be done with what, in the end, was just another core class they had to complete.

Also, we believe that further developing and incorporating materials that use System Dynamics simulation models to teach complexity will ultimately challenge the faculty who are teaching the classes. In our case, we always had access to faculty who were well trained in complex modeling and were able to fill in "on the fly" if the developed curricular materials hit a thin spot. We believe that the both the simulator and the supporting material will need to be more thoroughly developed and tested, possibly implemented through a web-based portal such as the Forio simulation portal [14] before such curricular innovations can become widespread.

5. Implications and Future Work

The use of the Pointe Claire SBLE described here supports the potential of SBLEs to teach complexity in public management education. The experience of the instructors and robustness of post simulation policy analyses indicates this simulation-based learning environment did help build a more complete and useful understanding of public policy complexity in public management students. We are moving forward with plans to improve and refine this SBLE in several ways:

- We are revising the background case material to make it into a more coherent set of background instructions as a response to student feedback and questions during the exercise. Initially, this will take the form of a unified packet of materials with hyperlinks, but we are moving in the direction of embedding all of these materials into a more integrated environment.
- We are working toward a simplified and revised version of the basic simulation itself that has improved clarity with respect to policy levers and feedback effects.
- Student final assignments are the best written record of what students have learned. We are experimenting with a sequence of assignments that might highlight learning in more of a "pre" and "post" environment in order to gain a better handle on overall learning.
- We are interested in examining what components of the SBLE were most effective, which were necessary to produce the desired outcome, and which might be unnecessary.

These types of SBLEs have the potential to secure thoughtful public engagement in sustainable planning across a wide range of domains that share features in common with coastal protection. The case described here focused on public management students, but the approach has potential for use with other groups, including community stakeholders. It will improve the ability of the public management workforce to engage the public in decision making about sustainable futures.

Acknowledgments: An earlier version of this paper was presented at the 31st International Conference of the System Dynamics Society, Cambridge, MA, USA, 21–25 July 2013. The authors thank Ventana Systems for providing the VENSIM simulation environment for this project.

Author Contributions: Michael Deegan developed the initial CoastalProtectSim model, worked with Rod MacDonald to adapt it for use in the class, and wrote the technical sections describing the model. David Andersen designed the SBLE curriculum materials around the model, conceptualized the use of the SBLE to teach complexity, and implemented the SBLE in the Rockefeller College MPA program together with Minyoung Ku. David Anderson, Krystyna Stave and Eliot Rich set the SBLE in a broader theoretical context and wrote the text describing the

SBLE and its broader implications. Minyoung Ku contributed to the alignment of the SBLE to NASPAA's core competencies and led the evaluation effort.

Conflicts of Interest: The authors declare no conflict of interest.

References

1. Comfort, L.K.; Wukich, C. Developing decision-making skills for uncertain conditions: The challenge of educating effective emergency managers. *J. Public Aff. Educ.* **2013**, *19*, 53–71.
2. National Association of Schools of Public Affairs and Administration, Accreditation Standards for Master's Degree Programs in Public Administration. Available online: http://www.naspaa.org/accreditation/NS/naspaaStandards.asp (accessed on 16 January 2014).
3. Lindblom, C.E. The Science of "Muddling Through". *Public Adm. Rev.* **1959**, *19*, 79–88. [CrossRef]
4. Couture, M. *Complexity and Chaos—State-of-the-Art; List of Works, Experts, Organizations, Projects, Journals, Conferences and Tools*; Defence Research and Development Canada: Valcartier, Canada, 2007.
5. Hu, Q.; Johnston, E.; Hemphill, L.; Krishnamurthy, R.; Vinze, A. Exploring the role of interactive computer simulations in public administration education. *J. Public Aff. Educ.* **2012**, *18*, 513–530.
6. Sterman, J.D. Learning in and about complex systems. *Syst. Dyn. Rev.* **1994**, *10*, 291–330. [CrossRef]
7. Kim, H.; MacDonald, R.H.; Andersen, D.F. Simulation and managerial decision making: A double-loop learning framework. *Public Adm. Rev.* **2013**. [CrossRef]
8. Ghaffarzadegan, N.; Andersen, D.F. Modeling behavioral complexities of warning issuance for domestic security: A simulation approach to develop public management theories. *Int. Public Manag. J.* **2012**, *15*, 337–363. [CrossRef]
9. Black, L.J. When visuals are boundary objects in system dynamics work. *Syst. Dyn. Rev.* **2013**, *29*, 70–86. [CrossRef]
10. Black, L.J.; Andersen, D.F. Using visual representations as boundary objects to resolve conflict in collaborative model-building approaches. *Syst. Res. Behav. Sci.* **2012**, *29*, 194–208. [CrossRef]
11. Sawyer, R.K. *The Cambridge Handbook of the Learning Sciences*; Cambridge University Press: New York, NY, USA, 2006.
12. Stave, K.; Beck, A.; Galvan, C. Assessing the effects of simulation-based learning on operational understanding of accumulation principles. *Simulat. Gaming* **2014**, in press.
13. Sterman, J.; Fiddaman, T.; Franck, T.; Jones, A.; McCauley, S.; Rice, P.; Sawin, E.; Siegel, L. Climate interactive: The C-ROADS climate policy model. *Syst. Dyn. Rev.* **2012**, *28*, 295–305. [CrossRef]
14. Forio Simulation Portal. Available online: http://www.forio.com (accessed on 16 January 2014).

![systems logo] *systems*

MDPI

Article

A Systems Engineering Methodology for Designing and Planning the Built Environment—Results from the Urban Research Laboratory Nuremberg and Their Integration in Education

Philipp Geyer [1,*], Jochen Stopper [2], Werner Lang [1,2,3] and Maximilian Thumfart [3]

[1] Center for Urban Ecology and Climate Change Adaptation, Technische Universität München, Munich 80333, Germany; w.lang@tum.de

[2] Center for Sustainable Building, Technische Universität München, Munich 80333, Germany; stopper@tum.de

[3] Energy-Efficient and Sustainable Planning and Building, Technische Universität München, Munich 80333, Germany; maximilian.o.e.thumfart@googlemail.com

* Author to whom correspondence should be addressed; p.geyer@tum.de;
Tel.: +49-89-289-23990; Fax: +49-89-289-23991.

Received: 6 November 2013; in revised form: 21 March 2014; Accepted: 1 April 2014; Published: 16 April 2014

Abstract: Sustainable urban development requires a long-term sector-integrative approach. This paper proposes a method of system analysis and partial simulation for urban structures for this purpose. It couples a discussion-based holistic approach for systems analysis and modelling of urban structures with quantitative modelling and simulation of partial scenarios that serve to examine specific questions regarding the long-term development of urban structures. In the first part, the application in the City Lab Nuremberg West, a multidisciplinary urban research laboratory, serves to develop the methodology and its illustration. The main objective is to examine the transition of the existing underperforming quarter to a sustainable and livable urban environment. Scenario-based experiments with respect to development paths determine robustness and risks of different configurations. The second part of the paper describes the transfer of the methodology to education. The approach serves to teach students in the Energy-Efficient and Sustainable Building master course program an integrative way of planning a sustainable built environment. The definition of educational objectives concerning the students' understanding and management of systemic interdependencies of sustainability help assess the use of the method in the classroom. The aim is to provide them with the competence to develop strategies for complex situations while planning a sustainable built environment.

Keywords: systems engineering; systems modelling; urban planning; long-term urban development strategies; integrative design and modelling for sustainability; research oriented teaching

1. Introduction: Sustainable Design and Planning in Research and Education

1.1. The Research Approach: Long-Term Urban Planning at the City Lab Nuremberg Western City

The impacts of global change are increasingly affecting cities and urban agglomerations. Economic, social, technological and ecological changes, such as climate change or the latest transformative changes to the energy policy in Germany (*"Energiewende"*) impose significant challenges that influence the conversion of existing neighborhoods and communities. Cities are highly complex spatial agglomerations. In order to adequately understand cities, a variety of levels and aspects have to be considered. These include urban planning, building design, infrastructure, functions, aesthetics and various others topics. In order to create a basis for an integrated view of options for the future development of Nuremberg West, we performed a fundamental analysis of the current situation. This included the interaction of different scales, disciplines and approaches. The knowledge of different working methods, levels of detail and references was crucial to create a basis for the interdisciplinary collaboration of the various disciplines and work areas, such as urban planning, landscape planning, resource consumption/energy efficiency and transport planning.

In this context, we developed a method of systems modelling that addresses the complex interdependencies and supports the development of strategic solutions for sustainable urban development. This development took place in the interdisciplinary research project City Lab Nuremberg West at the Technische Universität München and dealt with these challenges in order to establish long-term strategies for the development of a livable and sustainable future for this urban district, which has approx. 15,000 inhabitants.

The main purpose of this development is to derive a method to set up a systems model that supports decision processes in planning and designing the built environment and is tailored specifically for this purpose. This includes the derivation of the model in a discussion-based process between the disciplinary stakeholders and it describes the analysis and simulation of the systems model supporting the development of sustainable strategies in the planning context as an assisting tool. It allows the simulation of time-based transitions of the urban quarter such as those required for the *Energiewende*. The paper describes the methodology, its computer implementation and its transfer to education, which is outlined at the end of this section.

1.2. Importance of Long-Term Strategies

Based on the analysis and study of global trends, we developed three alternative visions, called development paths, for a plausible future aimed at the coming decades until the year 2050. Long-term strategies are crucial especially with regard to the development of key projects, sites and locations, as the short-term realization of supposedly appropriate projects on specific locations might prohibit the future viability of sustainable projects in these locations.

With regard to the realization of higher-level measures, such as the infrastructure of the city, including energy systems, individual and public transport as well as water supply and sewage systems, long-term thinking and strategic planning were crucial for the economic feasibility of these measures. In order to be able to propose and implement radical solutions in the planning process, longer periods of time are crucial for the economic feasibility of fundamental changes in the infrastructure that might be necessary to allow for the realization of sustainable concepts.

1.3. Integrated Urban Modelling in Research

The City Lab Nuremberg West places special emphasis on the 'livable city' as a major aspect of a sustainable urban development. It becomes apparent that many different sectors contribute to the emergence of a city worth living in, both in terms of content as well as in terms of the various administrative levels, such as the state, the city and the private level. It requires the integration of a very wide range of topics, such as economy, health, mobility, culture, identity, food supply, quality of the built environment and many other aspects.

Current research aims at sector-oriented modelling and simulation of the behavior of urban structures; Robinson [1] gives an overview of these developments. There is a history of sector-crossing systems modelling that also addresses the urban context with comprehensive general models, such as Urban Dynamics by Forrester [2] to name a prominent instance. However, large-scale approaches have often been criticized due to not being manageable and not being able to make correct predictions [3]. Nevertheless, they are still an important part of models predicting the behavior of urban systems in planning and decision-making, especially for land use and urban transport [4]. Furthermore, urban structures are seen as complex systems for which a systems approach provides the basis for current scientific examination [5,6].

Systems **2014**, *2*, 137–158

In contrast to large-scale comprehensive system models that aim for a general understanding of the behavior of urban structures, our approach uses problem-specific partial models for the specific planning demand and its inherent questions. Expert discussion serves to develop the systems model. For Nuremberg West, the discussion-based system definition focused on the sectors functionality, energy and resource consumption, mobility and urban quality. In addition to the sectoral analysis as part of long-term planning and control, an integrative view is also required. The dependencies of the many individual aspects of the various sectors and disciplines lead to a complex system that must be considered for long-term urban development. To detect and investigate the dependencies of the various factors, the method of sensitivity modelling as described by Vester [7] was applied, which forms an important step of the discussion-based setup of the system model. This methodology is used to detect the influences in an expert discussion between variables and trends of various sectors, and to map their effects.

1.4. Planning-Embedded, Time-Based Simulation

Cities are dynamically evolving structures and are constantly in transition due to continuous changes in many areas, such as population, functional requirements and economic conditions. Furthermore, global and local trends influence the development of a city. Based on these trends, the three different development paths mentioned above were developed to describe three fundamentally different, yet plausible alternative development paths for the coming decades until 2050. The alternative development paths depend on the following three economic patterns: (1) economic growth (knowledge-based economy hub), (2) economic standstill (managed care) and (3) economic decline (subsistence economy). In all of these three alternative visions of the future the concept of a livable city was used as an indispensable basis for the development.

Therefore, this paper—after performing systems modelling and analysis—proposes a method of systems modelling and partial simulation that is adapted to the specific situation of long-term urban planning and development. The purpose of the time-based simulation is to gain information about the interaction of the sectors and disciplines and to learn about the time-related development of the district in a long-term perspective. This includes information about the planned and expected effects in terms of their strength and timing but also the identification of unexpected side effects and development risks.

This use of the system simulation is embedded in the planning process and acts as a tool for decision-making. Therefore, embedding a detailed, but partial system simulation model in the decision process is a central aim of the approach. The model is derived from the planning process with its discussions and feeds its results back to this process. It is a tool to answer specific questions occurring in the planning process for which the method provides quantified intersectoral support to answer them appropriately. This helps overcome the usual arbitrary and implicit decision-making without a quantitative basis that often occurs in design and planning.

The method starts by modelling the system structure through expert discussion, as proposed by Vester [7]. The key variables and interdependencies as well as the objectives and external conditions—the latter described as development paths—result from this process. The next step is the definition of partial scenarios for simulation, again in experts' discussion. For systems modelling, this paper presents an adapted method for partial system simulation that differs from the method proposed by Vester, which is available as software by Malik [8]. The adapted method includes a continuous simulation approach in contrast to Vester's discrete simulation method; it allows different types of interdependencies and the linkage of the system scales and interdependencies to real values. A partial simulation for Nuremberg Western City was implemented based on the adapted method. The example results of this implementation demonstrate how the systems model with its simulation can support the planning process, providing answers to questions and examining risks and potentials for long-term urban planning.

1.5. The Education Approach: Integrative System-Based Understanding and Thinking for a Sustainable Built Environment

Interaction between different sectors and planning disciplines plays an important role in the education of architects, civil engineers and environmental engineers in sustainable planning. Many design and planning curricula now include mono-disciplinary views of sustainable planning and building, such as building services and thermal energy, transport, solar architecture, water management, *etc.* However, the integration of these views is lacking. Normally, students do not learn to assess interactions between the sectors and to weigh up sectoral benefits while considering that investments usually are limited and embedded in economic and social structures.

This was the situation for the Master's in Energy-Efficient and Sustainable Building course at the Technische Universität München. A lecture series in the module Sustainable Architecture, City and Landscape Planning (SACLP) provided sectoral views and included a seminar that bridges the sectoral view and introduces students to an integrative approach. Thus, the idea arose to transfer the methods of the City Lab Nuremberg West to education in this Master's course. The main challenge of this transfer was to introduce students to systems thinking, which we deem a core competence for sustainable building. The aim of the method transfer is to identify key parameters as well as strategies for sustainable built structures in a qualitative way as well as to provide students with the ability to quantitatively model sector-crossing interdisciplinary dependencies and their effects.

2. Systems Modelling in Research—City Lab Nuremberg West

The first step of the method developed in the research project City Lab Nuremberg West is to use the methodology of sensitivity analysis developed by Frederic Vester [7] as a starting point to build up the systems model and adapt it for urban structures. This approach is very appealing, especially for those not familiar with system engineering since it is easy to understand and uses many stakeholder discussion procedures. One major adaptation for long term planning is the use of development paths, which are described in Section 2.2.

As the second step after developing the structure of the systems model using Vester's approach, the method had to be significantly changed from a discrete event approach to a continuous dynamic simulation method. The subsection on quantitative systems modelling for partial simulation describes this continuous dynamic method. This development allowed mixed qualitative-quantitative modelling with the precision required for the challenge of a sustainable and livable urban structure as envisioned for Nuremberg Western City.

The discussion-based setup of the systems model, which is the first part of the methodology, led the team to a problem-specific partial setup of the systems model. This process took place in two systems modelling workshops and further regular project team meetings. These events defined the information in the Sections 2.1–2.3. The aim of the discussion process is to reach agreement among the stakeholders on the system and its parts, its description by variables and the relevant dependencies between the variables. Sections 2.4 and 2.5 describe the implementation of simulations.

2.1. Sensitivity Analysis, Systems Modelling and the Planning Process

The first step is the analysis of interdependencies by the influence matrix. For this purpose, the expert committee defines n variables describing the state of the system and, following the method of Vester, discusses and agrees on one effect strength between all n^2-n combinations in a matrix:

▼has effect on ►	V1	V2	V3	V4	Active sum
1-6 V1	-	2	1	2	5
V2	3	-	0	1	4
V3	0	1	-	2	3
V4	3	1	2	-	6
1-6 Passive sum	6	4	3	5	

Systems **2014**, *2*, 137–158

The matrix equals the methods of the design structure matrix (DSM), as proposed by Eppinger and Browning [9]. The result of this procedure, which was carried out for Nuremberg Western City in two workshops, is to define the role of the variables in the system. In detail, the active and the passive sums describe the extent to which variables influence one another. Figure 1 shows the role of the variables based on these sums.

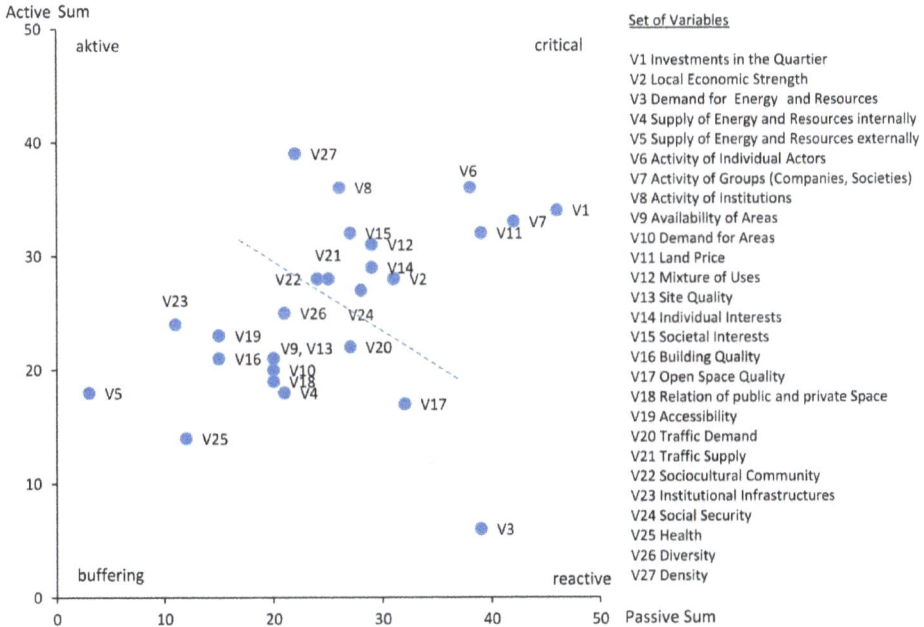

Figure 1. Role of variables in the system.

The role of variables allows us to select variables and relevant interdependencies for building the partial system model. Active variables, such as V27 Density, V6–8 Activity of Actors, V1 Investments and V11 Land Price, or reactive variables, such as the V3 Demand of Energy and Resources, are particularly interesting for setting up the system. Variables that are both active and reactive, and therefore critical, should also be included, but handled with care. The active variables are most interesting for the control of the system and for respective measures. Critical variables also allow for effective control of the system. However, as they react strongly to other variables, their adjustment tends to cause systemic instabilities. According to these considerations, variables above the dashed line are the primary candidates for the partial simulation.

2.2. Development Paths and Scenarios

One innovation in applying systems modelling in the long-term development of urban structures is to integrate a scheme of development paths and scenarios. Development paths define varying external and internal conditions of the urban district, which are mainly influenced by processes, decisions and states outside the district. They are a new feature of long-term urban planning that originated from the work by the Nuremberg Western City team [10].

Scenarios are subordinate to development paths and describe possible variations within them in order to examine risks and potentials. Scenarios form the basis for examinations in the partial simulation; they vary whereas the development paths represent fixed basic conditions for these examinations.

Systems **2014**, 2, 137–158

In the Nuremberg Western City project, the alternative development paths depend on the following three alternative economic development patterns: economic growth, economic standstill and economic decline. These three alternatives were named "knowledge economy hub", "managed care", and "subsistence economy". In all of these alternative visions, the concept of a livable city was taken as an indispensable basis for development.

Knowledge economy hub: The first path assumes that Nuremberg Western City evolves into a well-performing knowledge economy site. High economic activity takes place and leads to comprehensive investments.

Managed care: The second path describes a quarter mainly characterized by residential use that takes on a service role for other districts.

Subsistence economy: The third path is based on the assumption of widespread economic decline and the subsequent creation of an alternative circulation economy that features small local value-adding activities.

2.3. Quantitative Systems Modelling for Partial Simulation

After identifying the key variables for the three paths, the next step is to select variables for the effect structures and thus for the partial simulation model. The effect structure compiles all relevant dependencies in a graphic structure with their direction and sign but without magnitude, as shown in Figure 2. The occurrence and importance of qualitative as well as quantitative variables requires an intermediating approach. For this purpose, the approach uses substitute scales that normalize all variables to a range between 0 and 1 (for details see Geyer *et al.* [11]). The detailed definition of the scales of the real values and of the mapping to the substitute scale is required to determine the interdependencies, as described later in this section. Table 1 shows these definitions for the case Nuremberg Western City. Except in one case, a simple linear mapping is used for the scales. Only urban density is mapped using logarithmic transformation; as a result, except for table-defined dependencies, the interdependencies between this variable and the other variable are linear.

To model the interdependencies in detail for the simulation the approach proposed in this paper, in contrast to Vester [7], mainly uses a dynamic linear influence model including three types of interdependencies:

I. Direct or static dependencies provide a factor influence on a variable. In case of a variable v_1 influencing a second variable v_2, the following operation describes the influence with the influence factor a_{21} and the neutral point b_{21}:

$$v_2(t) = v_2(t) + \underbrace{a_{21}(v_1(t) - b_{21})}_{\text{interdependency term}} \qquad (1)$$

II. The first type of dynamic links provides an integrating interdependency:

$$v_2(t) = v_2(t) + \underbrace{\int a_{21}(v_1(t) - b_{21})dt}_{\text{interdependency term}} \qquad (2)$$

III. The second type of dynamic dependencies uses derivation:

$$v_2(t) = v_2(t) + \underbrace{\frac{d}{dt}(a_{21}(v_1(t) - b_{21}))}_{\text{interdependency term}} \qquad (3)$$

In some cases, the simple factor relation defined by a_{21} was replaced by more sophisticated functions described by tables or diagrams.

To determine realistic data for the factor *a* and the neutral point *b* per interdependency, three different strategies are applied. First, best quality systemic dependencies derive from simulations specifically made for the quarter under consideration. As part of the Nuremberg Western City project, results from a stochastic simulation of energy efficiency measures as described in [12] were modelled as interdependency and included for investments in buildings and building energy consumption. Secondly, empirical studies on specific dependencies in other urban contexts are the next source of interdependencies in the model. For example, results from Kenworthy and Laube [13] serve to model the interdependency of transport demand and density or data from Fischer [14] for the influence of density and mixture of use on social security. Thirdly, the evaluation of statistical data is a source to determine interdependencies, such as the influence of density on land value, which was determined by regression analysis of the standard land value and the number of inhabitants and workplaces in the area of Nuremberg [15].

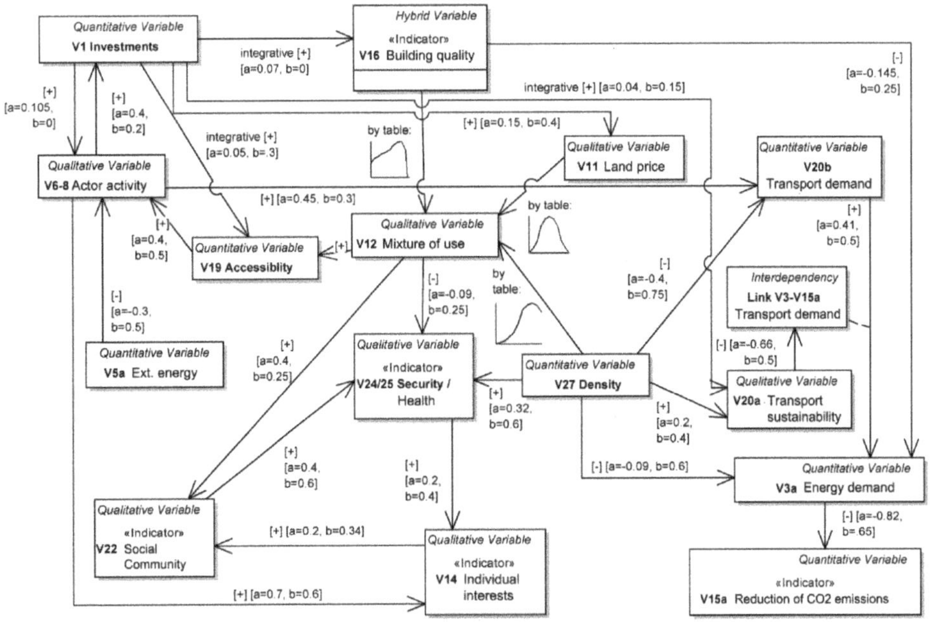

Figure 2. Effect structure modelled for Nuremberg Western City.

Table 1. Definition of the variables used for the partial simulation.

Variable	Description	Scale			
V1 Investments	Total investments per inhabitant/workplace	Quantitative: 500 … 10,000 EUR per cap. and yr.			
V3a Energy demand	Energy demand in the district	Quantitative: 5,000 … 75,000 kWh per cap. and yr.			
V5a External energy supply	The energy price describes the external energy supply	Quantitative: 50 … 200% (comp. to 2012)			
V6–8 Actor activity	Activity of individuals, groups (companies/societies) and institutions	Qualitative: 0% (passive) … 100% (active)			
V12 Mixture of use	Mixture of use describes the distance to most important uses in the city	Qualitative: 0% (monoculture) … 100% (mixed use)			
V14 Individual interests	Describes the realization of individual interests (e.g., employment)	Qualitative: 0% (restricted) … 100% (realized)			
V15a Reduction of CO_2 emissions	Common interest of reducing CO_2 emissions	Quantitative: 15 … 0 t CO_2-eq. per cap. and yr.			
V16 Building quality	Technical and spatial quality, construction cost as simplified measure	Quantitative: Residential: 750 … 1,500 € per m² gross areaOffice: 1,000 … 2,000 € per m² gross area			
V19 Accessibility	Average travel times per journey	Quantitative: 20 … 60 min			
		Qualitative:			
V20a Transport sustainability	Share held by ecomobility	Scale	Cycle	Public transport	Cars
		100%	0%	40%	20%
		0%	20%	10%	70%
V20b Transport demand	Weekly travelled distance per person.	Quantitative: 200 … 100 km per person and week			
V22 Sociocultural community	Integration of different groups of users and inhabitants	Qualitative: 0% (segregated) … 100% (integrated)			
V24/25 Social security/health	Social security and health of the users	Qualitative: 0% (low) … 100% (high)			
V27 Density	Inhabitants and users per area	Quantitative: 15 … 150 persons per ha (logarithmic scale)			

These strategies lead to information for all interdependencies included in the partial effect structure selected for simulation implementation. Figure 2 shows the effect structure and its interdependency values. This structure has a main focus on built structures and transport. Furthermore, it considers energy, investments, and social aspects. The interpretation of the simulation results will take this partial character into account.

2.4. Implementation

Besides the development of methodology, one aim of the research approach is to set up a systems modelling environment for buildings and urban structures. Therefore, experiments include testing of modelling and simulation environments using the visual programming approach. The structure of objects in this modelling environment was object oriented so that not only the environment with its graphic user interface and interactive procedures is developed, but also the elements of which the model is composed.

The visual user interface aims at representing a block diagram with objects as boxes and interdependencies as connectors in between, which is very close to an internal block diagram (ibd) of the Systems Modelling Language (SysML, [16]). The SysML is very suitable for the purpose for two reasons: First, it is a standardized way of modelling systems and representing systemic interdependencies; second, it is based on the software engineering Unified Modelling Language (UML), which eases later implementation. Another aim of the visual user interface was not only to represent the current state of the variables and their links, but also to allow for rapid, flexible and adaptive modelling and simulation of different configurations. Moreover, a powerful equation solver was required. After developing the structure as SysML diagrams, the *Simulink* environment within *MatLab* was chosen as an experimental platform because of its interactive user interface with a solver. It represents the instances of variables and the information flows between them visually, allowing interactive editing. At the same time *Simulink* provides access to powerful *MatLab* solvers allowing complex dynamic calculations.

The SysML model was implemented based on five classes (Class diagram, Figure 3). Each model variable is represented by an instance of the Variable class. The method "calculate" implements the update calculation of the variables; it gathers the values "factorInput", "integrationInput" and "derivationInput" according to the three dependency types described in Section 2.3 and generates the results "scaledValue" and "realValue". The class supports time-dependent or constant initial values ("initValue"/"timeBasedInitValue"). After calculation, the output value is available for other variables by using one or multiple instances of the Link class. The link implements linear scaling of interdependencies as shown in Equations (1–3) with the parameters a and b. Therefore, it requires the attributes link weight w, neutral point b, range a and a switch for using a lookup table instead of linear dependency definition. The output values of a variable can also be connected to the postprocessor, which will create and render a report. The class 'Init' hosts the time-dependent development of the predefined variables and some configuration settings for the postprocessor.

The implementation of the framework in *Simulink* sets up a systemic information flow model as shown exemplarily in Figure 4. The model represents system variables as instances of the Variable class (Variable A and Variable B). Each of them has one input port for time-dependent init values and three input ports for factor, integrative and derivative interdependencies. Both variables receive time-dependent initial values from the init instance. There are three output signals available: real, scaled and relative value. The real value contains the absolute value according to the variables unit; the scaled value contains the substitute scale value that is used for linking variables (for scales see Table 1). The relative value contains the percent change from the initial value for the report. An instance of the link class is required to create interdependency between two variables (Figure 4 Link). Its input port is connected to the scaled value output of variable B and its output signal is linked to the factor input of variable A. As a result, the scaled value of variable B has a static influence on variable A with the properties defined by the link's attributes. The scaled values of both variables are connected to the instance "PostProcessor", which creates a report describing the time-related development of the variables in the system.

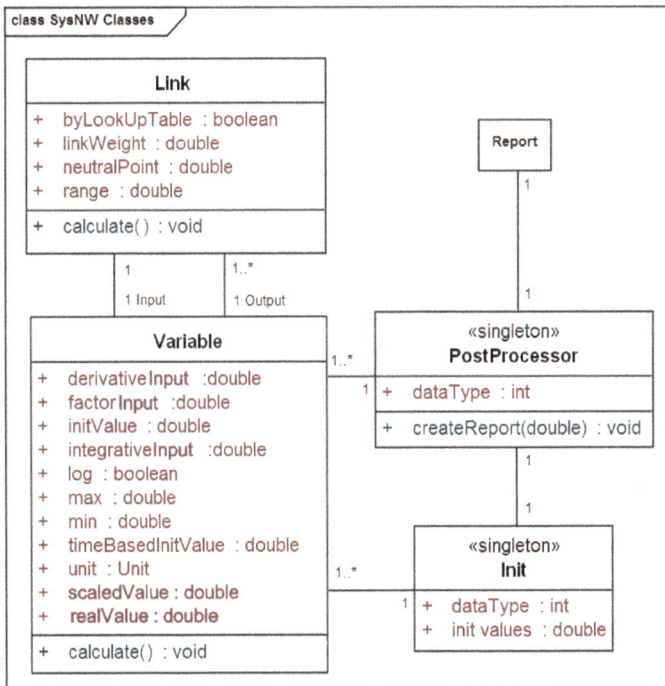

Figure 3. Variable and link classes.

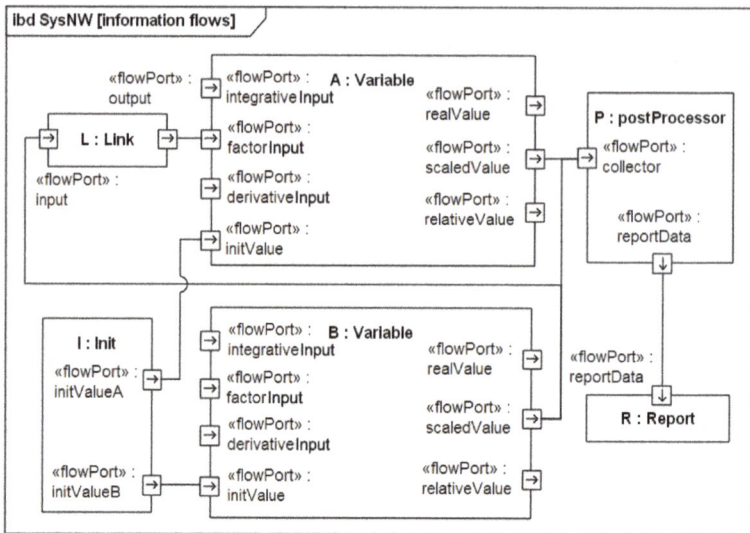

Figure 4. Internal block diagram (SysML) of an example model setup with information flows.

The variables are created and configured using Simulink's visual programming environment. Figure 5 shows an example of variable V1 Investments, with a time-dependent initial Value (Val) and a factor influence from variable V6–8. There are no integrative influences and derivative influences are not implemented yet, because the first does not apply to the variable and the second is not present in the Nuremberg Western City model. The attribute's values are also displayed in the variable instance, in this case, the substitute scale's maximum is set to 10,000.00 and the minimum to 500.00, the unit is set to "EUR/(cap·yr)". All outputs are passed on to the post processor, which collects results and provides a report. Furthermore, the scaled value is also connected to other variables. The attributes of the incoming link from V6–8 are also displayed in the instance representation in *Simulink*. Its range *a* is set to 0.40, the neutral point *b* is 0.20 and the link weight *w* is 1.00. The variable's attributes can also be changed by double-clicking the instance. If there is more than one link to one variable the signals are summarized first in order to merge them into one signal. Circular links are supported by the *Simulink* solver engine; in Figure 3, for example, variable A could be linked back to variable B leading to a mutual interdependency with complex systemic effects that represents control circuits as they are in the real world.

V1 INVESTMENTS

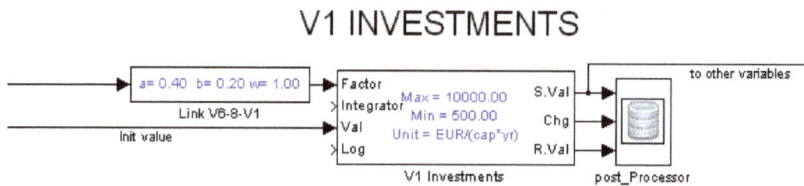

Figure 5. Variable 1 "Investments", its time-dependent initial Value (Val) and its Link from V6–8 "User Activity" in the Simulink implementation.

2.5. Simulation Results and Interpretation

This section presents one selected scenario and its simulation results for the development path "knowledge economy hub" conducted for Nuremberg Western City. The aim is to illustrate the information available using time-based partial system simulation and its interpretation. The path "knowledge economy hub" describes the trend of high economic activity based on knowledge-intensive and creative services. Bundling all economic activities of this kind and the respective investments from Nuremberg to this district is a prerequisite for this path, serving to achieve the required high investments (V1) as well as medium-to-high activity of the users (V6–8). A slight increase of the density (V27) in terms of urban redensification provides further support for this configuration.

For each path, experiments using different scenarios were carried out to determine its behavior under several circumstances. Figure 6 shows one experiment with the baseline results (orange line) of the partial simulation made for this path together with one scenario (blue line). The purpose of this experiment was to examine what effect a ten-year delay in investments has on the development of the district. This is a crucial question for city administration and planners as it determines how quickly they have to act to realize the development path if they decide in favor of it.

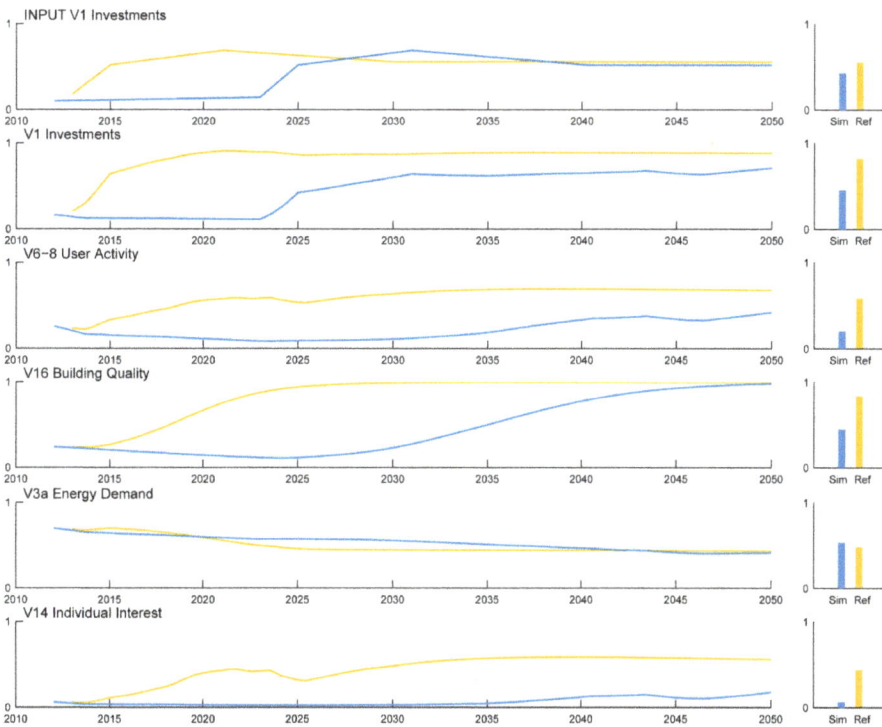

Figure 6. Results from the partial system simulation for Nuremberg Western City.

The results of the simulation (Figure 6) clearly show the risk related to this development path. Indeed, the investments (V1) and the activity of actors (V6–8) in the delay scenario reach a similarly medium-high level as in the baseline scenario. However, user activity in the first half drops to a low level leading to strong negative side-effects such as high unemployment rates and economic decay. Furthermore, the investments delay leads to deterioration of the building stock. Nevertheless, the demand for energy (V3a) is similar in both scenarios because the reduced transport demand caused by less user activity compensates for the higher energy demand of buildings due to their bad condition. However, due to the poor circumstances of the district, such as a high unemployment rate and an unlivable environment, personal contentment (V14) is very poor in the scenario with delayed investments. This illustrates that different urban developments with equal energy consumption can

Systems **2014**, *2*, 137–158

have very distinct qualities in terms of their livability. Finally, the described decline of the quarter increases the risk that investments will not be made at all with the delay of ten years; as a consequence of the poor district condition investors may choose another district.

The example experiment shows that if, given appropriate conditions in the near future, the city administration decides to realize the scenario "knowledge economy hub" they must ensure that they reach the necessary level of investments within a short time. Otherwise, they risk a further significant decline of the district. The district will not have far higher energy demand but they would endanger the livability of the district (shown by low realized personal interest, V14). This in turn has a negative effect on further investments, which puts the entire development path at risk of failure, leading to a poor-condition district (as shown by the blue curves in Figure 6). In summary, this reveals the urgency for action for this path—a characteristic that significantly differs from other paths.

This simulation and interpretation of the results is just an example of how to use the method and the model in the planning context to make planning decisions or to assess actions. Further effects on other variables, further experiments and further results for other paths will be shown in [12].

2.6. Discussion

The method developed enables the identification of key system interactions and driving variables. This provides a sound foundation for partial system simulation and systemic interpretation. The first step of the overall approach is the superordinate identification and definition of the system structure including a sensitivity analysis via expert discussion. The second step is selective analysis of relevant interactions including detailed analysis and the simulation. The experts' interpretation is an important step for the simulation to check the results for plausibility and to draw strategic conclusions. In this interpretation it is important that the simulation is not intended to exactly and absolutely predict the system state for a given moment in time. Instead it aims to observe the relative effects and interaction over the course of time. This both enables us to understand transitions, since it is a major requirement for the energy transition and the long-term urban planning situation in Nuremberg Western City and the experiments also allow us to examine the robustness of the system and identify risks and opportunities in these transitions. This enables us to carefully select development paths and to provide measures for the success of the selected development path.

3. Teaching Urban Systems Modelling—The Sustainable Architecture, City and Landscape Planning (SACLP) Course

3.1. Goals and Structure of the Seminar

The seminar Sustainable Architecture, City and Landscape Planning (SACLP), is part of the Master of Energy-Efficient and Sustainable Building [17] course at the Technische Universität München (TUM). The students, who come from different backgrounds with Bachelor's degrees in either architecture or civil or environmental engineering, work together in interdisciplinary groups. The seminar is accompanied by a SACLP lecture series, in which professors from different areas of expertise offer students insight into their respective areas of sustainable design, planning and building. The seminar has the function of integrating the separate perspectives.

This situation gave rise to the transfer of methods of systems modelling and analysis to education. The method is applied to concrete cases of sustainable building in accordance with Vester's Sensitivity Model. It is used to interpret cross-disciplinary relationships. For this purpose, the methodology developed in the City Lab Nuremberg West research project was adapted for use in the classroom. This transfer has taken place since the 2012/2013 winter term and the structure of the seminar is still under development. The following description represents the state of development at the end of the 2012/2013 winter term. Further developments of the seminar currently underway in the 2013/2014 winter term are outlined in the discussion in Section 3.5.

The seminar teaches students to analyze the complex relationships between different areas, sectors and disciplines, to determine the performance of a sustainable city and how to develop strategies to improve performance. The students are supposed to use an actual designing and planning case to analyze the impact of decisions in terms of sustainability and to quantify their general effect and interaction. Table 2 compiles the teaching objectives of the seminar; this is an updated version compared to the first description of the seminar in the master module made in 2012 [18].

Following the concept of Constructive Alignment [19], which highlights the importance of systematically aligning teaching and assessment to the intended teaching objectives for students, the following compilation of teaching objectives serves to verify the applied methods of systems analysis and modelling, to reflect the effect and to identify the need for further development. Implementing Constructive Alignment helps ensure that students actually acquire the previously defined skills in class and therefore represents one of the major selected concepts of TUM to assure and enhance teaching quality at university level [20].

Table 2. Compilation of the teaching objectives of the seminar "Sustainable Architecture, City and Landscape Planning" (SACLP).

No.	Description: The students are able …
1	to identify the discipline/sector-crossing interdependencies and the systemic boundary (Tax 1, 2, 3) [1]
2	to structure the dependencies of sustainable building for a specific case and to identify the lever in the system (Tax 4) [1]
3	to determine qualitative and quantitative systemic interdependencies (Tax 4, 5) [1]
4	to focus on a specific issue in sustainable building and to develop a solution strategy by means of system modelling (Tax 5, 6) [1]

[1] The "Tax" identifier shows the assessment of the cognitive level according to Anderson and Krathwohl [21].

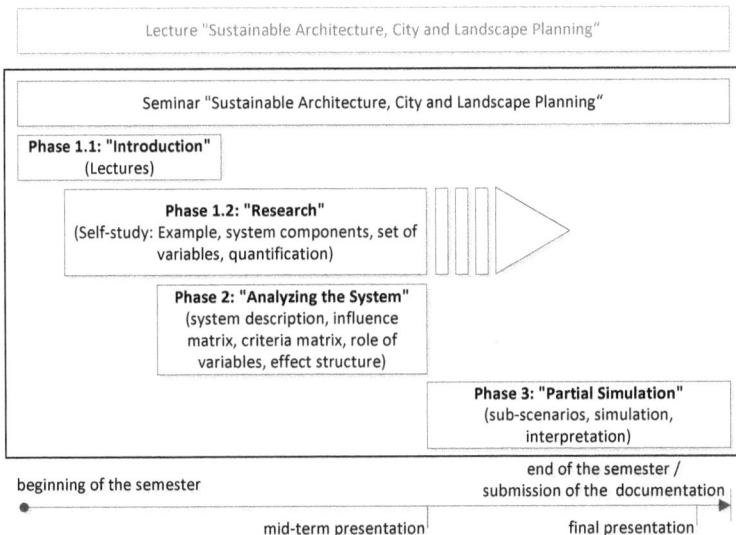

Figure 7. Concept of the seminar.

The seminar is divided into three overlapping phases, as shown in Figure 7. In the first phase, students are introduced to the methodology and the specific project through lectures. Alongside this, the students acquire the necessary background knowledge by carrying out independent literature research. In the second phase, the system is structured and analyzed in teacher-guided discussions among students with the help of the influence matrix. In the final phase, the interdisciplinary student groups select partial scenarios (see Figure 10 in Section 3.4) from the overall model, simulate these, and interpret their results.

3.2. Development of the System Structure

In the 2012/2013 winter semester, system relationships were examined using two examples of urban structures. The first example, the Munich quarter of Gärtnerplatz in the Isarvorstadt district is a dense downtown area. The second example was the garden city Gräfelfing in the county of Munich, a sprawling suburban quarter. Using the two examples, CO_2 emissions and CO_2 reduction potential were examined across all parts of life in dense and sprawling urban regions. The main aim the students were asked to work on was recognition of the principal controlling variables for the reduction of CO_2 emissions in the system of the urban structure. The software Malik Sensitivity Model Prof. Vester® [9] was used in the seminar to ease system analysis and simulation.

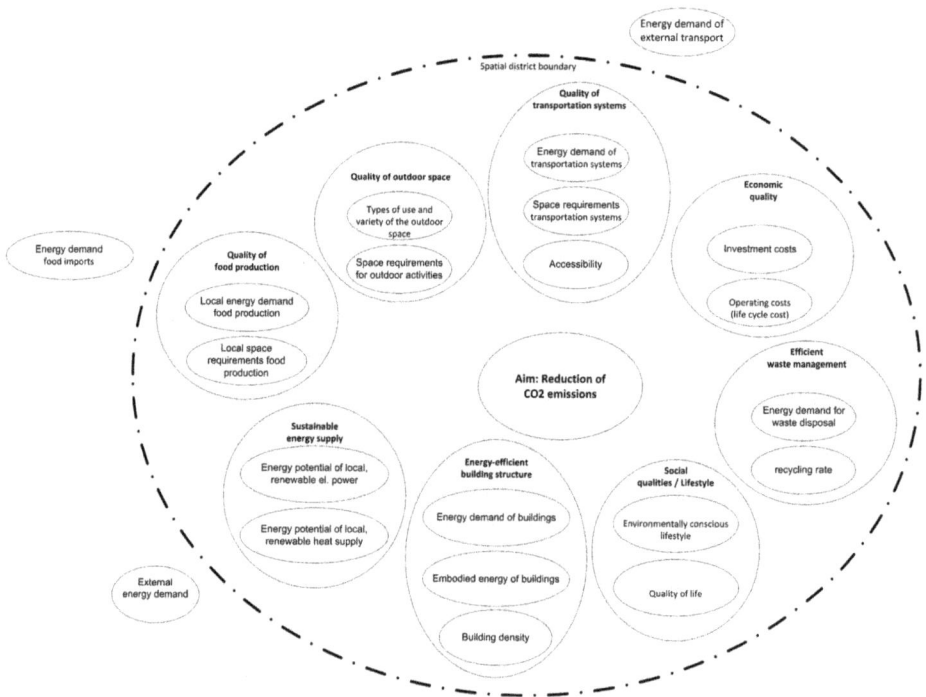

Figure 8. First sketch of the system description.

In the first phase, an introduction provides an overview of the methods and the students begin to develop the basis for system analysis, which investigates sector topics, elaborates the basic scheme of the system and defines performance criteria. Unlike the methodology developed by Vester, in order to achieve rapid understanding of the approach in one semester, an initial system description was provided as a basis for further discussions, as seen in Figure 8. The given topics also served as a template for systematic literature review in the first phase. The criteria catalog Neubau Stadtquartiere (Development of Urban Districts) by the German Society for Sustainable Building (DGNB) [22] was used as a reference for the system description and the objectives of sustainability in particular.

To achieve a manageable system, the initial system description was constantly aggregated step-by-step and kept with less than 30 variables.

3.3. Analyzing the System

In Phase 2 of the seminar, the students learn to analyze and to structure the dependencies of the city district as a system as described in Section 2.1. In order to introduce the method, each step started with a workshop. Afterwards the groups completed assigned work packages on their own. In a final discussion, all students agreed on a common result for each step. The results of phases one and two were presented by the students in the mid-term presentation. The students received complete documentation as a basis for further processing.

This phase addresses Teaching Objectives 1 and 2. The discussion process required to define the variables and complete the influence matrix refers to the knowledge from the lecture and fosters sensitivity for discipline/sector-crossing interdependencies as in Teaching Objective 1. In this discussion, the students have to argue the pros and cons of interdependencies in the system transcending all sector boundaries. In our experience, they often test different points of view that are very helpful for their holistic understanding. Furthermore, if they do not reach a consensus it is not detrimental; on the contrary, it can serve as a source of motivation for the next phase of the seminar to examine these questions in detail by quantified analyses and simulations. With respect to Teaching Objective 2, the analysis of the variables according to their roles in the system (Figure 9) and the setup of effect structure also provide them with tools for strategically structuring a system and give them an insight that some variables act as controllers in the system whereas others act as indicators or mediators. In addition to its applicability in later cases, the learned analysis method trains systemic thinking as a skill for sustainable planning through the identification of key variables, relevant interdependencies and dependency structure.

3.4. Partial Simulation

In the final phase, the groups produced their own partial simulation starting from the same basis. Each group chose a partial scenario (see Figure 10), which they modelled and simulated. Since the variable "political framework" turned out to be a very interesting controller in the system (see Figure 9), it was included in each selected scenario. The students investigated the influences of the 'political framework' by simulating their sub-scenario and critically discussed the results, which are shown, for instance, at the end in Figure 11.

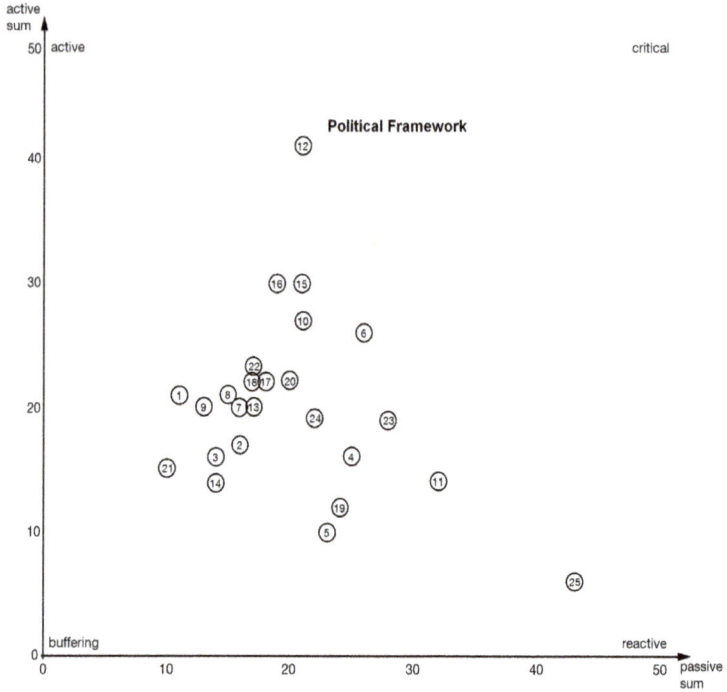

Figure 9. Role of variables in the systems for the urban districts Gärtnerplatz and Gräfelfing.

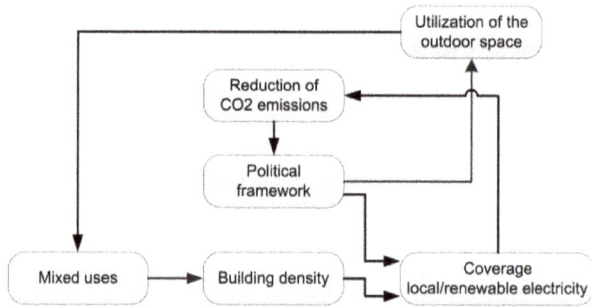

Figure 10. Partial scenario.

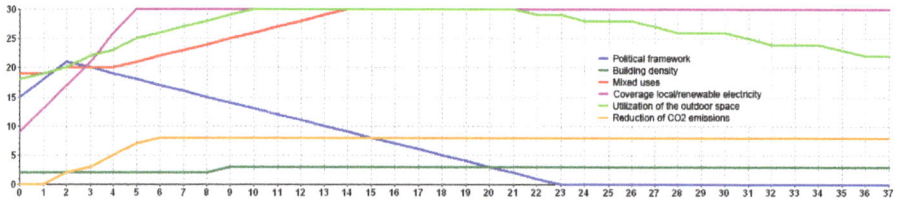

Figure 11. Results of the partial simulation.

Systems **2014**, *2*, 137–158

Unlike Vester's method, emphasis was put on the quantification of interdependencies. This fulfils Teaching Objective 3, which comprises an understanding and the ability to determine quantitative dependencies crossing disciplinary and sectoral boundaries. By compiling studies and data, they gain experience in the structure and magnitude of such dependencies. Furthermore, using a specific question of sustainability and setting up the required partial system model qualitatively and quantitatively enhances this skill of objectively and comprehensively assessing sustainability. This ability, which is part of Teaching Objective 4, enables the students to apply such a systemic approach in practice. The key for applying systems methods in planning decisions is not scientifically setting up a comprehensive, large system model, but developing purpose-tailored, question-driven partial models answering the specific questions of the planning process. Simulating partial scenarios, interpreting the results and scrutinizing their models foster an understanding of complex systemic interactions and trains students' abilities to find systemic integrative strategies for sustainable building.

3.5. Results and Discussion

In summary, systems modelling proved to be a suitable method for working on complex issues in the area of sustainable design and building not only in research, but also in the classroom. The students learn to identify relevant interdependencies and to define a system for representing them in a structured way. The seminar enables them to analyze the complex relationships between different areas within the overall system, such as a sustainable city, and to understand the effects within this structure. Beyond that, students gain insight into the mathematical relationships of the system components, which helps them to quantitatively estimate the effect of interdependencies. This provides them with experience in the strength of effects and the relevance of interdependencies. Therefore, besides methods of system analysis, modelling and simulation, the seminar trains their systemic thinking, which is a key skill in the field of sustainability since strategies for a sustainable built environment require a holistic discipline/sector-crossing assessment approach.

In the context of the narrow timeframe, only reduced system models make sense. The mathematical relationships of the variables in particular have to be simplified. For this reason, the quantitative results of the simulations should not be taken as absolute values but in their relative behavior. Nonetheless, these basic trends are very helpful for gaining better understanding of the system. It is crucial to communicate this fact very clearly from the beginning; otherwise students easily lose interest during the semester. Moreover, discussing each step during analysis, in order to reach consensus, turned out to be too time consuming for the short time period.

Since it is a seminar series, the education methods are continually improved. In the 2013/2014 seminar the process was simplified. Each group works independently throughout the entire semester and the discussions are held within each group. Then the results are discussed with the supervisors in weekly meetings. In addition, the case was narrowed down to a more clear arrangement, the WagnisART housing complex with five apartment buildings and large open spaces in the urban context of Munich. The seminar is closely related to an applied research project at the Institute of Energy Efficient and Sustainable Design and Building for this housing complex and thus has a positive influence on student motivation. Furthermore, the seminar is no longer based on the Malik software [9], but uses our own MatLab approach, which, compared to that presented in Section 2.4, is simplified. This enables a mathematically more precise definition of continuous interdependencies and is better suited for quantitative interdependencies.

4. Conclusions

The presented method of systems analysis, modelling and simulation serve as tools to support the development of strategies for sustainable and livable urban structures including quantitative and qualitative aspects. They were specifically developed to interconnect expert assessment in design and planning with a system model, its variables, interdependencies and their role in the system. From this setup, experts select relevant partial scenarios, model them in detail as effect structures and enrich them with detailed quantitative definitions by describing scales and interdependencies. This procedure leads to a systems model embedded in the planning discussion process, supporting its inherent decision-making in a holistic and understandable way. This is a prerequisite for making well-founded planning decisions for a sustainable built environment.

In the Nuremberg Western City research project the interpretation of results for Nuremberg Western City revealed what kinds of information can result from a partial system simulation. First of all, it is information about the intensity and timing of processes. Changing a variable controlling the system, as known from the previous analysis, helps to understand how to develop the urban quarter into a sustainable and livable neighborhood. Secondly, interpretation and reasoning of further consequences in other variables reveal strategies for this development and add a risk assessment. The application of system simulation is an interactive process of modelling systemic information, running simulations, interpretation and conclusions. It shows that partial system models and their interpretation by experts lead to the identification of strategies, potentials and risks in the different development paths. In particular, rather than guessing, we can now objectively test the overall systemic effect of actions, the intensity of the reactions and the time it takes until they have an effect. Therefore, the chief benefit of the method is that it supports systemic effects with documented and comprehensible results.

Understanding the interdisciplinary and sector-crossing dependencies of sustainability is the main objective for education in sustainable building. Systems thinking, in other words discussing the system and agreeing on a system description, identifying key variables and driving interdependencies, is the chief benefit of the learning process. Defining scenarios and testing them in environments of systems modelling and simulation provide the students with experience with relevant interdisciplinary connections and their time-based behavior. Furthermore, by partially quantifying such a system model, the students learn to develop strategies systematically and to make well-founded decisions instead of guessing at good solutions. This also teaches them to argue in favor of their solutions. Even without conducting systems simulation, we expect that students will gain competence in interdisciplinary systems thinking that is very valuable for sustainable building in their future in planning practice as well as in research.

In both cases, in research and education of sustainable building, the sensitivity and systems modelling methods turned out to vitally support intersectoral interaction and disciplinary integration. Together, both the method, with its inherent sector-crossing discussions, and the models are a vehicle to foster interdisciplinary reasoning for sustainability. Qualitative determination of sensitivities as well as quantitative support provides a holistic approach that is often lacking in the sustainable design of the built environment. Therefore, we deem a systemic approach an inevitable component of sustainable building that requires further development for education and research.

Acknowledgments: The specific results for the Nuremberg Western City district shown in the first part of this paper originate from the collaborative work of a project team at Technische Universität München consisting of members of the Centre and Chair of Energy-Efficient and Sustainable Planning and Building (ENPB), the Department of Urban Structure and Transport Planning, the Chair for Sustainable Urbanism, the Chair for Spatial Development, the Chair for Landscape Architecture and Public Space, the Chair of Energy Economics and Application Technology, the Chair of Climate Design, the Chair of Building Physics and the Chair of Urban Design and Regional Planning. The City of Nuremberg with the support of the State of Bavaria provided funding for the project and helped obtain local information in a dialogue. The course described in the second part of the paper was developed and conducted through a collaboration of the first two authors with Judith Schinabeck. For the conceptual work on systems modelling, the first author received a grant from the Volkswagen Foundation for the project Parametric Systems Modelling—A Method for Performance-based and Strategic Building Design. Finally, the authors would like to thank Daniela Popp from ProLehre, the Department for Teaching and Learning in Higher Education at the TU München for her suggestions for Section 3.

Author Contributions: Introduction: Sustainable Design and Planning in Research and Education by Philipp Geyer and Werner Lang;

Systems Modelling in Research-City Lab Nuremberg West by Philipp Geyer and Maximilian Thumfart;

Teaching Urban Systems Modelling—The Sustainable Architecture, City and Landscape Planning (SACLP) Course by Jochen Stopper and Philipp Geyer;

Conclusions by Philipp Geyer.

Systems **2014**, 2, 137–158

Conflicts of Interest: The authors declare no conflict of interest.

References and Notes

1. Robinson, D. *Computer Modelling for Sustainable Urban Design—Physical Principles, Methods and Applications*; Earthscan: London, UK, 2011.
2. Forrester, J.W. *Urban Dynamics*; MIT Press: Cambridge, MA, USA, 1970.
3. Lee, D.B. Requiem for large-scale models. *J. Am. Inst. Plan.* **1973**, *39*, 163–178. [CrossRef]
4. Timmermans, H.J.P. *Decision Support Systems in Urban Planning*; Taylor & Francis: London, UK, 1997.
5. Batty, M. *Cities and Complexity. Understanding Cities with Cellular Automata*; MIT Press: Cambridge, MA, USA, 2007.
6. Batty, M.; Torrens, P.M. Modelling and prediction in a complex world. *Futures* **2005**, *37*, 745–766. [CrossRef]
7. Vester, F. *The Art of Interconnected Thinking: Tools and Concepts for a New Approach to Tackling Complexity*; MBC Publishing House: München, Germany, 2007.
8. Malik Sensitivity Model Prof. Vester®. Available online: http://www.malik-management.com/en (accessed on 6 November 2013).
9. Eppinger, S.D.; Browning, T.R. *Design Structure Matrix Methods and Applications: Engineering Systems*; MIT Press: Cambridge, MA, USA, 2012.
10. Alaily-Mattar, N.; Thierstein, A.; Förster, A. "Alternative futures": A methodology for integrated sustainability considerations, the case of Nuremberg West, Germany. *Local Environ.* **2013**. [CrossRef]
11. Geyer, P.; Nemeth, I.; Lang, W.; Wulfhorst, G.; Roland, P. Systems Modelling Considering Qualities and Quantities for Strategies of Sustainable Development of a Liveable Urban District in Nuremberg. In Proceedings of EG-ICE Workshop 2012, Herrsching, Germany, 4–6 July 2012.
12. *Stadtlabor Nürnberger Weststadt: Endbericht*; Project Report; Technische Universität München: München, Germany, 2012.
13. Kenworthy, J.R.; Laube, F.B. Patterns of automobile dependence in cities: An international overview of key physical and economic dimensions with some implications for urban policy. *Transport. Res. Pol. Pract.* **1999**, *33*, 691–723. [CrossRef]
14. Fischer, J.H. *Stadtentwicklung und Umweltplanung: Dargestellt am Beispiel Hamburg*; (in German). Göttingen, Germay, 1985.
15. City of Nuremberg. Statistics of Nuremberg and Data Made Available by the City Administration Restricted to the Project Purpose Only. Available online: http://www.daten.statistik.nuernberg.de (accessed on 6 November 2013).
16. Object Management Group, OMG. *Systems Modelling Language: Specifications*, Version 1.3; Available online: http://www.omg.org/spec/SysML/1.3/ (accessed on 6 November 2013).
17. Master in Energy-Efficient and Sustainable Building. Available online: http://www.enpb.bgu.tum.de/en/master-enb/ (accessed on 6 November 2013).
18. Geyer, P.; Schinabeck, J.; Stopper, J. *Modulbeschreibung Seminar Nachhaltige Architektur-, Stadt- und Landschaftsplanung*; (in German). Technische Universität München: München, Germany, 2013.
19. Biggs, J.B.; Tang, C. *Teaching for Quality Learning at University: What the Student Does, SRHE and Open University Press Imprint*; McGraw-Hill: Maidenhead, Germany, 2011.
20. Bayer, T.; Fleischmann, A.; Spiekermann, A.; Strasser, A. *Constructive Alignment—Lernergebnisse, Lehrmethoden und Prüfungsformen optimal aufeinander abstimmen*; (in German). Technische Universität München: München, Germany, 2014.
21. Anderson, L.W.; Krathwohl, D.R.; Airasian, P.W. *A Taxonomy for Learning, Teaching, and Assessing: A Revision of Bloom's Taxonomy of Educational Objectives*; Longman: New York, NY, USA, 2001.
22. Deutsche Gesellschaft für nachhaltiges Bauen e.V (Hg). Neubau Stadtquartiere. In *DGNB Handbuch für nachhaltiges Bauen*; Version 2012.

systems

MDPI

Communication

Lessons Learnt from Educating University Students through a Trans-Disciplinary Project for Sustainable Sanitation Using a Systems Approach and Problem-Based Learning [†]

Janice Gray [1], Jennifer Williams [2], Prasanthi Hagare [3], Abby Mellick Lopes [4] and Shankar Sankaran [5,*]

[1]   UNSW Law, UNSW Australia (formerly the University of New South Wales, Sydney), NSW 2052, Australia; j.gray@unsw.edu.au

[2]   Division of Education, Arts and Social Sciences, University of South Australia, GPO Box 2471, Adelaide, SA 5001, Australia; jennifer.williams@unisa.edu.au

[3]   Faculty of Engineering and Information Technology, University of Technology Sydney, Ultimo, NSW 2007, Australia; prasanthi.hagare@uts.edu.au

[4]   School of Humanities and Communication Arts, University of Western Sydney, Locked Bag 1797, Penrith, NSW 2751, Australia; A.Lopes@uws.edu.au

[5]   Faculty of Design, Architecture and Building, University of Technology Sydney, Ultimo, NSW 2007, Australia

*   Author to whom correspondence should be addressed; shankar.sankaran@uts.edu.au; Tel.: +61-2-9514-8882; Fax: +61-2-9514-8051.

[†]   An earlier article "Sankaran, S.; Abeysuriya, K.; Gray, J.; Kachenko, A. Mellow yellow: Taking a systems thinking approach to designing research on transitioning to more sustainable sewage management. *Syst. Res. Behav. Sci.* **2013**, doi:10.1002/sres.2227" dealt with the research design aspect of the project described in this paper. This paper deals with the educational opportunities and outcomes associated with the research project.

Received: 24 December 2013; in revised form: 5 May 2014; Accepted: 16 May 2014; Published: 25 June 2014

Abstract: This article discusses how a Systems Thinking (ST) approach to student learning, employing Problem-Based Learning (PBL) interventions, at several different universities in Sydney, Australia was incorporated into a broader trans-disciplinary research project, the aim of which was to examine how urine diversion in an urban, institutional setting might form the basis of phosphorus collection—phosphorus being a non-renewable resource used in agricultural fertilizers. The article explores how the ST approach employed by the researchers themselves was adapted to embrace student engagement opportunities and how it permitted opportunities for Problem-Based Learning interventions. Five academics forming part of the research team consider the effectiveness of ST-styled student engagement via Problem-Based Learning in three action research cycles used in the research project. In sharing their experiences they provide an honest, "no-holds barred" review of what worked and what could be done more effectively with the benefits of hindsight.

Keywords: systems thinking; action research; systems education; legal studies; visual communication; civil and environmental engineering

1. Introduction

The student learning experiences described in this article may be envisaged as a set of actions that were planned as part of a sustainable sanitation research project. Philosophically the research was set in a Systems Thinking based intellectual framework (F) with Action Research as the Methodology

Systems **2014**, *2*, 243–272

(M) that guided the Problem-Based Learning interventions as the area of application (A) as shown in Figure 1 based on the FMA model proposed by Checkland [1] to set up any piece of research.

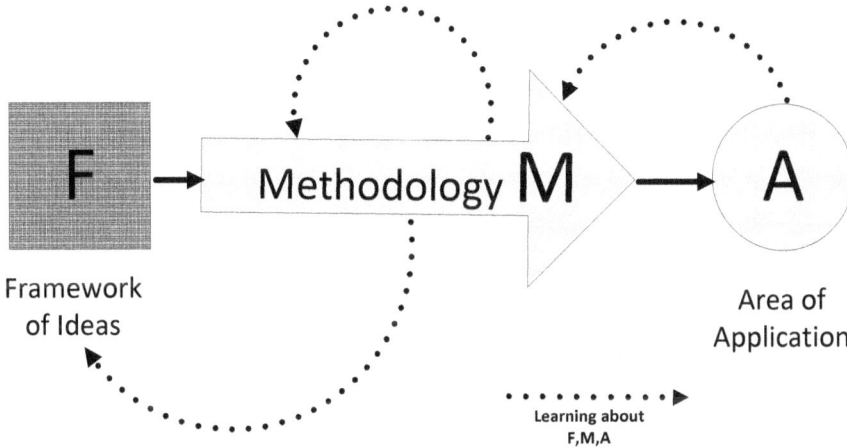

Figure 1. Elements of research (Based on [1]).

According to Savin-Baden and Howell [2], Problem Based Learning (or PBL) developed at a medical school at the University of McMaster in Canada as a new approach to medical education. The use of PBL spread to other medical schools across the world and from medical schools PBL spread to educating health workers. PBL spread further to professional preparation programs in engineering, architecture, economics, law and social work to name a few areas.

According to Barrows [3] the original model of PBL developed at McMaster had the following characteristics:

(1)   Learning is student-centered;
(2)   Learning occurs in small student groups;
(3)   Teachers are facilitators or guides;
(4)   Problems form the organizing focus and stimulus for learning;
(5)   Problems are a vehicle for the development of clinical problem solving skills;
(6)   New information is acquired through self-directed learning.

Boud and Feletti [4] clarified that "the emphasis of problem-based approaches is on learning processes of enquiry which proceeds by asking what needs to be known to address and improve a particular situation" and that "critical reflection is central to effective action". Rangachari [5] describes it thus: "The term PBL means different things to different people". "Shorn of all rhetoric, it is a format that encourages active participation by plunging students into a situation requiring them to define their own learning needs within broad goals set by the faculty. The students are presented with problem-situations that serve as springboards for learning. This is in sharp contrast to subject-based approaches that teach a body of knowledge prior to its application to specific problems".

PBL gained favor as an innovative idea when it was observed that students who used PBL to study in medical schools adapted more easily to medical practice because PBL activated prior knowledge [6].

While PBL was being developed in Canada, a variation of PBL based on project pedagogy was developed in two universities in Denmark. One of them, Aalborg University, used the variation to meet industry expectations of competencies of engineers. The concept that developed in Denmark was explained by de Graaff and Kolmos [6] as "a form of teaching in which students—in collaboration with teachers and others—explore and work with a problem in close relation to the social reality in which it exists".

The terms "problem-based learning" and "project-based learning" refer to models that have many similarities but the main difference between them is that while PBL is used to address open-ended and ill-structured problems (similar to the ones in which soft systems methodology plays a useful method of intervention) project-based learning refers to an assignment or task that students have to perform [6].

Savin-Baden [7] proposed five models of PBL:

(1) PBL for epistemological competence—knowledge is propositional and used for narrow problem scenarios;
(2) PBL for professional action—knowledge is practical and performance-oriented dealing with a real-life situation;
(3) PBL for interdisciplinary understanding where knowledge is both propositional and practical and the problem scenario requires a combination of theory and practice;
(4) PBL for critical contestability where knowledge is contingent, contextual and constructed by the learner for a given situation and the problem scenario is one that offers multidimensional possibilities.

De Graaff and Kolmos [8] reduce the main learning principles of PBL to three approaches:

(1) Learning approach—learning is organized around problems. It places learning in context and bases learning on learners' experiences;
(2) Contents approach—concerns interdisciplinary learning and crosses boundaries as learning leads to exemplary practice and the learning outcome is exemplary to overall objectives;
(3) Social approach in which team-based learning takes precedence and learning takes place through dialogue and communication.

As PBL developed it generated a number of debates that continue to raise questions of concern and/or interest. According to Savin-Baden [9] these include:

(1) The extent to which a course or a program needs to be problem-based.
(2) How it should be designed?
(3) What counts as PBL, ways of implementation and types?
(4) Should it be an instructional strategy or used only for curriculum design?

Savin-Baden [9] argues that PBL differs from other similar teaching methods such as project-based learning, problem solving, problem-solving learning, scenario-based learning, inquiry-based learning, problem-orientated learning, work-based learning and action learning. She is optimistic that PBL will continue to grow in higher education despite the various debates as its essential principles contribute to effective learning. It is, however, a difficult approach for students and teachers to grasp as it challenges them to accept that learning has to be managed in the midst of blurred boundaries and transitions. That was certainly the case in the sustainable sanitation project that forms the subject of this article.

For the purposes of contextualization, the following section details the particular sanitation project to which Systems Thinking (ST), Action Research (AR) and Problem Based Learning (PBL) were applied in an educational context.

2. Background

The sanitation project referred to above was the Transitioning to Sustainable Sanitation (TSS) Project or the Funny Dunnies Project, as it became affectionately known. It was a Sydney-based project that involved research by, and the participation of, academics and students at three universities as well as a range of industry partners. The project relied on AR within a ST framework and at different

Systems **2014**, *2*, 243–272

stages and in various circumstances, the academic members of the research team applied PBL to their students' learning.

The project was innovative at a number of levels including the scientific, environmental and technological endeavors it pursued, as well as the manner in which it sought to educate the students involved in it. The project's overall innovation was formally recognized when it won a New South Wales State government Green Globe Award for Innovation, in 2012.

What exactly did the TSS project aim to investigate?

The TSS project aimed to explore the possibility that urine diversion might become a viable concept in the urban environment.

Urine diversion and collection was considered important because urine contains high levels of phosphorus. Phosphorus is an element with a plethora of uses, and one key use is in modern agriculture where it is used in chemical fertilizers that support global food production.

As the world population increases, demands on phosphorus have increased. Yet, phosphorus is a non-renewable resource and mineral phosphate rock reserves are diminishing at such a rate that an anticipated peak in global phosphorus production will occur by 2035 [10]. Accordingly, the pressure to find alternative sources of phosphorus has escalated.

Aware that urine diversion permits the separation of nutrients as well as the potential recovery of approximately 80% of nitrogen and 50% of phosphorus in domestic wastewater [11], the multi-disciplinary and multi-institutional TSS research team (including students) embarked on a pilot project in urine diversion and capture in an institutional setting. Put simply, the research team set about capturing urine at an early stage in the sanitation process before it became mixed with other sewage components including feces, chemicals, paper and water because it was anticipated that this method would increase the percentage of urine captured and reduce energy consumption [12].

In order to facilitate this, not only did specially designed urine-diverting toilets (Figure 2) need to be installed at an appropriate site and location, but also plumbing needed to be modified, sampling equipment installed and collection undertaken. Additionally, the project had to develop and implement methods to encourage users to actually try out the new toilets. It then had to build into the broader methodology mechanisms for monitoring users' reactions and their adaptability to the new technology.

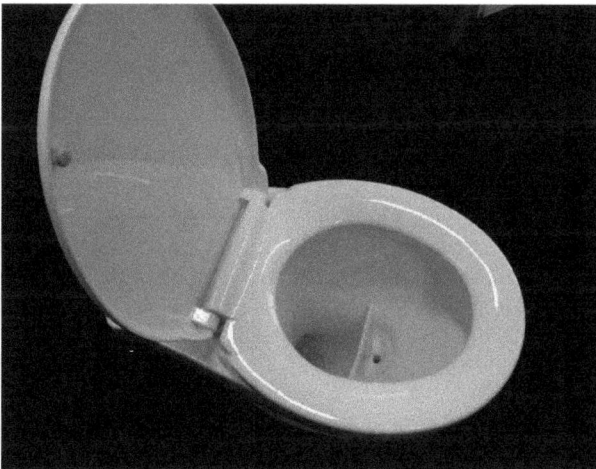

Figure 2. Wostman urine diverting toilet used during the pre-pilot trial. Urine is diverted into the front section of the partitioned bowl (*Image: Jennifer Williams*).

In this context, a range of matters were flagged as being potentially important. They included: ensuring that the legal, regulatory and institutional requirements for the installation of such toilets

Systems **2014**, 2, 243–272

and for the collection and storage of urine could be met; facilitating the uptake of the urine diverting toilets by stakeholders through appropriate and enabling design; monitoring the technical operation of the toilets and users' responses; and analyzing the urine collected. In particular, the research team sought to reveal the "range of independent factors that determine the successful uptake and potential scale-up of radical sustainable sanitation" [13].

Unlike many research projects that only involve academics or rely on the input of a handful of postgraduate students in one discipline, the TSS project incorporated both undergraduate and postgraduate students who were studying courses in a range of disciplines, and at three different universities. Students were a key part of the TSS project; they learnt a great deal and also contributed to knowledge creation and research. Learning and engagement in the project were associated with the five research strands into which investigators, partners and students had grouped. Because the project was trans-disciplinary, by nature it encouraged intersection and overlap between the strands. The strands were: (1) Regulation and Institutions; (2) Technology; (3) Visual Communication; (4) Stakeholder Engagement; and (5) Integration (Table 1). Three cycles of AR were designed. They were: (a) investigation and design; (b) contract and commission; and (c) operate, monitor, evaluate and decommission. Students had engagement with the project at various phases in the cycles.

This article addresses the question: What lessons have been learnt from engaging university students in a trans-disciplinary ST project, applying PBL and addressing key sustainability issues of the era?

Part One provides a description of where PBL interventions were applied via learning platforms across the three relevant strands of: (1) regulation and institutions; (2) visual communication; and (3) technology. It discusses the intended educational opportunities and then offers an evaluation of what *actually* happened in the instances where PBL was planned/intended to apply. This part, therefore, constitutes a first order reflection. The discussion following in Part Two deals with what could have been done better, providing a second-order reflection. Finally, Part Three of the article offers a holistic reflection across the three strands of the project; a project providing a site for educational innovation within a ST framework and in which the key focus was environmental sustainability.

Table 1. Research strands, disciplines, programs and student numbers (*Table: Jennifer Williams*).

Research strand	Academic Departments/University	Education Program	Number of students
Regulation and Institutions			
	UNSW Law, UNSW Australia (formerly known as University of	Bachelor of Laws (*from a university other than UNSW*)	1
		Masters in Environmental Law (*from a university other than UNSW*)	1
Technology			
	Faculty of Engineering & Information Technology	Bachelor of Engineering (Civil Engineering): Capstone Project	1
		Bachelor of Engineering (Civil & Environmental Engineering): Capstone Project	1
Visual Communication Design			
	Faculty of Design, Architecture and Building	Bachelor of Design (Visual Communication): Information Design	17
		Bachelor of Design (Visual Communication): Community Projects	5
	School of Humanities and Communication Arts University of Western Sydney Australia	Bachelor of Design (Visual Communication): Professional Design Studio	10
Stakeholder Engagement	**NO STUDENT INVOLVEMENT**		
Integration	**NO STUDENT INVOLVEMENT**		

3. Part 1: PBL Applications to Student Learning in the TSS Project

In this part we outline the innovative approaches to student learning and teaching that were introduced across three of the research strands of the TSS project mentioned above. In particular, we focus on PBL interventions that, although taking different forms in different research strands, were employed commonly across the project. They were employed to help foster co-operative learning [14], learning by doing [15] exploratory learning [16], social learning [17] and adaptive learning [18] among other things [19]. It was anticipated that such interventions would align well with the ST methodology used in the project; a methodology that we favoured because of its potential to serve students well in a rapidly changing society in which complexity characterizes many human endeavours. The following discussion is organized around the three research strands and outlines more specifically how the learning opportunities in a systems-focused space were designed.

3.1. Regulation and Institutions Strand

Van Buuren and others have noted that the literature on collaborative problem solving is deficient to the extent that it commonly underestimates the role, importance and characteristics of the governance system in which collaborative problem solving is employed [20,21]. The TSS project sought to address such neglect and deficiencies by devoting one strand to governance including regulation and institutional arrangements. The project, therefore, included a lawyer in the research team and it also sought to include the participation of law students in the Regulation and Institutions strand.

Regulation and Institutions Strand (UNSW Researcher—UNSW-R)

It was initially anticipated that in AR Cycle 1 (the investigation phase) later-year law students at UNSW Australia could, through involvement in the Regulation and Institutions strand, participate in the project by undertaking a comparative international review of institutional structures and legal frameworks that have been successfully adopted to facilitate resource recovery and re-use. It was also anticipated that student enrolment in a specific research thesis subject or in an elective—Environmental Law—which permitted students to design their own research task and sub-projects, would be the optimal way to proceed. It was envisaged that learning in this strand would build on PBL interventions employed in law teaching more generally where students are familiar with activities designed to simulate legal practice and legal problems so that, among other things, students learn to "think like a lawyer". Learning to think like a lawyer commonly involves the ability to "mentally problem solve, ask legally relevant questions and identify legal issues, search for coherence in fact patterns, think linearly, perceive ambiguity, appropriately engage in deductive and inductive reasoning, see all sides of an argument, and simultaneously pay attention to detail while recognizing which issues are more important than others" [22].

It was intended that students in this strand would formulate questions and develop a research framework based on both their direct engagement with the TSS project and their understanding of institutional enablers and blockers evident in comparative, international jurisdictions as well as in the domestic jurisdiction in which the TSS project was to operate. Real-life scenarios would encourage exploration of the nexus between practicum, theory, doctrinal law and institutional frameworks, so fostering and developing positive experiential learning. Student engagement with and involvement in the Regulation and Institutions strand, as in the other strands, was designed to rely on authentic learning, or learning in real situations, rather than purely hypothetical ones.

Authentic learning, which is commonly dependent on PBL (and project-based learning) interventions, involves a range of elements considered relevant to educating the TSS project students about environmental sustainability through a ST approach. It was hoped that the project would:

- Provide authentic contexts that reflect knowledge's use and application in the real world;
- Provide opportunities to undertake real tasks;
- Provide access to expert performances;

Systems **2014**, 2, 243–272

- Expose the need to take on multiple roles and or viewpoints;
- Support the collaborative construction of knowledge;
- Promote reflection to enhance the formulation of abstractions;
- Promote platforms for the articulation of tacit knowledge and thereby allow that knowledge to be made explicit; provide scaffolding by the educator at the point of need; and
- Provide for real world assessments of the learning [23,24].

Students were, therefore, to engage with "chunks" of the project depending on the cycle and phase of the project itself. Consequently different students would be dipping into the project at different times but their learning experiences would allow them to appreciate the holistic and integrated nature of the project overall, an outcome it was thought would be largely achieved through open dialogue, group work and regular meetings between different strand participants, along with effective reporting-back practices and procedures.

One key aspect of the plan was to offer the law students the opportunity to conduct applied research that focused on mapping the legal and regulatory framework under which the pilot project and later, non-pilot applications of it, would operate. Hence the law relating to urine collection, storage, transportation, experimentation and re-use, was relevant. The law needed to be laid out and its point(s) of intersection with the project, identified. This was envisaged as exploratory PBL. It was a potentially challenging task because the law governing areas of new technologies (such as sustainable sewage options) is commonly law designed for other more conventional purposes. That law needs to be transposed from one setting and applied in another new (and often unconventional) setting. Hence part of the PBL intervention was to involve students through an exploration of existing law in a range of jurisdictions, determining if that law had application in the context of sustainable sewage. Students were thus confronted with a complex problem that needed a creative approach to understanding and resolution. They had to adjust to the idea that the law was not waiting in neatly packaged compartments simply to be "discovered". In other words, the PBL interventions were designed to help students "construct" the relevant law.

It was also envisaged that as part of the TSS project and the PBL interventions, students would contribute to the law reform process. They would contribute by assessing and analyzing the legal and governance issues that they, the students, confronted through involvement in the project, coming to conclusions about which aspects of law and governance acted as blockers to and/or facilitators of, the introduction and implementation of sustainable sewage options. Developing law reform initiatives where necessary was therefore, another function of the project and in this aspect, as indeed in many others, the students, were to become problem-solvers.

PBL (and in some instances project-based learning) were to be relied on to encourage students to work out what legal issues were relevant to the technological, design and implementation aspects of the project. It was anticipated, therefore, that the law students would need to address questions such as the following: (a) what do I know already about sanitation regulation and governance? (b) what do I need to know about sanitation regulation and governance to contribute effectively to this project? and; (c) how might I find out what I need to know? UNSW-R, the academic researcher leading this strand, also intended that students would reflect on the fact that there would be some knowledge that students did not yet know that they needed to know. Some questions might not yet even be imagined. With this in mind it was anticipated that students would embark on their information discoveries and knowledge creation activities.

Accordingly, the project was rich with opportunities for students, including the opportunities to:

- Observe, respond to and analyze the interactions between complementary and competing pieces of legislation;
- Determine, in practical terms, which types of approvals needed to be sought throughout the project;
- Decide how and when such requirements could be satisfied in order best to progress the project;

- Apply the law to practical, real life issues that needed to be managed; and
- Observe and analyze the effectiveness of the institutional arrangements supporting regulation and governance, with a view to suggesting appropriate legal, regulatory and institutional reform.

It was anticipated that students would very much be project "insiders", working on practical aspects of the study such as contacting government agencies and institutions to ascertain what consent and approval forms were required under legislation as well as interpreting various statutes. It was envisaged that they would also need to work out the interaction between different legislative instruments and the common law. This way, it was hoped that students would receive the full range of benefits associated with legal experiential learning, PBL and authentic learning that took place in an adaptable ST based space. They would "learn by doing", benefitting from the approach by: taking responsibility for their work; gaining an appreciation of the importance of access to justice while developing professional ethics; and developing an awareness of the limitations of the law and legal practice. Involvement in the project was also designed to teach students civic responsibility and to strengthen communities [19,25]. Further, it was anticipated that student participation would provide a form of *service learning*—a learning and teaching strategy that blends or integrates "meaningful community service with instruction and reflection—[so as] to enrich learning experiences." Well implemented, it has the effect of teaching students the value of community service and civic responsibility, resulting in strengthened communities [26].

With these objectives in mind there would necessarily be a close relationship between the students in this strand and members of all the other strands but particularly with members of the technological strand. Why? Because students in this strand would, through their legal research, contribute ideas on whether the specific and technical approaches to be employed by the research team were in compliance with law and regulation. Hence, students in this strand would need to engage closely with the plumbers, engineers and designers, for example.

It was always imagined that students would, through PBL, work in groups and break down their engagement with the project into manageably sized interactions, in the same way as doctoral students are encouraged to think of their theses as a series of manageable chapters rather than one, large, amorphous problem that needs solving [27].

3.2. Visual Communication Strand

It was envisaged that the project would also engage University of Technology and University of Western Sydney students who were enrolled in either third (UTS) or fourth year (UWS) of their Visual Communication Design degrees. The objective of the Visual Communication strand was to design communications that would activate the involvement of participants in the TSS project and engage the imagination of the broader public in the issue of sustainable sanitation. In the well-known words of Herbert Simon; every design project is about converting existing situations into preferred situations [28]. It is important to note, therefore, that design thinking and practice was in synergy with the forward-looking and change-oriented dimensions of the TSS project.

The students would engage with the project through the development of a series of briefs as part of an industry partnership program. The visual tools to be designed would inform users about the "how" and "why" of the systems and develop a means of on-going, mutual communications with users, such as web tools. In keeping with the systems-based approach, students in the visual communication strand would seek feedback on the design elements so as to create improved and revised signage and tools.

Two researchers led the Visual Communication Strand: one each from UTS (UTS R1) and from the University of Western Sydney (UWS-R).

Systems **2014**, *2*, 243–272

3.2.1. Visual Communication Strand—UTS Researcher 1 (UTS-R1)

The TSS project ran across an academic year in two third year subjects of the 4-year degree program at UTS: Information Design, and Community Projects. In the former, 17 students were responsible for their individually formulated projects; in the latter, a 5-person group collectively produced a body of work, again steering the direction of their project.

In designing student participation in the TSS project for Information Design, the normative PBL approach of presenting the "ill-structured" problem [4,15] to students was tested. Not widely embedded in undergraduate design study—the more directive project-based learning being the model most commonly used [29]—PBL provided the impetus for students to construct their own visual enquiries by actively determining the most significant aspects of a given issue to investigate. The notion of utilizing a PBL approach was drawn from the structure of the TSS study itself, where visual communication was intentionally positioned at the strategic "fuzzy front end" rather than at the more usual production back-end of projects. This placement had the potential to disclose design's fuller disciplinary capacities, demanding an exploratory, speculative and provocative stance. It also demanded ongoing reflective engagement by the students over the arc of the project, as befitting both PBL and action research models.

Initially informed by subject expert briefings by the TSS project researchers, students framed their own projects through a questioning activity to determine the kinds of interventions that could benefit from design. They needed to be "metacognitively aware" [30] in order to: assess their existing knowledge; the deficit in their knowledge; and then evolve visual strategies in response. In this instance, two entwined issues were identified for enquiry: the global depletion of phosphorus and the rethinking of human waste as a resource. This more autonomous, self-directed approach was in contrast to traditional models of design education of "solving" pre-framed tasks dressed as "problems". It mirrors a limiting 20th century view of design as one of service provision rather than as a discipline employing a more expansive, nimble mindset to set agenda in a multi-faceted, trans-disciplinary enquiry where boundaries are fluid.

The TSS project was also foregrounded by a preparatory assessment task introducing students to information design systems, its pioneers, paradigm shifts in the discipline, plus its contemporary expansions, for example, experience design and interaction design. As part of their overall enquiry, students were encouraged to think beyond the comfort of disciplinary knowledge to quickly embrace many aspects of the TSS project; the intention here was to seed the idea of students framing their own projects.

Community Projects, run in the second semester, took on not-for-profit projects selected by UTS Shopfront (a gateway for community access to UTS); the cohort was divided into groups of five who were then allocated a project that is usually tightly controlled by the client. The group taking on the TSS project was advantaged with access to students from the first semester and to their research and projects; they were able to build upon knowledge grown by the first cohort. A key project team member also briefed them on soft systems. Again, they were required to assess critically the TSS research questions, determining where proposed design interventions could have the most traction for their chosen audience, in this instance, the UTS community. Each student was allocated roles within the project, and typical of PBL operating structure [29] the group was deliberately populated with a mix of strong, average and weaker students in order to offer learning opportunities in managing group dynamics, accountability, the giving and receiving of feedback from peers, and growing communication abilities.

3.2.2. Visual Communication Strand—UWS Researcher (UWS-R)

The TSS project was offered as a "Live Brief" to final year students in the Professional Strand of the Bachelor of Design (Visual Communications) degree in the School of Humanities and Communication Arts at UWS.

A group of seven students worked on the brief in the first semester and five in the second semester. UWS-R developed a project brief for students to respond to, and a key project team member based at

Systems **2014**, *2*, 243–272

UTS gave a briefing presentation, explaining the significance of the project in more depth. Students in the Professional Strand work in a studio environment that unlike the traditional classroom involves longer and more intensive periods of experimentation and research though practice. The design studio itself can be described as a problem-based learning environment with its emphasis on collaborative process, the ready application of concepts to practice and the validation of students' prior knowledge as they work to define the problems in the brief, in their own terms.

PBL is an approach where an "ill-structured" problem provides a stimulus for learning [4] The PBL intervention in the Professional Strand was in the nature of the problem embedded in the brief that students were commissioned to solve. This centered on the problem of "waste = food". Students had some background understanding of this concept from Braungart and McDonough's "cradle to cradle" thinking [31], which allowed them to grasp the central rhetorical challenge of the project: how can design help to recode what had been considered a waste product as a potentially precious resource for use in agricultural applications with a range of direct environmental and ultimately socio-cultural benefits? However, this problem was significantly more complex than those typically structured into curricula in the Professional Strand. Normally, students in this strand demonstrate their "industry-ready" professionalism and technical skills by solving relatively simple briefs in a direct service relation to the client. This is more akin to a traditional project-based learning approach wherein problems are tailored to the students' current knowledge base and written in a more prescriptive manner [29].

The TSS project provided students' with a rich "real world" set of problems that activated their critical problem solving skills. The "waste = food" problem demanded a significant amount of theoretical "skilling up" and students had quickly to acquire, share and apply new knowledge as they collaborated with each other to move toward the preferred solutions. Rather than these being decided in advance by the client and presented as a *fait accompli*, the link between critical thinking and action in this scenario came from the students' own self-directed learning.

3.3. Technology Strand

As part of the undergraduate engineering program, students are introduced to the concept of working on different types of projects in the real world. Some of these projects have defined specifications, or "a brief", while others are more open-ended. Students learn to deal with different types of projects in subjects such as Design and Innovation Fundamentals and Engineering Project Management. They are also exposed to problem-based learning and finding solutions to ill-structured projects while undertaking discipline-related subjects such as Environmental and Sanitation Engineering, and Pollution Control and Waste Management. Students usually work in groups and are required to undertake needs analyses while considering constraints, uncertainties and risks in order to establish priorities and goals in trying to solve the problem. This prior PBL knowledge was useful in helping students to work on the TSS project.

Technology Strand—UTS Researcher 2 (UTS-R2)

As part of the Technology strand, undergraduate engineering students of Civil and Environmental Engineering majors were considered ideal to be involved in the TSS project. These students are exposed to the theoretical aspects of challenges to sanitation issues, especially with respect to water conservation and resource recovery. The TSS project raised these issues and aspects of the project also related to risks to health and safety; issues with which UTS R2 wanted students to engage.

Students from undergraduate engineering programs and in their last stage of study were selected for this project. One of the key aspects of the project was to select an appropriate site for setting up the urine diversion toilet. As UTS is divided into ten different buildings, one student undertook a detailed survey of each. The data collected included information about space available, traffic movement, proximity to people, layout and water/wastewater pipeline accessibility and other related information. This student also designed a system enabling collection of urine from the UD toilet for sampling

Systems **2014**, *2*, 243–272

and analysis as well as undertaking a detailed literature review of urine diversion technology used elsewhere in Australia and overseas. The second student's work was related to identifying risks associated with using urine as a fertilizer, and techniques that can be used to reduce or avoid any risks to people and the environment.

In all cases students were encouraged to become part of the "would-be problem solvers" who intended to take purposeful action to address a "problematic" situation [32]. Academics also saw student involvement in the above-mentioned ways as assisting the mutual reinforcement of "institutional and socio-cultural transformations including new infrastructure planning processes, enabling regulatory and legal frameworks; and altered user practices" (Sankaran *et al.* [32]) [33].

In keeping with a systems-based focus that was embedded in the AR methodology, flexibility and re-orientation were to form key elements of the teaching/learning pedagogy informing student involvement—involvement that relied heavily on PBL. It was considered important to be able to adjust learning and research objectives, initiatives, directions and models throughout the project so that they better responded to developments that emerged. Such flexibility proved to be a very useful element of the methodology and as the discussion below indicates, ultimately permitted enhanced learning and research outcomes.

The following outlines more specifically how the learning opportunities in a systems-focused space were set up, particularly opportunities for PBL interventions.

4. Part 2: Evaluation of What Happened in Relation to the PBL Interventions in the TSS Project

As with many initiatives much happened "betwixt cup and mouth" and the student education component of the TSS project was no exception. This part of the article, therefore, takes the educational initiatives discussed above in Part One and evaluates them by discussing what happened according to plan and whether there were any surprises.

4.1. Regulation and Institutions Strand—UNSW-R

Very little happened according to plan in relation to student engagement in this strand of the project.

The opportunities for PBL (and project-based) interventions in this strand evaporated dramatically when no students at the relevant investigator's university took up the opportunity to be involved in the TSS project by enrolling in a course which would have accommodated the TSS project's learning experience. This outcome was largely the result of timetabling issues, which meant that no relevant environmental law courses (either undergraduate or postgraduate) were on offer at the right time to align with the AR cycles.

As a result, evaluation of the planned PBL interventions became difficult, but not quite impossible, to undertake. Why, not quite impossible? Because there was a surprise—an unintended happening which the AR model allowed the project to accommodate. The surprise element was the unexpected involvement of two students from a non-participating university. As a result of their involvement some evaluation of the PBL interventions in this strand became possible.

It is perhaps useful to appreciate how those two students came to be involved in the project and in what capacity, in order to understand some of the constraints that were imposed on their participation and engagement with the project. Their status arguably had some bearing on the evaluation of their engagement.

UNSW-R was contacted by: (1) an undergraduate law student, at a different university, who was keen to become a legal academic intern for a session; and UNSW-R was also contacted by (2) a postgraduate student, who was keen to use the TSS project as an example of applied research, for a Masters in Environmental Law, at an unrelated institution.

With the permission of the relevant academic administrators, UNSW-R supervised both interns as part of their university placements. With the interns' agreement, they were assigned to work on the TSS project. However, neither intern's progress was to be assessed and evaluated by the quality of her research alone nor by the skill with which she managed the PBL interventions but rather by other factors considered relevant to the effective completion of an internship, including the sufficient manifestation of attributes such as co-operation, diligence, commitment, punctuality, team-work capacity, ability to accept supervision and ability to assume responsibility, for example—all commendable assets but not necessarily the same attributes as the PBL intervention sought to foster. Hence there was a dissonance between evaluating the effectiveness of the intern's performance *qua* the internship and evaluating the effectiveness of the PBL interventions *qua* the teaching and learning methods by employed the ST based project. With these caveats in mind the following evaluation of the PBL applications' effectiveness is explored below.

UNSW-R initially encouraged the undergraduate intern to reflect on what she already knew about governance of the relevant field, recognizing that we "come into the world already theorizing" and that we bring some existing knowledge, no matter how little, to just about all that we do [34]. Basing PBL involvement on this supposition was designed to encourage the intern to see that she was not starting her research from a palimpsest—she could take comfort in the fact that she knew something from the outset. However, the approach was not entirely successful. The intern found it difficult to conceptualize what she knew already as being, in any way, relevant to the TSS project and consequently the (recognition of pre-existing knowledge) approach served to intimidate her, causing her to feel overwhelmed by the research task that lay ahead. Instead of taking "ownership of the project", the intern responded by seeking to transfer responsibility to UNSW-R with the intern asking questions such as, "What do *you* want me to do?" "Can *you* explain the law to me?" "What do I do today?" Review sessions regularly saw the intern responding that she simply did not know the answer and seeking teacher direction rather than teacher facilitation. When suggestions were made as to how she might frame relevant questions to assist progress, the intern resisted—not because she was difficult or cantankerous—but more because the internship was proving not to be of the nature that she had expected. There was an insufficient alignment between: (a) the intern's expectations about what embarking on an internship with a legal academic would mean, and; (b) the reality of participation in a ST project that relied on high levels of student involvement and the employment of problem solving, decision making and investigative activities. These participatory elements together with the relatively autonomous student learning environment that existed—all of which are hallmarks of PBL and project-based learning [35,36]—were not what the intern thought she had bargained for.

In evaluating what actually happened in terms of PBL implementation in this strand, it is relevant to turn to the issue of skills development. Communication skills that would assist in the creation of new environmental sustainability knowledge were skills that the project sought to develop in its student participants. In this regard, intern 1 (the undergraduate intern) was encouraged to reflect on the benefits of liaising with the project's industry partners with whom she could engage, in order to assist the development of a review of alternative sanitation options already in operation in Australia (e.g., waterless urinals). Industry partners' technical expertise could inform and enhance the development of legal knowledge in the sustainability realm and a reciprocal connection between problem solving and the surroundings to which the problem solving is connected could be established [20]. However, as de Jong and Boelens have pointed out (by reliance on the Alders table) mere recognition of the connection would not necessarily solve the political deadlocks that may ensue in relation to collaborative problem solving [21]. Greater attention would also need to be paid to "the decisive agency of new and evolving technologies within the entangled networks of sociality and materiality resulting in unprecedented, non-linear and fuzzy political problems" [21]. Given that the TSS project is a clear example of a new and evolving technology embedded in sociality and materiality, de Jong and Boelen's words arguably carry considerable force.

Aside from these theoretical concerns, there were also discipline-based concerns that arose in relation to intern 1's potential dialogue with industry partners. Oral feedback revealed that, part of the intern's reticence in pursuing dialogue with industry partners arose from a presumption that any such dialogue would be closed and limited by discipline-based thinking with which she was not familiar and where "involved actors" with "their own meanings and values that are fixed and securely anchored in their own contexts and interest, as in the histories of their surroundings" would prevail [21]. She thought it would be not unlike Hommels' description of "situations in which planners, architects, engineers, technology users, or other groups are constrained by fixed ways of thinking and interacting" [37] that may, in turn, lead not to "support and resilience solutions" but rather to "political deadlocks" [21].

Further, another limiting factor was the student's innate (or perhaps socially constructed) personal timidity and lack of confidence to make the necessary telephone calls to industry partners. She feared that her ignorance could be revealed and that embarrassment would ensue. Suggestions as to the benefits of scripting telephone conversations prior to making calls were not a success. The intern resisted and instead reverted to requests for teacher direction and teacher explanation. The attempt to introduce discovery learning through PBL was seemingly affected by the same difficulties as those described by Blumenfeld *et al.* [38]. They referred to the poor uptake of hands-on learning opportunities resulting from the relevant program not being sufficiently based "on the complex nature of student motivation and [the] knowledge required to engage in cognitively difficult work". They concluded that the lack of widespread acceptance of early discovery learning curricula was associated with insufficient attention being devoted to the students' viewpoint [38].

Additional opportunities for face-to-face and/or remote teacher-student engagement were not taken up and despite the provision of some initial references [17] designed to kick-start the research, the intern found it difficult to "own" the project in meaningful ways and to engage with the relevant field of law. In particular, she was uncomfortable with the notion of speculative responses. She instead, far preferred concrete outcomes. The flexibility, doubt, speculation and tentativeness that came to be associated with learning in the TSS project proved particularly challenging and UNSW-R greatly underestimated the implications of this.

Further, if evaluation of the PBL intervention were, in part, at least, also to be based on authentic assessment outcomes [39,40] then it would have to be said that the intervention was not highly successful. It did not deliver the desired outcomes. By the end of the internship, no framework for the governance of the relevant elements of the TSS project had been formulated by the undergraduate intern under UNSW R's guidance. Some aspects of the framework had been uncovered but the over-arching picture was still missing and no roadmap had been worked out which covered the existing plumbing codes of practice, guidelines, policies, legislation and regulations that operated to help manage the implementation of the TSS project.

The second surprise in the project (referred to above) was the involvement of a second student (Intern 2), not associated with a participating university. Intern 2 was enrolled in a postgraduate law degree (but not a professional law degree) and did not hold an undergraduate law degree. Although the trend to introduce non-professional postgraduate law degrees has many advantages, the intern's inexperience with black-letter law research, proved challenging for the student and disappointing for some of the project participants. While this particular intern clearly had some expertise in policy-oriented research, she was fairly unfamiliar with the range of, and the extent to which she would have to engage with, legal databases and employ fundamental skills such as those of statutory interpretation for example, if she were to participate effectively in her experiential learning opportunity.

Engaging with Intern 2 involved detailed reviewing of her hard copy work, suggesting outlines and planning frameworks, as well as guiding her towards specific legislation *etc*. An AR approach to such learning and teaching permitted an ongoing evaluation and re-evaluation of what was possible and not possible in the circumstances. Accordingly, the goals initially imagined needed to be re-set and re-determined. This proved to be one of the very positive aspects of employing PBL within a ST framework. While there were practical problems associated with generating the anticipated type and levels of research in this case, the SF framework, in which the PBL took place, proved to be a real asset in helping to educate for a sustainable planet.

4.2. Visual Communication Strand—UTS-R 1

The normal internal structures of both subjects needed some juggling to accommodate the flexible framework in which the TSS project would ideally operate. This was principally due to prescribed learning outcomes and time constraints imposed on subjects. Project design to this extent was unknown in the students' prior learning, and in their 4-year course, is only introduced in the final year of the program, though still highly scaffolded. Less travelled ground was PBL: encouraging students' autonomy and self-direction, providing a good degree of "intellectual space" to draw out and shape key communication issues, determining the most appropriate vehicle (media) and visual language best suited to carry content (also created by students). In practical terms this meant that students were far more responsible for a greater array of design decisions than the lecturer/client-driven brief might provide. They were asked to think and work more speculatively. For some, it was liberating, allowing them to move across disciplinary boundaries; for example, one student drew heavily on "experience design" and "fun theory" leading him to seek out advice in interaction design from specialists in the Architecture faculty. He had designed a heat- and motion-sensitive installation to explain "closing the loop" nutrient recovery cycle (Figure 3). Another student consulted with IT post-graduate students to make sense of speculative concepts for measuring usage of UD-installed toilets. Still another used burgeoning skills in motion graphics to develop a substantial animation piece explaining peak phosphorous and asking the UTS community to use the UD toilets; the work ultimately netted him a Gold AGDA Award—AGDA being the peak professional body of the Australian Graphic Design Association—and representation at the annual Society of Responsible Design's "Change" exhibition. Others created environmental graphics in toilet cubicles to explain the user's role and import in donating their urine.

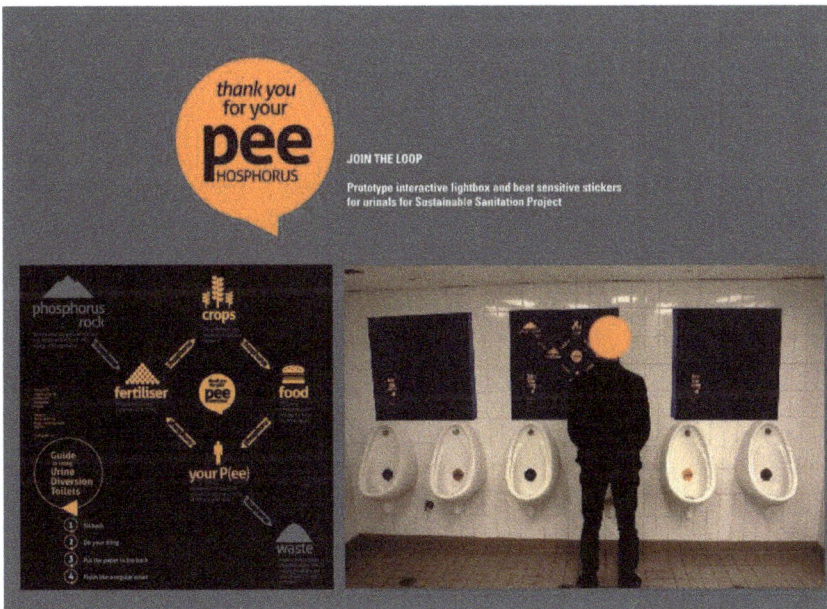

Figure 3. "Thank you for your pee" heat sensitive sticker, a still of "closing the loop" cycle, and *in situ* as motion sensor lightboxes in front of urinals (*Designer: Jethro Lawrence, UTS*). Reproduced with permission from [41], published by Elsevier, 2012.

Systems **2014**, *2*, 243–272

These types of students—highly intelligent, engaged, independent learners with excellent visual and aural communication skills—embraced the self-directed nature of PBL, though they still needed substantial guidance in constructing the parameters of their projects. However, this level of work required far more time from both students and UTS R-1 than the subject was designed to accommodate. As a result, and due to the commitment of all parties, work moved well beyond arbitrary timeframes imposed by the university timetable. Other students, though, were bewildered by blurred boundaries, finding comfort in designing familiar artifacts of limited value, such as posters and paper sculptures; this response was also to be expected. Some of the work was thoughtful and effective. Overall, the more successful work—"successful" in this instance was defined by identifying a need for communication between potential users using appropriate research methods, through to designing understanding and utilizing a visual language that would meet that need—from both cohorts was borne from expansive engagement with issues presented by the TSS project; the least effective work, unsurprisingly, defaulted to aesthetics and conventional typologies, such as branding, rather than communicating more pressing and relevant issues of concern.

The mentoring of the second cohort by several members of the first group was completely led by the students. The latter had become "subject experts" in extracting and navigating significant issues to address. So while the new cohort had access to TSS personnel, of equal import were the experiences and work previously produced by their peers, an informal kind of knowledge transfer and certainly true to PBL goals. Instead of thinking in subject silos and designing afresh, the new group built upon the first semester work, incorporating a bank of graphic symbols as well as furthering initial concepts. From there, they designed a system for whole-of-campus engagement with the testing of UD toilets that ranged from a re-thinking of "waste as resource" through to measuring usage of UD toilets and speculating on what the collected urine could actually yield in terms of produce.

4.3. Visual Communication Strand—UWS-R

The brief offered students a range of possibilities to pursue, including: the creation of a visual language for the story of "P" that could be used to "prime" audiences ahead of the trial; the creation of a modular visual identity for the project that could be used across a range of platforms; the creation of *in situ* signage to facilitate user adaption to the new technology (Figure 4); and the development of social engagement tools to elicit feedback and responses from end-users of the system. Students spent the first couple of weeks developing their contextual knowledge, working their way through the provided "starter" resources and exploring various visual approaches in relation to these possibilities. While it took longer than usual for students to claim ownership over the problems, the PBL approach saw students successfully directing their own learning on a "need to know" basis in the process of developing concepts, which Duggan and Dermody [29] refer to as "just-in-time learning", with instructors taking a facilitating rather than directive role.

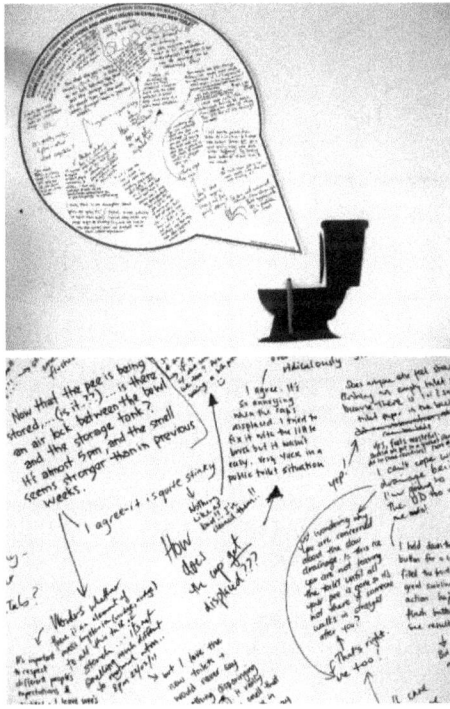

Figure 4. Graffiti board *in situ* and detail (*Designer: Yana Mokmargana, UWS*). Reproduced with permission from [41], published by Elsevier, 2012.

At the half-semester point, two key researchers based at UTS visited UWS for a client briefing session. Students presented their working concepts to the researchers that included a visual identity incorporating the closed loop of nutrient recovery and reuse and signage to encourage correct use of the urine diverting toilets. The researchers were invited to provide comment and feedback, and after some reflection, select preferred concepts. The plan was for students to "work up" these selected concepts for the remainder of the semester, for use in the trial.

In the second semester students developed on-demand communication tools such as the graffiti board that gathered social data across 26 weeks of the trial. It was empowering for students within the Professional Strand to see the impact their work could have beyond delivering on the stated requirements of a client brief. In a project as multidimensional and forward thinking as the TSS project, design became a critical tool for promoting ecological literacy and social learning. A value of PBL in a studio context was that it facilitated a constructive relationship between design and research, rather than research being "contextually severed" from the practice environment [29].

4.4. Technology Strand Evaluation—UTS-R2

Civil and environmental engineering undergraduate students were also selected to be part of the TSS project. Following PBL interventions it was envisaged that these students would employ "learning by doing" [15], by "exploratory learning" [16] and "adaptive learning" [18]. In order to foster those approaches, it was important to select students with the appropriate skills to work on the TSS project—a more open-ended enquiry, especially with respect to the Technology strand. For this purpose, the project was discussed within the Faculty of Engineering and Information Technology (FEIT) after which information sessions with students were established; these garnered keen interest from some students. While each undergraduate engineering student is required to undertake a six or twelve credit point capstone project—to be completed either in one or two semesters respectively—discussions with students revealed that not all had the requisite skills to undertake the extensive research aspects required by the project. One particular student, however, stood out and went on to be involved in the initial phase of the project where different sites were being sought to locate the urine diversion toilets. This student was also involved in identifying different designs used to set up systems so that urine samples could be collected for analysis. Other students were "interviewed" by a wider project team and were considered as not having the capacity to undertake the project. One of these students however, went ahead to complete a desk-based project highlighting the risks of resource recovery.

It was observed that all students involved in the Technology strand of the TSS project benefitted from PBL by "learning by doing" [15], "exploratory learning" [16] and "adaptive learning" [18]. The project aims were quite open-ended where students had to use design and technical skills acquired in other subjects together with their own experience to find appropriate pathways leading to a solution. Students also had to work in an environment where they had to consult, communicate and work with trans-disciplinary team members. This challenged them to work out of their comfort zone and helped them to gain important life-long learning skills. Overall, it can be said as part of the Technology strand the PBL interventions were successful. The reasons that the students were able to be engaged in the project were due to the initial dissemination of the objectives of the projects; proactive discussions by the project team; engagement of the project team in student discussions; and evaluation of student work. It was not possible to involve more students throughout the different stages of the project due to the following reasons: (a) student engagement required involvement, time, and education; (b) not all students were found capable of undertaking research at the level that the project team expected; and (c) the objectives of the topics that the students wanted to undertake did not completely align with the objectives of the project.

5. Part 3: Discussion of What could have been Done Better

5.1. Regulation and Institutions Strand

Regulation and Institutions Strand—UNSW-R

Participation Entry Requirements

In retrospect, more rigorous and project-specific screening processes for student participation in the TSS project would have been prudent. Evidence of a willingness to engage with a ST-based approach and an interest in sustainability issues should have been seen as obvious pre-requisites for participation in this strand, but because of the difficulties involved in attracting students referred to above, they were not so seen. Tough decisions about the suitability of students to the project needed to have been made but instead the driver of necessity prevailed. When it was feared that there would be no student participation at all in this strand, checks and balances for participation were largely waived and a very flexible attitude to involvement was embraced.

The planned system whereby students were funneled into the Regulation and Institutions strand via their enrolment in feeder elective subjects failed to yield students because, as noted, the timing of relevant, elective subjects did not align satisfactorily with the timing of the AR cycles. Whether this problem could be resolved in the future remains uncertain.

Copyright Issues

Another issue, which the benefits of hindsight suggest is worth ironing out before student involvement begins, is, in fact, a legal issue. It is the question of who owns the copyright in the research produced by an intern who is not associated with any of the participating universities? This is a similar, or at least related, question to that which arises in regard to academics' own research where that research is undertaken under grants involving industry partners. If the TSS project or a similar project were to run again, it would seem wise to seek an assignment of copyright at the point any parties joined the project. This may take some negotiating between institutions but is contractually possible and could, in some circumstances, greatly enhance the benefits and outcomes of the project.

A Different Attendance Model for the Undergraduate Intern Participation

Implementation of the PBL approach within the ST framework may have been more effective if the undergraduate internship had been designed to operate over several shorter periods during the week rather than over one whole day a week. Smaller/shorter interactions with the project and UNSW-R arguably may have created better opportunities for positive reinforcement and provided a more effective space for the absorption, calibration and recalibration of ideas; the latter being a fundamental aspect of ST. Greater opportunities for confidence building may have been another outcome of a revised attendance model because the project would possibly not have seemed so daunting if engagement with it was more often and in shorter bursts. When the project was isolated to a particular day per week the intern was less inclined to discuss issues with UNSW-R, set short-term goals, test propositions, evaluate them, and re-set goals and methods *etc*. Instead the intern set "big goals" because she had "big" workdays. When she could not achieve the outcomes set, she became dispirited and was inclined to relinquish responsibility, shifting it to UNSW-R. In retrospect, it may, therefore, have been more fruitful to employ a different attendance model. More emphasis would have been placed on the need for regular (perhaps daily) interactions with the teacher/supervisor, bearing in mind that such interactions needed only to be brief.

Alignment Issues—Methodology, Framework, Intervention and Skills Development

Some aspects of the AR methodology, the ST framework and the PBL interventions on which the project relied to educate students in the environmental sustainability sphere, appeared (superficially at least) to run counter to the actual skills that the project sought to develop and embed. For example, the project, in part, sought to teach law students to think linearly but it simultaneously employed PBL interventions in a ST framework that caused students to think non-linearly about sustainability issues. Under the ST framework students became experienced at finding only half the answer to a question or problem before moving to another question, only to return to the original question at a later date. They were forced to weave their way in and out of a labyrinth of regulatory and governance material, learning to bind half threads of thoughts and roughly hewn knowledge together in their quest for a coherence of fact patterns and to determine the ways in which the law applied to these facts. The employment of this non-linear approach to learning and teaching seemed to the interns to be at odds with the deductive and linear reasoning that the project, in part at least, sought to develop. There was a purported disconnect between the tools of teaching and the desired project outcomes. To the students (but not the educators) that was potentially confusing.

In retrospect, it may have been better to highlight the seeming contradiction between the PBL interventions within the ST framework (that is methodology and applications) on one hand, and the desired learning outcomes on the other and then to explain how these purported differences may be reconciled. Were this project to be undertaken again, better explanations would be given at the outset. As it was, however, student involvement of the nature that finally occurred was not planned and, therefore, was not as well integrated as it might have been.

The Law, the Limits of Student Participation and Unrealistic Expectations

Finally, in order to provide improved learning spaces for students, particularly interns whose learning involves legal research, it may also be useful to explain more effectively the nature of legal research and legal knowledge not just to the interns themselves but also to other investigators involved in the project. This suggestion is made because academics, like many others, sometimes tend to work in silos and do not necessarily understand the opportunities and constraints that exist in specialisms outside their own experience. As a result, a lack of understanding may give rise to unrealistic expectations of an intern from other researchers who do not share or adequately appreciate the intern's specialism. For example, in the legal domain, non-lawyers commonly think that the answer to a legal question already exists and that it is simply a matter of looking up legislation or a case and the answer is evident. Sometimes that is so but more commonly and particularly in relation to the law governing new technologies, the law has to be cobbled together from pre-existing law that has been designed to cover very different purposes and circumstances. Finding out whether there is already law governing a situation and what that law is, may involve detailed and complex research into cases in a number of different jurisdictions on varied topics, as well as the identification and interpretation of a range of interlinking statutes, regulations and other environmental assessment instruments, for example. Making all project participants aware of such issues may mean that interns/students do not bear the burden of unrealistic expectations. That is not to infer that any such difficulties, actually, arose in this project. It is, however, relevant to the question of what would be done differently next time—how things could be improved. In that regard pre-empting the likelihood of siloed knowledge and the unrealistic expectations which may go with that, would be likely to assist this or similar, future projects. Such awareness would potentially further enhance the breaking down of barriers across disciplinary boundaries, a key tenet of the TSS project.

5.2. Visual Communications Strand

5.2.1. Visual Communication Strand—UTS-R1

Not all students are capable of working in this field. Careful consideration needs to be given to recruiting student participation in trans-disciplinary work, how it could integrate with more traditional structures of university education as well as offering preparatory pathways to fully engage in such an opportunity. For projects such as the TSS project, there is a need to move beyond the arbitrary confines of both discipline silos and subject timeframes and towards a space that is year-round, physical as well as virtual, and multi-institutional.

The Achilles heel of visual communication design—privileging the aesthetic—was also in play throughout the TSS project. Some artifacts were self-indulgent, of questionable import to the overall goals of the project, and served primarily to display the technical prowess of the designers at the expense of communication. The idea of the "beautiful object" had, in essence, seduced them. It was safe and familiar territory. This comment arguably speaks to the current state of the discipline itself, still finding its way to greater capabilities. In the case of some students from the first semester cohort, the aesthetic response using traditional typologies was a refuge from the complexities of research demanded of a trans-disciplinary project beyond their capabilities at that stage of their development.

Giving students more guidance in asking the right questions is also key. The nature of action research and trans-disciplinary design is an unknown proposition to most design education activities, particularly at undergraduate level, as is privileging the "speculative prototype" as a legitimate outcome in itself. It is typical in visual communication design that only the commercially fabricated artifact is of value. However, working in a strategic space also yields an outcome, sometimes made tangible through an artifact or visualizing a system, and at other times through the interrogation of existing norms that mold a project differently.

5.2.2. Visual Communications Strand—UWS-R

As is common in PBL contexts, the learning outcomes become far more apparent at the end of the process rather than during it [29]. Students often felt out of their depth in the process, even though several student works from the TSS project were selected for exhibition in the Society for Responsible Design's graduate sustainable design exhibition and competition, "Change"—a clear measure of success.

Probably the key lesson from the application of PBL in this project is that students need more opportunities of this kind throughout their degree. The metaphor of the springboard is often used to describe the capacity of PBL to promote self-directed learning by immersing students in a complex situation that requires that they "define their own learning needs" [5]. This approach makes an important contribution to professional design education as critical problem solving skills and self-directed learning are increasingly valued graduate capabilities. The more traditional approach of project-based learning inducts students into design as a predominantly client-serving profession. However the professional landscape is changing. The multidimensional problems of the contemporary context, such as those embedded in the TSS project, push designers decisively out of their traditional client-serving role at the back-end of a design process into positions of leadership and concept generation at the front. A PBL approach helps to equip students with the knowledge and skills appropriate to respond to, and positively influence that context.

6. Technology Strand

Technology Strand—UTS R-2

Participation Entry Requirements

It was envisaged that more than three students, at different levels, would be involved in the project. However, as the TSS project "evolved", it was difficult to ascertain the entry requirement or what attributes students should have before they undertook the project. Nevertheless, students were interviewed prior to being engaged, and it was found that some students did not have sufficient "research skills" to participate in the project. This issue could be dealt with in a better way by identifying and specifying what attributes students should have, and disseminating this during presentation to students.

Conflict of "Time" Requirements

As student engagement required a considerable time commitment by the project team, continuing to engage students in the trial on the terms employed in this strand, proved not to be feasible on an on-going basis. One major drawback of the way students engaged in the project was that the same students did not continue throughout the project. As part of the undergraduate engineering program, students are allowed to undertake either a 6 months or a one-year project, while the main TSS project had a life span of 3 years.

The plan was to involve as many undergraduate engineering students as possible during every stage of the project. However, ultimately it was only possible to involve one student in the initial phases of the project and another student during the second stage of the project. If this "time" conflict could have been addressed at the proposal stage of the project, and attended to during the initial phases, we believe more students could have actively participated.

7. Towards Defining "Best Practice" in Trans-Disciplinary Projects

It is evident from the discussion above, that trans-disciplinary projects applying PBL, particularly in the sustainability context, still represent virgin territory, with "best practice" yet to be established. While there were several examples of progress, much exploratory work remains from at least two major perspectives. They are:

(1) Loosening arbitrary business-model university structures—such as time, money, competitiveness—in order to accommodate genuine collaboration in the search for new knowledge;
(2) Excavating the trans-disciplinary project itself in terms of how to plan engagement, as well as select and prepare students.

These thoughts are expanded upon, below.

Systems **2014**, *2*, 243–272

7.1. Time Commitments for Academics

In several strands, the issue of the labor and the time-intensive nature of student engagement with the TSS project came to the fore. The *quid pro quo* was questioned. In the Regulation and Institutions strand, for example, one of the internships unfortunately came to an end before very much had been achieved. This was disappointing for UNSW-R, the intern and any other team members dependent on anticipated, specific, research outcomes. On reflection, it would have been better if all parties had been able to ascertain, in more realistic terms, how much of a time commitment the TSS project would require. The situation was similar in the Technology strand. While the yield of work was strong in the Visual Communication strand, the time commitments for both academics and students also increased due to the demands of trans-disciplinary inquiry.

Whilst the academics supervising students in this project remained strongly committed to student engagement, acknowledging opportunities for independent learning and greater levels of inquiry, they, over time recognized that experiential, authentic, problem-based learning, as detailed above, places considerable demands on their resources. Those time constraints coupled with the fact that Australian universities presently operate on funding models which have seen reduced contributions from government and a consequent pressure to self-fund, also suggest that the likelihood of academics embedding experiential approaches to teaching and learning may diminish.

To explain, budgetary austerity, high student numbers and the resultant workload pressures arguably encourage the retreat to teaching and learning approaches which are less demanding on academics, less experimental and less focused on learning by doing. The tendency may be to opt for more time- and cost-efficient interventions, irrespective of their pedagogical strengths and weaknesses. One result may well be that large cohorts of students move through their university experience having been exposed to few interactions with PBL, self-directed learning and ST. If students are ultimately confronted with such exposure, it may come as a shock, being perceived as foreign, unfamiliar and frightening. They will not have been previously well acculturated to the style of learning and may find the exposure challenging in the same way as did intern 1 in the Regulations and Institutions strand of the project. However, the benefits of learning by doing, particularly when coupled with an AR approach are potentially great. AR permits for example, recalibrations and adaptations to accommodate better new or changed circumstances. It is reactive to events, permitting contextualized responses crafted to accommodate changed/changing circumstances and it would be disappointing to see such opportunities diminish.

7.2. Competitive/Uncollegial Practices

Unfortunately, in at least one instance, some uncollegial practices impacted on the project at a university level and served to hamper the effectiveness of student engagement. Competition between universities, a lack of understanding about the nature of the TSS project and a lack of collegiality may have been responsible for the necessary range of resources not being available to the relevant students. Where universities choose to emphasize market-based business objectives (relying on competition) in favor of educational drivers, such outcomes are arguably more likely to result.

7.3. Formal Student Evaluations

Although a final, reflective face-to-face interview was undertaken with intern 1 in the Regulation and Institutions strand, it proved impossible to undertake the same with intern 2. And in the Visual Communication strand, while formal university-led student evaluations were undertaken at the end of each semester and with excellent results (for example, 4.25/5.00 for Information Design (UTS)), their generic nature did not generate enough detail to inform future iterations of trans-disciplinary work. Were this project undertaken again, with the benefit of hindsight, the inclusion of more formal, written evaluative reflections from all students would be incorporated across all strands and at various intervals. By necessity these would need to be tightly drawn to reflect the trans-disciplinary demands of engagement.

7.4. Energy, Momentum and Positivity

One very positive outcome of the TSS project was that it forged on itself, irrespective of the less than optimal results in some strands. For example, in the Regulations and Institutions strand it forged on by reliance on the *ad hoc* assistance of some of the plumbers and other technicians involved in the project who had some ideas on how approvals should be sought and to whom parties should speak inside institutions. Indeed the way the broader project team worked its way through the regulatory, governance and compliance web seemed to replicate what individuals or small businesses (without legal teams) might have to do in the real world. Key members of the project team rang friends, contacts in government departments, councils and other agencies as well as contacting skilled tradespeople. They sought advice and pooled information. Some information was supplied officially and other information, unofficially. The end result was that there was sufficient compliance to satisfy regulators and approving agencies although planning for future obstacles was made difficult when "unknown unknowns" emerged. Although unintended, the project team had unwittingly put itself in the shoes of ordinary people and businesses that seek to engage with the legal and regulatory framework. Consequently, the project team experienced first-hand some of the barriers and facilitators relevant to the uptake of the urine diverting toilet technology. The energy and passion associated with the project, drove it. The ability of researchers and industry partners to work within the interstices demonstrated a powerful resilience that arguably was encouraged by the flexibility of the ST framework.

7.5. Contextualizing and Planning Student Involvement

The project was exciting due to the participation of the large number of stakeholders. It provided a good opportunity to test an AR-based approach because of the diversity of the group. However, as not all researchers were involved in the leadership of the project, it was hard to gauge at what stage the project was or where it was going. Student engagement was discussed neither at length nor formally in the planning stage with some of the researchers. As such it became difficult to contextualize student participation from the beginning to the end of the project. In any such future endeavour, it would be more effective to identify at least the type and number of student projects as well as time and resource commitment anticipated by the research project team. There would also need to be discussions about the level of student capability and the project members' expectations of students as well as the extent of student outcomes to be utilized in the project.

One other aspect to consider is the development of strategies to enable students from different strands to interact and learn from each other. Under the model used in the TSS project there was no opportunity for this. More rigorous initial planning in this regard would have been quite valuable. It would also enhance any future collaborative projects. Finally, the facility to include student reflection as part of the project outcomes would have been a helpful evaluative tool. The addition of an Education strand could alleviate such concerns, and set in motion a deeper, more demanding form of learning for participating students that could be transferred into further study and to industry.

8. Conclusions

In conclusion, this article has sought to reflect on the lessons learnt from the application of Problem Based Learning (PBL) within a Systems Thinking (ST) framework employing Action Research (AR) as the methodology. Its focus was on a trans-disciplinary research project involving a subset of university students and conducted across several universities and partner institutions in Sydney, Australia. It was designed to overcome the narrow and arbitrary delineations imposed by discipline boundaries, and hence deliberately brought together a trans-disciplinary research team, including academics engineers, lawyers and designers as well as technical staff. Importantly, it also incorporated a number of students

Systems **2014**, 2, 243–272

from a range of disciplines who were either enrolled in courses taught by the relevant academics or associated with those academics in some other way, such as through internship programs. Student engagement has formed the key focus of the discussion in this article.

The academic investigators forming part of the wider research team were particularly conscious that didactic, autonomous, discipline-based courses rarely seek to foster an advanced social networking culture among students; a culture which is commonly credited with promoting deep learning. This project, therefore, sought to extend the trans-disciplinarity of the academics and industry partners involved, to student involvement in the project. Hence, a number of students from a variety of disciplines contributed to the advancement of the project by undertaking learning tasks that it was anticipated would inter-link, reinforce and engage with the work of a range of academics, industry partners and other students. The tasks in which students were involved both cultivated and relied on an organic and adaptive approach to learning. The ST based approach employed by the research investigators was applied to the teaching and learning experiences offered to students.

The Transitioning to Sustainable Sanitation (TSS) project was premised on the pedagogical view that effective learning commonly involves *doing*, which many disciplines within the traditional curriculum development rarely incorporate, preferring instead to keep students as outside observers who learn passively rather than actively. As a result the article outlined and analyzed the effectiveness of various PBL interventions across a number of organizational strands within the ST framework. It also reflected on how effectively implementation of the project incorporated opportunities to revise, refine recalibrate and re-set direction—all of which are hallmarks of ST based approaches.

Implementation of the project revealed various problems, including the rigidity that tight, forward, course planning dictated, at times leaving little room for adjustment, change and experimentation in response to unanticipated situations and consequently foreclosing opportunities for creative, positive pedagogical initiatives. However, the overall conclusion is that despite problems associated with timetabling, the number of students involved and participation entry requirements for example, the project still created some very successful spaces for creative student engagement which promoted deep learning and sophisticated intellectual interactions in the sustainability sphere.

Acknowledgments: The authors would like to acknowledge the contribution of the research funders—University of Technology, Sydney (UTS) Research and Innovation Office, UTS Facilities Management Unit, Sydney Water, Caroma Dorf and UTS Institute for Sustainable Futures—of the UTS Challenge Grant Project. The UTS Sustainable Sanitation Project was designed and led by UTS Institute for Sustainable Futures—Professor Cynthia Mitchell, Dr. Kumi Abeysuriya and Dr. Dena Fam. It also involved faculty-based partner investigators at UNSW Australia (formerly known as the University of New South Wales, Sydney), UTS, and the University of Western Sydney, who are the authors of this article.

Author Contributions: Janice Gray is the lead author of this article. She managed the authorial team and was responsible for the sections on Regulation and Institutions. She was also responsible for the Background section, the introductory material in the PBL Applications to Student Learning section and the Conclusion. She was the primary author of the Towards Defining Best Practice Section (with some assistance from Jennifer Williams). Janice was also the primary authorial editor and Jennifer the assistant authorial editor. Jennifer was responsible for the Visual Communications sections that pertain to UTS, the graphic treatment of Table 1, as well as Figures 2 and 3. Prasanthi Hagare was responsible for the Technology sections and contributed to the text of Table 1. Abby Mellick Lopes was responsible for the Visual Communications sections pertaining to UWS and Figure 4, while Shankar Sankaran was responsible for the Introduction section, Figure 1 and overall guidance on Systems Thinking.

Conflicts of Interest: The authors declare no conflict of interest.

References

1. Checkland, P. Soft Systems Methodology and Its Relevance to the Development of Information Systems. In *Information Systems Provision: The Contribution of Soft Systems Methodology*; Stowell, F.A., Ed.; McGraw Hill: London, UK, 1995; pp. 1–15.
2. Savin-Baden, M.; Howell, M.C. *Foundations of Problem-Based Learning*; The Society for Research into Higher Education & Open University Press: Birkshire, UK, 2004.

3. Barrows, H.S. Problem-Based Learning in Medicine and Beyond: A Brief Overview. In *Bringing Problem-Based Learning to Higher Education: Theory and Practice*; Wilkerson, L., Gilselaers, H., Eds.; Jossey-Bass: San Franscisco, CA, USA, 1996.

4. Boud, D.; Feletti, G. *The Challenge of PBL*, 2nd ed.; Kogan: London, UK, 1997.

5. Rangachari, P.K. Twenty-up: Problem-Based Learning with a Large Group. In *Problem-Based Learning to Higher Education: Theory and Practice*; Wilkerson, L., Gijselaers, W.M., Eds.; Jossey-Bass: San Franscisco, CA, USA, 1996.

6. De Graaff, E.; Kolmos, A. *Management of Change: Implementation of Problem-Based and Project-Based Learning in Engineering*; Sense Publishers Rotterdam: Rotterdam, The Netherlands, 2007.

7. Savin-Baden, M. *Problem-Based Learning in Higher Education: Untold Stories*; SRHE and Open University Press: Buckingham, UK, 2000.

8. De Graaff, E.; Kolmos, A. Characteristics of problem-based learning. *Int. J. Eng. Educ.* **2003**, *19*, 657–662.

9. Savin-Baden, M. *A Practical Guide to Problem-Based Learning Online*; Routledge: London, UK, 2007.

10. Cordell, D.; Drangert, J.-O.; White, S. The story of phosphorus: Global food security and food for thought. *Global Environ. Change.* **2009**, *19*, 292–305. [CrossRef]

11. Larsen, T.A.; Peters, I.; Alder, A.; Eggen, R.; Maurer, M.; Muncke, J. Re-engineering the toilet for sustainable wastewater management. *Environ. Sci. Technol.* **2001**, *35*, 192A–197A.

12. Wilsenach, J.; van Loosdrecht, M. Impact of separate urine collection on wastewater treatment systems. *Water Sci. Technol.* **2003**, *48*, 103–110.

13. Institute of Sustainable Futures. *Transitioning to Sustainable Sanitation—A Transdisciplinary Pilot Project of Urine Diversion*; University of Technology: Sydney, Australia, 2013.

14. Slavin, R.E. *Cooperative Learning: Theory, Research and Practice*, 2nd ed.; Allyn & Bacon: Boston, MA, USA, 1995.

15. DuFour, R.; DuFour, R. *Learning by Doing: A Handbook for Professional Learning Communities at Work*; Solution Tree Press: Bloomington, IN, USA, 2010.

16. De Freitas, S.; Neumann, T. The use of 'exploratory learning' for supporting immersive learning in virtual environments. *Comput. Educ.* **2009**, *52*, 343–352. [CrossRef]

17. Reed, M.S.; Evely, A.C.; Cundhill, G.; Fazey, I.; Glass, J.; Laing, A.; Newig, J.; Parrish, B.; Prell, C.; Raymond, C.; Stringer, L.C. What is social learning? *Ecol. Soc.* 2010, 15, pp. 1–10. Available online: http://www.ecologyandsociety.org/vol15/iss4/resp1/ (accessed on 24 December 2013).

18. Midgley, C. *Goals, Goal Structures, and Patterns of Adaptive Learning*; Lawrence Erlbaum: Mahwah, NJ, USA, 2002.

19. Laurillard, D. *Rethinking University Teaching: A Conversational Framework for the Effective Use of Learning Technologies*; Routledge Falmer: London, UK, 2002.

20. Van Buuren, A.; van Boons, F.; Teisman, G. Collaborative problem solving in a complex governance system: Amsterdam airport Schiphol and the challenge to break path dependency. *Syst. Res. Behav. Sci.* **2012**, *29*, 116–130.

21. De Jong, B.; Boelens, L. Understanding Amsterdam airport Schiphol through controversies. *Syst. Res. Behav. Sci.* **2014**, *31*, 3–13. [CrossRef]

22. Steel, A.; Fitzsimmons, D. Answering Legal Problem Questions in a Grid Forma. *Marking Time: Leading and Managing the Development of Assessment in Higher Education*; Coleman, K., Flood, A., Eds.; Common Ground Publishing Pty. Limited: Champaign, IL, USA, 2013; pp. 77–90. Available online: http://works.bepress.com/alex_steel/25 (accessed on 24 December 2013).

23. Herrington, J.; Reeves, T.C.; Oliver, R. *A Guide to Authentic E-Learning*; Routledge: London, UK, 2010.

24. Herrington, J. Authentic Learning: Resources and Ideas about Authentic Learning and Authentic Learning. Available online: http://authenticlearning.info/AuthenticLearning/Home.html (accessed on 7 March 2014).

25. Giddings, J. *Promoting Justice through Clinical Legal Education*; Justice Press: Melbourne, Australia, 2013.

26. Evans, A.; Cody, A.; Copeland, A.; Giddings, J.; Noone, M.A.; Rice, S.; Booth, E. Strengthening Legal Education by Integrating Clinical Legal Experiences: Identifying and Supporting Effective Practices. Available online: http://www.olt.gov.au/resource-best-practices-Australian-clinical-legal-education (accessed on 24 December 2013).

27. David, E.; Paul, G.; Justin, Z. *How to Write a Better Thesis*, 3rd ed.; Melbourne University Press: Melbourne, Australia, 2011.

28. Schön, D.A. *The Reflective Practitioner: How Professionals Think in Action*; Basic Books: New York, NY, USA, 1983.

Systems **2014**, *2*, 243–272

29. Duggan, B.; Dermody, B. Design Education for the World of Work: A Case-Study of a PBL Approach to Design Education at Dublin Institute of Technology (DIT). *Handbook of Enquiry and Problem-Based Learning*; Barrett, T., Labhrainn, I.M., Fallon, H., Eds.; CELT: Galway, Ireland, 2005. Available online: http://www. nuigalway.ie/celt/pblbook/ (accessed on 21 March 2014).

30. Stanford University Newsletter on Teaching. Problem-Based Learning. In *Speaking of Teaching*; Winter: Stanford, CA, USA, 2001; Volume 11, p. 1.

31. Braungart, M.; McDonough, W. *Cradle to Cradle: Remaking the Way We Make Things*; North Point Press: New York, NY, USA, 2002.

32. Sankaran, S.; Abeysuriya, K.; Gray, J.; Kachenko, A. Mellow yellow: Taking a systems thinking approach to designing research on transitioning to more sustainable sewage management. *Syst. Res. Behav. Sci.* **2013**. [CrossRef]

33. Geels, F. Technological transitions as evolutionary reconfiguration processes: A multi-level perspective and a case-study. *Res. Policy* **2002**, *31*, 1257–1274. [CrossRef]

34. Garth, B. *Negotiating the Curriculum*; Boomer, G., Lester, N., Onore, C., Cook, J., Eds.; Falmer: London, UK, 1992.

35. Thomas, J.W. A Review of Research on Project-Based Learning. Available online: http://www.bobpearlman. org/BestPractices/PBL_Research.pdf (accessed on 19 March 2014).

36. Jones, B.F.; Rasmussen, C.M.; Moffitt, M.C. *Real-Life Problem Solving; A Collaborative Approach to Interdisciplinary Leaning*; American Psychological Association: Washington, DC, USA, 1997.

37. Hommels, A. Changing Obdurate Urban Objects: The Attempts to Reconstruct the Highway through Maastrich. In *Urban Assemblages: How Actor-Network Theory Changes Urban Studies*; Farías, I., Bender, T., Eds.; Routledge: London, UK, 2011; pp. 139–161.

38. Blumenfeld, P.; Soloway, E.; Marx, R.; Krajcik, J.; Guzdial, M.; Palinecsar, A. Motivating project-based learning: Sustaining the doing, supporting the learning. *Educ. Pyschol.* **1991**, *26*, 369–398. [CrossRef]

39. Moursund, D. *Project-Based Learning Using Information Technology*; International Society for Technology in Education: Eugene, OR, USA, 1999.

40. Lombardi, M.M. *Authentic Learning for the 21st Century: An Overview*. Oblinger, D.G., Ed.; Educause Learning Initiative, ELI Paper 1. May 2007. Available online: http://net.educause.edu/ir/library/pdf/eli3009.pdf (accessed on 17 May 2014).

41. Mellick Lopes, A.; Fam, D.; Williams, J. Designing sustainable sanitation: Involving design in innovative, transdisciplinary research. *Des. Stud.* **2012**, *33*, 298–317. [CrossRef]

systems

MDPI

Article

A Designed Framework for Delivering Systems Thinking Skills to Small Business Managers

Daowei Sun [1,*], Paul Hyland [2] and Haiyang Cui [3]

[1] The University of Adelaide Business School, 10 Pulteney Street, Adelaide 5005, Australia
[2] QUT Business School, The Queensland University of Technology, Brisbane 4001, Australia; paul.hyland@qut.edu.au
[3] ASEAN Research Institute, Guizhou University, Guiyang 550025, China; hosanna2004@163.com
* Author to whom correspondence should be addressed; daowei.sun@adelaide.edu.au; Tel.: +61-8-8313-1281.

Received: 6 February 2014; in revised form: 5 June 2014; Accepted: 12 June 2014; Published: 25 June 2014

Abstract: Many small businesses suffer from inadequate management skills which can lead to poor business performance and unsustainable businesses. Research to date has focused on traditional skills such as communication, time management and people skills, yet critically many business managers have no systems thinking skills. This paper presents a framework targeted at delivering systems thinking skills to managers of small businesses utilizing some key characteristic of small business managers. The design is also based on a systems analysis and guided by both adult learning theory and teaching theory. The quality of a training framework depends on the quality of the content design and the right training delivery methods. The systems thinking skills training framework structured systems thinking knowledge into three modules in order to meet the needs of different levels of managers. The framework advocates blended training delivery methods and it also presents possible pitfalls based on training experiences. Additionally, the framework incorporates a continuous improvement process for ongoing systemic improvement.

Keywords: small business manager; systems thinking; adult learning; systemic structure; mental model

1. Introduction

Small businesses make a significant contribution to the economic and social wellbeing of a society. For this reason, small businesses are often regarded as the backbone of the economy in many countries [1–3]. However, the small business sector continues to be plagued by relatively high failure rates and poor performance levels caused by the highly complex and dynamic business environment [1,3,4]. If a business is to achieve its desired outcomes and be sustainable in the long term, the dynamic complexity of business environment has to be successfully understood and addressed. The complexity of the business environment is not only due to multi-stakeholder involvement but also caused by the challenges from accelerating economic, technological, social, and environmental change, that require business managers to be equipped with systems thinking skills to effectively address these dynamic complexities [5–10]. For instance, in Sterman's view, effective business decision making and learning in a world of growing dynamic complexity requires business managers to be equipped with systems thinking skills to understand how the structure of complex systems creates their behaviour [8]. Unfortunately, empirical evidence suggests that the majority of business managers do not have systems thinking skills [11,12]. This is simply because our conventional education system, including schools and universities, has been focusing on teaching the traditional thinking skills of linear analysis [12]. Faced with such a dynamic and complex business environment large businesses are generally in a much better position to adapt themselves to the challenges compared to small businesses, since large businesses usually have both specialized management teams and access to the necessary resources.

Systems **2014**, *2*, 297–312

There is a clear trend showing that an increasing number of universities and schools have started to provide systems thinking courses (Please also refer to other papers in this special issue) yet the capacities for such formal training are far from sufficient [13]. However, there are very limited programs that suit or which are designed for small business managers. In our experience, many of the available systems thinking workshops and seminars for business managers are generally designed to solve specific problems and mainly target large businesses able to pay for the training. Our experiences from working closely with small businesses primarily in agricultural and service industries in Australia further supports the severe lack of systems thinking skills among small business managers. When provided with a brief introduction to systems thinking, small business managers quickly recognized the value this brings in the management of their business. This need for systems thinking and the recognition of its usefulness by managers provided the inspiration and motivation to design a framework to deliver systems thinking knowledge and skills specifically targeting small business managers. The involvement by some of the authors in bidding for the establishment of a Cooperative Research Centre for Managing Complex Projects and Programs in Australia has also provided further momentum to design this framework which will be implemented in the succeeding projects. The design of this framework was based on the authors' personal experiences through teaching and research, as well as their knowledge in the systems thinking and system dynamics area.

2. Different Types of Management Issues Faced by Small Businesses

The paper starts with the examination of some of the common issues that many small businesses face. This is done through the analysis of the hypothetical business scenarios presented below.

- Scenario 1: A rental real estate agent focuses mainly on attaining more properties that he/she can manage but cares little about the interests of the tenants.
- Scenario 2: Shops invest far more on sales marketing while spending little on after sale service.
- Scenario 3: Within a team, it is not uncommon for the team leader to favour some of the team members while overlooking some of the other members of the team.
- Scenario 4: A price war between two shops can lead to negative business performance for both.
- Scenario 5: It is extremely hard for a shop to keep steady stock levels for a certain product due to differing sales from day to day.

While there are many similar cases that could be used, these five cases demonstrate some of the common issues that small businesses are facing.

By using a systems thinking approach to analyse these scenarios we can easily identify that the problem in Scenarios 1 and 2 originate from small business managers' lack of holistic thinking when it comes to their business operation and management or their failure to truly understand the boundaries of their business systems. For example, in Scenario 1, the real estate agent does not realise how the unhappy tenants affect his/her business performance in the long run. Similarly, in Scenario 2, the shop manager does not recognise how the after sales service quality could affect his/her business performance in the long run.

There are commonalities among Scenarios 3, 4 and 5 which require systems tools to understand and structure the causes of these issues. However, Scenarios 3 and 4 can be addressed by using qualitative modelling techniques.

For example, the root causes can be identified through modelling using causal loop diagrams. Scenario 3 can be clearly explained by using the systems archetype of "success to the successful" while Scenario 4 can be effectively examined with the systems archetype of "escalation" [10]. When it comes to Scenario 5, qualitative systems modelling techniques will not help as much but instead quantitative systems modelling tools can be utilised.

In fact, these five examples can be categorized into three levels of typical business issues that small businesses are experiencing.

- The first level can be addressed by forming a holistic view and gaining basic knowledge of the systems nature (Scenarios 1 and 2).
- The second level of issues is more complex and addressing them requires not only a holistic view but systems tools to structure the issues (Scenarios 3 and 4). However, qualitative systems modelling tools are sufficient.
- Scenario 5 belongs to the third level of issues which is the most complex and requires quantitative systems modelling tools to unravel their dynamics and complexities.

3. The Design of the Framework

The design of a systems thinking knowledge delivery framework itself also uses a systems thinking approach [5]. A system analysis on the systems thinking knowledge delivery framework has been conducted which involved the key steps of identifying the key stakeholders, understanding the interactions among identified stakeholders, understanding the systemic structure and how different factors affect the system dynamics and system behaviour [5]. In this case, key stakeholders are mainly the designers of this framework, the knowledge recipients which are the small business managers, and the trainers who will deliver the systems thinking knowledge to the recipients. Interactions among these key stakeholders are mainly through the teaching, learning and assessment activities.

The design of a systems thinking delivery framework has taken the characteristics of small business managers into full consideration [4,14]. First of all, small business managers are commonly adult learners, thus the design process has been fully guided by adult learning theory [15]. It is understood that adult learners have characteristics that set them apart from "traditional" school or college learners. They come to courses with a range of experiences, both in terms of their working life and educational backgrounds and this impacts how and why they participate in learning. There is also an emphasis on structuring the systems thinking knowledge in the content design section [2]. Accordingly, the systems thinking skill delivery framework has the following characteristics.

(1) *Packaging systems thinking knowledge across different modules.* By structuring systems thinking knowledge into three modules, different levels of needs as well as different educational backgrounds can be better catered for to suit learners.

In this case, systems thinking knowledge is modularized into three levels which are in line with the identified three types of business issues. The modularisation of systems thinking knowledge is also conducive to the effectiveness of teaching and learning flexibility [16,17]. The need to modularize systems thinking knowledge is also supported by our research experiences. For example, one small business manager acclaimed that the most important innovation that happened in his business was attributed to a workshop which enabled him to see the business with a holistic view, which is to say a deeper understanding of the interactions between system components and system behaviours enabled him to manage his business in a more sustainable way. Similarly, we also came across business managers who possessed a systems view but who preferred to suffer a tentative heavy financial loss in order to achieve a healthy farm condition for sustainable business. In contrast, we have also come across businesses developed for short term financial gain but who jeopardize the sustainability of their business in the long run [18]. All these cases made us firmly believe that a model of systems thinking knowledge which enable small business managers to form a holistic view of their business is absolutely essential. As will be further explained in the later sections, because humans often lack the capability and inclination to deal with complexity, appropriate tools are needed to facilitate thinking to successfully address complexity and dynamic business issues [19]. Thus, two levels of systems thinking knowledge were aimed to address business issues with different levels of complexity and dynamics.

(2) *Course content aimed at practical knowledge.* Considering small business managers have abundant practical knowledge and life experiences, the course content is practical knowledge oriented. This is to say the course content utilizes examples from the related businesses as a vehicle to

deliver systems knowledge. Our interview with many small business managers in agriculture in Australia revealed that small business managers show much less interest in theoretical course content compared to practical ones. This was largely due to many small businesses being unwilling to risk their limited resources in trials, thus preferring to access verified knowledge and innovations [20–22].

(3) *Right length of systems thinking knowledge modules.* In terms of the size of the course contents, it needs to be able to be delivered in short time frames to suit the multiple roles of small business managers. The duration of each module is limited to two to three days because most small business managers are not only required to perform their management roles but also have to do the majority of the daily tasks themselves which means they are generally very busy [23]. Therefore, it is very difficult for them to allocate longer time periods to learning. Making things worse still are the uncertainties related to the global economy which forces small business managers to work longer rather than hire more staff in order to cut costs.

(4) *Paying attention to the systems thinking delivery process.* This can be achieved by selecting the right trainers, and training the trainer to make sure the knowledge can be delivered efficiently. The key is to select the right trainers who not only have high creditability to the trainees but also have the capability to use appropriate delivery methods to create a dynamic training and learning environment [24,25].

(5) *Working closely with industry to make use of industry networks as a vehicle to deliver the systems thinking knowledge.* There are several advantages of delivering training through industry bodies which include aligning the training to the industry needs, finding trainers with high credibility, possible cost sharing, large scale impact on industry and huge time savings in organizing a training activity.

(6) *Combine a continuous improvement process in the framework for further improvement.* Teaching and learning are two interactive aspects of the same process, while teaching aims to facilitate learning, in return learning results reflect the effectiveness of teaching. The quality of the designed framework will be further enhanced by the continuous improvement process through periodical review and reflection activities [26].

4. Elaborating the Framework

The designed framework consists of three interconnected components which are the content design, the training delivery design and continuous improvement for further improvement.

4.1. Modules of Systems Thinking Knowledge-Content Design

In this framework, one key component is to group systems thinking knowledge into three modules to target learners of primary, intermediate and advanced levels. The theory which underlie modularizing systems thinking knowledge is that "the most basic thing that can be said about human memory, after a century of intensive research, is that unless detail is placed into a structured pattern, it is rapidly forgotten" [2], (p. 24).

4.1.1. Primary Level

This level of systems thinking knowledge aims to equip small business managers with a holistic view through understanding the connectedness and interaction of components within a business-to-business system [27]. To achieve this, the module needs to cover knowledge on the right system boundaries, teach deep thinking about business issues using four levels of thinking and create an appreciation for the laws of systems thinking. The primary level of systems thinking knowledge is elaborated on later in this paper considering that research has shown that an understanding of fundamentals make a subject more comprehensible. Furthermore, understanding fundamentals appears to be the main road to adequate "transfer of training" [2].

- Defining the right system boundaries for a holistic view

While it is relatively easy for people to understand the inter-connectedness among different parts of the physical world, when it comes to the management area, the connections among different components of a system are no longer so obvious. However, correctly defining a system's boundary is of critical importance when using systems thinking to analyse complex issues [28]. The reason for this is that defining appropriate system boundaries determines whether a holistic view can be achieved. On the one hand, too small system boundaries mean that only part of the system can be examined and analysed. On the other hand, too large system boundaries result in wasted resources from non-value adding activities. More often people are inclined to define smaller system boundaries than is required (such as Scenarios 1 and 2 presented in Section 2).

- Four levels of thinking as a guide to deep thinking

There is another dimension of systems thinking which consists of four levels of thinking shown in Figure 1.

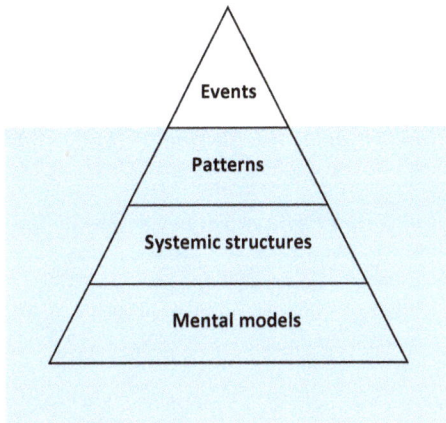

Figure 1. Four levels of thinking (Adapted from: Maani and Cavana [5], p. 16, Figure 2.1).

The four levels of thinking shows the depth of thinking in a vertical way by focusing on events, patterns, systemic structures and mental model levels [5]. The analogy of an iceberg is used to describe the four levels of thinking where the only visible part is the events level which often requires immediate attention [5]. In most situations, managers prefer to address issues at the events level because they are visible. However, the level of events thinking is the shallowest; actions based on events thinking are all reactive which can only temporarily address symptoms. A deeper level of thinking that reveals the pattern of events provides more insight into the whole "story". Interventions considering the pattern of the events are more effective than those based purely on a single event or at the events level. Interventions based on the pattern of events are characterized as adaptive. Further examination reveals that it is at the systemic structure level where the interplay of the systems components combines to cause the events and produce the pattern of the events. Interventions based at systemic structure level are characterized as generative, which are much more powerful than those based on events and their patterns. However, this is still not the root cause for any issue and the deepest cause lies in the main actors' mental models within the systems. The basis for sustainable interventions requires the full consideration of the mental models of different actors in the systems of interest.

- Laws of systems thinking

Other key components of the primary level of systems thinking knowledge are the laws of systems thinking. The influential systems thinking work by Senge [10] has suggested the following 11 systems laws that help people understand systems better.

➤ *Today's problems come from yesterday's "solutions".* In most cases, if solutions were not based on fully understanding the systems, they could merely shift problems from one part of a system to another often without being noticed. It is often the case that those who "solved" the first problem are different from those who inherit the new problem.

➤ *The harder you push, the harder the system pushes back.* This happens when well-intentioned low leverage interventions which were not based on fully understanding the dynamics of the research system, result in responses that offset the benefits of the intervention. Once this scenario happens, people tend to push even harder in order to achieve the expected results because people also hold the belief that hard work will overcome all obstacles. If fact, it is the pushing of the system in the wrong direction that produces the obstacles.

➤ *Performance grows better before it grows worse.* When low-leverage interventions are used to address systemic problems, symptoms disappear after a short time but problems will return after a certain period and, in most cases, problems will become even worse. This shows how the time delay between actions and the results explain why systemic problems are so hard to recognize.

➤ *The easy way out usually leads back in.* People tend to apply familiar solutions to problems encountered. Because root problems are seldom obvious, treating the symptoms by intervention cause the problems to reoccur. People tend to "stick to what we know best" but the system then usually becomes dependent on the intervener or the intervention, and the problem becomes chronic.

➤ *The cure can be worse than the disease.* When people do not really understand the cause of problems, all those well-intentioned efforts can actually make things worse. Non-systemic solutions increase the need for more interventions to the deteriorated problems.

➤ *Faster is slower.* Quick fixes to a systemic problem never last long. The problem will come back soon and leave the system fundamentally weaker than before and even more in need of further help.

➤ *Cause and effect are not closely related in time and space.* In many cases, people just simply mistake a symptom for the cause of the problem. However, a common fundamental characteristic underlying all of the complex problems is that "cause" and "effect" are not closely related—both in time and space.

➤ *Small changes can produce big results but the areas of highest leverage are often the least obvious.* Systems thinking shows that small, well-focused actions can sometimes produce significant, enduring improvements, but only if they are in the right place called "leverage points". Unfortunately, there are no simple rules for finding high-leverage changes, but there are ways of thinking that make it more likely. Learning to recognise the underlying "structures" rather than "events" is a starting point. Systems archetypes suggest areas of high leverage change.

➤ *You can have your cake and eat it too, but not at the same time.* It is rare that one change in a complex system will produce immediate results. In fact, a series of interventions are often required for achieving the overall result. In many cases, people need to be prepared for deterioration of the situation before the improved system shows better results.

➤ *Dividing an elephant in half does not produce two small elephants.* A system needs to have integrity and the character of a system depends on the whole system rather than part of it. It is always helpful to keep the big picture in mind because most of time people get into trouble due to only focussing on a small part of the picture.

➤ *There is no blame.* This simple statement is meant to remind people that encountered problems and their causes are part of the same system, even in cases where there is obvious competitive intent.

Systems **2014**, 2, 297–312

The implication is that people have to recognize the power of systemic structure in influencing their choices and behaviour.

Mastering the law of systems thinking [10] facilitates the learning of casual loop modelling techniques which are planned to be the key knowledge and skills transmitted at the intermediate level. Our experiences with teaching systems thinking courses to university students showed that fully understanding the laws of systems thinking is essential for students to be able to identify system archetypes. The successful identification of archetypes in causal loop models is a key step to reveal the systemic structures of systems being studied [5,10,29].

4.1.2. Intermediate Level

Forrester [30] asserted that the human mind is incapable of truly understanding the behaviour of complex social systems without the assistance of tools and technology. At this level, the systems thinking knowledge is about using qualitative systems tools to unravel complex issues [5,31].

The flexible and useful tools are causal loop diagrams which are diagrams used to demonstrate the feedback structure of systems in any domain by showing the causal links among variables with arrows from a cause to an effect [8,31]. Causal loop diagrams are qualitative systems tools that enable complex systems to be described in terms of cause-and-effect relationships [5,10]. The use of causal loop diagrams to describe the complexity of real systems highlights the connectedness of the component parts which also provides a platform for discussion, communication, and policy formulation. Causal loop diagrams can also help people identify the most appropriate way of influencing the system of interest by using systems archetypes and their associated mental models for leverage points [31,32]. As a result, poor decisions like quick fixes can be avoided.

Systems archetypes are generic systems models or the templates that represent a wide range of situations. Systems archetypes provide a high-level map of dynamic processes. Systems archetypes can provide valuable hints for systems intervention normally referred to as leverages [10,32]. The contents of this level of systems thinking knowledge is designed to teach small business managers how to use qualitative systems tools such as the causal loop diagrams to model complex issues in order to understand the feedback systemic structure. Causal loop diagrams are excellent for quickly capturing stakeholders' hypotheses about the causes of dynamics; eliciting and capturing the mental models of individuals or teams; communicating the important feedback that people believe is responsible for a problem [8].

For demonstration purposes, scenario four is modelled using a causal loop diagram. Assuming two shops are A and B and their price war relates to selling TV sets. The model is shown in Figure 2.

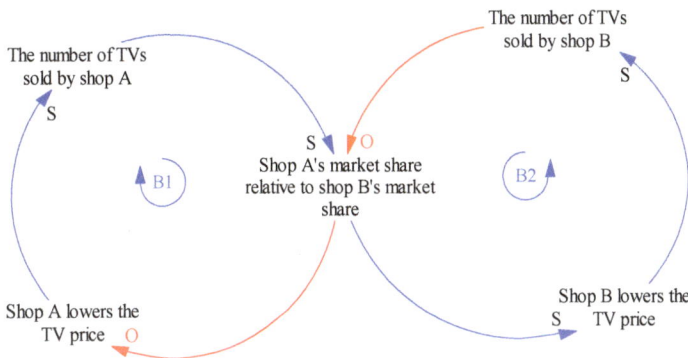

Figure 2. TV price war between shop A and shop B. Legend: S (same direction), O (opposite direction), B (balancing feedback loop) Arrows: (cause or affect relationship).

Systems **2014**, *2*, 297–312

The model in Figure 2 shows an "escalation" archetype [10] of which the competition between two shops is going to damage both shops' business performance. Considering the implications for intervention based on this archetype, we need to examine whether perceptions of the opponent's intent is accurate. Instead of competing with each other, both sides should understand that overcoming this structure requires cooperation toward a larger goal that benefits both competing parties.

Nine systems archetypes were summarized by Senge which are the results of different combinations of two basic feedback loops, namely the reinforcing loop and the balancing loop [10]. To learn the causal loop modelling techniques, Sherwood's work was found to be very useful due to the case-based step-by-step illustration on how to use causal loop models to model business issues [31]. Plenty of examples can be found where real life complex issues have been successfully addressed by using causal loop models [5,8,10,29,33].

4.1.3. Advanced Level

The key shortcomings of causal loop diagrams are that they are static and cannot be used to describe how the properties of a system evolve over time [8,31,34]. This is because most problem structuring methods yield qualitative models showing causal relationships but omitting the parameters, functional forms, external inputs, and initial conditions needed to fully specify and test the model [8]. In contrast, addressing many management issues require more than just structuring the complexities, and eliciting and mapping the participants' mental models. In fact, it requires many of the inputs in quantitative formats for an optimized scenario. In these circumstances, system dynamics simulation becomes the only reliable way to test hypotheses and evaluate the likely effects of policies. Therefore, the systems thinking knowledge covered at the advanced level is about how to simulate business management issues quantitatively using system dynamics modelling techniques [35].

The key advantage of system dynamics computer models is that it enables the time-dependent behaviour of complex systems to be explored under a range of different assumptions [5,8,31,36]. System dynamics modelling allows people to simulate how a complex system, which is expressed as a causal loop diagram, is likely to evolve over time. The scenario analysis serves the same function as a laboratory, but this laboratory is about the future of the system under consideration. System dynamics modelling enables people to test the likely consequences of different actions, decisions, or policies before really committing to them [31,36]. In comparison, causal loop diagrams emphasize the feedback structure of a system while system dynamics simulation emphasizes their underlying physical structure.

To fully understand scenario five requires system dynamics modelling, however it needs different data sets to populate the model and those data sets are not accessible here. However, there is a classic "Beer Distribution Game" model which is referred to in several textbooks [5,8,34]. Nevertheless, there are also plenty of cases available on the use of system dynamics to address dynamic and complex issues [37–40].

4.2. The Training Delivery

Equally important to the content design is the process to deliver the content. Key issues of delivering the content are choosing the most suitable delivery methods, training the trainers and making good use of industry networks as a vehicle to improve training efficiency.

4.2.1. Choosing the Delivery Methods

The choice of the delivery methods is fully guided by the teaching theory [15]. Choosing the delivery methods basically concerns when and how to deliver the training contents. While there are various delivery methods available for training, their effectiveness depends on the contents to be delivered and the characteristics of the trainers and participants. While most training methods have their pros and cons, past experiences from various training programs indicate that using blended delivery methods for each training session appears to be the most effective way to help participants learn and retain information. Key experiences when delivering different modules of systems thinking knowledge were:

- Instructor-led training is necessary for delivering each of the three modules in order to get the key messages through to the participants.
- Small group discussion is the most effective way to enhance understanding.
- Case studies with issues from their own business are the most preferred part of the training.
- After training, support is crucial and communication technologies have made this very easy and effective.

Thus, the training methods require the trainers to be able to shift their roles gradually from presenters from the beginning of the training sessions through to active facilitators towards the end of the training sessions.

4.2.2. Train the Trainers

There needs to be a train the trainer procedure in place to ensure the quality of the training delivery. The critical point is more about choosing the right trainers than training them, because we found that all trainers can easily grasp the designed training content and training methods. However, the effectiveness of the training delivery was largely affected by how the group of trainees judge the trainers' credibility. Our survey conducted in the agricultural area showed that when it comes to trainers, the following factors negatively affect the efficiency of the training delivery and are therefore important to keep in mind.

- Young graduates as trainers lack creditability due to a lack of on the ground experiences.
- Academics from research organizations also suffer from lack of on the ground experiences.
- Private consultants were regarded as profit oriented as well as failures (too often) in the businesses.

In contrast, government funded practitioners from the industry were highly trusted for their relatively natural roles.

4.2.3. Using the Industry Body as a Vehicle to Increase Training Impact

Many industries in Australia have their own industry bodies. Small businesses generally join the industry body that can assist them. One of the key roles of these industry bodies is to provide technical support to their members. The continuous interaction between the members and the industry body builds good relationships and over time these relationships form social networks. The social networks within industry bodies enable deep learning so that the advice and suggestions provided by the industry bodies and their networks are highly trusted by their members. The social networks of industry bodies associated with small businesses can easily increase the scale and impact of the training and they promote interactions between participants as well as ongoing learning. The design of this systems thinking knowledge delivery framework took into account the training delivery through industry bodies and national funded research and development projects, such as different cooperative research centres.

There are clear advantages of delivering training through industry bodies including increased impact and sharing the cost of training. However, importantly, by working with networks in industry bodies, the learning becomes more sustainable and it is easier to recruit trainers from these business champions.

4.3. Continuous Improvement Process to Improve the Framework

Even though the design of this systems thinking delivery framework was based on a systems analysis, it can be further improved. Therefore, the framework design itself consists of an improvement process, namely the continuous improvement process.

This is to say once the designed framework is put into practice it will be continuously evaluated by collecting feedback from both the trainer and the trainees. There is a reflection procedure to be used by the designers of this framework for further improvement that addresses identified issues. Then, the improved framework will be put into practice and continuously reviewed. This process continues to ensure better and more effective training outcomes and impact.

4.4. The Structure of the Design Framework

The structure of the designed framework can be shown by putting it into a model as illustrated in Figure 3.

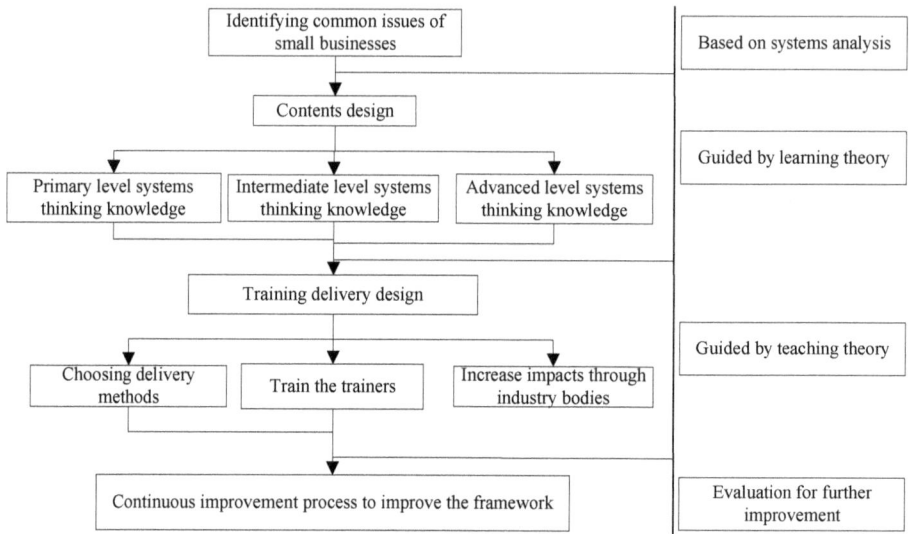

Figure 3. The designed framework for systems thinking skills delivery.

5. Conclusion

Simply delivering the same traditional skills to small business managers as universities and training organisations have done in the past will see a continuation of the same problems and the same outcomes that often lead to business failure. Most traditional training packages take a modular approach to business skills training, looking at the issues facing managers from a fragmented rather than holistic stance. Systems thinking by its very nature seeks to examine business systems holistically so that a deeper and more analytical understanding of the issues the business needs to address can be achieved. This paper has sought to describe and explain the approach taken to design a systems thinking delivery framework for managers in small businesses.

The design process used a systems thinking approach by seeking to identify the key stakeholders, understand the interactions among identified stakeholders, understand the systemic structure and how different factors affect the system dynamics and system behaviour [5]. By using this process, the framework has sought to achieve a more sustainable outcome. The need for stakeholder involvement in both the design and delivery is essential to the ongoing and sustainable success of the training delivery. The process has also been enhanced by the inclusion of a continuous improvement element that ensures the feedback from stakeholders is incorporated into ongoing improvements in the modules and in the delivery. By involving industry bodies in the design and delivery, the training was able to incorporate powerful and influential social networks that enhance learning both in the short and long term. This approach and this program address the challenge of building capacity in small businesses to rapidly

Systems **2014**, *2*, 297–312

analyse and understand the systemic issues facing their business by providing managers with the tools needed to address issues at a systems level in order to provide long term sustainable interventions.

It needs to be clarified that while the systems thinking knowledge incorporated in this framework belongs to system dynamics, on a broader level, systems thinking has many streams. In practice, the delivery of systems thinking knowledge can place emphasis on certain levels based on the needs and profiles of small business managers. Our limited research, training and teaching experiences in systems thinking revealed that for a large number of small business managers, the most valuable knowledge lays in the primary and intermediate level, and that majority business issues can be successfully addressed by using these levels. The important point is that fully grasping the primary and intermediate levels of systems thinking knowledge does not require sophisticated calculation and advanced computer skills. Moreover, the advanced level of systems thinking knowledge is only necessary for those small business managers who have a need to understand quantitative change or the magnitude of dynamic change.

The authors are also aware that the designed framework still needs to be fully tested to achieve creditability. However, efforts have been made to incorporate our first hand teaching and training experiences into the framework, which are also supported by the most influential teaching and training theories that overcome this limitation.

Acknowledgments: This research has been supported by the National Natural Science Foundation of China, Titled "Evolution mechanism and development pattern research on ethnic cultural ecological community in southwest China", Project Grant No. 41361033.

Author Contributions: The article is based on the collective experience and knowledge of all authors. Daowei Sun conceived and was involved in the development of the framework based on his experience developing and delivering the training. Paul Hyland provided input on issues relating to the management of small business based on his experience working with farm businesses and reviewed and edited the article. Haiyang Cui's expertise enabled refinement of the framework and assisted with integrating scenarios into the research.

Conflicts of Interest: The authors declare no conflict of interest.

References

1. Jocumsen, G. How do small business managers make strategic marketing decisions?: A model of process. *Eur. J. Market.* **2004**, *38*, 659–674. [CrossRef]
2. Bruner, J.S. *The Process of Education*, 25th ed.; Harvard University Press: Cambridge, MA, USA, 2009.
3. Australian Government. *Australian Small Business: Key Statistics and Analysis*; Department of Industry, Innovation, Science, Research and Tertiary Education: Canberra, Australia, 2012.
4. Watson, K.; Hogarth-Scott, S.; Wilson, N. Small business start-ups: Success factors and support implications. *Int. J. Entrep. Behav. Res.* **1998**, *4*, 217–238. [CrossRef]
5. Maani, K.E.; Cavana, R.Y. *Systems Thinking, System Dynamics: Managing Change and Complexity*, 2nd ed.; Prentice Hall: Auckland, NZ, USA, 2007.
6. Bosch, O.J.H.; Maani, K.; Smith, C. Systems Thinking—Language of Complexity for Scientists and Managers. In *Improving the Triple Bottom Line Returns from Small-Scale Forestry, Proceedings from an International Conference*; Harrison, S., Bosch, A., Herbohn, J., Eds.; The University of Queensland: Brisbane, Australia, 2007; pp. 57–66.
7. Jackson, M.C. *Systems Approaches to Management*; Kluwer Academic/Plenum: New York, NY, USA, 2000.
8. Sterman, J.D. *Business Dynamics: Systems Thinking and Modeling for a Complex World*; McGraw-Hill Higher Education: Boston, MA, USA, 2000.
9. Boardman, J. *Systems Thinking: Coping with 21st Century Problems*; CRC: Boca Raton, FL, USA, 2008.
10. Senge, P.M. *The Fifth Discipline: The Art and Practice of the Learning Organization*, 2nd ed.; Currency Doubleday: New York, NY, USA, 2006.
11. Ackoff, R.L. Why few organizations adopt systems thinking. *Syst. Res. Behav. Sci.* **2006**, *23*, 705–708. [CrossRef]
12. Greer, B. Overview of the papers: Why is linear thinking so dominant? *Math. Think. Learn.* **2010**, *12*, 109–115. [CrossRef]

13. Bosch, O.; Nam, N.; Sun, D. Addressing the critical need for 'new ways of thinking' in managing complex issues in a socially responsible way. *Bus. Syst. Rev.* **2013**, *2*, 48–70. [CrossRef]

14. Gorman, G.; Hanlon, D.; King, W. Some research perspectives on entrepreneurship education, enterprise education and education for small business management: A ten-year literature review. *Int. Small Bus. J.* **1997**, *15*, 56–77. [CrossRef]

15. Knowles, M.S.; Holton, E.F.; Swanson, R.A. *The Adult Learner: The Definitive Classic in Adult Education and Human Resource Development*, 5th ed.; Elsevier Inc.: Oxford, UK, 2005.

16. Lee, R. Modularisation and the curriculum: Flexibility and empowerment in teaching and learning. *J. Geogr. High. Educ.* **1991**, *15*, 205–210. [CrossRef]

17. Lundin, R. Flexible Teaching and Learning: Perspectives and Practices. Proceedings of the Australian Conference on Science and Mathematics Education (formerly UniServe Science Conference), Sydney, Australia, 9 April 1999; Available online: http://openjournals.library.usyd.edu.au/index.php/IISME/article/view/6655/7301 (accessed on 6 February 2014).

18. Cui, H. *Human and Rice Paddy: Dong People's Traditional Livelihoods*, 1st ed.; Yunnan People's Publishing House: Kunming, China, 2009.

19. Miller, G. The magical number seven, plus or minus two: Some limits on our capacity for processing information. *Psychol. Rev.* **1956**, *63*, 81–97. [CrossRef]

20. Covin, J.G.; Slevin, D.P. Strategic management of small firms in hostile and benign environments. *Strat. Manag. J.* **1989**, *10*, 75–87. [CrossRef]

21. Naldi, L.; Nordqvist, M.; Sjöberg, K.; Wiklund, J. Entrepreneurial orientation, risk taking, and performance in family firms. *Fam. Bus. Rev.* **2007**, *20*, 33–47. [CrossRef]

22. Walker, E.; Redmond, J.; Webster, B.; Clus, M.L. Small business owners: Too busy to train? *J. Small Bus. Enterprise Dev.* **2007**, *14*, 294–306. [CrossRef]

23. Wade, M. Fewer Workers Doing the Long Grind—But Still Far Too Many. Available online: http://www.smh.com.au/federal-politics/political-news/fewer-workers-doing-the-long-grind--but-still-far-too-many-20130529-2nbwx.html (accessed on 6 February 2014).

24. Silberman, M.L.; Auerbach, C. *Active Training: A Handbook of Techniques, Designs, Case Examples, and Tips*, 3rd ed.; John Wiley & Sons: Hoboken, NJ, USA, 2011.

25. Salas, E.; Cannon-Bowers, J.A. The science of training: A decade of progress. *Annu. Rev. Psychol.* **2001**, *52*, 471–499. [CrossRef]

26. Bessant, J.; Caffyn, S.; Gilbert, J.; Harding, R.; Webb, S. Rediscovering continuous improvement. *Technovation* **1994**, *14*, 17–29. [CrossRef]

27. Kim, D.H. *Introduction to Systems Thinking*; Pegasus Communications: Acton, MA, USA, 1999.

28. Midgley, G. *Systemic Intervention: Philosophy, Methodology, and Practice*; Kluwer Academic/Plenum: New York, NY, USA, 2000.

29. Meadows, D.H. *Thinking in Systems: A Primer*; Chelsea Green Publishing: White River Junction, VT, USA, 2008.

30. Forrester, J.W. Counterintuitive behavior of social systems. *Theor. Decis.* **1971**, *2*, 109–140. [CrossRef]

31. Sherwood, D. *Seeing the Forest for the Trees: A Manager's Guide to Applying Systems Thinking*; Nicholas Brealey Pub.: London, UK, 2002.

32. Meadows, D. *Leverage Points: Places to Intervene in a System*; The Sustainability Institute: Hartland, VT, USA, 1999.

33. Senge, P.; Roberts, C.; Ross, R.; Smith, B.; Kleiner, A. *The Fifth Discipline Fieldbook: Strategies and Tools for Building a Learning Organization*; Currency, Doubleday: New York, NY, USA, 1994.

34. Forrester, J.W. *Industrial Dynamics*; Pegasus Communications: Cambridge, MA, USA, 1961.

35. Richmond, B.; Peterson, S. *An Introduction to Systems Thinking*; High Performance Systems, Inc.: Honolulu, HI, USA, 2001.

36. Sterman, J.D. System dynamics modeling: Tools for learning in a complex world. *Calif. Manag. Rev.* **2001**, *43*, 8–25. [CrossRef]

37. Ford, A. *Modeling the Environment*, 2nd ed.; Island Press: Washington, DC, USA, 2010.

38. Madachy, R.J. *Software Process Dynamics*; IEEE Press: Piscataway, NJ, USA, 2008.

39. Homer, J.B.; Hirsch, G.B. System dynamics modeling for public health: Background and opportunities. *Am. J. Publ. Health* **2006**, *96*, 452–458. [CrossRef]
40. Ghaffarzadegan, N.; Lyneis, J.; Richardson, G.P. How small system dynamics models can help the public policy process. *Syst. Dynam. Rev.* **2011**, *27*, 22–44.

systems

MDPI

Opinion

Systems Education for a Sustainable Planet: Preparing Children for Natural Disasters

Kevin R. Ronan [1,*] and Briony Towers [2]

[1] School of Health, Human and Social Sciences, CQ University Australia, Rockhampton, QLD 4701, Australia
[2] School of Mathematics and Geospatial Science, RMIT University, Melbourne, VIC 3000, Australia; briony.towers@rmit.edu.au
* Author to whom correspondence should be addressed; k.ronan@cqu.edu.au.

Received: 29 November 2013; in revised form: 3 January 2014; Accepted: 15 January 2014; Published: 24 January 2014

Abstract: This paper first reviews research linked to the United Nations International Strategy for Disaster Reduction focusing on "child-centred disaster risk reduction" (CC-DRR), highlighting systemic aspects of disaster prevention and preparedness educational programming to date. However, it is also pointed out that education evaluated to date largely assumes a linear, mechanistic approach to preparedness and related resiliency outcomes. Thus, the main thrust of this paper is to elucidate means by which hazards and disaster preparedness education programs for children can shift to systems-based models, those that incorporate both systemic epistemologies but also more systems-based, and interconnected, curricula. This includes curricula that help children connect the physical world and science with the social world and human factors. It also includes the more systemic idea that natural hazards are but one example of a larger category of problems in life related to risk and uncertainty. Thus, a main aim of a systems educational approach is to help children equip themselves with knowledge, skills, motivation and confidence that they can increasingly manage a range of risks in life. This includes an increasing understanding of the added value that can be gained from approaching problems with systemic tools, including producing increasingly effective and sustainable solutions to what public policy refers to as wicked problems.

Keywords: disaster prevention and preparedness; systems education; children and youth

1. Introduction

In systems thinking, physical and the social worlds are treated as interconnected. In education in the Western world, academic subjects are treated largely in isolation [1]. This includes the subject of natural hazards and disasters [2]. Amongst other things, a split often exists between the physical systems linked to naturally occurring events and the social systems that are connected to their anticipation, occurrence and aftermath [3]. What follows in this paper is first a selective review that starts within the social system, namely "hazards education" programs for children and youth. More specifically, following some background for context, it starts with the notion of a fairly specific type of hazards education for children and youth, that of disaster resilience education done during the "prevention and preparedness" phase of the disaster cycle (*i.e.*, before a disaster's occurrence). A main aim of these programs for youth is to increase young people's resilience to disasters, helping them to prepare so that they, and their families, might respond and recover more effectively. As the review aims to demonstrate, while there are seeds of systems-based thinking and education within this area, it is largely underpinned by a linear, mechanistic model that tends to treat interconnected problems in isolation or simply ignore them.

2. Promoting Preparedness for Disasters in Youth

In an attempt to reduce the impact of hazardous events, published research since about the turn of the century [4,5] has begun to focus on hazards and disaster education programming for children. It is a well-established finding that households and communities typically do not attend to prevention and preparedness, including recommended risk reduction activities and safety measures [6]. This low rate of documented preparedness in households and communities includes for those in vulnerable groups in a community and in established high hazard areas (e.g., for earthquakes including San Francisco Bay Area; and Wellington, New Zealand) [3,7].

Additionally, in terms of youth themselves, research has demonstrated that larger scale hazards create vulnerability for children. For example, research on childhood fears has consistently found that the most feared situations for children tend to vary across age groups. However, some fears tend to be stable across age groups, particularly those that reflect threats to survival. Thus, research in the 1980s [8,9] found that of the eight most feared situations across 8–17 year-olds, a number of them were related to natural or man-made disasters, either directly (earthquakes; bombing attacks; fire—being burnt to death) or indirectly (not being able to breathe; falling from a high place). In addition, in the aftermath of a disaster, children tend to have more intense fears including of the same or other disasters occurring. For example, when asked an open-ended question about fears they or children their age have, children who were both exposed and not exposed to Hurricane Katrina named future hurricanes or tornadoes [10].

Following a disaster, children have also been identified in a large scale review as the most vulnerable demographic group for severe reactions [11]. Even in a relatively benign hazard, a significant minority of children have been found to have moderate to more severe reactions. For example, after a series of volcanic eruptions, where there was no loss of life, over 10% of a sample of 118 schoolchildren met the self-reported criteria for acute and post-traumatic stress syndromes [12]. In addition to children being cited as a particularly vulnerable sample, the Norris *et al.* review [11] also identified families with children as another vulnerable group. It is also worth noting that one of the strongest risk factors, if not the strongest, for a child having negative reactions to a hazardous event is a parent's reactions [13–15]. Linked to this idea, children with emotional and behavioral difficulties tend to have parents with similar problems (e.g., anxiety) [2,3]. A final link here is that these factors—emotional, behavioural, decision-making/problem-solving—are systemically related to each other. For example, parents of anxious and aggressive children have been found to reinforce unhelpful problem-solving strategies (avoidant and aggressive, respectively) [16]. In another study, parents of anxious children were also rated as less granting of autonomy to their child, perhaps linked to a tendency also found in parents of anxious children to be over controlling or overprotective [17].

Such findings have underpinned moves to reduce vulnerability in children and families, before, during and after a hazardous event [2,3]. The focus in this article is on risk reduction through pre-disaster prevention and preparedness education programs aimed at reducing vulnerability through reducing risk while increasing physical and emotional preparedness. In addition to reducing vulnerability, another rationale for these programs is that today's youth are tomorrow's adults. However, in more current discussions, children are also a source of enthusiasm and motivation that potentially can help mobilize households and communities to act. This is important in light of the findings that show convincingly that community preparedness is low and further suggest motivation to be a central problem e.g., [18–21].

3. Disaster Preparedness Education: What Do We Know Thus Far?

A recent review ([22], see also [3]) suggests that school-based preparedness programs can assist to increase motivation and actual preparedness [23,24]. For example, an early cross-sectional study [4] examined the effect preparedness education had on a number of factors in a reasonably large sample of schoolchildren ($n = 460$). Participation in a preparedness education program was related to more realistic perceptions of risk and increased knowledge of appropriate safety behaviours. Another finding was that children who participated in preparedness programs also reported lower levels of fears in relation to hazardous events compared to children who had not participated. These children also were less likely to perceive their parents as having hazards-related fear.

Another study [5] also found that participation in preparedness education programs is related to a number of benefits, including replicating a number of findings of the first study. Additionally, the study found that children who reported involvement in a preparedness program, *versus* those who were not involved in a program, reported more preparedness activities at home as did their parents. That study also empirically identified predictors of increased preparedness activities including: (1) involvement in more recent and a greater number of preparedness programs; (2) more knowledge of risk reduction activities and safety behaviours; and (3) more interaction at home (*i.e.*, discussions between children and parents) linked to learning in a preparedness program. More recent cross-sectional [25] research has extended earlier findings.

In addition to correlational research, experimental findings have also supported the value of education programs increasing resilience indicators [23,26,27]. For example, the first of these used a quasi-experimental design with classrooms randomly assigned to one of two conditions. The first was based on usual school curricula, focused on a reading and discussion format about special topics, the topic here being disasters. The second condition added a more specific emergency management focus to the reading and discussion format. This included specific discussions and activities focused on preparedness activities that youth could do independently or with parents. One exercise was a homework activity designed to be done with parents to encourage a number of specific preparedness activities. In terms of findings, both the usual conditions (UC) and emergency management-focused (EM) programs led to significant benefits on a number of indicators. In terms of knowledge and home-based preparedness activities, the EM condition was seen to significantly out-do the UC condition. In terms of emotional factors, both the EM and UC conditions led to benefits and did not differ from each other. Given that both conditions led to changes suggests that preparedness programs don't by themselves raise fears and, further, can be beneficial [2]. These experimental findings [26] have also been replicated and extended [23].

Given findings overall in this area based on a recent systematic review [23], there is evidence-based promise for children's involvement in hazards education programs, albeit in a limited number of studies, a number of which have limited methodologies [22]. Despite that issue, preparedness education programs that involve children appear to be increasingly common globally, endorsed by the United Nations International Strategy for Disaster Reduction (UNISDR) as part of a "child-centred disaster risk reduction" (CC-DRR) emphasis. As confirmation of increasingly widespread CC-DRR activities, a recent UNESCO and UNISDR supported mapping exercise reported on and described preparedness programs across 30 countries [28]. While most programs to date do not have accompanying research findings, they do appear to have potential based on the research that has been conducted. As a most recent illustration to highlight the potential, a recent study [27] used a quasi-experimental and benchmarking design and methodology and found an increase of 6 parent-reported home-based hazard risk reduction activities. Children were found to increase their hazards-related knowledge by 39%. These increases were after a quite brief four session interactive preparedness program held at a youth centre. It is worth noting that this study was done with a sample from a lower SES stratum, including about half of the youth involved not being engaged with education or vocational training. Given that SES is a major risk factor for poor adjustment to a disaster [11,29], disaster preparedness programs for children and youth have increasingly documented potential as a gateway for increasing resilience in some of the most vulnerable sectors of a community.

4. Moving to a Systems Focus

Some of the findings to date in disaster preparedness education implicate systemic features, including education involvement and increased knowledge being linked to lower fear levels [4,23,26,27] but also linked to greater risk perceptions about injuries [4] and more frequently occurring events [25].

This finding implicates systemic relationships between factors that are sometimes thought about in simpler cause-effect terms. For example, in focus group research, some teachers have expressed concerns that exposing children to hazards-related risk information might raise both children's concerns about risk and, in doing so, scare them [30]. In children as young as 7, exposure to hazards risk information in an education program actually has been shown to produce increased accurate knowledge and increased risk perceptions (e.g., increased perception of risk of injury). However, in contrast to teacher focus group perceptions, multiple studies have demonstrated that these same children also report significantly reduced levels of fear in relation to those hazardous events compared to those who have no exposure to risk information [4,23,26,27]. Further yet, there is an additional correlational link that has been found between increased knowledge (or search for knowledge) and increased action, including increased preparedness activities done at home [5,26] (and an increased sense of control in relation to preparedness [27]). Thus, starting at a relatively early stage of development, children have been shown to be quite capable of learning about risk in ways that promote emotional and physical resilience. Another of the findings here implicating systems features is the notion that children can take a preparedness mindset with them into the home setting to promote further benefits. A cross-sectional study done in Japan further demonstrates this potential, linking children's learning not only to the home but also to larger community benefits [24].

On the other hand, disaster preparedness education for children to date largely rests on notions that child- and home-preparedness is the "royal road" in preparedness terms. Another is that education programs themselves can often be quite simple and revolve around the theme of a "disaster as a discrete event that leads to potentially destructive effects that child-, school- and home-based preparedness will mitigate" linear sequence [23]. From a systemic view of disasters (and of risk more generally) [31,32], this sequence just simply does not account for the complexities involved in disasters. That is, disasters are an example of what public policy might refer to as a "wicked problem" [33]. To illustrate first systemic issues in disasters, two examples are provided in relation to floods and fires, respectively. Then, in subsequent sections, consideration of the building blocks necessary to help children begin to develop the increasing capacity to solve these sorts of complex challenges is taken up.

Starting with examples of disasters as wicked problems, and firstly in relation to floods, a common mitigation measure in populated areas is levee construction [34]. However, a lack of systems thinking has invited a number of problems with this mitigation measure. In what is called the "levee syndrome", the building of levees may protect an area from a flood event. However, even if it does, the water eventually will have to go somewhere. Thus, there are many documented occurrences where farmers' and others downstream from a levee site get inundated [2]. Another problem with such a mitigation measure is related to an implicit idea that humans can control nature. In the case of a levee, they tend to be built to withstand certain intensity flood events (e.g., 100 year floods). Thus, when an event exceeds the planned capacity (e.g., a 1000 year flood), or if the levee is engineered poorly, the levee itself will be overwhelmed [34]. A corollary of this "humans can control nature" theme is that the building of levees can give the impression that it is safe to live in the area. Thus, the building of levees can invite increased building, settlement and populations. When a levee fails, it can then further lead to a host of problems that are not anticipated [34].

In the case of bushfires, to cite an example from Australia, analysis done by Brian Ashe, John McAneny and colleagues at Risk Frontiers at Macquarie University, shows the value of a systems approach. First, since 1900, fires in Australia have stayed relatively constant in terms of frequency, intensity, spread. Loss of life has also stayed fairly constant, as have other factors (e.g., risk of losing houses). Loss of life from bushfires is currently at rate of 14 per annum (low by international standards) [35], far less than some other fatality risks (e.g., structural fires, 100 per annum; road fatalities, 1600 per annum) [36]. The relatively low rate of fatalities and other losses is despite increased population and related infrastructure (e.g., homes, buildings) in areas of high bushfire risk. A main reason appears to be that public investment in risk mitigation procedures has increased significantly over time. However, the cost effectiveness of current investment has been questioned, including by experts engaged in a "structured expert judgement exercise" [35]. Experts all agreed that there was no net benefit from increasing investment and most indicated that reducing the investment would yield increased net benefits. Interestingly, as politicians and others might point out, over-investment should not be a problem if lives are saved. However, systems analysis shows that "compliance with costly government interventions affects the consumption of risk-reducing goods and services in the same way as a decline in wealth" (p. 2) [35]. Such a reality is also not going to assist people becoming motivated to prepare, including a perception that large-scale government investment in risk mitigation is largely going to fix the problem. The current investment itself has been attributed at least in part to public perceptions, where the public has been found to over-estimate bushfire-related fatalities and these perceptions then having a knock-on effect to political and policy decisions affecting funding [36]. Finally, a study benchmarking Australian investment in risk mitigation against 11 other countries showed no significant relationship between government spending and losses from fire. This suggests other factors are responsible, including human settlement patterns [37]. In fact, one of the reasons for increased problems linked to a range of hazardous events, including floods and bushfires, is increasing human settlement and development (In the case of volcanoes, the problem has become such that an entire conference series starting in the shadow of Mt. Vesuvius (Naples) in 1998—Cities on Volcanoes—deals directly with the problem of increasing human settlement worldwide in areas vulnerable to volcanic eruptions).

This includes through policies that do not deter settlement but in fact subsidise settlement in a sense through government rather than household-financed risk mitigation and response costs. This includes both *costs in anticipation* (e.g., prevention measures) and *costs in response* (e.g., firefighting resources; compensation to victims) [37]. Contrast the investment in bushfire risk mitigation with the situation in relation to structural fire losses. Research shows that for structural fires, most of which are residential fires, those who experience them tend to be some of society's most vulnerable populations (e.g., from the lowest SES strata) who reside in accommodation with higher levels of fire risk [38]. However, despite increased fatalities linked to structural fires, this problem gets less attention than does bushfires, in both research and in the media. In Australia, the risk of dying in a structural fire is seven times that of dying in a bushfire. Thus, overall, it appears that risk mitigation in terms of government investment in reducing fire risk tends to be unequally distributed across a society, raising social issues (e.g., equity) [36].

Nevertheless, risk reduction education campaigns and programs are encouraged and promoted in both bushfire and urban locations (where residential fires are more common). However, as is found in other countries and for other hazards, preparedness for fires is generally quite low, implicating low motivation. As pointed out by Ashe and colleagues [36], the motivation to engage in increased safety behaviours may be not be high in either setting, but for different reasons. High government subsidy in bushfire prone areas may reduce a sense of increased personal responsibility (In the case of bushfires, while average annual deaths in Australia average 14 per year, catastrophic fires lead to spikes in the form of increased deaths and destruction. The main risk factor in these instances appears to be proximity to bushland, either being within bushland itself or in very close proximity (within 10 m) [39]. One implication of this finding is that creating a perimeter around a home by clearing bush is advantageous for saving lives and property, particularly when, as is quite commonly the case, land use planning policies are deficient and government subsidises risk by heavy investment in both costs in anticipation and costs in response [36]).

In structural fire prone areas, other more pressing daily living requirements may reduce a sense of urgency about fire safety ([38]; see also [36]). In addition, even if mitigation measures are available in residential settings, they may not help. For example, in a study looking at residential fires in Surrey, British Columbia [40] while one third (36%) of residences that experienced fires did not have smoke alarms, the rest did. However, of those 1,554 residences that did have alarms, almost half (49.5%) were not activated during the fire. Further yet, various factors are known to militate against appropriate response to smoke alarm activation (e.g., young and old age; impairment and disability;

being asleep) [40]. In addition, a smoke alarm may provide an illusory sense of control that then proves a deterrent to additional prevention and safety behaviour in the home (e.g., related to acquiring information about how to prevent and mitigate risk in relation to the known causes of residential fires including factors mostly related to human negligence including cooking-, open flame-, smoking-related factors and others [36,40]. These examples could continue to be elaborated (Examples will be returned to in subsequent sections to highlight ways that education programs for children might help them consider ways to solve some of the problems considered in this section).

However, the point here is to illustrate that preparedness and disaster preparedness education for children will benefit from a more holistic perspective. One that links physical with social systems more effectively and helps them begin to understand that problems related to risk reduction and increased preparedness are not based on a simple cause and effect approach but rather based on a range of physical and social factors that are interconnected. To anticipate later discussions, it is worth pointing out that children at younger ages have not developed the cognitive capacity to think in adult, or systemic, terms. For young children entering school, this will include a focus on appealing to their lifeworld and their level of development, focusing on simple knowledge and linking that to preparedness understanding and activities aimed at keeping them and important people safe. Over time, this foundation can be built on as children's development takes on more cognitive complexity and moves from a more purely egocentric view to one that increasingly incorporates, and can accommodate, more systemic, civic, and abstract concepts and views of life [41].

4.1. A Systems Educational Approach

As reviewed in a previous section, research supports the value of disaster preparedness education in changing risk perceptions, knowledge and behaviour, as reported by children and their parents. However, research to date has focused mainly on standalone education programs that themselves are focused more singularly on disaster awareness and preparedness. The two forms of preparedness generally emphasized are child and family safety behaviours as well as home-based risk mitigation activities. This is as opposed to an educational approach that has disaster preparedness as one part of a an interconnected model of education and incorporates but also goes beyond safety behaviour and risk mitigation activities. An approach that embeds disaster preparedness education as part of a larger focus on helping children understand their worlds from a holistic ontological, epistemological and scientific perspective: One that links learning in one sphere (disaster risk reduction) to larger organizing themes and that becomes increasingly interconnected over time. In current views around the philosophy of science and its disciplines (including education), whereas Pepper [42] discussed four traditions (formism, contextualism, mechanismic, organismic), some current models have collapsed across these four and now emphasise two: split *versus* relational models [43].

Thus, emphasizing a relational (organismic-contextual) philosophical and educational approach, one premise related to this mindset is that disaster preparedness education can be seen merely as one smaller part of a larger theme of helping children develop capacity (*i.e.*, knowledge and skills) to understand, accept and manage risk and uncertainty in life more generally. Thus, the idea underpinning the organizing theme of "understanding and managing risk and uncertainty" here is linked to a relational philosophy, where education is able to help children make connections between topics that are typically more siloed. This includes through introducing a systemic way of thinking and processing information but also includes the content of courses themselves. Preparedness and the management of risk also implicate a systemic relationship between learning, emotions and behaviour, including motivational factors. What follows are sections devoted to these factors, starting with an overview of the how and what of these programs.

4.2. The How and What of a Systemic Approach to Education: Process and Content

The first of the factors introduced just above, systemic thinking processes focuses on the "how", or the means underpinning a systems view of the world. Thus, the idea here is to help children develop the tools, and an increasingly differentiated capacity, to understand and manage risk and uncertainty, including effective disaster preparedness and risk reduction. Various approaches are available from different disciplines. From environmental science, one scheme focuses on dealing with problems through development of "cognitive interdisciplinary skills" linked to science education [44]. Another set of approaches focus on using problem-solving approaches. One of these schemes, drawn from a social science perspective, deals with problems through primary *versus* secondary appraisal and problem-solving skills [45]. Another problem-solving model is drawn from an educational perspective and focuses on inclusive and evolutionary themes [46]. In addition to systemic thinking processes, more interactive educational models that stress experiential and enactment learning are recommended [2,47]. Through "seeing, learning, practicing and doing" [2], cognitive and affective learning within a social context can be emphasized, including the connections between thinking, feeling and behaviour in the world (e.g., mastery links to feelings of well-being; knowledge about and approaching feared objects or problems tends to reduce anxiety; talking with others about problems can help solve problems and help one feel supported).

One form of learning introduced earlier that might be particularly emphasized is framing hazards and risk as community-based "problems to be solved" *versus* insurmountable threats. In fact, presenting problems as "challenges *versus* threats" has a good deal of empirical support [48]. The main idea here is that emotional factors link directly to problem-solving capacities. Challenge appraisals promote facilitative feelings and arousal configurations that promote "approach" behaviour; threat perceptions promote more avoidance. Thus, when one is motivated *versus* scared and feels a problem does have potential solutions, it is then more likely that s/he can recruit physiological and cognitive processes that lead to successful task performance [48] (According to Blascovich and colleagues [49], challenge *versus* threat appraisals are related to the balance between perceived resources and demands one experiences in dealing with any stressful event: "When perceived resources exceed perceived demands, a state of challenge is invoked. Challenge states are typically associated with better performance, positive affect, and, importantly (in the context of potential responses to in-group deviants), a heightened desire to approach positive goals actively (for reviews, see [50,51]). Conversely, when demands exceed resources, a state of threat is typically invoked. Threat is associated with negative affect, limited focus, and a state of approach or avoidance [48]. Challenge and threat represent opposite ends of a continuum, such that relative differences in challenge and threat (e.g., greater *vs.* lesser challenge) are meaningful. Changes in the balance of resources and demands affect neural and adrenal pathway activation (specifically, sympathetic adrenal medullary and pituitary adrenal cortical axes activation; see [48] for a thorough review). Activation of these pathways leads to distinctive patterns of cardiovascular responses that are used to index challenge and threat, respectively." (p. 106).

Thus, in helping children mobilize inner resources that help them approach *versus* avoid risks, this includes helping them develop a sense of control and "agency", the sense that "I can do this, I can solve this problem." Thus, from a very young age indeed, longitudinal research demonstrates that children's sense of agency (self-efficacy) can be raised or lowered through healthy approach coping environments *versus* more threat-based environments. For example, in a study of predictors of toddler self-efficacy, greater maternal behaviours (acceptance; responsiveness) at 5 and 17 months of age predicted greater self-efficacy behaviours at 17 months whereas greater maternal anxiety predicted decreased self-efficacy behaviours [52]. Similarly, school settings can promote risks as problems to be approached and as challenges to be solved.

In addition to the process (or "how") of a more systemic approach to preparedness education, there is also the content itself (the "what"). As inter-disciplinary process knowledge and skill development can help children develop the ability to connect the physical and social worlds so too can the manner of presenting the educational content itself. Thus, moving disaster preparedness education from one off, standalone programs to that which is embedded across curricula is the theme here. One that integrates both horizontally and vertically [47]. Such integrated curricula then has potential to help children acquire knowledge in a given area while gaining an increasing understanding of the world from a more connected perspective (As an aside, it is worth pointing out that even in standalone disaster resilience education programs, where risk reduction and preparedness are the main themes, there is room for increased connectedness).

Main themes in a more integrated curriculum would include helping children [2]:

(1) To understand the science related to hazards and risk—knowledge has been linked to promoting reduced fear and increased approach coping (e.g., home-based risk reduction activities);
(2) To build systemic problem-solving capacities for managing hazards and risk;
(3) To build motivational and emotional competencies necessary to solve problems related to risk, including seeing hazards, risk, and uncertainty as individual and community-based challenges *versus* threats.

4.2.1. A Systemic Educational Approach: Understanding Science, Developing Capacity

Drawing on current models of education that can be linked to reducing risk and increasing preparedness in relation to disasters, various approaches are possible to draw from [53] including the following:

- The Earth-System-Science (ESS) Model [54,55];
- Holistic disaster preparedness and resilience educational models [2,29,47].

Developed by the NASA Advisory Council's Earth System Science Committee [54], the ESS model has three main themes [55]:

- Earth and its place in the universe;
- Earth systems;
- Earth in relation to human activities.

And, three steps to connect these themes:

- Step 1: Understanding the four earth systems in terms of the "spheres" (atmo, bio, hydro, litho);
- Step 2: Add an event (e.g., natural hazard);
- Step 3: Tools to develop understanding of connections within and across systems;

  ○ Guiding questions (what changes? how does it change? why does it change?);
  ○ Connection keywords that help students think like "scientists thinking about and discovering earth-system connections";

    ▪ Causes, effects;
    ▪ Increases, decreases;
    ▪ Changes, impacts.

In the ESS model, as an Event is entered, it can then be understood in terms of its relationships to each of earth's spheres, as in the following diagram (see Figure 1).

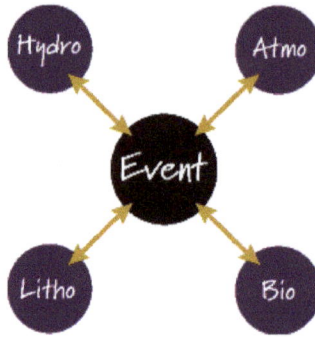

Figure 1. Event-sphere connections. Illustration courtesy of Exploring the Environment® (http://ete.cet.edu).

Over time, and with increasing sophistication and child cognitive development, increasing connections can then begin to be made (see Figure 2).

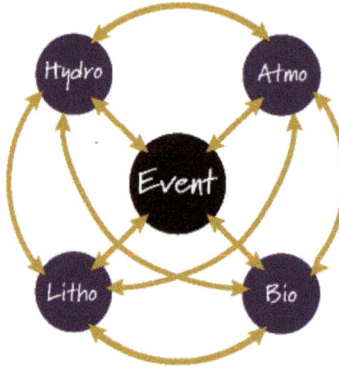

Figure 2. Elaborated event-sphere connections. Illustration courtesy of Exploring the Environment® (http://ete.cet.edu).

Building on and extending the ESS model, an additional node can then be added to link earth systems and the event with human systems (see Figure 3).

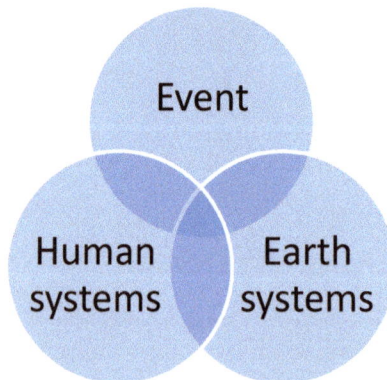

Figure 3. Event-earth-human systems connections.

Filling in the human systems node can include a number of systemic strategies that are process- or structurally-based. One type of process model would take account from prior to the event through to following the event and be able to delineate resilient *versus* vulnerable pathways. This could be quite specific pathways linked to natural hazard events specifically or more generally delineating resilient *versus* vulnerable "risk and uncertainty" pathways. This could then be accompanied by guiding questions and connection keywords to help students understand vulnerable *versus* resilient pathways and how one is more likely to be on one pathway *versus* another. These guiding questions and connection keywords could be drawn from those of the ESS model:

(1) What changes are related to being on risk *versus* resilient pathways?
(2) How and why does change happen to be on one path *versus* the other?
(3) Connection keywords:

    a. Causes, effects;
    b. Increases, decreases;
    c. Changes, impacts;
    d. Parts, parts-whole.

A more structural human systems model would delineate between different human systems, making links between them similar to the ESS's event-spheres diagram. This structure could be anything from individual- to more community-level focused and become increasingly sophisticated over time, congruent with children's development and increasing understanding. Thus, for younger children, connections could be made to help them understand themselves and their families more systemically. Thus, an event (e.g., storm with high winds) could first be understood in terms of child nodes (thoughts, behaviours, feelings, bodily reactions). Over time, with increasing development, they could then be further connected to "outside the child" nodes (e.g., schools node, friends node, "family and home" node). Thus, as the child develops more mature thinking (see next section), more community-level models can start to be introduced. For example, Norris and colleagues [29] have a community-based model that has four main nodes: economic development, social capital, community competence, information and communication. While Norris *et al.* developed their model in relation to disasters, these main nodes have more general application. Each node can have any number of sub-nodes in relation to a particular event being mapped. In terms of promoting resilience to disasters, the sub-nodes that Norris [56] emphasises are the following:

- Economic development;

    ○   Resource level;
    ○   Resource equity;
    ○   Resource diversity.

- Social capital;

    ○   Social support and networks;
    ○   Social participation;
    ○   Bondedness and commitment to the community.

- Information and communication;

    ○   Trusted sources of information that are linked together;
    ○   Responsible media;
    ○   Good information infrastructure.

- Community competence;

    ○   Collective sense of control and efficacy;

    ○   Sense of empowerment;

    ○   Collective and cooperative decision-making and actions.

Reflecting systems thinking, Norris herself states that "resilience to disaster ... rests not only or even primarily on traditional preparedness activities but on building economically strong communities whose members can work together and use information to make decisions and act" [56]. In moving to systemic educational approaches, Ronan and Johnston's Strengthening Systems (SS4R) model ([2]; see also [3]) emphasizes an educational platform involving the strengthening of relationships through "spreading activation networks" within communities. An important network in any given community is the school-youth-household network, one that generally involves the majority of residential households.

4.2.2. Starting Simple and Building over Time: Stages, Modes of Learning, Problem-Solving Tools

Helping children move to a systems- and community-level understanding of how to manage risk and uncertainty in relation to natural hazards and other events needs by necessity to start at the basic in younger years. When children are aged 5–6, they are typically in the pre-operational level of cognitive development, a time characterized by egocentrism and "perceptual centering" [57]. Thus, they are incapable of understanding problems in more adult, systemic ways and require an approach that appeals to their capacity and their lifeworld. Starting simple, a sequenced approach then can keep pace with the child's growing competencies and add more complexity over time. Thus, it can help move disaster preparedness, and related, education along a developmental continuum that helps children begin to develop basic understandings of uncertainty, risk and risk mitigation first from a child-focused and family perspective and ultimately to a community-level focus. This should start with simple ideas for younger children in early school years (*i.e.*, from age 5–6). Simple ideas can then be elaborated to develop an increasingly sophisticated understanding of the science linked to physical and human systems. In teaching the science of hazards and disasters, it is worthwhile to help children also understand that increased understanding and knowledge is also linked to increased "solutions" (e.g., increased willingness to engage in risk reduction activities and an increased sense of control [5,26,27]).

Children at school entry level need to be taught about hazards at their level of understanding: first through simple scientific knowledge (e.g., floods happen because rain can cause waterways to rise). Second, a related emphasis would include helping them learn that hazards can be managed in ways that children at these ages would understand and appreciate. In particular for children at this developmental stage, it would focus on promoting increased safety. Thus, levees get in the way of rising water and can keep people safe, installing home alarms can detect smoke and help people get out of a burning building and bringing a safety plan home to fill out with parents can "help keep me and my whole family safe."

As children start to enter concrete operations from about age 7 [57], they are better able to accommodate the seeds of systemic thinking, including thinking in more relational terms (e.g., conservation). Thus, scientifically-based connections can help children begin to understand that a solution can also have a drawback. A built levee can solve one problem (protecting communities) while introducing another that can be described, discussed, and even demonstrated (e.g., downstream flooding). Additionally, a self-help, safety metaphor used with younger children can begin to increasingly incorporate a "good citizenship" focus that also develops during this stage of development, including basic links to nodes in models such as the Norris *et al.* model described earlier. This could include basic depictions of numerous modes that appeal to and encourage a civics-based mindset, part of the growing lifeworld at this stage of development (e.g., community participation and bondedness; responsible and trusted information networks that work together; working together to make cooperative decisions to help those in a community). One example of a civics-related problem might be learning about complacency around preparedness. This problem can be like other problems linked to both the science of flooding (e.g., flood return periods; structural integrity of levees) and human factors (e.g., levees can discourage additional home-based adjustment activities based on the perception of a levee as a "cure all"). Solutions can then be problem-solved through various classroom and teaching modes (e.g., brainstorming, discussion, homework exercise with parents; community motivational exercise; see also below).

In addition, as children begin to be able to think in more logical, relational terms, systemic thinking approaches can also start to be introduced. For example, there are events to think about in terms of their parts (analytic thinking; how things are different) and there are connections between events in terms of how they work together (synthetic thinking; how things are the same) (Given a systemic model favouring a combination of analytic and synthetic approaches, helping children start to develop a systemic mindset can involve helping them think in terms of both differences and similarities. This could start with simple concrete objects or living things (e.g., dog and cat, how are they different? how are they the same?). Over time, more sophisticated approaches can then be introduced (e.g., posing a problem and then asking for different solutions; writing solutions on the board and asking how are individual solutions different from each other but also how are they the same? Sometimes the best answer to a problem is a singular solution, sometimes a more synthetic solution that cuts across different possibilities). Over time, these can incorporate hazards- and risk-related topics).

As children continue to advance cognitively, and move to the stage of being able to think more conceptually, other problems that appeal to a more adolescent, formal operational level of thinking [57] might be introduced. Of many possibilities, one example is social justice (e.g., those who typically live in flood plains, and near levees that may or may not be well maintained, can also be from more vulnerable sectors of society (e.g., Ward 9, New Orleans in Hurricane Katrina)). Another set of topics might draw on social science findings [10,11,29,56,58,59] and discuss and problem-solve around the idea that those who do prepare effectively at the individual and household level might nevertheless continue to be at risk of other unanticipated community-level impacts (e.g., vicarious trauma; economic effects; social cohesion that can be accompanied or followed by elements of polarization and breakdown).

To summarise the foregoing discussion, a systems approach would link up the value of an increasingly sophisticated understanding of the science of hazards with social factors, starting with simple self-help strategies at earlier ages and increasingly sophisticated community- and civic-minded problems, views and actions at later ages. With advancing age, children begin to enter the concrete operational stage of thinking (from ages 7–8 [57]), and the increasing ability to consider different dimensions of a problem (*i.e.*, moving from "perceptual centredness" on one aspect of a problem to "decentering" and the ability to consider different elements of a problem simultaneously). At about this age, the relationship between self-help and community-focused actions can be introduced and considered. With advancing age and development, more complexities can then be added (e.g., community complacency; social justice; economic implications). Alongside and as part of this approach, helping children understand that helping oneself and collectively helping others can have numerous benefits, including reduced physical, socio-emotional and financial/economic impacts at both the individual and community levels. In addition, helping oneself and "collective helping" have been shown to lead to other more generalisable benefits, including positive feelings and an increased sense of mastery, efficacy, control, and connectedness [2,41,59]. In fact, at more advanced ages (high school), the link between collective helping and problem-solving can be illustrated by a discussion of research that suggests that policies that are developed through collaborative strategies *versus* other means (e.g., authoritative or competitive strategies) are thought to be more effective for solving wicked problems linked to risk and other complex problems [33], including disasters and in educational contexts [60].

To supplement learning in the classroom, discussion points, examples, simulations and a variety of in- and out-of-class experiential learning approaches can be used. Selby and Kagawa's [28] mapping of disaster risk reduction approaches in school curricula in 30 countries highlight numerous types of interactive learning that have been used to date. (These include "various forms of interactive learning (brainstorming as well as pair, small group and whole group discussion on disaster risk/climate change topics); inquiry learning (team case study research, internet searches, project work); surrogate experiential learning (filmic experience, board games, plays, drama, simulations on disasters and climate change; field experiential learning (field visits to disaster support services, hazard mapping, vulnerability assessment in school and community, community hazard transects and surveys); action learning (poster campaigns, street theatre around disasters and climate change, holding public meetings, risk reduction campaigns and projects, such as tree planting)" (p. 214) [47]).

Whatever the form of interactive learning, helping with increased connectivity to the home and to the community would assist as would connections between scientific and social/societal aspects. This might include working through known examples of problems linked to disaster risk reduction and response. For example, drawing on both flood and fire examples from earlier, the opportunities, and opportunity costs, linked to flood levees and to fire safety could be used to help connect the science with an increasing set of risk reduction competencies, which range from simple and safety-focused at young ages to more systemic and connected at older ages. To assist teachers, published "case examples" here are available in relation to levees (e.g., New Orleans) [33] and in relation to fire safety in Australia [35–38] and Surrey, British Columbia [40,61]. In the case of the latter, the case study of Surrey not only speaks to systemic issues related to fires and fire safety, it also presents research around solving some of those problems through an interactive, community-level campaign [61] that was based on an evaluation of systemic problems identified [40]. Such case examples could be drawn from, with material adjusted to the age level of the child, and used to frame a problem that then is turned over to students to solve.

As part of this process, more simple problem-solving tools can be introduced at younger ages with more advanced ones introduced over time (This might include a basic problem-solving sequence for younger children that defines the problem in basic terms: what choices are available to solve the problem, consequences for each choice, choosing of best alternative (e.g., family emergency plan). Over time, rather than simply choosing one alternative as is usually done, an emphasis on increasingly synthetic, systemic solutions can start with brainstorms for a large number of alternatives and then help children start to find the themes that cut across these alternatives (e.g., combination of prevention strategies in the home with more community-focused, collective solutions). Additionally, as children get more towards adolescence, more systemic problem-solving tools can start to be introduced to build on the more simple problem-solving approach. For example, the theory of constraints [62] adds questions to a problem-solving process such as what to change? what to change it into?; how to bring about change and then sustain and improve on it?; why change? In this model, a number of more specific tools are also available (e.g., evaporating cloud; core conflict cloud, future reality tree; positive reinforcement loop). Numerous other approaches and tools are also available [63]).

In flood (New Orleans), fire (Australian, Surrey) or other examples, students could have a "go" at problem solving pitched at the appropriate age level (e.g., young ages, how do we protect ourselves in our home?; older ages, how do we protect ourselves and others in our community and why are both important?) that is complemented with discussion, argument, identification of problem themes and solutions that have agreed upon value. Then, elements of the "solution" (e.g., from Surrey example) can be presented and discussed, including "what else could be done here?" Following case examples, attention could then be turned to a local problem related to some risk, hazards or otherwise, that uses a similar process and incorporates experiential learning including interactive efforts to motivate households and a community to act.

On the issue of motivation, it is an essential issue in preparedness for disasters given universally low levels of preparedness including in high hazard areas [6]. One reason of course is complacency, based on competing priorities or low levels of risk perception. In relation to risk more generally, risk perceptions have been found to motivate protective behaviours in the public but have also been found to have a negative relationship (*i.e.*, promote avoidance [64]). Thus, a perception of risk, particularly higher levels, can invite for some negative emotions like fear and anxiety. High anxiety and its link to avoidance behaviour is well-established [65]. Anxiety has also been related to higher levels of perceived risk [66]. Children with higher levels of fear have been found to have lower hazards knowledge [4] and increased perceptions of not being prepared [27]. Recall also the finding that family settings with highly anxious children tend to have adults with similar problems, including a family environment that supports avoidant solutions to problems [16]. Thus, if anxiety, or "risk concern", is too low or high, it can motivate avoidant behaviour or inhibit approach behaviour, consistent with a well-known maxim in psychology called the Yerkes-Dodson law [67]. By contrast, moderate levels of anxiety or concern invite the adaptive features of that emotional state, inviting increased willingness to engage in behaviours to solve problems and to engage in behaviours that successfully solve those problems. As introduced earlier, then, framing hazards as challenges *versus* threats [48] would be thought to help invite the pattern of arousal and accompanying cognitive and behavioural readiness that promotes consideration of change and actual change behaviours. However, motivation is more than challenge *versus* threat perceptions. In addition, owing to the critical role of motivation in preparedness, a more explicit focus on its role in a systems educational approach is warranted.

4.2.3. The Role of Motivation in Systemic Education and Risk Management

A simple view of behaviour change of any sort reflects two main elements, (1) competencies necessary to enact change (knowledge and skills) that is (2) "fuelled" through emotional factors (Psychology textbooks include in their definition of emotions the idea of emotions as "behavioural tendencies". That is, a primary function of emotion is to motivate particular types of behaviour [65]). That fueling function is generally referred to as motivation. For any change behaviour, it assumes that a person "can do" the behaviour (*i.e.*, has competence to think through and perform the behaviour) but it also assumes that a person wants to carry out some behaviour, the "will do" factor.

According to the motivational interviewing (MI) model, Miller and Rollnick [68] extend the can do and will do ideas to a sequence that emphasises being "willing, able, and ready" to make change. Willingness to change is tied to one's emotional investment. In terms of the can do or ability factor, this represents an individual's capacity and sense that a behaviour itself (e.g., hazard preparedness activity) can be effective (general efficacy), alongside confidence that they are able to carry out the behaviour (self-efficacy) [20]. The "ready" factor reflects the idea that changing behaviour now is better than doing it later.

The MI model focuses on the idea of "developing discrepancy" as part of the process to increase one's willingness to consider change. The idea is to create a noticeable discrepancy between one's current status and a value or a goal state. The more the discrepancy, the greater potential for motivation and the carrying out of some change behaviour, Representing an underlying philosophy that is relational (*versus* split) [43], there is a connection (*i.e.*, a relationship) drawn between a current state of affairs and its degree of discrepancy from an imagined future. The "discrepancy space" itself represents motivational space. Thus, the idea of helping people "develop and amplify" discrepancy is intended to elicit motivation. Motivation that is intrinsic (from within) *versus* extrinsic (e.g., "I need to prepare because my teacher tells me I have to") is the focus here (In terms of hazards mitigation, it is worth noting that we also favor extrinsic motivation (e.g., mandated land use planning, building codes and so forth). Mandated activities can co-exist with voluntary activities that children and families can adopt to help them protect themselves and their households in the event of a major hazardous event, mindful that regulation in relation to hazardous events comes with opportunities, opportunity costs, tipping points and so forth [36]).

As a discrepancy is first widened through discussions, it can then be "resolved" through "change talk." This can include consideration of the advantages (and disadvantages) of change and begin to promote change talk that has increasing "commitment strength". Increasing commitment strength can then help a person, classroom, or community to move along in the "stages of change" continuum [69].

Support for a motivational approach in the hazards preparedness literature has come from research that implicates increased motivation as key to initiating change (see review [3]). Thus, disaster preparedness education programs can include such discussions to help motivate children while at the same time providing them with a set of motivational tools for use in other contexts.

Preparedness education programs that introduce the idea of hazards and risk as challenges *versus* threats can also incorporate "discrepancy tools" to help children work from a current state of affairs to a more desirable future, including delineating vulnerable *versus* resilient pathways to the future. As part of that process, it could then further help them begin to learn about problems (*i.e.*, current state of affairs) through a systemic and scientific understanding and then be able to picture and map an imagined future. Then, with the assistance of problem-solving tools, children can then begin to discuss and map out movement from present to future, mindful in the case of wicked problems [33] that the process quite often is non-linear.

As a result, as children develop more mature thinking, this process should include the idea that problems related to risk tend to get more effectively solved with holistic solutions: Ones that take account of both physical and human systems, employ systemic thinking strategies, use collaborative problem-solving, and so forth. Related to collaborative efforts, developing relationships and strengthening links between systems within a community would be thought to help develop a shared sense of motivation for both personal and collective action. This could of course include leveraging the school-youth-family network to initiate a community-wide focus on a problem. Thus, as children carry their learning, their motivation and growing sense of efficacy and mastery home with them, they can at the same time understand that schools and households are embedded in communities that are interconnected socially, occupationally, economically and in other ways. Helping them understand how to connect within a community would be thought to enhance their own learning while also potentially helping contribute to community-level competence, efficacy, and action. This can include for problems related to hazards preparedness and resilience [29] and a host of others. In other words, children can leverage their learning to help motivate their homes, and their communities, to act in important ways [2,47].

5. Summary

To summarise important ideas presented in this paper, in a systems educational approach, various concepts first taught on their own merits can become increasingly inter-connected over time including:

(1) That science, research, and increased understanding are basic tools to help deal with problems linked to risk and uncertainty in life;

(2) Linking various factors with each other including:

   (a) Physical with human systems in relation to disasters and other risks;

   (b) The child with the home, the home with the community, the community within a region, the region within a country and so forth;

   (c) Preparedness activities with more effective response and recovery;

   (d) Physical preparedness and response with psychosocial preparedness and response; linking risk mitigation with living within a world of others;

   (e) The idea of learning and behavioural change with emotional factors (e.g., motivation, confidence, sense of one's efficacy); linking knowledge and skills (e.g., increased physical preparedness) with increased confidence and sense of control that can assist quality decision-making under duress;

   (f) Preparedness for hazards with the larger theme of developing the knowledge, skills, motivation and self-efficacy to underpin a growing holistic ability to think through and solve problems in life linked to risk and uncertainty;

Systems **2014**, 2, 1–23

(3)   That managing risk and uncertainty can have both local solutions (e.g., a sense of personal responsibility; preparedness at home) and wider systemic solutions (e.g., increased community development, linkages, and collective helping; land use planning; policy development and practices that understand opportunities, opportunity costs, tipping points, relationships between various physical and human systems).

With respect to preparedness education currently, most education programs focus on fairly simple themes related to "what you and your family can do to keep safe". While this is definitely a useful starting point, particularly for younger children, a systems perspective would go beyond that to help children develop an increasingly sophisticated understanding of the context of natural hazards. This includes complexities linked to this particular wicked problem. One main one is that human beings are part of the disaster cycle, not just passive recipients. We are part of the problem as well as part of the solution. Consistent with ideas linked to the UNISDR's CC-DRR approach [28], it can help children and adolescents become increasingly empowered with knowledge and skills that hazard events are challenges that can be approached *versus* avoided.

We see interactive components of education programs as one of their greatest strengths. As findings from our own research program have demonstrated, linking children's learning and enthusiasm with the family and home preparedness has potential in terms of both physical preparedness and emotional readiness. However, this link certainly merits extending beyond the school-youth-family network to the wider community [24]. Initiatives to promote increasing connectedness include collaborative networking between schools and others in a community [2]. These discussions have potential for increasing the discrepancy between the current status (e.g., low preparedness within the community) and an ideal status or goal, the increased protection of that local community (including its children) from those local hazards that threaten it. An area for future research is assessing the added value of preparedness education in schools as part of a larger community-based campaign (Our team is starting a three year project, 2014–2016, in the area of CC-DRR, funded by Australia's Bushfire and Natural Hazards Cooperative Research Centre. In particular, this project aims to inform practice, policy and research first through a large scale review and scoping process followed by development and evaluation of hazards education programming for children. One aim of this project is to move preparedness education programs to more systemic models as discussed in this paper. This includes linking preparedness education to community-level initiatives and solutions).

As it relates to children and families, and their increased risk status, such initiatives may well create road maps for a planned and effective household response to a disaster that includes linkages to larger community efforts. A systems approach to preparedness education can also promote outcomes for children that help them become increasingly effective, confident systems thinkers and doers and as they move towards adulthood. Those who are able to deal with specific problems like natural hazards but, equally, are also willing, able and ready to deal with a range of challenges that life presents.

Acknowledgments: The preparation of this paper was supported in part through funding from the Australian Bushfire and Natural Hazards Cooperative Research Centre and from the New Zealand Government in association with the Natural Hazards Research Platform.

Author Contributions: Both authors made contributions to this paper in accord with order of authorship. Kevin Ronan wrote the majority of the paper while Briony Towers contributed through adding her own expertise in working with children to each of the major sections of the manuscript to supplement, extend, provide an alternative view to early drafts.

Conflicts of Interest: The authors declare no conflict of interest.

References

1.   Nguyen, N.; Bosch, O. The art of interconnected thinking—Starting with the young. *Systems* **2014**, in press.
2.   Ronan, K.R.; Johnston, D.M. *Promoting Community Resilience in Disasters: The Role for Schools, Youth, and Families*; Springer: New York, NY, USA, 2005.

3. Ronan, K.R.; Crellin, K.; Johnston, D.M.; Finnis, K.; Paton, D.; Becker, J. Promoting child and family resilience to disasters: Effects, interventions, and prevention effectivenes. *Child. Youth Environ.* **2008**, *18*, 332–353.

4. Ronan, K.R.; Johnston, D.M.; Daly, M.; Fairley, R. School Children's Risk Perceptions and Preparedness: A Hazards Education Survey. Available online: http://www.massey.ac.nz/~trauma/issues/2001-1/ronan.htm (accessed on 8 October 2013).

5. Ronan, K.R.; Johnston, D.M. Correlates of hazard education programs for youth. *Risk Anal.* **2001**, *21*, 1055–1063.

6. Lindell, M.K.; Arlikatti, S.; Prater, C.S. Why people do what they do to protect against earthquake risk: Perceptions of hazard adjustment attributes. *Risk Anal.* **2009**, *29*, 1072–1088. [CrossRef]

7. Mileti, D.S.; Darlington, J.D. The role of searching in shaping reactions to earthquake risk information. *Soc. Probl.* **1997**, *44*, 89–103. [CrossRef]

8. Ollendick, T.H. Reliability and validity of the Revised Fear Survey Schedule for Children (FSSC-R). *Behav. Res. Ther.* **1983**, *21*, 685–692. [CrossRef]

9. Ollendick, T.H.; Matson, J.L.; Helsel, W.J. Fears in children and adolescents: Normative data. *Behav. Res. Ther.* **1985**, *23*, 465–467. [CrossRef]

10. Burnham, J.J.; Hooper, L.M.; Edwards, E.E.; Tippey, J.M.; McRaney, A.C.; Morrison, M.A.; Underwood, J.A.; Woodroof, E.K. Examining children's fears in the aftermath of Hurricane Katrina. *J. Psychol. Trauma* **2008**, *7*, 253–275. [CrossRef]

11. Norris, F.H.; Friedman, M.J.; Watson, P.J.; Byrne, C.M.; Diaz, E.; Kaniasty, K. 60,000 disaster victims speak: Part I. An empirical review of the empirical literature, 1981–2001. *Psychiatry* **2002**, *65*, 207–260.

12. Ronan, K.R. The Effects of a "Benign" Disaster: Symptoms of Post-Traumatic Stress in Children Following a Series of Volcanic Eruptions. Available online: http://www.massey.ac.nz/~trauma/issues/1997-1/ronan1.htm (accessed on 8 October 2013).

13. Hock, E.; Hart, M.; Kang, M.J.; Lutz, W.J. Predicting children's reactions to terrorist attacks: The importance of self-reports and pre-existing characteristics. *Am. J. Orthopsychiatr.* **2004**, *74*, 253–262. [CrossRef]

14. Huzziff, C.A.; Ronan, K.R. Prediction of Children's Coping Following a Natural Disaster—The Mount Ruapehu Eruptions: A Prospective Study. Available online: http://trauma.massey.ac.nz/issues/1999-1/huzziff1.htm (accessed on 8 October 2013).

15. Ronan, K.R. The effects of a series of volcanic eruptions on emotional and behavioural functioning in children with asthma. *N. Z. Med. J.* **1997**, *110*, 11–13.

16. Dadds, M.R.; Barrett, P.M.; Rapee, R.M.; Ryan, S. Family process and child anxiety and aggression: An observational analysis. *J. Abnorm. Child Psychol.* **1996**, *24*, 715–734. [CrossRef]

17. Siqueland, L.; Kendall, P.C.; Steinberg, L. Anxiety in children. *J. Clin. Child Psychol.* **1996**, *25*, 225–237. [CrossRef]

18. Karanci, N.; Aksit, B.; Dirik, G. Impact of community disaster awareness training program in Turkey: Does it influence hazard-related cognitions and preparedness behaviors. *Soc. Behav. Personal.* **2005**, *33*, 243–258. [CrossRef]

19. Kelly, B.; Ronan, K.R. Engaged *versus* passive public education for disaster preparedness. 2014; submitted for publication.

20. Paton, D. Disaster preparedness: A social-cognitive perspective. *Disaster Prev. Manag.* **2003**, *12*. [CrossRef]

21. Peek, L. Children and disasters: Understanding vulnerability, developing capacities, and promoting resilience—An introduction. *Child. Youth Environ.* **2008**, *18*, 1–29.

22. Johnson, V.A.; Ronan, K.R. Evaluations of disaster education programs for children: A methodological review. 2014; unpublished work.

23. Ronan, K.R.; Crellin, K.; Johnston, D.M. Community readiness for a new tsunami warning system: Quasi-experimental and benchmarking evaluation of a school education component. *Nat. Hazards* **2012**, *61*, 1411–1425. [CrossRef]

24. Shaw, R.; Shiwaku, K.; Kobayashi, H.; Kobayashi, M. Linking experience, education, perception, and earthquake preparedness. *Disaster Prev. Manag.* **2003**, *13*, 39–49.

25. Ronan, K.R.; Crellin, K.; Johnston, D.M. Correlates of hazards education for youth: A replication study. *Nat. Hazards* **2010**, *53*, 503–526. [CrossRef]

26. Ronan, K.R.; Johnston, D.M. Hazards education for youth: A quasi-experimental investigation. *Risk Anal.* **2003**, *23*, 1009–1020. [CrossRef]

27. Webb, M.; Ronan, K.R. A quasi-experimental investigation of a hazards education program for youth in a low SES community. 2014; submitted for publication.
28. Selby, D.; Kagawa, F. Disaster Risk Reduction in School Curricula: Case Studies from Thirty Countries. Geneva/Paris: UNICEF/UNESCO, 2012. Available online: http://www.educationandtransition.org/resources/unicefunesco-mapping-of-global-drr-integration-intoeducation-curricula-sustainability-frontiers/ (accessed on 8 October 2013).
29. Norris, F.; Stevens, S.P.; Pfefferbaum, B.; Wyche, K.; Pfefferbaum, R.L. Community resilience as a metaphor, theory, set of capacities, and strategy for disaster readiness. *Am. J. Community Psychol.* **2008**, *41*, 127–150. [CrossRef]
30. Johnson, V.A.; Ronan, K.R. Experiences of New Zealand school teachers and displaced children following the 2011 Christchurch Earthquake. *Nat. Hazards* **2014**, in press.
31. Helbing, D. Globallly networked risks and how to respond. *Nature* **2013**, *497*, 51–59. [CrossRef]
32. Salmon, P.M.; Goode, N.; Archer, F.; Spencer, C.; McArdle, D.; McClure, R. New perspectives on disaster response: The role of systems theory and methods. In Proceedings of the Australian and New Zealand Disaster and Emergency Management Conference, Brisbane, Australia, April 2012; pp. 353–367.
33. Australian Public Policy Commission. *Tacking Wicked Problems: A Public Policy Perspective*; Commonwealth of Australia: Canberra, Australia, 2007.
34. Adams, V.; van Hattum, T.; English, D. Chronic disaster syndrome: Displacement, disaster capitalism, and the eviction of the poor from New Orleans. *Am. Ethnol.* **2009**, *4*, 615–636.
35. Ashe, B.; Macaneney, K.J.; Pittman, A.J. Total cost of fire in Australia. *J. Risk Res.* **2009**, *12*, 121–136. [CrossRef]
36. Ashe, B.; de Oliveira, F.D.; McAneney, J. Investments in fire management: Does saving lives cost lives? *Agenda* **2012**, *19*, 89–103.
37. Ashe, B.; Macaneney, K.J.; Pittman, A.J. Is the allocation of resources towards mitigation and response to fire in Australia optimal? *J. Risk Res.* **2011**, *14*, 381–393. [CrossRef]
38. Brennan, P. Victims and survivors in fatal residential building fires. *Fire Mater.* **1999**, *23*, 305–310. [CrossRef]
39. Crompton, R.P.; McAneney, K.J.; Chen, K.; Pielke, R.A.; Haynes, K. Influence of location, population and climate on building damage and fatalities in Australian bushfire: 1925–2009. *Weather Clim. Soc.* **2010**, *2*, 300–310. [CrossRef]
40. McCormick, A.V. *Residential Fires in Surrey BC, 1988–2007*; School of Criminology and Criminal Justice, University of the Fraser Valley: Abbotsford, BC, Canada, 2009.
41. Ben-Zur, H. Coping, affect and aging: The roles of mastery and self-esteem. *Personal. Individ. Differ.* **2002**, *32*, 257–372. [CrossRef]
42. Pepper, S. *World Hypotheses*; University of California Press: Los Angeles, CA, USA, 1942.
43. Overton, W.F. A coherent metatheory for dynamic systems: Relational organicism-contextualism. *Hum. Dev.* **2006**, *50*, 154–159. [CrossRef]
44. Fortuin, K.P.J.; van Koppen, C.S.A.; Kroeze, C. The contribution of systems analysis to training students in cognitive interdisciplinary skills in environmental science education. *J. Environ. Stud.* **2013**, *3*, 139–152. [CrossRef]
45. Smith, C.A.; Kirby, L.D. Putting appraisal in context: Toward a relational model of appraisal and emotion. *Cognit. Emot.* **2009**, *23*, 1352–1372. [CrossRef]
46. Chapman, J.D.; Aspin, D.N. A problem-solving approach to addressing current global challenges in education. *Br. J. Educ. Stud.* **2013**, *61*, 49–62. [CrossRef]
47. Kagawa, F.; Selby, D. Ready for the storm: Education for disaster risk reduction and climate change adaptation and mitigation. *J. Educ. Sustain. Dev.* **2012**, *6*, 207–217. [CrossRef]
48. Blascovich, J. Challenge and Threat. In *Handbook of Approach and Avoidance Motivation*; Elliot, A.J., Ed.; Psychology Press: New York, NY, USA, 2008; pp. 431–445.
49. Frings, D.; Hurst, J.; Cleveland, C.; Blascovich, J.; Abrams, D. Challenge, threat, and subjective group dynamics: Reactions to normative and deviant group members. *Group Dyn. Theory Res. Pract.* **2012**, *16*, 105–121. [CrossRef]
50. Blascovich, J.; Mendes, W.B.; Seery, M. Intergroup Threat: A Multi-Method Approach. In *From Prejudice to Intergroup Emotions: Differentiated Reactions to Social Group*; Mackie, D.M., Smith, E.R., Eds.; Psychology Press: New York, NY, USA, 2002; pp. 89–109.

51. Blascovich, J.; Mendes, W.B. Challenge and Threat Appraisals: The Role of Affective Cues. In *Feeling and Thinking: The Role of Affect in Social Cognition*; Forgas, J.P., Ed.; Cambridge University Press: New York, NY, USA, 2000; pp. 59–82.

52. Oppenheimer, J.E. Understanding Early Vulnerabilities for Anxiety: Predictors of Self-Efficacy in Toddlers. Unpublished Ph.D. Dissertation, University of Oregon, Eugene, OR, USA.

53. Swann, J. *Learning, Teaching and Education Research in the 21st Century*; Continuum: London, UK, 2011.

54. Earth System Sciences Committee (ESSC). *Earth System Science: A Program for Global Change*; NASA: Washington, DC, USA, 1988.

55. Gagnon, V.; Bradway, H. Connecting earth systems: Developing holistic understanding through the Earth-System-Science model. *Sci. Scope* **2012**, *36*, 68–76.

56. Norris, F.H. Capacities that promote resilience. Plenary presentation: What makes a resilient community. In Proceedings of the Fourth Annual Department of Homeland Security Network Summit, Washington, DC, USA, March 2010.

57. Lerner, R. *Concepts and Theories of Human Development*, 3rd ed.; Lawrence Earlbaum: Mahwah, NJ, USA, 2002.

58. Kemmelmeier, M.; Broadus, A.D.; Padilla, J.B. Inter-group aggression in New Orleans in the immediate aftermath of Hurricane Katrina. *Anal. Soc. Issues Public Policy* **2008**, *8*, 211–245. [CrossRef]

59. Drury, J. Collective Resilience in Mass Emergencies and Disasters: A Social Identity Model. In *The Social Cure: Identity, Health and Well-Being*; Jetten, J., Haslam, C., Haslam, S.A., Eds.; Psychology Press: New York, NY, USA, 2012.

60. Tong, T.M.T.; Shaw, R.; Takeuchi, Y. Climate disaster resilience of the education sector in Thua Thien Hue Province, Central Vietnam. *Nat. Hazards* **2012**, *63*, 685–709. [CrossRef]

61. Clare, J.; Garis, L.; Plecas, D.; Jennings, C. Reduced frequency and severity of residential fires following delivery of fire prevention by on-duty fire fighters: Cluster randomized controlled study. *J. Saf. Res.* **2012**, *43*, 123–128. [CrossRef]

62. Goldratt, E.M.; Cox, J. *The Goal: A Process of Ongoing Improvement*; North River Press: Great Barrington, MA, USA, 2004.

63. Dettmer, H.W. *The Logical Thinking Process: A Systems Approach to Complex Problem Solving*; ASQ Quality Press: Milwaukee, WI, USA, 2007.

64. Rimal, R.N. Perceived risk and self-efficacy as motivators: Understanding individuals' long-term use of health information. *J. Commun.* **2002**, *51*, 633–657. [CrossRef]

65. Barlow, H.D.; Durand, V.M. *Abnormal Psychology: An Integrative Approach*, 5th ed.; Wadsworth/Cengage Learning: Belmont, CA, USA, 2009.

66. Chaffee, S.H.; Roser, C. Involvement and the consistency of knowledge, attitudes, and behaviors. *Commun. Res.* **1986**, *13*, 373–399. [CrossRef]

67. Yerkes, R.M.; Dodson, J.D. The relation of strength of stimulus to rapidity of habit formation. *J. Comp. Neurol. Psychol.* **1908**, *18*, 458–482.

68. Miller, W.R.; Rollnick, S. *Motivational Interviewing: Preparing People for Change*; Guilford Press: New York, NY, USA, 2002.

69. Prochaska, J.O.; DiClemente, C.C.; Norcross, J.C. In search of how people change: Applications to addictive behaviors. *Am. Psychol.* **1992**, *47*, 1102–1114. [CrossRef]

systems

MDPI

Communication

Organizational Learning in Health Care Organizations

Savithiri Ratnapalan * and Elizabeth Uleryk

Division of Emergency Medicine, Clinical Pharmacology & Toxicology, The Hospital for Sick Children, 555 University Avenue, Toronto, ON M5G 1X8, Canada; elizabeth.uleryk@sickkids.ca
* Author to whom correspondence should be addressed; savithiri.ratnapalan@sickkids.ca;
  Tel.: +416-813-7532; Fax: +416-813-5043.

Received: 7 January 2014; in revised form: 11 February 2014; Accepted: 17 February 2014;
Published: 24 February 2014

Abstract: The process of collective education in an organization that has the capacity to impact an organization's operations, performance and outcomes is called organizational learning. In health care organizations, patient care is provided through one or more visible and invisible teams. These teams are composed of experts and novices from diverse backgrounds working together to provide coordinated care. The number of teams involved in providing care and the possibility of breakdowns in communication and coordinated care increases in direct proportion to sophisticated technology and treatment strategies of complex disease processes. Safe patient care is facilitated by individual professional learning; inter-professional team learning and system based organizational learning, which encompass modified context specific learning by multiple teams and team members in a health care organization. Organizational learning in health care systems is central to managing the learning requirements in complex interconnected dynamic systems where all have to know common background knowledge along with shared meta-knowledge of roles and responsibilities to execute their assigned functions, communicate and transfer the flow of pertinent information and collectively provide safe patient care. Organizational learning in health care is not a onetime intervention, but a continuing organizational phenomenon that occurs through formal and informal learning which has reciprocal association with organizational change. As such, organizational changes elicit organizational learning and organizational learning implements new knowledge and practices to create organizational changes.

Keywords: organizational learning; system based learning; healthcare organizations; knowledge management

1. Introduction

"A health system consists of all organizations, people and actions whose primary intent is to promote, restore or maintain health" according to the World Health Organization WHO [1]. Health care systems vary by country and are financed by varying compositions of public and private sector funding. Health care organizations such as hospitals and academic health centers (university affiliated teaching hospitals) form a major component of a healthcare system, regardless of the country or funding arrangements.

Healthcare organizations are composed of health care professionals from multiple disciplines forming several interconnected care teams that strive to provide safe and consistent care [2]. The care teams have to coordinate and communicate amongst their team members and with other teams to function in a cohesive manner to execute the highly coordinated and high risk activity that is called patient care. Health care organizations have to be able to modify their activities based on sudden changes in the condition of their patients or sudden demands due to public health disasters such as pandemics (Severe Acute Respiratory Syndrome, 2002–2003), without compromising patient safety or quality of care. New knowledge creation, technology advances and other market changes can add new and unexpected demands in health care delivery. Health care organizations have to maintain stability following institutional protocols but have to assess their performance and evaluate protocols to create and incorporate new knowledge.

Organizational learning is described in several ways. It is said to be the cumulative product of the learning of small groups or teams [3]; and the collective learning that occurs in an organization that has the capacity to impact an organization's performance [4,5]. It is also described as a process of increasing organizational effectiveness and efficiency through shared knowledge and understanding [6], which is a system-level phenomenon that stays in the organization regardless of the changes in health care teams or team members [2,7].

Organizational learning can be viewed as a modified context specific learning by multiple teams and team members to translate knowledge to action and to evaluate those actions to create shared knowledge within an organization/institution. Individual and team learning complement organizational learning but do not produce organizational learning because these learnings often occurs in professional or team silos without knowledge sharing with other groups within an organization. Organizational learning can occur either as a result of organizational change or as a precursor to organizational change and has been explained by change or system's theories and knowledge management theories respectively.

Peter Senge, introduced the term "learning organization" a scenario in which people are continuously learning together for the best possible outcomes from the organization [8]. A successful learning organization in Senge's system's theory has the capacity to change and manage change where individuals in an organization adopt system thinking, attain personal mastery, share mental models, have a shared vision and learn in teams [7] Nonaka and Takeuchi proposed a model of organizational learning as the process of knowledge management where they discuss the knowledge spiral in which tacit knowledge of an individual becomes explicit knowledge through a process of socialization and externalization which is in turn disseminated through the organization which promotes the organization to learn [9].

The importance of organizational learning in health care systems is to provide the framework for complex interconnected dynamic systems where all operational units have to learn and execute their assigned functions to collectively improve safe patient care. Policies and procedures are developed in healthcare organizations to reduce errors and improve patient safety. Regulated health professional are expected to engage in continuing education to maintain and update knowledge and skills to provide safe patient healthcare as continuing education of health care professionals has shown to be related to improved patient outcomes [10]. Conversely, there is no explicit mandate to engage in continuing education for the support or administrative staff in healthcare institutions although many organizations provide and expect ongoing professional development to improve efficiency at an individual level or local level. Organizational learning forms the backdrop to weaving these diverse groups and mandates into a cohesive platform to advance patient care.

The delivery of quality patient care and patient safety is dependent on the healthcare system in which care is provided. For example, administrative staff such as registration clerks are crucial for timely registration before patient care is initiated. Patient service aids or housekeeping staff are responsible for cleaning patient rooms after discharge or transfer or the operation room after surgery, to get the rooms ready for the next patient. Stores and transport system staff are crucial for logistics of equipment, dressings, linen and several other items. As such, any improvements in efficiency have to include participation and learning among clinical, nonclinical and administrative staff who work within a system. A study examining a systems approach where multiple, multilevel clinical and administrative staff were involved in redesigning processes and roles has been shown to increase organizational capacity and efficiency in hospitals [11]. Identifying and including all diverse groups involved in the delivery of services in reducing waste and improving efficiency of the system using the "Lean methodology" been shown to increase efficiency and safety in healthcare institutions [12].

2. Teams within a Health Care Organization

Teams within a health care organization are not generally consistent in scale or membership. They can be homogenous and heterogeneous teams. Heterogeneity exits within what may be called a homogenous team such as a team of surgeons, where it may not be possible to replace one member with another, as training level, specialty and sub-specialties may vary. These teams can be visible teams that provide frontline patient care such as physicians and nurses or ancillary care teams such as phlebotomists, laboratory technicians, radiographers and radiologists or frontline nonclinical teams such as security, registration and information clerks, patient service aids, housekeeping, or invisible teams such as the biomedical engineering, information technology, kitchen staff or the plant operation team. These interconnections and interdependence are not apparent or appreciated in the large scope of daily activities. For example if the tube system that transport specimens and medications or the information technology (IT) systems that manages all the computers, telephone and paging systems in the hospital breakdown, there is a disruption and loss of communication, compromising standard care in a timely manner by frontline workers. As such the smooth functioning of a health care organization is dependent on multiple diverse teams learning and working towards a shared goal. There are several reports on improvements in the quality of healthcare and patient safety when inter-professional and team based learning have been implemented [13,14].

Health care organizations' central role is to provide safe and effective health care. They are equally charged with generating new knowledge and approaches to complex issues while educating future generations of health professionals. However, all healthcare institutions recognize that learning as an organization, is an essential function in complex organizations to manage and make system changes, Individual and team learning alone cannot produce the desired effect nor stave off stagnation which could threaten service excellence and patient safety. Individuals and teams in an organization do not learn the same thing at the same time. Information, knowledge transfer, experiences and processes are chosen and adapted to fit their own working environment to complete their task at hand [15]. Organizational learning occurs as the teams learn and execute a series of processes to produce the desired outcome and evaluate their outcomes to make changes in their processes and procedures.

This paper will describe organizational learning in health care in two contexts; the first as reaction to change or as a precursor to change, the second discussing the facilitators and barriers that influence organizational learning

3. Organizational Change Leading to Organizational Learning (Change Management)

Organizational learning is linked to organizational changes and its management of the change process [16]. Organizational change and restructuring due to economic and political reasons is becoming more common in many countries. In a recent survey, 88% of the 263 American hospitals that were surveyed, were engaged in restructuring changes to improve cost efficiencies, quality, or both [17]. This study showed that a "stronger orientation to learning and innovation had a statistically significant and positive relationship with the ability to sustain the restructuring changes and that a control orientation decreased organizational consensus on the perception of improved costs, but did increase perceptions of organizational ability to sustain the effort". Some of the factors identified as control in the study included "the importance to follow existing rules, avoiding risk, and using budgets to motivate employees". The authors caution that the usual habit of health care organizations to become more control oriented during times of change is not beneficial as it may create ineffective change [17].

Health care organizations have to be dynamic to accommodate changes to their system and service delivery models due to changing demands brought on by several factors but not limited to globalization, migration trends, travel and changing socio-cultural landscape of urban and rural areas.

For example the patient populations in several urban centers have changed requiring an increased use of translators to service the multicultural group. Translators need to communicate in a culturally sensitive manner and ascertain the breadth and variety of potential disease exposures endemic to the patient's home country. Healthcare staffs, through the interpreters, need to accurately convey the nuances of these interactions and find the right terms.

Similarly, if a change to improve ambulance wait times in emergency rooms (ER) is mandated, the whole organization has to learn and change its practices to make this happen. For example discharge delays can affect schedules for next day surgeries as bed availability for post operative care is compromised, which in turn results in either delaying or cancelling the surgery. The ripple effect of in-patient discharge delays also impacts ER bed availability as acute care beds are blocked by admitted patients. ER services are delayed and wait times are increased. Increased ER wait times and ER bed scarcity places a strain on emergency medical services (EMS) who need to re-route ambulances to other hospitals. As ER wait times increase, government funding may be withheld as in Canada or hospital may be fined as in the United Kingdom (UK) which impacts the financial health of the institution. The chain reaction of seemingly minor delays caused by late discharges affects the various internal and external arms of the health care system. Targeted quality improvement initiatives such as discharge planning schedules are prime candidates for organizational learning.

Adverse critical events such as privacy breaches or medical errors are some of the most unfortunate yet powerful reasons for health care organizations to reevaluate their practices and engage in organizational learning. The tragic death of Betsy Lehman from chemotherapy overdoses at The Dana Faber Cancer Institute, in Boston sent shock waves, across the institution, oncology community, and the public in 1995. The system changes that occurred at Dana-Faber Cancer Institute following this critical incident and the ongoing organizational learning to improve safe care were reflected in a 10-year report which shows the evolution of systems thinking and safety as a system property in a healthcare organization [6].

Learning from failures does not happen routinely in health care organizations and is hindered by pervasive barriers such as a lack of psychological safety and a culture of blame [3]. Leadership that accepts that failures are bound to happen, proactively develops context-specific strategies to prevent them and promote a culture of safety for admitting and reporting errors, facilitates organizational learning and consequently patient safety [18].

At times, systems changes can be the result of public efforts; for example the acknowledgement of the harmful effects of sleep deprivation on physicians' performance and shortening of duty hours in residency training in North America were due to a distraught father's relentless campaign following the death of his daughter from a drug prescription error [19].

Organizational change in health care does not happen in isolation; routine work is expected to continue during the change process. Iterative design methodology requires repeated testing and refinements which can affect performance [3]. To confound matters, disruptive innovations such as, robotic surgery, telemedicine, self monitoring and self management of chronic conditions such as diabetes, the use of ultrasound by non radiologists, reading glasses in retail stores, medical tourism and retail medical clinics are changing how health care is accessed by the public and delivered by the system. Many inpatient procedures are delivered in outpatient settings now and the need for hospital care is decreasing while home care needs are increasing. Health care organizations have to learn and change with these new innovations to survive the market changes [18].

4. Organizational Learning Leading to Organizational Changes (Knowledge Management)

Another approach to organizational learning associates the organizations' ability to actively create and use knowledge with outcomes [16]. Knowledge management is an important aspect of learning in health care organizations; as new discoveries and knowledge become available professionals in their respective fields will have to acquire, transmit, retain and use that knowledge. For example, until the mid 1990's surgery was the standard treatment for severe peptic ulcer disease. Organizational policies and procedures were in place to ensure patient safety for these surgeries. Surgeons practiced and perfected their skills to reduce operative complication and the rest of the team followed policies and procedures to ensure patient safety. The discovery that Helicobacter pylori infection is the cause of peptic ulcer disease by two Australian physicians changed the management for peptic ulcer disease from surgery to antibiotic therapy [20]. As such, peptic ulcer diseases became the responsibility of general practitioners and gastroenterologists with surgical teams being consulted only on rare occasions.

There is often a lag time between knowledge creation and knowledge translation in health care. The guideline movement and knowledge translation aspect of research in health care is intended to provide patients with the best evidence-based care in a timely manner. What is perceived as best patient care may change temporally and challenging the status quo and exploring alternate ways should be encouraged to provide the best possible patient care. In this example, it took almost a decade for basic research plus knowledge translation to intersect to drive a change in peptic ulcer disease treatment from cutting the vagus nerve to treating with antibiotics [21].

Institutional policies and protocols based on guidelines are expected to standardize routines, reduce errors and provide consistent care. However, health care organizations should be careful about strict adherence to policies and procedures as it will not promote new thinking and delay innovative discoveries and their use as illustrated by the following interview with Barry Marshall, who discovered Helicobacter pylori and was the winner of the Nobel prize for medicine in 1998.

"The courage to experiment"

"You're Australian, and you were working against a pretty strong North American medical group. Did that play into it?"

Barry Marshall: "Yes, and no. If I'd discovered the initial findings in the United States, I might have just discounted them. There's a very structured and very conventional gastroenterology program in the United States. If your head's just full of that conventional learning (50% of which is incorrect), it's very difficult to get a new concept in" [22].

5. Organizational Memory

Organizational learning also encompasses old knowledge and institutional memory that is held within organizations of how things were done and what the consequences were. The level of expertise and experience of nursing staff in a hospital, determines the infrastructure, functioning and learning as an organization [19]. Healthcare organizations have institutional memory which has traditionally been held by nurses and passed on verbally. Some of the practical knowledge from the nursing pool was compiled into institutional policies and procedures which were updated, modified or changed as needed. Nursing shortages seem to be a global phenomenon and shortage can lead to overwork, burn out and high turnover [12,23]. Burn out and high turnovers can negatively impact organizational learning as tacit knowledge transfer and institutional memory are compromised. As such, organizational learning has to be actively encouraged to share tacit knowledge and maintain institutional memory [24].

6. The Process of Organizational Learning

A qualitative study examined the process of organizational learning in primary health care innovation in two Canadian provinces studying how health care managers, physicians and other health professionals work and share knowledge. The authors conducted 170 interviews over 3 years and examined documents associated with each of the sites involved in primary health care innovation projects [15].

The authors found that organizations that were able to choose and adapt existing knowledge, experiences and processes (bricolage) to solve the problem at hand; implement supportive mechanism and create the "right kind of space" for learning; strengthen learning through experimenting; manage the rivalry between medical professionalism and management; and balance power differences by the local leaders were successful in facilitating both organizational learning and the spread new ideas on providing primary health care services [15]. The authors caution that "organizational learning takes time; patience and persistence are essential. Setbacks and challenges are inevitable, and finding ways to cope with them is an important factor in overall success" [15].

7. Leadership in Organizational Learning

Senior management and formal leaders such as "Chief Executive officers, Presidents, and Chiefs of Staff", sets the tone for institutional learning but middle management (line managers), such as divisional chiefs and unit leaders play a more important role in encouraging and supporting practical experiments and ensuring psychological safety to acknowledge and rectify individual and system issues [6].

Innovation in health care can often come from frontline workers and other informal leaders. Sister Ward a frontline worker observed that sunshine decreased neonatal jaundice. She shared this observation with Doctors R. H. Dobbs the consultant paediatrician and Cremer, the paediatric registrar, during a ward round [25]. This observation and other incidents where blood samples kept in the sunlight had reduced levels of bilirubin (the cause of neonatal jaundice) led to collaboration with the biochemist Mr. Perryman and his team, where they scientifically studied the effects of sunlight on serum bilirubin and developed the phototherapy lamps, which in turn revolutionized medical care of neonatal jaundice world-wide [26].

A second example from Bellevue hospital (New York City) illustrates a similar learning opportunity. Bellvue had strict protocols for treating infants with exchange transfusions if the total serum bilirubin levels (TSB) were above 25 and basing exchange transfusions on a test called salicylate displacement tests at lower levels, illustrates the role of informal leaders in system changes [27].

A child treated in the Bellevue NICU (Neonatal Intensive Care Unit) had an extremely high TSB (total serum bilirubin) (well over 20) but "ample sites" by salicylate displacement. As per protocol, he was not treated. The infant soon developed seizure like activity, an early manifestation of kernicterus. After this, the six senior residents decided to change protocol unofficially; for any TSB > 20, they would perform exchange transfusion regardless of salicylate binding results. To appease the NICU mandate, they continued to perform exchange transfusions in cases of low TSB but saturated albumin sites. In time, quality assurance tests revealed the poor reproducibility of salicylate displacement. Bellevue stopped doing the test but for years remained partial to exchange transfusion over phototherapy [27].

These six senior residents (postgraduate trainee physicians) were the informal leaders who evaluated their practice of performing exchange transfusions basing their decisions on the results of salicylate binding sites, a test of insignificant value, which resulted in a bad outcome for a baby. They were able to persuade their colleagues to follow their unofficial protocol to prevent another tragic outcome, until quality assurance studies found the test unreliable.

Informal network leaders are the community builders who weave organizations together. With little or no formal position or authority, they turn this weakness into strength by demonstrating commitment when they act from personal conviction [2,28]. These informal leaders can be bedside nurses, social workers in an inpatient ward, senior residents, attending staff physicians or any other healthcare professional with a passion to make a change to improve patient care. They have to be able to convince and create a team to address the cause, assign responsibilities and accountability, make the changes and evaluate outcomes to foster organizational learning [29]. It is important that senior management ensures that line managers do not stifle these informal leaders by their rigid adherence to what they consider unbreakable rules and priority projects.

Local unofficial leaders are also called opinion leaders or educational influentials in medical education literature. A systematic review of 18 studies involving close to 300 hospitals and over 300 primary care practices showed that the use of "opinion leaders alone or in combination with other interventions may successfully promote evidence-based practice; effectiveness of the interventions varied both within and between studies" [24]. Informal leaders and opinion leaders are important to promote, sustain and evaluate organizational learning within each group of professionals or teams. For example, to sustain a hand hygiene guideline implementation aimed at reducing spread of infection in a hospital, informal local leadership will be needed at each and every department, division, unit, ward, clinical and nonclinical area, to promote, monitor and evaluate the initiative. The success of the initiative depends on it being a system wide practice so that hand hygiene is observed even in a non-patient care area such as the hospital library. If a librarian touched a door knob on her way to work and does not practice hand hygiene in the library, she can spread the infection through other clinical staff who frequent the library.

8. Conclusion

Health care professionals have the responsibility to look after the interests of their patients, the public, the profession and the organization in that order. As healthcare systems respect and advocate this hierarchy of accountability, patient safety and quality care becomes part of the system. Organizational learning in health care should focus on understanding how it was done, perfecting how it is done and exploring how it can be done to optimize patient care without compromising patient safety.

Acknowledgments: The authors wish to thank Suba Sivakumar, at The Center for Engineering Education Research, Michigan State University, for her for their insightful comments and contributions to the manuscript.

Author Contributions: Savithiri Ratnapalan was responsible for the conception, design, drafting the article, revising it critically and final approval of the version to be published. Elizabeth Uleryk was responsible for the design, revising it critically and final approval of the version to be published.

Conflicts of Interest: The authors declare no conflict of interest.

References

1. World Health Organization (WHO). Everybody's Business. Strengthening Health Systems to Improve Health Outcomes: WHO's Framework for Action. Available online: http://www.who.int/healthsystems/strategy/everybodys_business.pdf (accessed on 7 January 2014).
2. Peirce, J.C. The paradox of physicians and administrators in health care organizations. *Health Care Manag. Rev.* **2000**, *25*, 7–28. [CrossRef]
3. Levinthal, D.A.; March, J.G. The myopia of learning. *Strat. Manag. J.* **1993**, *14*, 95–112. [CrossRef]
4. Goh, S.C.; Chan, C.; Kuziemsky, C. Teamwork, organizational learning, patient safety and job outcomes. *Int. J. Health Care Qual. Assur.* **2013**, *26*, 420–432. [CrossRef]
5. Bapuji, H.; Crossan, M. From questions to answers: Reviewing organizational learning research. *Manag. Learn.* **2004**, *35*, 397–417. [CrossRef]
6. Conway, J.B.; Weingart, S.N. *Organizational Change in the Face of Highly Public Errors. I. The Dana-Farber Cancer Institute Experience*; Agency for Healthcare Research and Quality: Rockville, MD, USA. Available online: http://www.webmm.ahrq.gov/perspective.aspx?perspectiveID=3 (accessed on 7 January 2014).
7. Krejci, J.W. Imagery: Stimulating critical thinking by exploring mental models. *J. Nurs. Educ.* **1997**, *36*, 482–484.
8. Senge, P.M. *The Fifth Discipline: The Art and Practice of the Learning Organization*; Doubleday/Currency: New York, NY, USA, 1990.
9. Nonaka, I.; Toyama, R.; Konno, N. SECI, *Ba* and leadership: A unified model of dynamic knowledge creation. *Long Range Planning* **2000**, *33*, 5–34. [CrossRef]
10. Mazmanian, P.E.; Davis, D.A.; Galbraith, R.; American College of Chest Physicians Health and Science Policy Committee. Continuing medical education effect on clinical outcomes: Effectiveness of continuing medical education: American College of Chest Physicians Evidence-Based Educational Guidelines. *Chest* **2009**, *135*, 49S–55S. [CrossRef]
11. MacKenzie, R.; Capuano, T.; Durishin, L.D.; Stern, G.; Burke, J.B. Growing organizational capacity through a systems approach: One health network's experience. *Joint Comm. J. Qual. Patient Saf.* **2008**, *34*, 63–73.
12. Kimsey, D.B. Lean methodology in health care. *AORN J.* **2010**, *92*, 53–60. [CrossRef]

13. Wilhelmsson, M.; Pelling, S.; Uhlin, L.; Owe Dahlgren, L.; Faresjo, T.; Forslund, K. How to think about interprofessional competence: A metacognitive model. *J. Interprof. Care* **2012**, *26*, 85–91. [CrossRef]

14. Pettifer, A.; Cooper, J.; Munday, D. Teaching interprofessional teamwork in palliative care—A values-based approach. *J. Palliat. Care* **2007**, *23*, 280–285.

15. Reay, T.; Casebeer, A.; Golden-Biddle, K.; Hinings, C.R.; Denis, J.-L.; Lamothe, L.; Langley, A. Organizational Learning in Primary Health Care Innovation. Available online: http://www.business. ualberta.ca/TrishReay/Research/~/media/business/FacultyAndStaff/SMO/TrishReay/Documents/ CIHR78710OrganizationalLearning.ashx (accessed on 7 January 2014).

16. Aramburu, N.; Saenz, J.; Rivera, O. Organizational learning, change process, and evolution of management systems: Empirical evidence from the basque region. *Learn. Organ.* **2006**, *13*, 434–454. [CrossRef]

17. Walston, S.; Chou, A.F. CEO perceptions of organizational consensus and its impact on hospital restructuring outcomes. *J. Health Organizat. Manag.* **2011**, *25*, 176–194.

18. Christensen, C.M.; Bohmer, R.; Kenagy, J. Will disruptive innovations cure health care? *Harv. Bus. Rev.* **2000**, *78*, 102–112.

19. McCall, T.B. No turning back: A blueprint for residency reform. *JAMA* **1989**, *261*, 909–910. [CrossRef]

20. Warren, J.R.; Marshall, B. Unidentified curved bacilli on gastric epithelium in active chronic gastritis. *Lancet* **1983**, *321*, 1273–1275. [CrossRef]

21. Ratnapalan, S. Cutting the vagus nerve: Clinical practice and research in medicine. *Can. Fam. Physician* **2008**, *54*, 748.

22. Academy of Achievement. Interview: Barry Marshall—Nobel Prize in Medicine. Available online: http://www.achievement.org/autodoc/printmember/mar1int-1 (accessed on 7 January 2014).

23. Donald, J. What makes your day? A study of the quality of worklife of OR nurses. *Can. Oper. Room Nurs. J.* **1999**, *17*, 17–27.

24. Flodgren, G.; Parmelli, E.; Doumit, G.; Gattellari, M.; O'Brien, M.A.; Grimshaw, J.; Eccles, M.P. Local opinion leaders: effects on professional practice and health care outcomes. *Cochrane Database Syst. Rev.* **2011**. [CrossRef]

25. Cremer, R.J.; Perryman, P.W.; Richards, D.H. Influence of light on the hyperbilirubinaemia of infants. *Lancet* **1958**, *1*, 1094–1097.

26. Dobbs, R.H.; Cremer, R.J. Phototherapy. *Arch. Dis. Child.* **1975**, *50*, 833–836. [CrossRef]

27. Weiss, E.M.; Zimmerman, S.S. A tale of two hospitals: The evolution of phototherapy treatment for neonatal jaundice. *Pediatrics* **2013**, *131*, 1032–1034. [CrossRef]

28. Carroll, J.S.; Edmondson, A.C. Leading organisational learning in health care. *Qual. Saf. Health Care* **2002**, *11*, 51–56. [CrossRef]

29. Bohmer, R.M. Leading clinicians and clinicians leading. *New Engl. J. Med.* **2013**, *368*, 1468–1470. [CrossRef]

![systems logo] *systems* MDPI

Article

Emergy Evaluation of Formal Education in the United States: 1870 to 2011 †

Daniel E. Campbell [1],* and Hongfang Lu [2]

[1] USEPA, Office of Research and Development, National Health and Environmental Effects Research Laboratory, Atlantic Ecology Division, 27 Tarzwell Drive, Narragansett, RI 02882, USA

[2] South China Botanical Garden, Chinese Academy of Sciences, 723 Xingke Rd., Tianhe District, Guangzhou 510650, China; luhf@scbg.ac.cn

* Author to whom correspondence should be addressed; campbell.dan@epa.gov; Tel.: +1-401-782-3195; Fax: +1-401-782-3030.

† An earlier version of this article "Campbell, D.E.; Lu, H.F. The Emergy Basis for Formal Education in the United States. In *Emergy Synthesis 5, Theory and Applications of the Emergy Methodology*; Brown, M.T., Sweeney, S., Campbell, D.E., Huang, S.L., Ortega, E., Rydberg, T., Tilley, D.R., Ulgiati, S., Eds.; The Center for Environmental Policy, University of Florida: Gainesville, FL, USA, 2009" was presented at the 5th Biennial Emergy Research Conference, Gainesville, FL, USA, January 2008.

Received: 2 April 2014; in revised form: 4 July 2014; Accepted: 16 July 2014; Published: 24 July 2014

Abstract: We evaluated the education system of the United States from 1870 to 2011 using emergy methods. The system was partitioned into three subsystems (elementary, secondary and college/university education) and the emergy inputs required to support each subsystem were determined for every year over the period of analysis. We calculated the emergy required to produce an individual with a given number of years of education by summing over the years of support needed to attain that level of education. In 1983, the emergy per individual ranged from 8.63E+16 semj/ind. for a pre-school student to 165.9E+16 semj/ind. for a Ph.D. with 2 years of postdoctoral experience. The emergy of teaching and learning per hour spent in this process was calculated as the sum of the emergy delivered by the education and experience of the teachers and the emergy brought to the process of learning by the students. The emergy of teaching and learning was about an order of magnitude larger than the annual emergy supporting the U.S. education system (*i.e.*, the emergy inflows provided by the environment, energy and materials, teachers, entering students, goods and services). The implication is that teaching and learning is a higher order social process related to the development and maintenance of the national information cycle. Also, the results imply that there is a 10-fold return on the emergy invested in operating the education system of the United States.

Keywords: emergy evaluation; formal education; teaching and learning; United States

---

1. Introduction

Emergy is a universal accounting quantity, which was derived by Odum [1] (Chapter 3) from the first and second laws of thermodynamics and Lotka's maximum power principle [2–4]. In this paper, the evaluation of the formal education system of the United States was carried out by first determining the available energy, material, and information inputs used up both directly and indirectly to make a product or service within the U.S. education system in their native units (e.g., joules, grams, *etc.*) and then converting these quantities to solar emjoules (semj) by multiplying by the appropriate UEV or emergy per unit value (e.g., semj/J, semj/g, semj/$). The emergy unit is the solar emjoule, which is a solar equivalent joule that has been used in the past as contrasted with a joule of available energy within a product or service, which is potential energy that can be used in the present.

Odum characterized human beings as Earth's information processors [1]. He pointed out that humans arose late in the evolutionary process of the Earth and that they have highly developed

Systems **2014**, 2, 328–365

information processing organs and use social mechanisms for group information processing, e.g., art, music, sports, *etc.* Perhaps because of their facility in developing and using information, as well as, the opening of vast fossil energy resources for use in supporting human activities in the Industrial Age, human beings have come to control many of the living and nonliving system operations on the surface of the Earth. For this reason, the world has become a human-dominated system [5–7], in which human agency accounts for and controls the majority of many material and energy flows [8,9] of the biogeosphere. Because of the magnitudes of anthropic effects on the environment and anthropic demands for environmental resources to support economic and social activities, discovering more accurate methods for valuing the contributions of the environment to human wellbeing has become an imperative for ecological-economic research.

Past research has shown that the environmental, economic, and social costs and benefits of alternative economic and environmental policies can be quantified in equivalent terms based on the relative ability of various individuals, products and services to perform work in a system [1,10–13]. These equivalent work potentials are measured by emergy, which is quantified as the available energy of one kind, e.g., solar joules, that is used-up in the process of making a product or service. In this paper, we used the standard calculation methods for quantifying emergy (Odum 1996) [1] to estimate the emergy delivered to the system in the knowledgeable work of people, which underlies all kinds of human service; and which, at present, is most often measured in terms of money. The end result of determining the emergy required to produce individuals with varying amounts of knowledge (*i.e.*, as measured in this study by an individual's education) is that we will be able to estimate the emergy potentially delivered to a national system, e.g., the United States, by individuals employed in the workforce. When this information is applied in an emergy evaluation, it will result in more accurately quantifying the relative contributions of the work of people and the work of the environment in operating a system such as the United States.

An assumption underlying the potential usefulness of the results reported in this paper is that the work performed by individuals in carrying out economic and social activities is primarily a function of their knowledge and experience. Thus, we assume that the knowledgeable work done by people employed in social and economic activities underlies all kinds of human service. The work done by people is dependent on a storage of information (*i.e.*, their knowledge and experience), which requires an information cycle [1,14] for its development and maintenance. Because of the operation of the second law of thermodynamics, which causes the degradation of information carriers and the pressure for innovation caused by evolutionary competition, all living systems include an information cycle, which is needed to maintain the information controlling the structure and function of the system and to prevail in competition with other systems. The information maintenance cycle includes the following processes: depreciation, extraction, copying, dispersion of copies, operation, testing in use and selection [1] (Figure 12.2). As a result, human knowledge and experience have unique properties that require us to consider the role of time in their creation. First, the knowledge base of an individual or of a nation cannot be generated in the course of a single year, which is the standard temporal unit used for most emergy analyses. In general, individuals go through many years of school or other training, while they accumulate enough knowledge to profitably enter the workforce. In a similar manner, the stored knowledge and experience of the people of a nation cannot be generated quickly. Even if the information has been derived earlier in another time and location, it still requires at least a generation for those trained in the various fields of knowledge to reach their full potential and to train the next generation of students to establish a more advanced level of knowledge in the system.

A second unique aspect of human knowledge is that it is not diminished by use; in fact, it increases as individuals learn more about their fields through the application of what they have learned. Thus, the information that individual workers contribute grows throughout their career and as a result the emergy of their knowledge increases as does the transformity of their work, *i.e.*, the emergy delivered per joule of metabolic work. The storage of knowledge and experience of a people is diminished, ultimately, by death. In addition, unemployment and sickness diminish its application in carrying out economic and social activities in any given year. Retirement changes the way that the knowledge of an individual is used by society and, sadly, aging begins to erode the knowledge of many.

The work of people with varying levels of education and experience plays a fundamental role in determining the kinds of economic and social activities that can be carried out within a system. The emergy required for much, but not all, of the information stored in human knowledge can be evaluated through an analysis of the formal education system of a nation. In this study, we evaluated the formal education system of the United States from 1870 to 2011 using emergy methods [1,15] to provide information critical for establishing the equivalence between the emergy contributed to a system by the work of people and the emergy contributed to the system by the work of the environment. This study is also the second step on a research path to produce an integrated method of environmental accounting based on a combined emergy-money unit as defined in [16].

In this study, we assumed that a person is paid for the information (knowledge and experience) that they deliver in their work, and that the emergy equivalent of this information can be calculated by summing the emergy required for the education of an individual up to a particular time. First, we determined the emergy required annually to support each level of education, *i.e.*, elementary, secondary, and college/university. Second, we calculated the emergy required to train an individual up to the various levels of education of interest to us, *i.e.*, pre-school through the professional and doctoral degrees. This was accomplished by summing the emergy required to support a student each year, over the years that the student spent in school up to the time when they graduate or dropout. Finally, we estimated the emergy required for the process of teaching and learning at elementary, secondary and college/university levels, *i.e.*, the cumulative emergy of the students and teachers brought to the classroom. The activity of teaching and learning was found to be a higher order social process dependent on the emergy required for the transfer and reproduction of information. We provided a table of Unit Emergy Values (UEVs) for individuals with various levels of education from 1870 to 2011 for use in subsequent emergy analyses.

2. Prior Methods and Studies Related to the Evaluation of the Emergy of Human Service

Odum (1996) [1] applied the term "human service" to a broad spectrum of human activities including the emergy delivered by different levels of education and experience, emergy accounting for schools and universities, the emergy of teaching and learning, the emergy of television and information transfer (e.g., the internet), and the emergy in culture. In this study we consider the first three aspects of human service listed above. In general, human service of all kinds is often a high quality (*i.e.*, high transformity or high emergy per unit available energy) feedback, interacting with lower quality material and energy resources to make value added products of intermediate transformity.

Our concern in this paper is primarily with ways of quantifying the work done by individuals with various amounts of knowledge and experience, *i.e.*, in this case, with varying levels of education. For example, money, *i.e.*, income and wages, is only paid to people for their work and as a result the emergy of "human service" can be approximated by multiplying the money flow accompanying the work performed in carrying out a given task by the emergy to money ratio of the system within which the work was performed. However, Odum [1] states that this method is only valid when the service is performed by a person with the average level of knowledge and experience found in the system being evaluated. Another method that Odum [1,17,18] used to evaluate the work delivered by people with different amounts of knowledge and experience was to divide the total national emergy flow (or national empower as semj/y) in a given year by the number of people that possessed a given level of education or higher. In this method he calculated the emergy per individual based on the number of people in the population who have attained a given number of years of education. The transformity (semj/J) of an individual's labor was then determined by dividing the annual metabolic energy (J) of an individual into the emergy (semj) of an individual with a given level of knowledge. Odum [1] (p. 232) presents the results of this calculation for the United States in 1983.

Systems **2014**, *2*, 328–365

Both of these methods of estimating the emergy delivered in the work of people are rough approximations. The commonly used method of multiplying the money flows by the emergy to money ratio essentially uses the information of the money flow to scale the emergy estimate, rather than the process that Odum [1] originally defined, which was to use the emergy flows to scale the money flows in an economy, thereby showing the source of buying power. The second method may be more accurate, because it is based on the emergy flows supporting the national system in a given year. However, it is based on the assumption that the knowledge system of the nation is in steady state and that the current cumulative distribution of people who have attained a given number of years of education can be taken as the output of the education process. This calculation method implies that all the emergy inputs to the nation in a given year and only those inputs are required to produce all the people that have attained a given number of years of education or greater. However, since the data demonstrate that the U.S. national education system has not been in a steady state over the period from 1870 to 2011 and since we show that there is a time requirement for the creation of knowledge, a more accurate method for determining the emergy required for the knowledge and experience delivered by an individual's work may be to analyze the education system required to generate and transfer knowledge.

In an earlier version of this paper, we developed and applied a more accurate method of assessing the emergy of education levels in the U.S. based on evaluation of detailed models of elementary, secondary, and college/university education in the nation from 1870 to 2006 [19]. In this study, we used modeling methods to construct the time series of data needed to evaluate the system. Also, we accessed most of the data from the U.S. Statistical Abstracts 1870 to 2009 [20], which combined with key additional data sources allowed us to calculate and then sum the emergy requirements for each level of education over the time in school to gain a particular degree or level of training. In the present study we have reported, for the first time, five additional years of data (2007 to 2011), which allowed us to examine the effects that the Great Recession of 2008 (GR08) had on the education system of the U.S., and to check and refine our earlier methods and calculations so as to increase the accuracy of the results.

Berquist *et al.* [21] pointed out that a complete approach to evaluating human knowledge must be able to evaluate local traditional and informal knowledge [22,23] as well as formal education. They proposed that the calculation of UEVs for human labor should consider four factors: caloric intake, the quantity and quality of knowledge, how knowledge is transferred between individuals and in the broader society, and the cultural context within which the knowledge is applied. They illustrated this process with a hypothetical calculation of the development and transfer of knowledge of millet farming in a traditional system of subsistence agriculture. However, they state that we [19] believe "that human knowledge is created when individuals carry out economic processes … ", rather we would say that human knowledge is applied or in some cases accumulated (e.g., through education) in the system when individuals carry out economic processes. In one sense, the authors of [21] are correct, because knowledge is created when economic processes are carried out to the extent that learning through experience occurs as the work is done. Furthermore our research implies that knowledge is created within the social and cultural context of all education systems (formal, traditional, or informal) supported by the emergy of the resource inputs needed to carry out the process of teaching and learning. Thus, in this study and in [19] we used a similar approach to that put forward in [21] to evaluate formal education in the U.S. However, in our study we assumed that the available energy expended in metabolic work of an individual delivers the emergy of that individual's knowledge and experience to perform a task, for which they have been trained.

Abel's work on expanding the scale of estimates for the transformities of human work [24] established by Odum [1,18] based on education level are relevant to this study. Abel [24] applied Odum's method to quantify the emergy supporting various levels of social organization in the world as a whole. In this way he estimated transformities for a range of individuals from the world's poor to the world's super elites, *i.e.*, the 55 most powerful people in the world. This hypothetical calculation was based on a global emergy inflow of 15.83E+24 semj/y and a world population of 6.11 billion people, allowing for nine levels of transformity from 5.5 billion to 55 individuals with the first level split into two parts, 1 billion poor and 4.5 billion others. Abel [24] argued that the household, not school, might provide a better location for evaluating the production of people. He calculated household emergies in a county, and produced an emergy pyramid or hierarchy using the data. While he did not calculate an associated hierarchy of human transformities, he did calculate one transformity (for the average household) as a demonstration of the method that could be used at every location in the hierarchy.

3. Models of the U.S. Education System and of Teaching and Learning

Education covers a portion of Odum's [1,14,18] model of the information cycle. We agree with Abel [25] (Figure 8), who represented formal education within the information cycle model of Odum [1]. In this model [25], formal education covers that part of the information cycle in which information is selected from operating systems through a determination of what is successful within the existing milieu of society and science. Teachers then extract this working information in accordance with their various disciplines into a form that can be communicated to students through the process of teaching and learning, *i.e.*, the reproduction of knowledge or copying. Graduates containing the copied information are then released back into the world once they leave the education system, carrying their part of the shared information to use in operating the system. The university education system plays an additional role in the information cycle, in that part of its work is the creation of new knowledge in the cycle as shown in [1] (Figure 12.1). This aspect of the U.S. education system is not evaluated in this study.

3.1. Model of the U.S. Education System

An Energy Systems Language, (ESL) model [26] of the education system of the United States is presented in Figure 1, where the system is divided into three subsystems: elementary, secondary, and college/university education. Each subsystem has its own inputs and outputs, which are quantified in the figure using values for 1983. We chose 1983 as the year to illustrate our calculations, because this was the year upon which Odum [1] based his initial evaluation of the U.S. education system. Each pathway is also marked with a pathway coefficient, the subscripted letter, k; which in turn is entered as a line item in Table 1, where the definition of the pathway is given along with its value. The letter k with the same subscript is repeated for similar flows in each subsystem. While the model was evaluated for 1983, values for the model output in any year can be found by consulting Appendix B given below.

The emergy inputs required to run the U.S. education system at each level are shown as emergy flows from external sources or from internal storages that enter the box marked "Operations" (Figure 1). Sources include the emergy inputs from: the environment, k_0; the energy used to operate the system, k_1; the energy, k_9, and the materials (lumber, paper, chemicals, petroleum products, stone, glass, concrete, primary metal and fabricated metal), k_{10}, used in building construction; the new students enrolling in school, k_5; students returning to school, k_6; the goods used in construction (*i.e.*, machinery except electrical, electrical machinery, instruments and related, misc. manufactured items), k_{11}; the services used in construction, k_{12}; the goods and services used to operate the schools, k_3; libraries and equipment, k_4; and teachers, k_7. The total annual emergy supporting the education carried out within a subsystem is given by the pathway coefficient, k_8. The outputs of the education systems are graduates, k_{15}, and dropouts, k_{14}. College/University (Figure 1c) was evaluated as a combined system with outputs ranging from a two year associate degree, k_{14}; through college graduates, k_{15}; master's degree, k_{16}; 3-year professional degree, k_{17}; to the Ph.D., k_{18}. College dropouts, k_{14}, were assumed to have, on average, an education equivalent to the 2-year degree. The emergy per individual was modeled based on the time that a student remains in school. Thus, the difference between a Ph.D. and an average dropout with two years of college is the emergy required to support the doctoral graduate in the school system for an additional 6 years. Doctoral candidates, who spend more time in school or who complete post-doctoral fellowships, have greater emergy per individual. We also determined the emergy of individuals who had had 2 years of postdoctoral experience and the emergy required for medical doctors (not shown in Figure 1c), who generally spend 4 years in medical school followed by a year internship and an average residency of 4 years. Assuming a 30 year replacement time for school buildings, the depreciation in a given year (for example, k_2 in Figure 1c) represents the contribution of college infrastructure to the emergy required for the education process. Books and equipment are shown as a separate storage for all subsystems, but because of the limited data available, libraries were the only aspect of this storage that we quantified explicitly, and this was done only for colleges/universities. The storage of books and equipment was quantified as part of the general expenditures on services for the other subsystems, and the emergy of the equipment in college buildings was included as a part of overall college services.

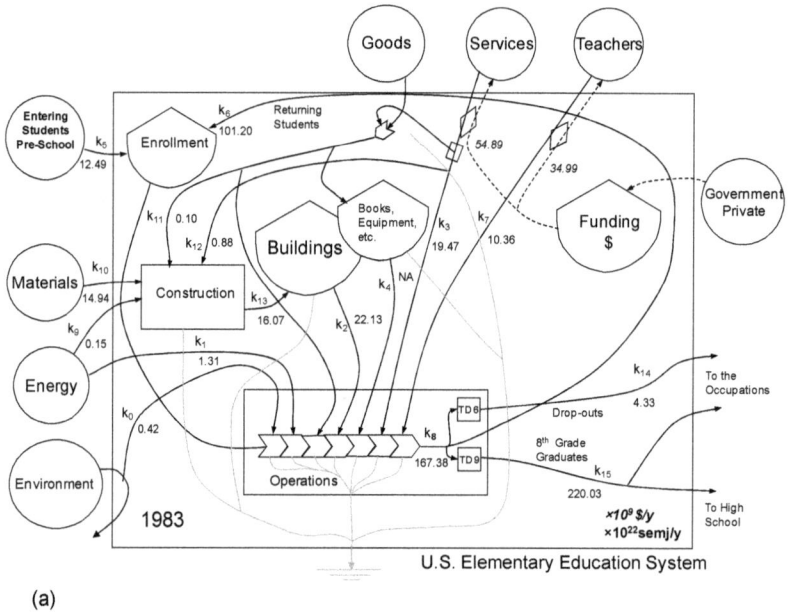

(a)

Figure 1. *Cont.*

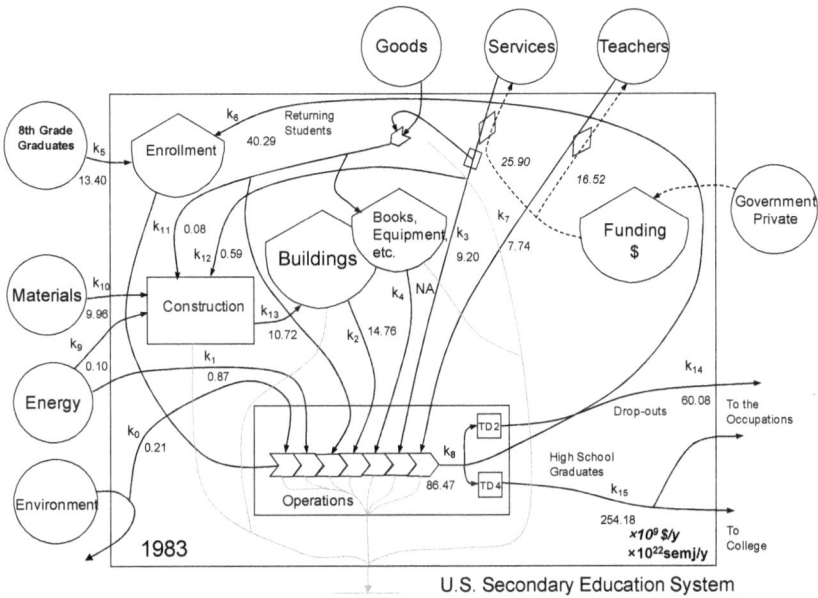

(b)

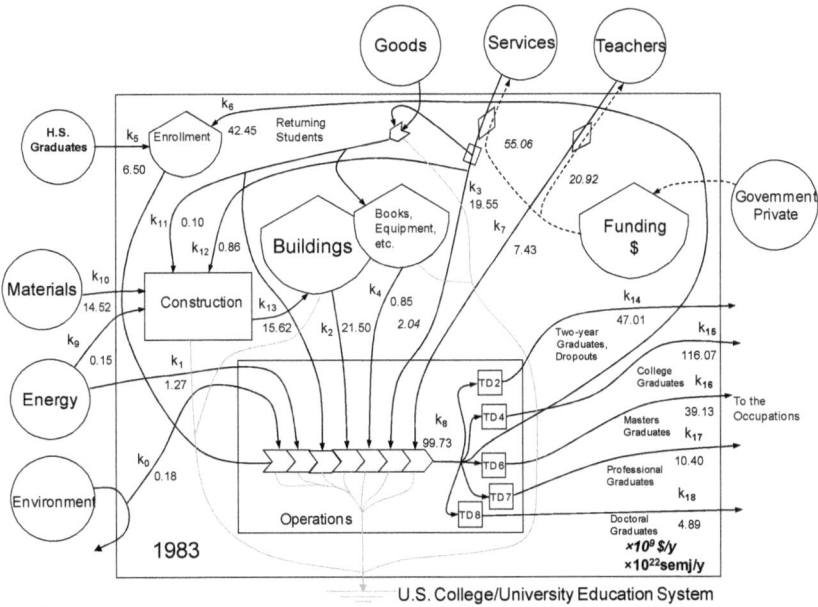

(c)

Figure 1. An evaluated Energy Systems Language (ESL) [26] diagram of the formal education system of the United States showing three subsystems: (**a**) Elementary education, kindergarten to eighth grade; (**b**) Secondary education, grades 9 to 12; (**c**) College/University education. The values on the diagram are for 1983 and the model pathways are defined in Table 1. Plain text is emergy flow in solar emjoules per year $\times 10^{22}$ (semj/yr) and italics shows annual money flows in nominal dollars $\times 10^{9}$ ($/yr).

Table 1. Definition of the pathways in the ESL models of the education subsystems of the United States (Figure 1). Note the emergy of k_0 to k_7 sum to k_8 the annual emergy required for school operation at an education level, the emergy of k_{14} dropouts and k_{15} to k_{18} school completers is the sum of the emergy support over the years spent in school (1983 + all prior years), and k_9 to k_{13} evaluate building construction put in place in that year.

Pathway	Definition of Emergy Flow	Value $\times 10^{22}$ (semj/y)
Elementary Education (Figure 1a)		
k_0	Renewable resources used on the school grounds	0.42
k_1	Consumption of fuel and electricity to run the schools	1.31
k_2	Depreciation of school buildings (0.0333 per year)	22.13
k_3	Service support required in addition to teachers	19.47
k_4	Books and equipment (lumped with other services in k_3)	NA
k_5	Support for pre-school students entering school in the fall	12.49
k_6	Support for students returning to school in the fall	101.20
k_7	Support for teachers (purchased with their salaries)	10.36
k_8	Total emergy required to support elementary education	167.38
k_9	The energy used in building construction	0.15
k_{10}	The materials used in building construction	14.94
k_{11}	Goods purchased for building construction	0.10
k_{12}	Services used in building construction	0.88
k_{13}	Total emergy of new construction	16.07
k_{14}	Emergy of dropouts with an average fifth grade education	4.33
k_{15}	Emergy of students completing the eighth grade	220.03
Secondary Education (Figure 1b)		
k_0	Renewable resources used on the school grounds	0.21
k_1	Consumption of fuel and electricity to run the schools	0.87
k_2	Depreciation of school buildings (0.0333 per year)	14.76
k_3	Service support required in addition to teachers	9.20
k_4	Books and equipment (lumped with other services in k_3)	NA
k_5	Support for eighth grade graduates entering high school in the fall	13.40
k_6	Support for high school students returning to school in the fall	40.29
k_7	Support for teachers (purchased with their salaries)	7.74
k_8	Total emergy required to support high school education	86.47
k_9	The energy used in building construction	0.10
k_{10}	The materials used in building construction	9.96
k_{11}	Goods purchased for building construction	0.11
k_{12}	Services used in building construction	0.59
k_{13}	Total emergy of new construction	10.72
k_{14}	Emergy of dropouts with an average 10th Grade education	60.08
k_{15}	Emergy of students completing high school	254.18
College/University (Figure 1c)		
k_0	Renewable resources used on the school grounds	0.18
k_1	Consumption of fuel and electricity to run the schools	1.27
k_2	Depreciation of school buildings (0.0333 per year)	21.50
k_3	Service support required in addition to teachers	19.55
k_4	Library books	0.85
k_5	Support for high school graduates entering college in the fall	6.50
k_6	Support for college students returning to school in the fall	42.45
k_7	Support for teachers (purchased with their salaries)	7.43
k_8	Total emergy required to support college education	99.73
k_9	The energy used in building construction	0.15
k_{10}	The materials used in building construction	14.52
k_{11}	Goods purchased for building construction	0.10
k_{12}	Services used in building construction	0.86
k_{13}	Total emergy of new construction	15.62
k_{14}	Emergy of associate degrees and college dropouts	47.01
k_{15}	Emergy of college graduates	116.09
k_{16}	Emergy of masters graduates	39.13
k_{17}	Emergy of professional graduates	10.40
k_{18}	Emergy of doctoral graduates	4.89

3.2. Model of Teaching and Learning

Following the ideas of Odum (1996) [1] the higher order social process of teaching and learning (Figure 2) is modeled as a system interaction, in which a few high quality transmitters (the teachers) transfer information to many lower quality receivers (the students).

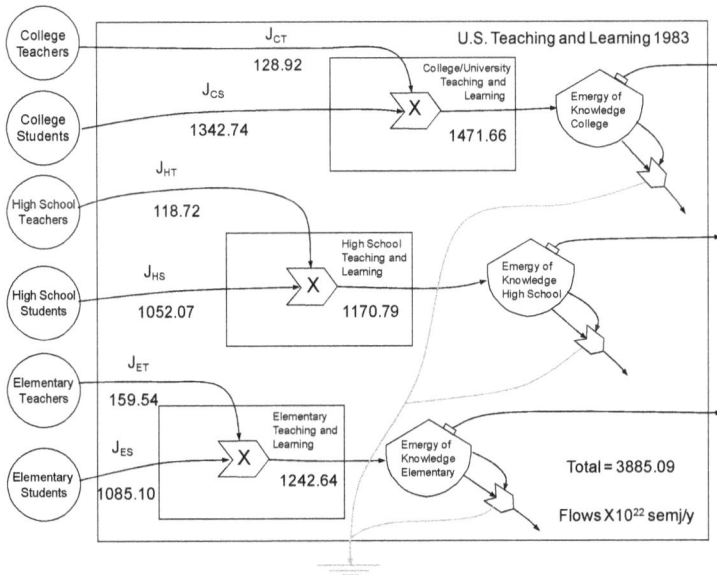

Figure 2. An emergy evaluation of the process of teaching and learning that occurred within the elementary, secondary, and college/university education subsystems of the United States in 1983.

The emergy of teaching and learning was quantified as the sum of the emergy delivered during the time spent transmitting information plus the emergy brought to the learning process by the receivers, *i.e.*, the students. We assumed that the emergy of the teaching and learning process was all that was required to increase the total knowledge in the system. The energy requirements for maintaining organized information increase in proportion to the number of possible combinations of connections in the system, which is proportional to the square of the number of units organized [26]. Thus, since knowledge is a form of information, the energy requirements for maintaining useful or organized knowledge must increase quadratically to balance losses as shown by the quadratic drains on the knowledge storages in Figure 2. The algorithms for calculating the emergy required for the teaching and learning process are given in Appendix A under *Emergy of Teaching and Learning*.

4. Methods

The standard methods of Emergy Analysis [1,15,27,28] were used to evaluate the education system of the United States. The methods used were those appropriate for evaluating a production process [1]. These methods were applied independently to each of three subsystems, elementary, secondary, and college/university, that together comprise the U.S. education system. The first step in performing an emergy evaluation of a production process is to diagram the process (Figures 1a–c and 2) using the symbols of the ESL [26]. In the process of creating the diagram appropriate spatial and temporal boundaries are determined. The spatial boundaries of this study were set to be the territorial boundaries of the United States including the 48 contiguous states, Alaska and Hawaii. The temporal boundaries of the study were set by the time period evaluated, *i.e.*, 1870 to 2011. The time period for each discrete evaluation of the subsystems was one year. The model components, outputs and the required inputs to the education subsystems were determined from our general knowledge of the structure and function of education systems and from a prior study of the University of Florida reported in [1] (p. 233).

In this case, the second step in the evaluation was to decide on the method that we would use to estimate the emergy of the graduates from the three subsystems. We decided that, for this analysis, the fundamental aspect of students was their capacity to store information through learning, so the emergy required to transfer information to the students in a given year could be captured by the sum of the annual emergy inputs required to run the school subsystem. In this method, the emergy of an individual student's education was calculated as the sum of the emergy required for an individual to complete each year of education summed over the time spent in school through graduation or dropout.

The third step was to systematically evaluate each of the inputs required to produce individuals with the various levels of education. Most of the raw data used to evaluate the subsystems were found online in the Statistical Abstracts of the United States: 2012 and Earlier Editions [29], as well as in the Statistical Abstracts of the United States 2012–2013, 131st edition [30] and ProQuest Statistical Abstracts of the United States 2014 [31]. All volumes issued from 1870 to 2014 were used in this evaluation. In addition, we used data on the U.S. education system compiled by [32]. Furthermore, various sources were used to fill-in critical information that was not recorded in the Statistical Abstracts of the United States, e.g., Olsen [33] provided data on the material and labor requirements for building construction. The second task in evaluating the inputs was to determine the algorithm to be used to calculate each input (see Appendix A). The amount of each input was determined first in the units in which it is commonly expressed, e.g., individuals for people, grams for mass, joules for energy, and $ for economic flows.

The fourth step in evaluating the education process of the U.S. was to convert the values for the inputs from their common units into emergy by multiplying by the appropriate Unit Emergy Value (UEV), *i.e.*, the emergy per person (semj/ind) for people, the transformity (semj/J) for energy, the specific emergy (semj/g) for mass, or the emergy to money ratio (semj/$) for money flows. The emergy inputs to each subsystem were then summed to determine the emergy required to support the educational process at that level in any given year. The emergy per individual for graduates or dropouts from any subsystem was determined by summing the annual emergy use required for their support during their time in school. The emergy required for all earlier education, including pre-school, was included in the emergy of an individual who had attained higher levels of education. The transformity (semj/J) of the work done by an individual with a given number of years education was calculated by dividing the emergy per individual by the metabolic energy expended by an individual in a year. The implicit assumption for this calculation to be valid is that a person will draw upon the majority of the information that they possess in the performance of the work done over the course of a year and that all of the daily activities of the person are necessary to support their ability to apply their knowledge and experience during their working hours. Other choices for these parameters are also plausible, but were not investigated in this study.

"Teaching and learning" was evaluated as a higher order social process requiring the emergy of both interacting inputs (see Appendix A). The emergy delivered in the teachings conducted in a subsystem is the emergy of the teacher's education and experience per individual times the fraction of hours spent on teaching times the number of teachers. The student's emergy, which is required to receive the information, is the emergy of their average education level per individual times the fraction of hours spent learning times enrollment. The sum of these two inputs is the emergy of "teaching and learning" that occurs within each subsystem. The sum of the three subsystems is the emergy of teaching and learning occurring within the formal education system of the United States in any given year.

5. Results

The primary results of this study are reported in Appendix B as a table of values showing the emergy required to educate individuals to achieve varying levels of education from preschool to the doctoral degree with 2 years postdoctoral experience. The values of the emergy per individual are based on the emergy inputs to the U.S. given in [34,35]. Other results of this study are reported in the text, figures and tables presented below.

The large scale pattern of growth in the empower (*i.e.*, emergy flow in semj/y) of all three levels of education in the U.S. (Figure 3) has been driven by population growth as shown by the growth in enrollment (Figure 4) and by the expansion of the fuel and mineral resources supporting the U.S. economy [34,35]. Within this large scale pattern we can observe some interesting features. In 1983, the empower of elementary education was 1.94 times that of high school and 1.68 times that of the college/university education subsystem (Figures 1 and 3). This relationship has varied over time, but elementary education's empower has exceeded that of the other two subsystems over the entire period. College education's empower first exceeded high school education in 1980, when it was 5.7% greater. After 1983, the emergy supporting both college and elementary education began to increase rapidly, but the time of rapid increase was delayed until 1993 for high school as the increase in elementary enrollment moved through the system (Figure 4). The structure of the inputs to all three subsystems followed a similar general pattern with some differences. The emergy of returning students was always the largest input to all subsystems, but the second largest input varied among the subsystems, e.g., in 1983 (Figure 1) the second largest input to the elementary and college subsystems was purchased services, whereas entering eighth grade graduates supplied the second largest emergy input to secondary schools. Purchased services, as a percent of total emergy use, are relatively more important in the college/university subsystem than in the elementary and secondary subsystems.

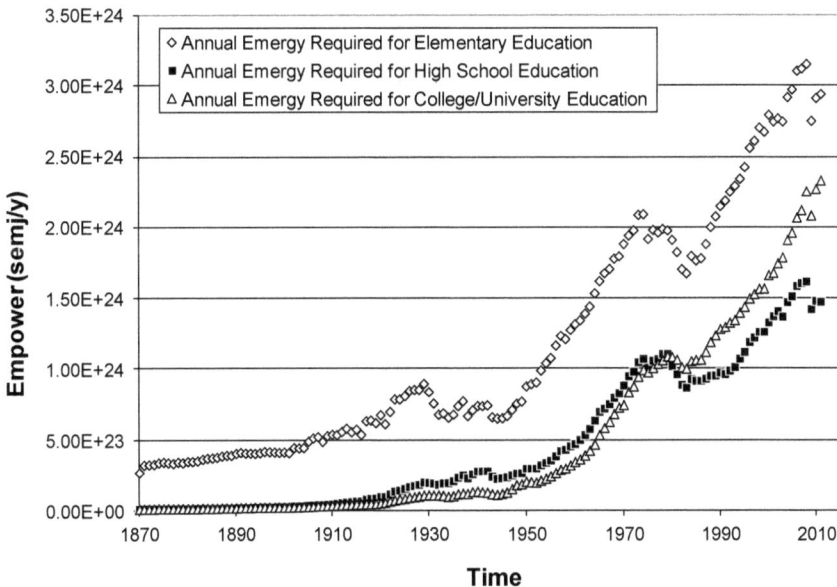

Figure 3. The annual emergy required to support the elementary, secondary, and college/university subsystems (the k_8 pathways in Figure 1) of the education system of the United States from 1870 to 2011.

In general, the emergy of the inputs to all three education subsystems followed an increasing trend from 1870 to 2011 with periods of decline and fluctuation corresponding to sometimes different and sometimes similar sensitivities to the major socioeconomic events of the past 142 years (Figure 3). Note the marked decline in emergy supporting elementary education during the Great Depression (GD) and the GD's smaller effect on the emergy supporting secondary and college education. In contrast, the emergy support for all three subsystems drastically declined in 2009 in response to GR08; however the annual empower of the college subsystem recovered to its 2008 level in 2010 while the emergy flow supporting the elementary and secondary levels remained depressed through 2011. An observation that helps explain this pattern in emergy use by the subsystems is that enrollment in college markedly increased in 2008 (Figure 4), while elementary and secondary enrollment continued to follow the existing trends established by the population of elementary and secondary students.

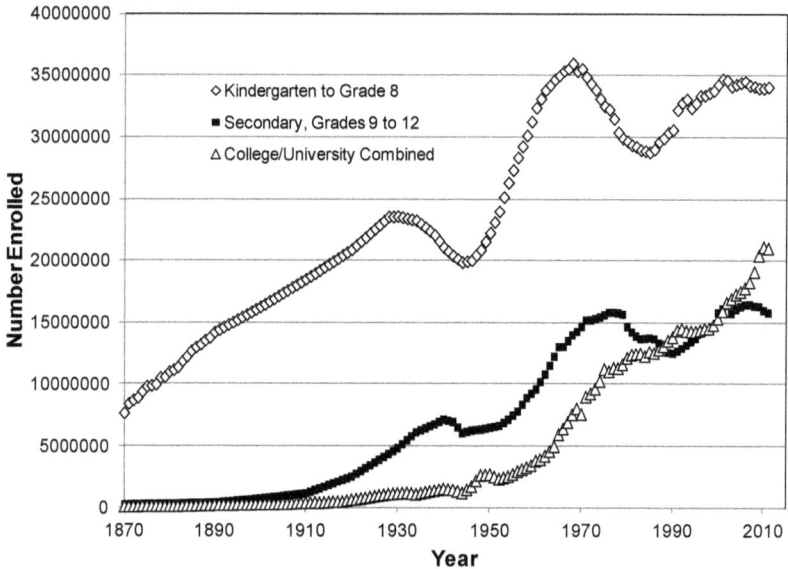

Figure 4. Annual enrollment in the elementary, secondary, and college/university subsystems of the education system of the United States from 1870 to 2011.

The amount of information transferred as measured by the emergy of the process of teaching and learning in the 1983 school year is shown in Figure 2. The annual emergy required to support teaching and learning in the elementary school subsystem exceeded the secondary school subsystem by 6.1%; whereas, the emergy supporting teaching and learning at the college/university level exceeded secondary school subsystem by 25.7% and the elementary subsystem by 18.4%. In 1983, the emergy of the process of teaching and learning exceeded the annual emergy required for school operations by 7.4 times for elementary, 13.5 times for secondary, and 14.8 times for college/university education (Figures 2 and 5). The unweighted average with the standard deviation of these ratios is 11.9 ± 3.95, which is approximately an order of magnitude difference.

Figure 5 shows the time history of variation in the emergy of teaching and learning in the three U.S. education subsystems (Figure 2). Until 1977, the emergy of teaching and learning is greatest at the elementary level. After 1977, high school briefly accounted for the largest emergy flow until 1980 when the emergy of teaching and learning at the college level became the largest. Since 1980, teaching and learning in the college/university subsystem has continued to increase, maintaining its position as the largest educational activity in the U.S. as measured by the emergy of the information transferred. The emergy of teaching and learning in the elementary subsystem declined slowly from 1976 to 1986 after which it began to increase. The high school subsystem declined from 1979 to 1989 and then after 1991 it began to increase at a rate similar to the increase of the emergy of teaching and learning in college/university and elementary subsystems. After 1995 the rate of increase in the emergy of teaching and learning in the college/university subsystem became more rapid, separating it from the rates of increase of both the elementary and secondary education subsystems. This rapid growth continued until 2011, the last year of data available to us, when it suddenly stopped, *i.e.*, the emergy of teaching and learning at the college level in 2011 was almost the same as in 2010.

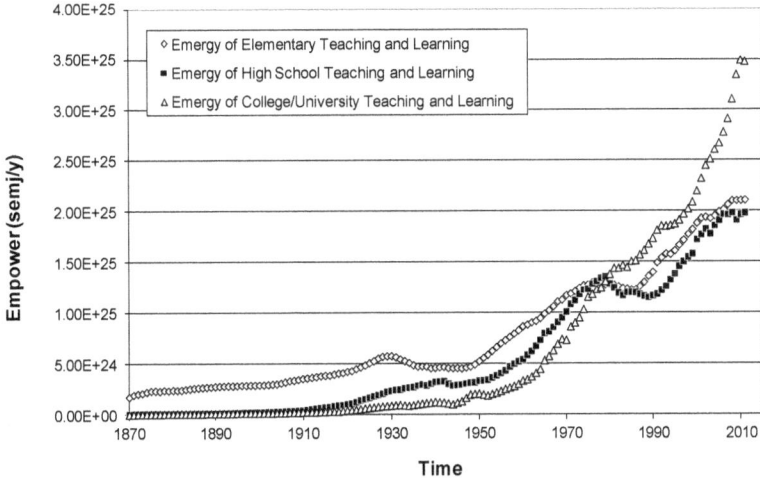

Figure 5. The annual emergy flow (empower) of teaching and learning in the elementary, secondary and college/university education subsystems of the United States from 1870 to 2011.

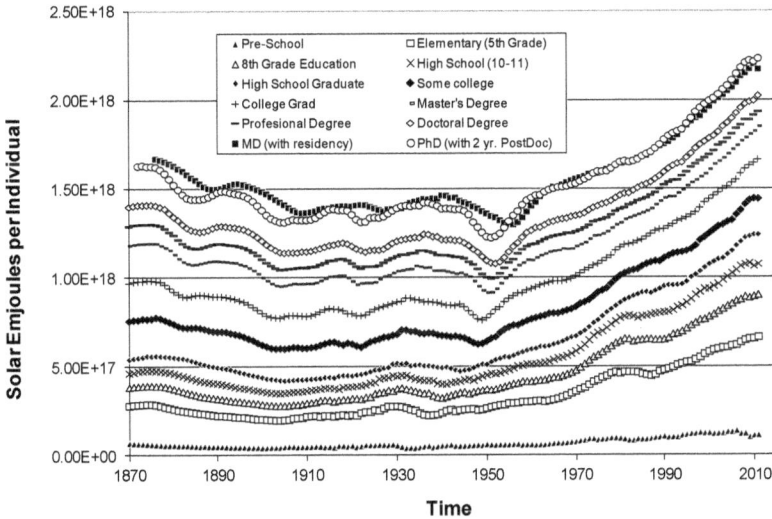

Figure 6. The emergy per individual required to create knowledge (*i.e.*, by storing information with the instructions on how to use it) at twelve levels of education (*i.e.*, primary, secondary, college/university and their subsets) within the United States from 1870 to 2011 (see Appendix B).

Time series of the emergy per individual for twelve education levels from pre-school to the doctoral degree plus 2 years postdoctoral experience are shown in Figure 6 (see Figure 1 for 1983 values). The numerical values for the emergy per individual at these education levels are given in Appendix B in tabular form for use in future emergy analyses. The emergy per individual in this table is the summation of the emergy required annually at each level to support the student up to the point he or she leaves school. The emergy of education per individual in all categories declined from 1870 to varying inflection points, which occurred in most cases during the first 5 years of the new century. After this time, the emergy of education per individual began to increase and it continued to do so in most categories until varying times during the Great Depression. From this high point, the emergy per individual declined with some variation depending on education level to an inflection point occurring around 1950. After this time the emergy of education per individual for high school graduates and higher has increased almost monotonically to the present time. A general pattern is noticeable in the data, in which the inflection point in the emergy required per graduate is lagged in time for higher levels of education, *i.e.*, longer times in school. For example, after WWII, the turnaround in emergy support for education was later for progressively higher education levels (*i.e.*, 1945 for high school graduates, 1952 for graduate degrees and 1957 for MDs).

Table 2. Emergy per individual and the transformity or the emergy delivered per joule of metabolic work for different education levels in the United States in 1983.

Attainment	Odum 1996 [1] ^		This study [#]	
	Emergy/ind. (E+16 semj/ind./y)	Transformity [*] (E+6 semj/J)	Emergy/ind. (E+16 semj/ind./y)	Transformity [*] (E+06 semj/J)
Preschool	3.4/5.7	8.9/14.9	8.63	22.6
School	9.4/15.8	24.6/41.2	47.3	123.8
College Graduate	28.0/46.9	73.3/122.8	119.7	313.3
Masters			135.0	353.4
(Post College Ed.)	131.0/219.5	343.0/574.6		
Professional			142.2	372.3
Ph.D.			149.2	390.6
Public Status	393.0/658.4	1029.0/1723.9	552.5	1446.3
Legacies	785.0/1315.1	2054.0/3441.1		

^ The emergy and transformity values for the levels of educational attainment from [1] are reported first using the emergy base for the U.S. (7.70E + 24 semj/y) as determined by Odum [1] and second using the emergy base for the U.S. for 1983 (1.29E + 25 semj/y) as determined in this study. Also, these values are generally consistent with the calculations for levels 3–5 in Abel [24]. [#] In this table, school assumes education through grade 5, college assumes 2 years study, professional assumes a 3 year degree and public status assumes that 1% of the population meets this criterion. [*] Energy per individual (ind.) [1] (p. 232): (2500kcal/day) × (365days/yr) × (4186J/kcal) =3.82E+09 J/ind/yr.

We compared the emergy per individual and the transformity of the work done by individuals with various levels of education as calculated in this study to earlier results from Odum [1] (Table 2). A solidus or slash separates Odum's results as he originally calculated them from the values obtained after adjusting his calculation using the emergy base for the United States in 1983 given in [34,35]. The emergy inflows to the U.S. reported in an earlier version [35] of [34] are slightly different from those used in this study. Estimates from this study exceed the adjusted estimates from Odum [1] for preschool, school, and college education by 1.56, 3.07, and 2.27 times, respectively. However, Odum's adjusted estimate for post-college education exceeds our average post-college estimate by 1.52 times. If one percent of the population has attained public status as we assumed, Odum's estimate for the emergy of an individual with public status is 17% greater than the estimate made in this study. "Public Status" implies that an individual controls energy, material, and information flows that are larger than expected for a person with their education level, e.g., for a public official managing a National Park, or a CEO of a large company, experience may be the largest factor in determining the transformity of their work.

6. Discussion

In most published databases, flows of energy, materials and labor are quantified in monetary units; whereas, emergy analysis primarily needs information quantified in physical units of mass, energy or information. Consequently, estimating the emergy equivalent of a monetary flow is sometimes the only possible way to quantify all the inputs to a production process or a territorial system, e.g., a nation, state, or county. In an emergy evaluation, the Emergy to Money Ratio (EMR) is the metric commonly used to convert a money flow expressed in dollars to an estimate of the associated emergy flow; however, this conversion is only a rough approximation of the emergy of the human work required to produce the item. With this concern in mind, we wanted to make an independent estimate of the emergy for which a quantity of money is paid, assuming that money is paid only for the knowledge and experience delivered by the intellectual and physical labor required to produce a product or service.

In this study the education level of the worker is largely responsible for our estimates of the quality-adjusted work performed by individuals (Appendix B); however, we recognize the importance of experience and we included it in this study, when possible, as explained in the next section. In any case, the emergy of an individual's experience could be documented in the same manner as we determined the emergy of an individual's education, *i.e.*, by calculating the emergy required to support the time spent in learning while on the job (Appendix A: *Emergy of Teaching and Learning*).

6.1. Comparison of Estimation Methods

Our estimate of the transformity of knowledge was based on quantifying the emergy required for the education of an individual, which we assumed captured most of the emergy delivered in the work done, for which money was paid. As described above, the knowledge of individuals was quantified through performing an emergy analysis of the U.S. education system from 1870 to 2011. In the future, the value of experience also should be quantified to obtain the best estimate of the emergy delivered in a joule of a person's metabolic work. However, we quantified both the average number of years of education and experience of the teachers in each subsystem as a model input and as part of the internal calculations within the model (see Appendix A). We quantified the experience of students as they passed through the education subsystems to graduation; however, in this case we considered their education and experience to be the same thing. The emergy of the experience of doctors performing internships and residencies was quantified as was the experience of a Ph.D. in postdoctoral study. In both cases, we assumed that the emergy required to gain experience was similar to that required to educate university students. Similar methods might be used to quantify the emergy of experience for other occupations as this method matures. In this study, we proposed that a quasi-independent estimate of the emergy flow for which money is paid, *i.e.*, the emergy of the knowledge and experience delivered in the work of individuals, would allow us to calculate the emergy of educational attainment in the United States over time and to include this input as part of the emergy basis for characterizing and analyzing socioeconomic activities of the nation and of people [36,37].

Odum [1] estimated the emergy delivered by the work done at various education levels by assuming that the total emergy inflow to the nation in a year supported the observed distribution of educational attainment. The number of people that had achieved each level of attainment was divided into the emergy base for the nation in that year to estimate the emergy per individual with a given number of years of education. The output was a series of transformities that increased with education level, because almost everyone had achieved a preschool level of education, but only 6 million people had post college education. This method assumes that the system is in steady state and that all of the emergy input to the nation is what was required to produce the hierarchy of observed education levels in the year evaluated. In this paper, we estimated the emergy of human service based on an emergy evaluation of the education system in the United States under the assumption that the emergy supporting an individual in this system, when summed over the time spent in school, captured the emergy required to produce an individual with a given number of years of education. In this method, we do not need to assume that the system is in steady state, because we have the data to document the change in the state variables of interest in each year, nor must we assume that the entire emergy of the nation is required to produce the individuals at each education level. Even though the variables of interest are in flux from year to year, we have used the assumption of steady state when estimation or extrapolation was used to obtain missing values. Our method, which is based on determining the cumulative emergy required for a given level of education, resulted in a higher assessment of the emergy per individual for college, high school, elementary and preschool, but a lower estimate for post-graduate education than found in [1]. This result is, in part, due to the use of the total number of people who had attained an education level as the basis for Odum's calculation compared to our use of summation over the years in school up to the final level of education attained. Odum's method is more holistic and top-down in that it relies only on the emergy use of the nation and educational attainment to estimate the emergy per individual, but it has some significant difficulties related to the reasonableness of its underlying assumptions, *i.e.*, it assumes that the education system of the U.S. is in steady state and that the details of the system are not important and perhaps unchanging, if his numbers for 1983 are applied to other years and places. The method used in this paper makes the plausible argument that all students learn from their time in school and that all other things being equal the emergy required for a step in learning is proportional to the emergy required to support the students and the school system during their time in school. Of course, all other things are not equal because students vary in intelligence, dedication to their studies, learning styles as well as in other ways. These secondary factors were not considered in this analysis. Given the fact that the two methods use different approaches, it is encouraging that the results from both methods are in the same "ballpark" and that the variation is consistent with the differences expected from the inherent characteristics of the calculation methods used. For example, since our calculations are more detailed and ostensibly more complete, one would expect our numbers to be higher than Odum's and this is true for education levels below post-graduate. However, Odum's numbers for the emergy of an individual with a post-college education are somewhat higher than ours, possibly because of the smaller number of people in this class and because he used the entire emergy of the nation to determine the emergy per individual rather than the emergy actually used to support their education.

6.2. Temporal Patterns in the Emergy Measures of the Education Subsystems

We observed patterns in the time series of variables used to characterize the three education subsystems. For example, we noticed a broad pattern of increase in all inputs to all subsystems over the entire period of the analysis except for the input from the environment to the elementary education subsystem and to a lesser extent from the environment to the secondary education subsystem. Input from the environment to the elementary school system peaked from 1927 to 1929 after which it rapidly declined, apparently due to the consolidation of small schools into larger ones, thus requiring less total land area. Also, we observed a pulse with a long period of increase and rapid decline, which is seen in the temporal pattern of the emergy required to support the elementary and secondary school systems from 1950 to the late seventies, which can be explained, in part, by the population cycle driven by the post WWII "baby boom". The consistent decline in the emergy of education per individual with a given level of education at all education levels from 1870 to 1900 is due to factors not related to the efficacy of the work performed by a person of a given educational status. This pattern is seen because the number of students enrolled in school at all levels increased rapidly during this period, while the emergy of the inputs to the educational system increased less rapidly.

Systems **2014**, *2*, 328–365

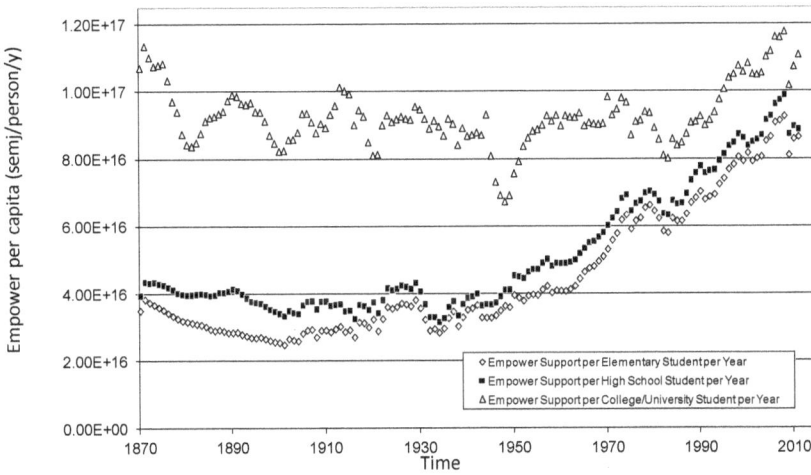

Figure 7. The emergy per student per year used by each subsystem of the education system of the United States from 1870 to 2011.

A different perspective on education in the United States can be gained from examining the emergy invested per student per year in each subsystem (Figure 7). The pattern of annual emergy use to support a college/university student remained relatively constant from 1901 until 1983 varying between 8.0E+16 and 1.0E+17 semj/ind./yr with the exception of the period from 1945 to 1951, when soldiers were returning to school on the GI bill. After the transition decade from 1974 to 1983 during which petroleum was replaced as the largest energy source for the United States by electricity from nuclear power and coal [34,35] and the rapid growth in the use of personal computers starting in the early 1980s, which ushered in the Information Age; the annual expenditure of emergy per college student began an almost linear increase that continued until 2008. Two fluctuations occurred along this path: a minor decline associated with the recession of 1991 and a larger decline (2001–2003) associated with the bursting of the internet or "dot-com" bubble of inflated values in the stock market and in society as a whole. This linear advance ended with a precipitous decline in the emergy invested per student for all education subsystems beginning in 2009 and from which the subsystems had not recovered by 2011.

The emergy support per student in the elementary and secondary subsystems shows a closely related pattern over the time examined that is different from the pattern exhibited by college/university education. The emergy invested per student declines from 1870 to 1900 for the reasons given above, but from 1901 until 1929 the emergy invested per student generally increased with some fluctuations. From the middle of the GD (1929 to 1934), emergy expenditures on primary and secondary education decline. After 1934 the emergy invested per student rises, first with a linear trend, which was interrupted by the 1957–1958 recession and then with an apparently exponential trend, which continues until 1974, the beginning of the transition period mentioned above. From 1974 to 2011, elementary and secondary education follow a pattern similar to that described for college/university education. The most striking characteristic of the pattern of annual emergy use per student in elementary and secondary education is that it remained in a relatively constant relationship with college education from 1900 to 1934, with expenditures varying from 30% of college expenditures in 1901 for elementary education to 45% in 1929 for secondary education. However, from 1934 to 2008 the amount of emergy invested per student rose in both the elementary and secondary subsystems until, in 2008, society's emergy investment in elementary and secondary education per student was 79% and 84%, respectively, of that invested in college education. The rapid growth of the emergy invested per student from 1983

Systems **2014**, *2*, 328–365

to 2008 may reflect the resource expenditures necessary to support the transition of the nation into the Information Age. This transition was characterized first by learning to incorporate computer use into daily activities (1981 to 1995) and second by learning how to use access to the knowledge available on the internet (1995 to the present) to increase the effectiveness of our work in an increasingly complex world, and thereby strengthen the fabric of society.

6.3. Technical Obstacles

One of the primary obstacles that had to be overcome in carrying out this research was that we wanted to estimate the emergy of an individual with a given number of years of education in a manner that was as independent as possible from estimates based on monetary measures of the inputs. Therefore, we needed to make the calculations without using the emergy to money ratio of the nation to determine the emergy supporting the education levels. We imposed this condition on our analysis, because we intend to use the emergy required for the education of an individual as a measure of the emergy that this individual contributes to society through the knowledge delivered in the work that they do and for which they are paid. If the estimate of the emergy of education is relatively free of monetary influences, we can use the emergy required to produce the information delivered in the paid work done by people at a certain education and skill level as an independent estimate of the emergy delivered to the economy in that work, which in turn will allow us to establish a relatively unbiased complete emergy base for a national economy, *i.e.*, an emergy base that includes the emergy of the material and energy inputs from the environment and the emergy of information delivered in both the intellectual and physical work of people in a manner that is not confounded [16].

6.3.1. Why the Method is Quasi-Independent of Monetary Measures

The complete avoidance of monetary measures proved to be a task beyond our capabilities; therefore, we settled for a quasi-independent estimate using the EMR only when absolutely necessary. The EMR of the U.S. was used to estimate two important inputs to the analysis. First, we used it to estimate the emergy required to support students and teachers. In the former case, we used the share of the emergy of the nation as represented by the disposable income per individual to estimate the emergy that could be used to support an average student. In the latter case, the emergy used to support teachers was calculated using their salary and the EMR in the year being evaluated. In the former calculation, an error is introduced by assuming that a student of any age will get an equivalent share of disposable income within a family. Also, we might have made a more accurate estimate of the emergy used to support students by using the median instead of the average disposable income in the estimation. Thus, our estimate of the emergy required for student support may be somewhat too high and biased by overestimating the annual support needed for an elementary school student and underestimating that needed for a college student. In the latter calculation, the emergy that can be purchased by a teacher's salary is probably a fairly accurate estimate of the resources available for their support.

Second, the service required for school operations and construction was estimated using the current EMR in the year evaluated. In this case, we estimated the material and energy flows separately and the dollars paid for services should reflect the emergy required for the purchased work of people, if the services are being delivered by labor with the average transformity of the system. Most other inputs were estimated from the emergy of energy, material and information flows; and therefore, we believe that we have made a reasonable first-order, quasi-independent estimate of the emergy per individual at the various education levels in the United States from about 1900 to 2011. We do not recommend that the years from 1870 to 1899 be used as accurate estimates of the emergy per individual at the various education levels, since we allotted this time for the calculation to stabilize (see below).

6.3.2. Method Used to Deal with Unknown Initial Conditions

A second difficulty, in performing these calculations, was that we needed to know the initial condition of several variables, e.g., the emergy of school buildings, the emergy of teacher's education, *etc.*, in order to make an accurate estimate of the annual emergy flows required for education in the first year of the analysis. We dealt with this problem by starting our analysis in 1870 rather than in 1900, when the storages, e.g., school buildings, enrollment, number of teachers, *etc.*, were very small compared to later years. By starting the analysis in 1870 when storages and flows were small, errors in the initial estimates were not so important, and we could allow the evaluation to "spin up" as each year of new data was added, in a manner similar to the simulation of a mathematical model with uncertain initial values. In about 10 years the output variables had stabilized and were following reasonable trends. Our initial estimates might be improved in the future by applying an iterative approach to the calculation of the emergy of the education levels by constructing a model and feeding back the current estimates as initial conditions and annual inputs iteratively until a stable value for the emergy per individual at each education level is reached.

6.3.3. Lack of Consistency in Some Measurements

There is a lack of consistency in some of the numbers currently used in our evaluation for some years. These variations occur because the U.S. Census Bureau reports many different versions of a number like elementary enrollment. In addition, one accounting method will be used for a series of years and then changed, leading to different methods for making the estimate. Furthermore, the values that are first reported often are refined in subsequent years, so it was difficult to eliminate all inconsistencies from the reported values of some variables. Wherever possible we have tried to remove inconsistency by checking numbers against more than one source in the database; however, inconsistency in reporting still leads to some noise in the data, but it is small compared to the first and even second order trends, *i.e.*, we do not believe that the discrepancies in the data are large enough to affect the results of the study. In general, variations of our estimates are within the ±10% bounds acceptable for emergy analyses [15,28]. Also, many variables that were used in this analysis had missing data for one or more years. We handled missing data using three techniques, interpolation, extrapolation, and estimation. Interpolation and extrapolation were used when we had values for many years over the 142 year period. Estimation was used when we had little information and needed to impute reasonable values for a variable. Linear interpolation between two known values and proportionate extrapolation using the relationship between a known variable and the unknown to assign values to the unknown were used to assign values to the years with missing data.

6.4. The Emergy of Teaching and Learning

Odum [1] described the method for calculating the emergy of teaching and learning, and we followed his method in our spreadsheet calculations. Our calculation of the emergy of teaching and learning is one of the first calculations of the emergy of a higher order social process, but see [38]. We refer to "teaching and learning" as a higher order social process because it depends on a complex underlying series of energy transformations supporting education, and it evaluates with transformities that are approximately an order of magnitude greater than the underlying annual support for operating the education system (e.g., for elementary education in 1983 (Figures 1 and 2) we have, 1320.72 semj/171.41 semj = 7.7, for the ratio of the annual emergy of elementary teaching and learning to the annual support emergy for elementary education. The emergy of teaching and learning is a measure of the emergy required for copying or transferring information [1,14] vital to the functioning and continuance of society, and as such it is a higher order social function, which has a transformity approximately an order of magnitude greater than that required for the annual support of the U.S. education. The implication of this result is that the emergy spent annually on education has about a 10:1 return on investment in terms of the overall benefits gained by society

Systems **2014**, *2*, 328–365

through the transfer of information vital for its continuance. The importance of teaching and learning to maximizing empower of the nation is particularly apparent in the exponential increase of teaching and learning empower at the college/university level during the Information Age (1981 to present).

7. Conclusions

We developed a model-based empirical evaluation method for tracking the emergy required for an individual to achieve various levels of education in the United States from 1870 to 2011. We provided a data table giving the emergy required to produce individuals at 12 different levels of education for each year from 1870 to 2011 for use in subsequent emergy evaluations. We demonstrated that our method gave results that were plausible when compared to the earlier results of Odum [1], which were determined using a different method. We evaluated "teaching and learning" in elementary, secondary and college/university subsystems of the U.S. education system and we characterized it as a higher order social process with an emergy amplification effect 10 times the emergy invested in operating the school systems. Temporal patterns of the emergy invested per student per year were indicative of educational priorities; practical realities, such as wars and population cycles; as well as the necessity of providing better education to help society incorporate the advances of industrial and information technology over the past 142 years. By quantifying the emergy of the information delivered to a national system by the work of individuals with various levels of education, we have taken a first step toward making a quasi-independent estimate of the emergy supplied to that nation through the knowledge delivered from the educational attainment of its workers in their work performed annually within the system boundaries.

Acknowledgments: This paper is tracking number ORD-008032 of the U.S. EPA's Office of Research and Development, National Health and Environmental Effects Research Laboratory (NHEERL), Atlantic Ecology Division (AED). Although the research in this paper was funded, in part, by the USEPA, it has not been subjected to Agency-level review; therefore, it does not necessarily reflect the views of the USEPA. Giancarlo Cicchetti of AED, Walter Galloway formerly of AED (now retired) and Denis White of NHEERL's Western Ecology Division (now retired) and three anonymous reviewers provided helpful reviews of this paper.

Author Contributions: Dan Campbell was the primary author of this paper and principal researcher accounting for 90% of the writing and 75% of the research and analysis. Hongfang Lu gathered data and performed some of the analyses. She carried out and checked the spreadsheet calculations, read and criticized the draft paper, and provided intellectual input in developing the theory and methods used in the paper. Her contribution was 10% of the writing and 25% of the emergy evaluation and methodology.

Conflicts of Interest: The authors declare no conflict of interest.

References

1. Odum, H.T. *Environmental Accounting: Emergy and Environmental Decision Making*; John Wiley and Sons: New York, NY, USA, 1996.
2. Lotka, A.J. Contribution to the energetics of evolution. *Proc. Nat. Acad. Sci. USA* **1922**, *8*, 147–151. [CrossRef]
3. Lotka, A.J. Natural selection as a physical principle. *Proc. Nat. Acad. Sci. USA* **1922**, *8*, 151–154. [CrossRef]
4. Lotka, A.J. *Physical Biology*; Williams and Wilkins: Baltimore, MD, USA, 1925.
5. Vernadsky, V.I. The biosphere and the noösphere. *Am. Sci.* **1945**, *33*, 1–12.
6. Vitousek, P.M.; Mooney, H.A.; Lubchenco, J.; Melillo, J.M. Human domination of Earth's ecosystems. *Science* **1997**, *277*, 494–499. [CrossRef]
7. Campbell, D.E.; Lu, H.F.; Knox, G.A.; Odum, H.T. Maximizing empower on a human-dominated planet: The role of exotic *Spartina. Ecol. Eng.* **2009**, *35*, 463–486. [CrossRef]
8. Vitousek, P.M.; Aber, J.D.; Howarth, R.W.; Likens, G.E.; Matson, P.A.; Schindler, D.W.; Schlesinger, W.H.; Tilman, D.G. Human alteration of the global nitrogen cycle: Sources and consequences. *Ecol. Appl.* **1997**, *7*, 737–750.
9. Campbell, D.E.; Lu, H.F.; Lin, B.L. Emergy evaluations of the global biogeochemical cycles of six biologically active elements and two compounds. *Ecol. Model.* **2014**, *271*, 32–51. [CrossRef]
10. Brown, M.T.; McClanahan, T.R. Emergy analysis perspectives of Thailand and Mekong River dam proposals. *Ecol. Model.* **1996**, *91*, 105–130. [CrossRef]

11. Brown, M.T.; Ulgiati, S. Emergy measures of carrying capacity to evaluate economic investments. *Popul. Environ.* **2001**, *22*, 471–501. [CrossRef]

12. Lu, H.F.; Campbell, D.E. Ecological and economic dynamics of the Shunde agricultural system under China's small city development strategy. *J. Environ. Manag.* **2009**, *90*, 2589–2600. [CrossRef]

13. Lu, H.F.; Lin, B.L.; Campbell, D.E.; Sagisaka, M.; Ren, H. Biofuel *vs.* Biodiversity? Integrated emergy and economic cost-benefit evaluation of rice-ethanol production in Japan. *Energy* **2012**, *46*, 442–450.

14. Odum, H.T. Limits of Information and Biodiversity. In *Sozialpolitik und Okologieprobleme der Zukunft, Festsymposium der Osterreichischen Akademie der Wissenschaften analaslich ihres 150jahrigen Jubilaums 14. Bis 16. Mai 1997*; Loffler, H., Streissler, E.W., Eds.; Verlag der Osterreichischen Akademie der Wissenschaften: Wien, Austria, 1999; pp. 229–269.

15. Campbell, D.E.; Ohrt, A. Environmental Accounting Using Emergy: Evaluation of Minnesota. USEPA Project Report, EPA/600/R-09/002. 2009. Available online: http://www.epa.gov/nheerl/download_files/publications/MNEmergyEvalfinal2009_1_16.pdf (accessed on 2 April 2014).

16. Campbell, D.E. Keeping the books for the environment and society: The unification of emergy and financial accounting methods. *J. Environ. Account. Manag.* **2013**, *1*, 25–41.

17. Odum, H.T. Living with complexity. In *Crafoord Prize in the Biosciences, 1987*; Crafoord Lectures, Royal Swedish Academy of Sciences: Stockholm, Sweden, 1987; pp. 19–85.

18. Odum, H.T. Self-organization, transformity, and information. *Science* **1988**, *242*, 1132–1139.

19. Campbell, D.E.; Lu, H.F. The Emergy Basis for Formal Education in the United States. In *Emergy Synthesis 5, Theory and Applications of the Emergy Methodology*; Brown, M.T., Sweeney, S., Campbell, D.E., Huang, S.L., Ortega, E., Rydberg, T., Tilley, D.R., Ulgiati, S., Eds.; The Center for Environmental Policy, University of Florida: Gainesville, FL, USA, 2009; Presented at the 5th Biennial Emergy Research Conference; Gainesville, FL, USA, January 2008.

20. The 2012 Statistical Abstract: Earlier Editions. Available online: http://www.census.gov/compendia/statab/past_years.html (accessed 2 April 2014).

21. Bergquist, D.A.; Ingwersen, W.; Liebenow, D.K. Emergy in Labor—Approaches for Evaluating Knowledge. In *Emergy Synthesis 6: Theory and Applications of the Emergy Methodology*; Brown, M.T., Sweeney, S., Campbell, D.E., Huang, S.L., Ortega, E., Rydberg, T., Tilley, D.R., Ulgiati, S., Eds.; The Center for Environmental Policy, University of Florida: Gainesville, FL, USA, 2011; Presented at the 6th Biennial Emergy Research Conference; Gainesville, FL, USA, January 2010, pp. 501–507.

22. Martin, J.F.; Roy, E.D.; Diemont, S.A.W.; Ferguson, B.G. Traditional Ecological Knowledge (TEK): Ideas, inspiration, and designs for ecological engineering. *Ecol. Eng.* **2010**, *36*, 839–849. [CrossRef]

23. Diemont, S.A.W.; Martin, J.F.; Levy-Tacher, S.I. Emergy evaluation of Lacandon Maya indigenous swidden agroforestry in Chiapas, Mexico. *Agroforestry Syst.* **2006**, *66*, 23–42. [CrossRef]

24. Abel, T. Human transformations in a global hierarchy: Emergy and scale in the production of people and culture. *Ecol. Model.* **2010**, *221*, 2112–2117. [CrossRef]

25. Abel, T. Culture in cycles: Considering H.T. Odum's 'information cycle'. *Int. J. Gen. Syst.* **2013**, *43*. [CrossRef]

26. Odum, H.T. *Ecological and General Systems: An Introduction to Systems Ecology*; University Press of Colorado: Niwot, CO, USA, 1994; Revised edition of Systems Ecology; Wiley: Malden, MA, USA, 1983.

27. Brown, M.T.; Ulgiati, S. Emergy analysis and environmental accounting. *Encyclopedia Energ.* **2004**, *2*, 1–25.

28. Campbell, D.E.; Brandt-Williams, S.L.; Meisch, M.E.A. Environmental Accounting Using Emergy: Evaluation of the State of West Virginia. 2005. Available online: http://www.epa.gov/nheerl/download_files/publications/wvevaluationposted.pdf (accessed on 2 April 2014).

29. U.S. Census Bureau. The 2012 Statistical Abstract: Earlier Editions. 2012. Available online: http://www.census.gov/compendia/statab/past_years.html (accessed on 2 April 2014).

30. U.S. Dept. Commerce. *Statistical Abstracts of the United States: 2012–2013*, 131st ed.; Sky Horse Publishing, Inc.: New York, NY, USA, 2012; pp. 143–192.

31. ProQuest. *ProQuest Statistical Abstracts of the United States 2014*; Bernan, Rowman and Littlefield: Lanham, MD, USA, 2014; pp. 155–205.

32. Snyder, T.D. *120 Years of American Education: A Statistical Portrait*; National Center for Education Statistics, U.S. Department of Education: Washington, DC, USA, 1993. Available online: http://nces.ed.gov/pubs93/93442.pdf (accessed on 2 April 2014).

33. Olsen, J.G. Labor and Material Requirements for Federal Building Construction. Monthly Labor Review Productivity Reports. 1981, pp. 47–51. Available online: http://www.bls.gov/opub/mlr/1981/12/rpt2full.pdf (accessed on 2 April 2014).

34. Campbell, D.E.; Lu, H.F.; Walker, H. Energy and emergy as forces driving money flow in the United States from 1900 to 2011. *Frontiers Energ. Syst. Pol.* **2014**. submitted.

35. Campbell, D.E.; Lu, H.F. The Emergy to Money Ratio of the United States from 1900 to 2007. In *Emergy Synthesis 5, Theory and Applications of the Emergy Methodology*; Brown, M.T., Sweeney, S., Campbell, D.E., Huang, S.L., Ortega, E., Rydberg, T., Tilley, D.R., Ulgiati, S., Eds.; The Center for Environmental Policy, University of Florida: Gainesville, FL, USA, 2009; pp. 413–448, Presented at the 5th Biennial Emergy Research Conference; Gainesville, FL, USA, January 2008.

36. Campbell, D.E.; Lu, H.F.; Kolb, K. Emergy Evaluation of Educational Attainment in the United States. In *Emergy Synthesis 6: Theory and Applications of the Emergy Methodology*; Brown, M.T., Sweeney, S., Campbell, D.E., Huang, S.L., Ortega, E., Rydberg, T., Tilley, D.R., Ulgiati, S., Eds.; The Center for Environmental Policy, University of Florida: Gainesville, FL, USA, 2011; pp. 483–500, Presented at the 6th Biennial Emergy Research Conference; Gainesville, FL, USA, January 2010.

37. Campbell, D.E.; White, D.; Fonyo, C. Emergy of the Occupations. In *Emergy Synthesis 7: Theory and Applications of the Emergy Methodology*; Brown, M.T., Sweeney, S., Campbell, D.E., Huang, S.L., Kang, D., Rydberg, T., Tilley, D.R., Ulgiati, S., Eds.; The Center for Environmental Policy, University of Florida: Gainesville, FL, USA, 2013; pp. 381–404, Presented at the 7th Biennial Emergy Research Conference; Gainesville, FL, USA, January 2012.

38. Higgins, J.B. Emergy analysis of the Oak Openings region. *Ecol. Eng.* **2003**, *21*, 75–109. [CrossRef]

39. Filardo, M. *Good Buildings, Better Schools*; EPI Briefing Paper #216; Economic Policy Institute: Washington, DC, USA, 2008.

40. Dober, R.P. *Campus Planning*; Reinhold Publishing Corporation: New York, NY, USA, 1962. Available online: http://www.questia.com/PM.qst?a=o&docId=54331549 (accessed on 2 April 2014).

41. Schulman, A.; Peters, C.A. GIS analysis of urban schoolyard land cover in three U.S. cities. *Urban Ecosyst.* **2008**, *11*, 65–80. [CrossRef]

42. Energy Information Administration (EIA). Monthly Energy Review (MER)—Long-Term Historical Statistics All in One Place. Release Date: 26 February 2014. Available online: http://www.eia.gov/totalenergy/data/monthly/ (accessed on 2 April 2014).

43. Energy Information Administration (EIA). Historical Data. Available online: http://www.wou.edu/las/physci/GS361/electricity%20generation/US_consumption_1635-1945.htm (accessed on 2 April 2014).

44. Energy Information Administration. Available online: http://www.eia.gov/totalenergy/data/annual/showtext.cfm?t=ptb0209 (accessed on 2 April 2014).

45. Campbell, D.E.; Garmestani, A.S.; Hopton, M.E. Chapter 5. Emergy. In *San Luis Basin Sustainability Metrics Project: A Methodology for Evaluation Regional Sustainability*; EPA/600/R-10/182; Heberling, M.T., Hopton, M.E., Eds.; USEPA, Office of Research and Development, National Risk Management Research Laboratory: Cincinnati, OH, USA, 2010; pp. 77–162.

46. Stein, R.G. Energy cost of building construction. *Energ. Build.* **1977**, *1*, 27–29. [CrossRef]

47. Scheuer, C.; Keoleian, G.A.; Reppe, P. Life cycle energy and environmental performance of a new university building: modeling challenges and design implications. *Energ. Build.* **2003**, *35*, 1049–1064. [CrossRef]

48. Arnold, A. Energy Use during Construction. Available online: http://www.google.com/url?sa=t&rct=j&q=&esrc=s&frm=1&source=web&cd=1&ved=0CCQQFjAA&url=http%3A%2F%2Fregion5.ascweb.org%2Farnold%2520ppoint.ppt&ei=y-YYU5K7NIHM0wG064HQAg&usg=AFQjCNHzTJ1SFJFai1ey0AZzN8ASqTX-tA&bvm=bv.62577051,d.dmQ (accessed 2 April 2014).

49. Destre, G.; Levy-Garboua, L.; Sollogoub, M. Learning from experience or learning from others? Inferring informal training from a human capital earnings function with matched employer-employee data. *J. Socio-Econ.* **2008**, *37*, 919–938. [CrossRef]

Appendix A. Calculation of the Emergy Inputs to Each Level of the U.S. Education System

This Appendix is organized by input, so that the calculation methods, data and sources for all subsystems are discussed within each input category.

Environment

The area supporting each of the education subsystems was estimated by multiplying the average area of the school grounds by the number of schools active in a given year. The total number of schools in each subsystem was determined from data recorded in the U.S. Statistical Abstracts. Estimates for the average acreage of U.S. elementary (1 acre for 1 room and 10 acres for multi-room schools) and secondary (15 acres) schools are from [39]. Data on the average area of different types of U.S. colleges were found in [40]. The number of schools in different categories of colleges was multiplied by the average number of acres for a school of that type (61 acres for private colleges and 154 acres for public colleges) the categories were summed to estimate the total land area for colleges in the U.S. The renewable empower for the United States and the emergy of erosion [34,35] were used to quantify the emergy contributions of the environment to support the education subsystems. Total use of renewable emergy and the emergy input due to erosion were divided by the area of the nation to obtain the average empower density (semj/m^2) of environmental inputs. We assumed that 68% of the school grounds was school yard and subject to erosion based on a study by Schulman and Peters [41]. The environmental emergy contributing to each education subsystem was calculated by multiplying the school grounds area (m^2) by the renewable empower density of the U.S. and adding 0.68 times the area times the empower density of erosion.

Energy Consumed

The energy used to operate the buildings in each education subsystem was estimated using data obtained from the Energy Information Administration [42]. Statistics were available on commercial energy use in the United States from 1949 to 2011. The data were given as BTUs consumed by energy type, including, biomass, coal, petroleum, natural gas, and electricity. Longer term data on energy consumption in the U.S. from 1635 to 1945 were also found on the EIA website [43]. The area of school buildings in each subsystem from 1870 to 2011 was estimated below, under building construction. The average fraction of total commercial energy use accounted for by education in the five energy types mentioned above was given for eight years within the time period 1979 to 2003 [44]. These data were used to estimate the energy used by education buildings in each of the 5 energy types. After 1948 the emergy used in each subsystem was calculated by multiplying the average number of BTUs used, annually, within each type of energy by the fraction of the total building area accounted for by that subsystem, times 1055 J/BTU, times the transformity of the energy used. The transformities of the types of energy used in this study were: biomass, 28200 semj/J; coal, 37800 semj/J; natural gas, 43500 semj/J; petroleum, 65800 semj/J and electricity, 130500 semj/J [15,16,34]. Detailed data on education and commercial building energy use were not available prior to 1949; therefore, the average rate of energy use per square foot for education buildings from 1870 to 1948 was assumed to be similar to that calculated for 1949. Prior to 1949, the algorithm for determining the emergy of energy use was to multiply the average total energy use per sq. ft. by the fraction of that type of energy used nationally, times the area of buildings in the subsystem, times the conversion from BTUs to joules, times the transformity of the energy type. In both algorithms given above, the summation over all energy sources in a year gave the emergy used to support the buildings of the education subsystem in that year.

Building Construction

U.S. Census Bureau [29] contains estimates of the dollar value of new public and private construction put in place from 1915 to 1970. The value of public education buildings put in place was given from 1919 to 1970. In addition, the value of contracts awarded in education and science and the floor space to be built were also recorded. From these data the average cost of construction per square foot was determined. The average cost per sq. ft. was divided into the cost of public school construction put in place to estimate the area of public school buildings built in a given year. From 1993 to 2011, [29–31] give detailed data on the cost of public and private school construction. The average fraction of private to public construction costs was used to adjust the area of schools built, under the assumption that the cost for building a school was about the same regardless of the source of funds.

The value of all new construction awarded in the U.S from 1870 to 1919 was available in the U.S. Statistical Abstracts [29]. We applied the ratio of education construction to total construction in 1919 back to 1870 to estimate the value of new school construction. We applied the average cost per sq. ft. ($6.05 sq. ft.) during the relatively stable period from 1919 to 1943 to estimate the area of public education buildings constructed during that time. The area of schools built from 1870 to 2011 was partitioned into subsystems using the detailed data on public and private school construction by education level that was reported from 1993 to 2006 [29]. This information was also used to calculate the fraction of total cost that applied to each subsystem. About 14% of the construction costs were assigned to other education buildings, e.g., museums, public libraries, *etc.* and these costs were not counted as inputs to the education subsystems.

The emergy inputs to the school buildings built in each subsystem were determined using the material and labor requirements for constructing public buildings [33]. The classes of material inputs along with their emergy per unit values are as follows: (1) Minerals and raw materials including lumber and wood products, 5.18E+08 semj/g; paper, 2.15E+09 semj/g; chemicals, 2.75E+09 semj/g; petroleum refining and related products, 6.58E+04 semj/J; stone, glass, and concrete, 2.39E+09 semj/g; primary metal, 6.91E+09 semj/g (assume 2/3 steel and 1/3 aluminum); and (2) Goods including fabricated metal, 1.78E+10 semj/g; machinery except electrical, 7.76E+09 semj/g; electrical machinery, 1.46E+10 semj/g; instruments and related products, 1.46E+10 semj/g; and misc. manufactured products, 7.76E+09 semj/g. References for the specific emergies used for these materials are given in [12] and [45]. The transformity for electrical machines is a new estimate that is available from the authors on request. The same transformity was applied to instruments. The emergy of the services required for construction was calculated using the average dollar value of construction times the emergy to money ratio for the year in which the construction was put in place. The energy cost of building construction was originally taken from Stein [46], who estimated that 1.3 E+06 BTUs were required per sq. ft. built. In this study we checked this number using data from Scheuer *et al.* [47] and [48]. The fraction of energy (336 GJ/m^2) in material placement and transport for a high rise (7) floors (0.2% of total use, [44]) was corrected by a factor of 0.217 for an average education building 2 to 3 stories [48] We used the estimate of 1.21E+6 BTU/square foot from the latter estimate in this study. This value was applied uniformly over time, using the area built to estimate energy requirements for building construction. The emergy of the energy used in construction was determined by multiplying the energy required for the area built by the fraction of energy of each type available to support building construction in that year times the transformity of the energy used. The emergy requirements for construction were summed to determine the emergy of the school buildings constructed in each year. New construction was summed to estimate the area of buildings in service at any given time after diminishing the existing area by 0.033, a factor equivalent to a 30 year replacement time. New construction put in place was assumed to come into service on the half year, thus new construction was also subject to depreciation of 0.0167 per year. The emergy lost through the depreciation of the buildings in service, given a 30 year lifetime, was assumed to be the emergy supplied by building infrastructure in support of the education process carried on by each subsystem.

Services

The total expenditures for public elementary and secondary schools from 1870 to 2011 are recorded in [28–30]. Private school expenditures were recorded in some years from 1910 to 1970, after which they were recorded annually. We used linear interpolation to fill in the missing years, and we estimated private expenses prior to 1910 assuming that private expenses on education were about 10% of the public expenses (as estimated from years when both values were known). Expenditures were divided into elementary and secondary categories based on enrollment. The dollar values of elementary and secondary expenditures minus teacher salaries were considered to be the service input to these education subsystems. Dollar values were converted to emergy using the EMR calculated in [34]. We estimated the emergy to dollar ratio of the U.S. from 1870 to 1899 for this study and we applied it to make estimates of the emergy equivalent of dollar values for the years before 1900. After 1930, college expenditures were recorded and several different aggregations were reported. For this study we used the largest measure of expenses and diminished it by the cost of teacher salaries and library operations. Library operations were added into the emergy of college/university inputs as a separate item. Before 1900 college/university expenses were not recorded, so we estimated the values for earlier years using the ratio of college/university expenses to combined elementary and secondary expenses in 1900, and extrapolated back to 1870.

New Students Entering

The average disposable income per capita in the U.S. economy in the year evaluated, times the EMR for that year [34] was used to determine the support emergy allocated to each student in all subsystems. The new students entering elementary school in the fall were estimated by adding the entering kindergarten students to the first grade students and subtracting last year's kindergarten students. Data on kindergarten and first grade enrollment were taken from [32], although these data also appear in [29–31]. The new students entering elementary school were multiplied by the emergy per capita (as determined above) to estimate the emergy supporting the students entering elementary school. Eighth graders going on to high school were estimated as ninth grade enrollment in the fall. The emergy supporting new students entering high school was calculated as for elementary students. Data on the number of students graduating from high school each year was found in the U.S. Census Bureau data [29–31]. The percent of high school graduates going on to college was given in one format from 1931 to 1979, and in another format from 1984 until 2003. Missing data from 1979 to 2003 were supplied by linear interpolation; the number of recent high school completers going on to college was given in [30,31]. A linear regression of the data set from 1931 to 2011 was used to extrapolate values back to 1870. The number of new students entering college was multiplied by the emergy per capita used for their support to determine the emergy support for newly entering college students.

Returning Students

The emergy of returning elementary students was calculated as last year's enrollment minus the eighth graders going on to high school minus dropouts. The support emergy assigned to returning students in all three subsystems was the emergy per capita calculated from disposable income, and the EMR in that year. Initially returning high school students were calculated as high school enrollment in the previous year, minus high school graduates, minus dropouts. Because of irregularities in the data we changed the method of estimating returning high school students by adjusting the number of dropouts so that enrollment of new and returning students would give the correct enrollment in a given year. We handled returning college students in a manner similar to that used for high school students, *i.e.*, high school graduates entering college, and returning students, were forced to sum to enrollment using dropouts as the adjustment factor. In some years, this implied that "Dropouts" was a positive number in the balance and thus the extra students had to matriculate from other sources, e.g., former dropouts returning to or former high school graduates entering college.

Teachers

Data on public elementary and secondary teachers have been recorded by the U.S. Census Bureau [29,30] since at least 1870 and now by ProQuest [31]. The ratio of public to private enrollment was used to estimate the total number of teachers from the number of public school teachers. The total number of teachers was separated into elementary and secondary subsystems based on elementary and secondary enrollment assuming that the student to teacher ratio was similar. Salaries for public school teachers have also been recorded since 1870. We used the salary estimates for both elementary and high school teachers and multiplied by the number of teachers and the EMR for the economy in the appropriate year to determine the emergy supporting teachers at the elementary and secondary levels. College/University teacher salaries have been recorded since 1958 [29–31]. Between 1930 and 1958 college salaries were not recorded, but we estimated them from the number of teachers and the total expenses for instruction. Prior to 1930, college teacher salaries were estimated using the ratio of college salaries to elementary and secondary salaries in 1930. The emergy supporting college teachers was determined in a manner similar to that used for elementary and secondary teachers.

Dollar Flows

The dollar flows shown in Figure 1 were taken from U.S. Census Bureau data [29]. Data on public school expenditures are complete back to 1870. Missing data on private expenditures were handled in a manner similar to that described for estimating private enrollment and teachers. Data on revenues were not quite as complete as that for expenditures. To simplify the analysis, unknown revenues were estimated from their ratio to expenditures in the closest series of years when both were known.

Emergy of Teaching and Learning

The emergy per individual at any level of education is the summation of the emergy used to keep the student in school for the period of time needed to attain that level. The average education level and years of teaching experience for elementary and secondary school teachers are given in U.S. Census Bureau data for certain years [29–31] The emergy of a teacher's education was quantified in a manner similar to that used to calculate the emergy of an individual with a given level of education, *i.e.*, by summing the required emergy inputs over the actual years that the teacher was in school, which was determined based on the average experience level of the work force at the time the data was taken.

Destre *et al.* [49] found that within 10 years workers can learn almost 100% of the new knowledge available to them after taking a new job. Based on this observation, the emergy of the teachers' experience at any time was estimated assuming that teachers learn something new about 10% of the time, while they are performing their jobs. As a result, the emergy of teachers working at any given time is the emergy of their education level determined based on the average time they spent in school, plus 10% of the emergy to support their teaching activities in a year summed over their years of experience from graduation to the present time. Thus, both the emergy of a teacher's education and experience are determined using appropriate summations over past years when they obtained their knowledge and experience. Missing data on teacher education and experience was estimated using linear interpolation between known values.

The emergy per individual that students bring to the learning process was determined similarly. A student's level of knowledge is the sum of the emergy used to support their education up to the current year. A student is still learning, so they do not also get credit for experience, since their experience is captured in their learning. In the calculation of the emergy of learning during internship and residency, we assumed that a MD would spend half of their time learning and the other half of their time doing routine work; whereas, for a postdoctoral researcher the entire time was assigned to learning.

When determining the emergy of the teaching and learning process, the emergy per individual for the students and teachers was divided by their metabolic energy use in a year and multiplied by the metabolic energy used per hour of work to give the emergy delivered per hour of participation in the teaching or learning activity. The emergy delivered per hour of work was multiplied by the hours of work (teaching and learning) and then multiplied by the number of individuals engaged in this activity to give the annual emergy of this process in a subsystem of the U.S. education system. The sum over all subsystems gives the emergy of teaching and learning in the United States as a whole in any given year.

Systems **2014**, 2, 328–365

Appendix B.

Table A1. The emergy per individual for different education levels in the United States from 1870 to 2011. Numbers are in 10^{16} semj/ind. Some college means 2 years or an associate's degree, the professional degree is 3 years, and the MD degree assumes the completion of residency (5 years beyond medical school), postdoctoral experience is 2 years study beyond the Ph.D.

Year	Pre-School	Elem. Fifth Grade	Eighth Grade	High School 10-11	High School Grad.	Some College	College Grad.	Master's	Professional Degree	Doctoral Degree	MD with Internship Residency	Ph.D. with 2yr. Post Doc.
1870	7.3	28.2	38.7	46.5	54.4	75.8	97.3	118.7	129.4	140.1	NA	NA
1871	7.1	28.5	39.0	46.9	54.8	76.5	97.9	119.3	130.0	140.8	NA	NA
1872	6.9	28.8	39.2	47.7	55.2	76.5	98.2	119.6	130.4	141.1	NA	163.1
1873	6.8	28.9	39.4	47.9	55.6	77.2	98.3	119.7	130.4	141.1	NA	163.5
1874	6.6	29.0	39.5	48.0	56.3	77.0	98.8	119.8	130.5	141.2	NA	163.0
1875	6.4	29.1	39.5	48.0	56.2	77.1	98.6	119.9	130.6	141.3	NA	162.9
1876	6.3	28.8	39.4	47.9	56.3	77.9	98.3	119.9	130.2	141.0	167.3	162.6
1877	6.1	28.1	39.3	47.7	56.2	77.3	97.9	118.7	129.6	140.0	166.7	161.1
1878	6.0	27.5	39.0	47.4	56.1	76.3	96.4	117.4	128.1	139.0	165.7	159.1
1879	5.9	26.9	38.5	47.0	55.8	75.3	94.4	116.1	126.2	136.8	164.6	155.9
1880	5.9	26.3	37.7	46.5	55.5	74.2	92.5	113.6	124.5	134.6	163.3	152.7
1881	5.8	25.7	37.0	45.6	55.2	72.9	91.0	111.2	122.0	132.9	161.7	150.0
1882	5.7	25.2	36.2	44.9	54.9	72.3	89.8	109.3	119.7	130.5	160.4	147.3
1883	5.7	24.8	35.5	44.2	54.4	72.0	89.5	108.2	118.1	128.5	158.4	145.3
1884	5.5	24.5	34.9	43.5	53.6	72.1	89.9	107.7	117.3	127.2	156.6	144.5
1885	5.4	24.2	34.3	42.8	52.8	72.3	90.5	107.9	116.9	126.6	155.3	144.4
1886	5.3	23.9	33.7	42.1	52.1	71.9	90.8	108.4	117.1	126.2	153.3	144.5
1887	5.3	23.6	33.3	41.6	51.4	71.3	90.5	109.1	117.7	126.5	151.7	145.0
1888	5.3	23.4	32.9	41.3	50.8	70.7	90.1	109.5	118.5	127.1	150.7	145.7
1889	5.2	23.0	32.5	41.0	50.3	70.2	89.8	109.7	119.3	128.2	150.4	147.0
1890	5.2	22.6	32.2	40.7	49.9	70.0	89.8	109.7	119.6	129.2	150.3	148.3
1891	5.2	22.5	31.9	40.4	49.6	70.0	89.7	109.6	119.6	129.4	150.7	149.1
1892	5.0	22.4	31.4	39.9	49.2	69.7	89.5	109.3	119.2	129.2	151.5	149.0
1893	4.9	22.2	31.0	39.3	48.6	69.1	88.9	109.0	118.9	128.8	152.6	148.3
1894	4.8	21.9	30.7	38.6	47.9	68.4	88.3	108.7	118.6	128.6	153.3	147.8
1895	4.8	21.7	30.5	38.2	47.2	67.9	87.5	108.0	118.1	128.0	153.3	147.3
1896	4.8	21.6	30.2	37.9	46.5	66.9	86.7	107.1	117.4	127.5	152.8	146.6
1897	4.7	21.3	29.9	37.6	45.8	66.0	85.4	106.0	116.3	126.5	152.0	145.3
1898	4.6	21.0	29.7	37.0	45.3	65.0	83.8	104.5	114.7	125.0	151.1	143.5
1899	4.6	20.6	29.4	36.6	44.8	63.6	82.2	102.6	112.9	123.2	150.0	141.0
1900	4.6	20.5	28.9	36.3	44.2	62.4	80.3	100.5	110.8	121.2	148.9	138.3

Table A1. *Cont.*

Year	Pre-School	Elem. Fifth Grade	Eighth Grade	High School 10-11	High School Grad.	Some College	College Grad.	Master's	Professional Degree	Doctoral Degree	MD with Internship Residency	Ph.D. with 2yr. Post Doc.
1901	4.4	20.3	28.5	35.7	43.6	61.5	78.9	98.6	108.7	119.1	147.6	135.8
1902	4.7	20.2	28.3	35.3	43.3	60.7	78.3	97.1	107.2	117.3	146.0	133.8
1903	4.7	20.1	28.2	35.2	43.0	60.4	77.9	96.0	105.7	115.8	144.4	132.6
1904	5.0	22.4	31.4	39.9	49.2	69.7	89.5	109.3	119.2	129.2	151.5	149.0
1905	4.9	22.2	31.0	39.3	48.6	69.1	88.9	109.0	118.9	128.8	152.6	148.3
1891	4.8	21.9	30.7	38.6	47.9	68.4	88.3	108.7	118.6	128.6	153.3	147.8
1892	4.8	21.7	30.5	38.2	47.2	67.9	87.5	108.0	118.1	128.0	153.3	147.3
1893	4.8	21.6	30.2	37.9	46.5	66.9	86.7	107.1	117.4	127.5	152.8	146.6
1894	4.7	21.3	29.9	37.6	45.8	66.0	85.4	106.0	116.3	126.5	152.0	145.3
1895	4.6	21.0	29.7	37.0	45.3	65.0	83.8	104.5	114.7	125.0	151.1	143.5
1896	4.6	20.6	29.4	36.6	44.8	63.6	82.2	102.6	112.9	123.2	150.0	141.0
1897	4.6	20.5	28.9	36.3	44.2	62.4	80.3	100.5	110.8	121.2	148.9	138.3
1898	4.4	20.3	28.5	35.7	43.6	61.5	78.9	98.6	108.7	119.1	147.5	135.8
1899	4.7	20.2	28.3	35.3	43.3	60.7	78.3	97.1	107.2	117.3	146.0	133.8
1900	5.0	20.1	28.2	35.2	43.0	60.4	77.9	96.0	105.7	115.8	144.4	132.6
1901	4.9	22.4	31.4	39.9	49.2	69.7	89.5	109.3	119.2	129.2	151.5	149.0
1902	4.8	22.2	31.0	39.3	48.6	69.1	88.9	109.0	118.9	128.8	152.6	148.3
1903	4.6	21.9	30.7	38.6	47.9	68.4	88.3	108.7	118.6	128.6	153.3	147.8
1904	5.1	20.0	28.2	35.1	42.6	60.5	77.8	95.7	104.8	114.5	141.4	131.7
1905	5.2	20.2	28.2	35.2	42.5	60.4	78.6	96.0	105.0	114.2	139.9	131.5
1906	5.3	20.5	28.4	35.6	42.6	60.7	79.1	96.5	105.3	114.4	141.4	132.5
1907	4.8	21.2	28.6	35.9	42.8	61.2	79.2	97.1	105.6	114.4	138.5	133.1
1908	5.1	21.2	28.7	36.0	42.9	61.0	79.1	97.0	105.8	114.3	137.3	132.8
1909	5.1	21.4	29.0	36.0	43.0	60.7	78.8	97.0	106.0	114.9	136.8	132.7
1910	5.0	22.2	29.7	36.5	43.2	60.7	78.7	97.0	105.9	114.9	136.9	132.7
1911	5.2	22.4	29.9	37.1	43.3	61.0	78.9	97.0	106.3	115.2	137.2	133.2
1912	5.3	22.5	30.1	37.2	43.6	61.4	79.9	97.5	106.6	115.9	137.8	134.1
1913	4.9	22.1	31.0	37.5	43.8	62.2	81.1	98.6	106.7	116.7	138.8	135.6
1914	5.0	22.6	31.2	38.2	44.2	63.3	82.4	100.0	108.7	117.7	139.4	137.4
1915	4.7	22.6	31.3	38.2	44.2	63.9	83.2	101.1	109.9	118.6	139.5	138.7
1916	5.6	22.3	30.5	38.0	44.0	64.1	82.8	101.3	110.1	118.9	140.2	138.9
1917	5.6	22.7	31.3	37.4	44.9	63.1	82.5	101.7	110.7	119.5	140.6	138.5
1918	5.3	23.0	31.5	38.6	45.3	62.5	81.8	101.5	110.9	120.0	140.7	138.4
1919	5.7	22.6	31.5	38.7	45.3	63.6	80.2	100.3	110.0	119.4	140.7	138.1
1920	4.9	23.1	32.1	38.8	45.1	63.0	80.2	98.4	108.4	118.1	140.6	135.9
1921	5.4	22.7	32.1	39.2	45.6	61.9	79.2	96.5	106.6	116.5	141.0	133.1
1922	6.0	24.2	32.0	39.4	46.0	61.3	79.0	97.3	105.5	115.6	141.5	131.8
1923	5.9	24.6	32.8	40.0	46.7	62.8	79.6	97.5	106.6	114.8	141.2	131.9
1924	6.0	24.8	33.1	41.1	47.5	64.3	81.1	97.4	106.6	115.7	140.4	134.0
1925	6.0	25.8	34.9	41.3	48.3	65.0	82.6	97.9	106.6	115.8	139.4	134.2
1926	6.1	25.4	35.5	43.3	48.6	65.8	83.5	99.6	107.1	115.8	138.6	134.1
1927	6.1	26.7	35.7	43.9	49.5	66.8	84.2	101.0	108.7	116.3	137.7	134.7
1928	5.9	27.7	36.8	44.1	49.8	67.1	85.1	101.8	110.2	117.9	138.8	136.3
1929	6.3	27.8	36.5	45.2	51.8	67.8	85.8	102.9	111.4	119.7	139.1	138.1
1930	5.7	27.9	37.7	44.9	52.2	68.5	86.8	104.1	112.4	120.8	139.1	139.5
1931	5.0	27.7	38.3	45.4	51.9	70.8	87.1	104.4	113.3	121.6	139.4	140.6
1932	4.3	26.8	37.5	45.3	52.1	70.8	88.9	104.9	113.3	122.2	141.0	140.8
1933	4.4	26.0	36.9	44.1	50.8	70.0	88.9	105.2	114.1	122.5	142.5	140.5
1934	4.4	25.5	36.4	43.4	51.1	70.2	88.1	107.0	114.1	123.0	143.2	141.0
1935	4.6	24.1	35.5	42.8	51.3	68.9	87.8	106.5	115.7	122.8	144.0	140.9
1936	5.1	23.1	35.0	42.4	50.8	68.7	86.8	106.0	115.7	124.8	144.7	142.5

Table A1. *Cont.*

Year	Pre-School	Elem. Fifth Grade	Eighth Grade	High School 10-11	High School Grad.	Some College	College Grad.	Master's	Professional Degree	Doctoral Degree	MD with Internship Residency	Ph.D. with 2yr. Post Doc.
1937	5.5	22.7	35.2	42.4	50.7	69.2	87.0	106.0	115.0	124.7	144.6	142.6
1938	4.6	22.9	33.8	42.3	50.3	69.0	86.6	104.2	114.4	123.4	145.1	141.6
1939	5.1	23.2	32.9	40.9	49.9	68.2	86.3	104.3	113.2	123.3	144.9	140.8
1940	5.6	24.1	32.5	40.5	49.7	67.7	85.8	104.2	113.0	121.8	146.7	139.1
1941	5.8	25.2	33.3	40.3	50.0	67.5	85.0	103.7	112.9	121.7	146.5	139.3
1942	6.0	26.0	33.9	41.2	49.3	67.0	85.0	103.2	112.5	121.7	145.3	139.1
1943	5.4	24.9	34.6	41.5	48.3	67.5	84.5	102.5	111.9	121.2	145.4	138.7
1944	5.4	25.7	35.4	41.9	47.7	66.8	85.5	103.0	111.8	121.2	143.6	138.7
1945	5.4	26.1	35.8	42.8	48.2	66.3	84.1	101.9	111.1	119.9	142.8	137.9
1946	5.5	26.1	34.8	43.2	48.6	65.1	81.7	100.8	109.2	118.4	141.9	135.8
1947	5.7	26.3	35.8	42.4	49.6	63.6	79.3	98.4	107.8	116.1	140.4	131.5
1948	5.9	25.7	36.5	43.8	50.8	62.9	77.3	95.4	105.1	114.5	139.2	128.7
1949	5.7	26.0	36.8	44.7	51.6	63.2	76.5	93.0	102.3	112.0	137.6	125.7
1950	6.3	26.7	37.5	45.4	51.4	64.5	77.7	91.7	100.5	109.8	136.4	123.5
1951	6.1	27.4	37.1	46.5	53.0	66.1	80.0	92.0	99.7	108.4	134.9	122.9
1952	5.9	28.0	37.6	46.0	54.1	66.9	82.4	94.0	100.3	108.0	134.2	123.5
1953	6.1	28.6	38.2	46.7	54.9	69.3	83.9	97.0	102.6	109.0	132.7	125.3
1954	6.1	28.7	39.0	47.6	55.8	71.1	86.7	99.8	105.8	111.4	131.1	128.4
1955	6.1	29.6	39.8	48.4	55.6	72.4	88.8	101.6	108.7	114.6	130.3	132.1
1956	6.4	29.6	40.6	49.4	56.5	73.5	90.2	104.6	110.6	117.7	130.3	135.4
1957	6.4	29.8	41.0	50.5	57.6	73.5	91.7	107.1	113.9	119.9	131.5	137.8
1958	6.0	30.3	42.0	50.8	58.5	74.8	91.9	108.6	116.2	123.0	134.2	141.3
1959	6.1	30.4	41.9	51.7	59.4	76.0	93.2	110.1	117.9	125.5	137.5	143.9
1960	6.0	30.5	41.9	51.7	60.2	76.9	94.2	110.1	119.1	126.9	140.7	145.3
1961	6.0	30.9	42.5	51.7	60.5	77.7	95.1	111.5	119.4	128.4	142.8	146.7
1962	6.1	31.0	42.6	52.3	61.6	78.5	96.2	112.7	120.7	128.6	146.0	146.9
1963	6.2	30.5	42.9	52.6	61.6	79.0	96.9	113.6	122.0	130.0	148.5	148.5
1964	6.1	31.1	43.6	53.1	61.9	80.0	97.6	114.8	123.0	131.3	149.9	149.8
1965	6.5	31.5	44.2	54.2	62.9	80.2	98.4	115.3	123.8	131.9	151.3	150.5
1966	6.9	32.2	44.3	55.1	63.7	80.3	98.3	115.6	124.3	132.8	151.5	151.2
1967	7.1	33.0	45.2	55.4	64.4	81.0	98.4	116.5	124.6	133.4	152.7	151.4
1968	7.3	33.9	46.0	56.4	65.7	81.8	99.0	116.3	125.5	133.7	153.9	151.8
1969	7.6	35.2	47.0	57.5	66.8	82.5	99.8	116.5	125.4	134.6	154.9	152.6
1970	7.8	36.4	48.3	58.8	67.4	83.8	101.4	117.9	126.3	135.2	156.0	153.3
1971	8.3	37.5	49.9	60.5	68.9	85.6	102.9	119.0	127.2	135.6	156.7	154.5
1972	8.6	38.6	51.8	62.5	70.5	86.5	104.4	120.2	128.5	136.7	157.4	155.8
1973	9.3	40.1	53.9	65.0	72.5	87.7	105.8	122.2	130.0	138.3	158.6	157.0
1974	9.6	41.8	55.8	67.6	74.7	89.8	107.2	123.9	131.8	139.6	158.7	158.9
1975	8.8	42.8	56.9	69.2	76.5	92.0	108.1	124.1	132.6	140.6	159.0	160.0
1976	9.2	44.2	58.4	70.1	78.6	93.1	109.8	125.0	133.2	141.7	159.9	160.1
1977	9.4	45.2	60.1	71.9	80.7	94.3	111.3	126.4	134.1	142.4	161.3	160.2
1978	9.9	46.6	61.7	73.8	82.6	96.9	112.8	128.3	135.8	143.5	162.5	161.8
1979	10.0	47.3	63.6	75.7	84.4	99.2	115.6	130.1	137.7	145.1	163.5	163.7
1980	9.6	46.7	64.7	77.6	86.1	101.4	117.5	131.1	139.0	146.6	164.4	165.4
1981	9.3	47.4	65.9	78.4	87.8	102.7	118.9	133.1	139.7	147.6	164.6	165.8
1982	8.7	47.3	65.8	79.0	88.8	103.6	119.3	134.1	141.2	148.2	165.0	165.3
1983	8.6	47.3	64.5	78.5	89.9	104.5	119.7	135.0	142.1	149.2	166.2	165.9
1984	9.4	47.1	65.2	77.6	90.9	104.9	121.1	135.9	143.6	150.7	167.4	166.8
1985	9.3	46.3	65.4	78.6	92.0	106.5	121.9	136.7	144.3	152.0	168.4	168.5

Table A1. *Cont.*

Year	Pre-School	Elem. Fifth Grade	Eighth Grade	High School 10-11	High School Grad.	Some College	College Grad.	Master's	Professional Degree	Doctoral Degree	MD with Internship Residency	Ph.D. with 2yr. Post Doc.
1986	9.3	45.6	65.8	78.7	92.2	107.9	123.4	137.9	145.2	152.8	168.9	169.8
1987	9.6	45.1	65.7	79.4	91.5	108.8	125.1	139.1	146.7	153.9	170.9	170.8
1988	10.1	45.9	65.4	80.0	92.9	109.4	126.7	141.2	148.2	155.8	172.6	173.0
1989	10.4	47.7	65.5	80.4	94.0	109.3	127.6	143.3	150.3	157.3	174.3	175.1
1990	10.8	48.4	65.7	80.8	95.4	111.0	127.7	145.0	152.6	159.6	175.4	177.8
1991	10.2	49.0	66.6	81.0	96.0	112.3	129.3	145.9	154.0	161.6	176.7	179.9
1992	10.4	50.1	68.4	81.8	96.0	113.7	130.5	145.9	155.0	163.2	178.7	181.4
1993	10.5	51.3	69.0	83.7	96.1	114.1	132.2	147.8	155.2	164.4	180.6	182.5
1994	11.4	52.0	70.1	84.6	96.5	114.5	133.2	149.6	157.6	165.0	183.3	183.5
1995	11.7	53.0	71.6	86.2	97.9	115.3	134.4	152.0	159.7	167.7	185.9	186.8
1996	12.2	53.1	73.6	88.2	100.5	116.3	135.7	153.7	162.4	170.1	188.2	189.9
1997	12.5	54.3	74.9	90.4	101.9	118.4	137.2	155.3	164.2	173.0	190.1	193.4
1998	12.9	55.6	76.5	92.1	103.8	121.4	139.7	157.0	166.0	175.0	191.2	195.9
1999	12.6	57.5	76.9	93.9	105.8	123.2	142.8	158.6	167.6	176.6	194.2	197.9
2000	12.9	58.7	78.4	93.9	107.8	125.1	144.6	161.1	169.4	178.4	196.7	199.8
2001	12.3	59.7	79.6	95.3	109.1	127.3	146.5	164.1	171.6	179.9	199.6	201.4
2002	12.5	60.4	81.5	96.7	110.6	129.1	148.3	165.6	174.6	182.1	201.5	203.5
2003	12.6	61.0	82.7	98.8	111.0	130.1	150.2	167.5	176.2	185.2	203.3	206.2
2004	13.3	61.1	84.3	100.6	113.4	131.7	151.7	169.9	178.6	187.2	205.4	208.3
2005	13.4	62.2	85.6	102.7	115.3	132.6	153.9	172.4	181.1	189.8	207.4	211.4
2006	14.1	62.5	87.2	104.5	118.3	135.6	155.5	174.6	184.0	192.7	210.1	214.9
2007	12.2	63.9	88.0	106.6	120.5	138.1	158.8	177.1	186.2	195.6	213.8	218.5
2008	12.4	65.2	89.6	107.6	122.8	141.5	161.5	178.9	188.9	198.0	215.4	221.2
2009	10.5	66.0	89.0	108.2	123.5	143.9	163.5	180.8	189.0	191.1	217.8	222.5
2010	11.3	66.1	89.8	106.7	124.5	144.8	164.8	182.4	191.5	199.8	220.4	221.7
2011	11.5	66.8	90.5	107.6	124.4	144.5	166.6	185.3	193.5	202.6	217.5	223.5

Systems **2014**, *2*, 328–365

systems

MDPI

Article

One Way Forward to Beat the Newtonian Habit with a Complexity Perspective on Organisational Change

Sam Wells * and Josie McLean

The University of Adelaide Business School, 10 Pulteney Street, Adelaide, SA 5005, Australia;
josie@the-partnership.com.au
* Author to whom correspondence should be addressed; sam.wells@adelaide.edu.au;
  Tel.: +61-8-8313-8336; Fax: +61-8-8223-4782.

Received: 11 September 2013; in revised form: 14 October 2013; Accepted: 16 October 2013;
Published: 23 October 2013

Abstract: We face a global crisis of un-sustainability—we need to change trajectory, but have so far displayed a collective inability to do so. This article suggests that one reason for this is our entrenched approach to change, which has inappropriately applied mechanistic Newtonian assumptions to "living" systems. Applying what has been learned about the behaviour of complex adaptive systems, we develop a pragmatic model for students of sustainability, who want to facilitate profound organizational and community change towards sustainability on the ground. Our model, "one way forward", does not purport to be the only way but one possibility, grounded in a different understanding of the nature and dynamic of change as seen through the lens of complexity. In this way, it challenges more conventional change management practices. One way forward is a model facilitating evolutionary change in a social ecology—one possible expression of a "culture of community self-design" as expressed by Banathy. Its theoretical foundations and its practical application (it is designed for practice) both have their source in a systemic view and in the principles that reflect the paradigm of complexity. Four central components of this new model—envisioning, core messages (values), indicators of progress, and experimentation—are explored in more detail.

Keywords: sustainability; systemic change; paradigm shift; complex systems; envisioning; values; indicators; strategic experiments

---

"If you do not change direction, you may end up where you are heading".

Laozi

1. The Case for a New Approach

In a recent article Starik and Kanashiro refer to Academy of Management meetings "in which numerous scholars proposed various justifications and aspects of one or more new sustainability management theories" ([1], p. 11). They go on to explore the challenge of developing management theory that can truly influence practice—that enables individuals, organizations and society to make the shift towards "sustainability" in its most profound expression. They pose a question that reflects that challenge "How can social and environmental sustainability management phenomena be integrated for "total" or "holistic" sustainability approaches, whether through integrated sustainability indicators, approaches, policies, values, strategies, programs, or results?" ([1], p. 24). What follows is one response to that question, specifically in regard to the dynamics of the organizational and community paradigm shift to sustainability, and how students of sustainability can learn how to exercise their leadership by better understanding and engaging with the dynamics of that profound change.

Organizational literature on change reports the "success" rate of conventional planned change initiatives as between 70% and 90% failure [2–4]! We might expect that this lack of success would have

Systems **2013**, *1*, 66–84

propelled us collectively to inquire more closely into the nature and dynamic of change, but it seems we have been exhibiting what has been described as "insanity"—doing the same thing over and over and expecting different results.

If for no other reason than that planned change initiatives appear to fail so often and so comprehensively, we should be looking at new ways of perceiving, being and doing—but our global state of unsustainability provides a further and urgent imperative. What prevents us from bringing about the necessary transformation of ourselves and our organizations? This paper seeks to explore that question and propose, not the "correct" approach, but one possibility—*one way forward*.

2. The Paradigm Shift—From Newton to Complexity

Thomas Kuhn, in his account of the way in which scientific "revolutions" have taken place in the past, provides a useful starting point, in the form of one precious insight. He describes how an existing "paradigm" perseveres even when the evidence from nature suggests that it is flawed. The disconfirming evidence mounts, but instead of abandoning the paradigm, scientists make changes at the margins of their existing theoretical framework—so that it appears to accommodate the new data. Kuhn observed that the shift away from a flawed paradigm only occurred when a new paradigm was articulated (and sometimes when the major leader of the old paradigm passed away!)—a new paradigm that explained the evidence better. Revolutionary change did not take place to escape inadequacies in the established paradigm, but to embrace a new possibility [5].

This article attempts to draw on Kuhn's insight in two ways. First, the model described here itself reflects a paradigm shift, a new possibility in terms of how we understand and engage with transformational change. Second, the way in which the model proposes that we exercise our leadership to facilitate that change—the actual dynamics of change—reflects Kuhn's observation that profound shifts in thinking and action are the product of embracing a beckoning future, rather than eschewing a flawed present.

What is the old paradigm? Many writers have described it, and it permeates management training and education in our organizations as pervasively as it has permeated our wider society for three hundred years [6–10]. It is referred to as the "Newtonian paradigm", or the "mechanistic paradigm". On one level, this paradigm has undeniably worked well for the modern Western world. It has helped to generate living standards that even our grandparents' generation is astonished by, but like so many worldviews, its strengths are also its Achilles' heel—it has created its own problems and, with them, the imperative to explore an alternative [11].

As a new paradigm emerges, however, it is useful to pause and reflect upon the assumptions, often unconscious, that characterize the Newtonian paradigm, and to consider how those assumptions underpin the demonstrated failure of the majority of conventional planned change management initiatives.

Sir Isaac Newton believed that the universe was a piece of clockwork—a machine. The rules or laws that governed how the machine operated were assumed to be fully discoverable and it was inferred that if we understood them, we could then understand, predict and control the behaviour of the machine. In this certain and predictable world, causation is "linear"—cause and effect are related consistently, predictably, on a commensurate scale and in one direction, from cause to effect. These assumptions have reinforced the desire to control processes in order to deliver the desired or preferred and predetermined outcomes—to provide a sense of certainty.

The machine's function was understood to be no more than the sum of its parts. To understand the function, the machine could be reduced to its parts, and each part reduced to smaller and smaller parts, viewed in isolation from each other. This "reductionist" approach has helped us in mechanical systems, but it is becoming apparent that when it comes to helping humanity to deal with systems that are "living" and non-mechanical, it has serious limitations. Indeed we now may view these mechanistic assumptions, applied inappropriately to environmental and social systems, as having created more problems than they have solved [12,13].

Knowledge and understanding of living systems has been accumulating since scientists started exploring the "ecology" of natural systems in the 20th century. The world of complex systems is as uncertain as Newton's world was certain. (We use the term "systems" here as a way of recognizing areas of focus or concern that are bounded for practical problem solving purposes—the "system of interest"—but we also recognize that given the "incompressibility" of complex systems, the notion of boundaries between different social and environmental "systems" is conceptual. It could be argued that there is but one, all-encompassing system [14]).

Small changes in a starting point can produce wide fluctuations in outcome—"sensitivity to initial conditions". It is often impossible to track the path from cause to effect and the effect may not be at all commensurate with the cause—"non-linear causation". The popular story of the butterfly flapping its wings on one side of the world and creating a tornado on the other side—Lorenz's *butterfly effect*—describes this dynamic of causation that contributes to the inconsistency and unpredictability of complex systems [15]. We cannot hope to predict the precise nature and timing of outcomes by modelling these systems. Modelling can explore scenarios, but not certainties [12]. Reductionism does not help us when it comes to understanding the behaviour of complex systems. In breaking them into parts, we lose the very quality that makes them what they are, that makes them "whole"—we lose the relationship between the parts. If we are to understand them, we must understand them as a whole, while surrendering any pretension to prediction or control.

The paradigm shift from a mechanistic to a complex systems view can be tracked in the organisational change literature. In 1995, John Kotter published a Harvard Business Review article on leading change that was to become the darling of management educators and consultants, and the touchstone for "best practice" [16]. It could be argued that Kotter's model was the epitome of the mechanistic paradigm—certain, linear, controlling. Just follow the eight steps in order and you can unerringly navigate your organisation from point A to point B.

(1) Establish a Sense of Urgency
(2) Forming a Powerful Guiding Coalition
(3) Creating a Vision
(4) Communicating the Vision
(5) Empowering Others to Act on the Vision
(6) Planning for and Creating Short-Term Wins
(7) Consolidating Improvements and Producing Still More Change
(8) Institutionalizing New Approaches

In 2012, Kotter published another HBR article about the need for a second "operating system" that "accelerates strategic change" [17]. It builds on the original eight-step model, but we can see in his eight "accelerators" the unmistakable signs that the science of complexity and living systems has begun to influence Kotter's thinking:

> "There are three main differences between those eight steps and the eight "accelerators" on which the strategy system runs: (1) The steps are often used in rigid, finite, and sequential ways, in effecting or responding to episodic change, whereas the accelerators are concurrent and always at work. (2) The steps are usually driven by a small, powerful core group, whereas the accelerators pull in as many people as possible from throughout the organization to form a "volunteer army". (3) The steps are designed to function within a traditional hierarchy, whereas the accelerators require the flexibility and agility of a network". ([17], p. 95)

Meanwhile, the systems community, while not yet occupying the orthodox centre stage still dominated by Newtonian linearity, was already coming to grips with the profound implications of complexity for how we understand and engage with change. Donella Meadows was encouraging us to "dance" with systems:

Systems can't be controlled, but they can be designed and redesigned. We can't surge forward with certainty into a world of no surprises, but we can expect surprises and learn from them and even profit from them. We can't impose our will upon a system. We can listen to what the system tells us, and discover how its properties and our values can work together to bring forth something much better than could ever be produced by our will alone.

We can't control systems or figure them out. But we can dance with them!. ([18], p. 2)

We can envision what we really want, not what we are willing to settle for ([19], p. 4), and then learn how to bring that vision "lovingly into being", in a world of systems that requires "our full humanity—our rationality, our ability to sort out truth from falsehood, our intuition, our compassion, our vision, and our morality" ([18], p. 2).

Bela Banathy was writing in very similar ways about vision as "design", and emphasising the role of conversation in co-creating the design of our future:

What do we do in communities and in education that will lead us toward conscious evolution? In other words, what approaches will help us make connections, find common ground, create images of desirable futures, and select and plan to make those images come to life?. ([20], Chapter 6, p. 7)

Banathy contrasted the process of self-design in a complex environment with our objective, logical, linear inheritance:

- Designing is different from planning or trying to fix what exists. It involves imagining new possibilities.
- Designers use reason and intuition, depend on judgments rather than decisions, are proactive rather than reactive, and embrace diversity of viewpoints.
- Most situations of importance are dynamic and complex and require systems thinking.
- To be able to work together we need to uncover and understand our own and each other's assumptions, beliefs, and values...
- Conversation represents a new way of being together. It is a powerful tool for designing, systems thinking, and uncovering assumptions, beliefs, and value. It offers much to the development and ongoing work of communities and education.
- Conscious evolution might be manifested in a global culture of community self-design ([20], Chapter 6, p. 9).

One way forward seeks to take the next step on the path lit up by Meadows and Banathy. In fact, we hope that it does not break stride. In presenting a practical model for exercising sustainability change leadership, *one way forward* proposes vision or design not as the starting point in a linear planning process, to be followed by a quite distinct implementation process, but as a container, deftly cradling the components of a dynamic that reconnects "planning" and "implementation" and honors the behaviour of complex systems. All the components of this dynamic are in a continuous process of interaction and refinement. There is no beginning or end, but a constant becoming. It is a model for facilitating evolutionary change in a social ecology—one possible expression of a "culture of community self-design".

3. Engaging with Complexity

In order to grapple with challenges like climate change, pollution, poverty, social dysfunction and organisational sustainability, in its broadest sense, humanity must learn the lessons of complexity. Delivering predetermined outcomes by controlling complex systems is not possible—this becomes more apparent as we expand geographical and temporal horizons. Does that mean we give up and metaphorically "turn out the lights"?

We could choose that response, or we could attempt to *influence* outcomes proactively, by engaging with the challenges in a different way. It is no coincidence that the contemporary champions and exponents of systems thinking have been drawn inexorably, and seamlessly, to these challenges of sustainability. Nowhere do the qualities of connectedness and complexity come more naturally to the fore than in attempts to nourish those complex living systems that both encompass human community and in which human life on earth is embedded. And it follows that the dynamics of transformational change for sustainability, in particular, are best influenced from that same perspective. We cannot control complex systems, as the mechanistic paradigm assumes we can, but we can, as Meadows proposes, learn to "dance" with them [18]—to interact with them in a spirit of humility, patience, experimentation and learning. Where we cannot predict, we can still learn how the system behaves by trial and error—or "trial and error, error, error" as Buckminster Fuller described it (in [18]).

Further, we suggest that, rather than accepting our lack of control reluctantly, grudgingly, we can joyously surrender the desire for direct control, because it is self limiting—limited by the capacity of our stand-alone efforts and by the boundaries of whatever specific outcome we are seeking to dictate—whereas the art of influencing systemically involves recognizing and learning to work with the powerful self-organizing forces already operating within the system. If we can learn to work with those forces, in a spirit of humble facilitation and liberation, we gain access to the transformative power of the system itself, so much greater than the power of our own (illusory) control. The surfer and the gardener know what it is to encounter forces that cannot be controlled, but which can be learned about and worked with in a way that renders the desired outcome more likely, and which open the door to possibilities that could not be contemplated as the end point of control, even if control were possible.

The notion of managing and exercising leadership in a way that influences rather than controls is a challenging one for managers, not least because they have been trained, educated and "performance managed", in alignment with the assumptions of the Newtonian paradigm, to believe that they *should* be able to exert control and deliver predetermined outcomes. One of the most challenging implications of the shift from a mechanistic to a complexity perspective lies in recognizing the ways we have been socialized, within the Newtonian paradigm, to think about the nature and dynamic of change itself. Within this paradigm, which favours the objective and concrete world, change has come to be thought of as an object, leading to a future state that can be predetermined, planned, scheduled, implemented and achieved. Corporate language reflects this way of thinking, with phrases such as "driving change", "rolling out change" and "shifting the levers of change".

Within the paradigm of complexity, however, change may be understood as a response of the system to a stimulus, and better thought of as an emergent quality of the living system itself. It is intangible and occurs when participants (agents) within the system make sense of new information [21], and decide to act differently based upon reference to the system's "DNA" or, in the context of an organization, its organizational vision and values [10]. This different perception of "change" demands a different type of leadership and management—one that can shape a human environment in which desirable change may emerge.

We suggest that the perception of change as an object within the mechanistic paradigm, failing to grasp the real nature and dynamic of emergent change, is a significant contributor to the poor success rate of planned organizational change initiatives. The perception or assumption that change is an object leads to the design of change initiatives best suited to incremental change or change where little learning is required to be undertaken—"technical challenges" in Heifetz's language [22].

In developing the following model of transformational change for sustainability we have honoured the "adaptive" quality of the challenges [22], and the nature and dynamic of emergent change as perceived through the lens of complexity.

4. One Way Forward: A Model for Proactively Facilitating Systemic Change

How *do* we go about "influencing" systemic change—without submitting to our Newtonian habits of thought and self-limiting, mechanistic assumptions?

Our "*One way forward*" has emerged from an abductive process of engaging with the literature, building a conceptual model, trying things out in practice and reflecting critically on what does and does not work. Its very development has been an exercise consistent with the proposed model itself, in that our actions have been consistently informed by the principles of complexity, and we have tried not to be seduced by the allure of the familiar—by the "old" paradigm. We present this overview as one organizational expression of the emerging paradigm of complexity.

The model described here is informed by what we understand about the behaviour of complex systems. It has emerged from a deep inquiry into the challenge of catalysing transformational change for sustainability. Its apparent simplicity conceals an appreciation of how adaptive change emerges—a fundamental shift in perspective that challenges much received wisdom, reflected in models like Kotter's eight steps as previously described, and institutionalized in activities like strategic planning, change management and organizational communication. In practice, this framework requires that those employing it be prepared to "unlearn" many things previously held to be true—and step into a sometimes impenetrable world of ambiguity that demands new learning and "adaptive work" [23]. In his Adaptive Leadership Framework, Heifetz indicates that one characteristic of an adaptive challenge, in which fundamentally new learning is required, involving shifts in orientation, is that the people with the problem, are the problem, ... and the solution [23]. Our model and the accompanying facilitated process incorporate the principles of adaptive change.

Students of management may be *assisted* and guided in this process by developing an understanding of the principles underpinning the complexity paradigm. That involves not just a conceptual understanding, but also appreciating the practical importance of timing and the practical value of personal qualities like trust, patience, and humility. Combined with emotional intelligence and the interpersonal skills to work with and through people, these qualities shape the capacity to exercise leadership, which will enable the whole system (community of interest or organization) to bring a shared vision into being.

The *one way forward* model provides an understanding of how to engage in transformational change for sustainability, building on the special characteristics of complex adaptive systems. It simultaneously encompasses conventional "planning" and "implementation", which are seen as separate activities in the Newtonian paradigm. Planning and implementation become one dynamic and converge with management practices that generate a "sense of ownership" of solutions. This approach is also consistent with our understandings of autopoietic (living and self-generating) systems, where change may be viewed as a response made by all agents within the system, when they make sense of the need for a different response. System wide participation is a fundamental principle that emerges from this understanding [10,21]. *One way forward* emphasizes the importance of *genuine* ownership and the acceptance of appropriate responsibility within the system.

Consistent with the principles of complexity, our approach reflects notions of working with the whole system and employs *holarchy* rather than hierarchy as an organizing principle [24–26]. Within the holarchy, the design of Figure 1 assumes a temporal dimension of "now". We might view all time as being present in only one moment—this moment, or "now". Past actions reflecting the path that has brought us to this moment and our current state; choices and actions we might take in this moment; the future that we really want as it exists in us at this moment; and the various choices available that will lead to that "future moment" that are already present within this moment, but not yet unveiled.

Systems **2013**, *1*, 66–84

One way forward

In every moment, each holon is in a continuous dynamic influencing all other holons

Figure 1. One way forward.

We have deliberately avoided the depiction of our process as a linear progression over time, because we are seeking more appropriate ways of expressing the new paradigm. Using "old" paradigm flowcharts and arrows may have made the process seem more familiar (and therefore acceptable), because it encourages the employment of entrenched linear, mechanistic and reductionist mental models—these need to be opened to the air if we are to explore new possibilities [7]. Another important reason for framing our model within the "now" is the recognition, emphasized by Stacey and others, that complex adaptive systems (the metaphor for organizations and society that Stacey employs) are inherently unpredictable [8,27]. As soon as we develop a planning process with pre-determined, concrete outcomes determined for a future time, we are falling back into the Newtonian world.

Within complex systems, across the longer periods of time and greater spatial spans that are characteristic of sustainability challenges, predetermined paths, goals and milestones are a mirage, even though we may be deeply socialized to believe they are the only way to plan. Our model explores another way. In complex systems the future unfolds unpredictably. Our model honors both that unpredictability and the impulse to influence the emergent future, proactively.

4.1. One Way Forward

4.1.1. Revealing a Shared and Responsible Vision: "What We Really Want, Not What We'll Settle for"

The most obvious place to start is envisioning, because a shared vision, once created, has embedded within it all the other elements we propose are useful for moving forward. It cradles the entire model, and prepares and sustains a group (organization, community or team) that is seeking to influence the unpredictable unfolding of the future. It is the rich soil in which the other elements are planted and with which they exchange nourishment.

In her presentation on "envisioning for a sustainable world" [19], Donella Meadows highlighted the absence of vision as a major source of failure in addressing environmental issues and there is no evidence to suggest that this absence has since been addressed [28]. Possibly drawing on the work of her Dartmouth colleague, Elise Boulding [29], she went on to describe the principles and benefits of envisioning a *responsible* shared vision. In doing so she inspired our current approach.

The idea of vision and of leaders being visionary is not uncommon in leadership literature, but there is a fundamental difference between that type of top-down vision that the followers "buy into" [30], and the vision that we are describing. *One way forward* begins with the co-creation of a vision that brings together all the relevant stakeholders within the system.

Systems **2013**, *1*, 66–84

In a paper primarily focused on two questions—what constitutes a vision? and how does a vision work?—van der Helm identifies seven different types of vision, one of which is community based and designed to "produce a common ground from which to build programmes of action" ([30], p. 98). The vision we are describing is of this type.

Visions, as they are understood in *one way forward*, are also values-rich stories, rather than the pithy one-sentence "vision statements" that have come to pervade the corporate world. They are stories, capable of reflecting complexity, that describe what we really want to experience, and because values are central to decision making and behavior, vision of this kind also stirs energy within people and prompts the translation of energy into action. It is precisely because the vision is values rich and idealistic that it moves people with a sense of "divine discontent"—compelling action and change. In this sense we argue that idealistic shared visions are the most "realistic" and "pragmatic" way forward.

As Peter Senge quotes Kazuo Inamori of Kyocera, "It's not what the vision is, it's what the vision does" ([7], p. 207) and Meadows is more specific when she describes how a vision at the level of feeling (values) unites people rather than dividing them over less important "concrete" details [19]. She observed, and our own work has consistently confirmed, that at the level of fundamental values—"what we really want"—there is a great deal in common among people who might otherwise be at odds.

The *one way forward* envisioning process addresses the need for "emancipation", one of the central focuses of critical systems thinking—"denouncing situations where the exercise of power, or other causes of distorted communication, are preventing the open and free discussion necessary for the success of interaction" ([31], p. 141). Perceived differences in priority or "agenda", and perceived power differentials operating outside the envisioning process, succumb to the leveling impact of story-telling, in which each voice is equally honoured and every story is "gathered up" in the process of shaping a shared story or vision that is not "consensus" or "lowest common denominator", but tells everyone's story in one.

Nevertheless, facilitators need to be alert at the point of invitation that perceived power imbalances do not discourage some stakeholders from accepting. Every effort should be made to encourage participation by all stakeholders—invariably, the experience is one of surprise at how little such power issues persist into the envisioning process. There are a few points in the process where established power dynamics might try to assert themselves, but this can be readily forestalled by a watchful facilitator simply re-establishing the primacy of the story-telling process, in which all voices have equal weight.

On one occasion, we facilitated an envisioning workshop for a group of about 50 diverse stakeholders in the NRM (natural resource management) space—from state government policy makers and federally funded agencies, to scientists and consulting practitioners. We had been warned to expect conflict and potential implosion, such were the perceived differences. The entity funding that research sent an "observer" (he intended to observe, but could not help participating in the process). He was unaware of the political, philosophical and personal tensions that had been at work in this group before the workshop. As he left, he observed that it was impressive how smoothly the process went in a group of such like-minded stakeholders, but it would be interesting to see how well it performed in the regions where there were starker differences of perspective!

Of course, there will still be disagreements about the actions to be taken—the "strategic experiments"—in order to bring the shared vision into being, but the common ground, established at the most basic level of meaning making, provides a constant orientation for the debate and ensures that the dynamic is one in which differences enrich rather than diminish.

A shared vision channels the collective energy for change, for trying something new. In complex circumstances where we want to assume a proactive attitude, yet cannot predict or dictate a defined path to our desired future, a vision provides a light or touchstone to orientate and guide action [30].

The reason we seek to envision a new possible state is because we are dissatisfied with the existing one but, referring back to Kuhn, we recall that the emergence of a clearly articulated new paradigm is the trigger for change that enables most people to let go of the old and move to the new. So, in any transformational change initiative, the creation of a shared vision is important.

Without detailing here how this envisioning is most effectively facilitated, the central characteristics of the process are as follows:

(1) An invitation to be a part of the envisioning extended to as many as possible of the stakeholders within the system of interest.

(2) road participation by everyone who accepts the invitation.

(3) A facilitation process that by-passes the more analytical thinking and encourages more heartfelt, "feeling" responses.

(4) A vision of how we want to *experience* sustainable living—for example, how we want to experience working together—rather than the concrete details of what everything will actually be like (that is, a dynamic and evolving state—there is no definitive, concrete end point).

(5) Articulating individual visions through conversations about *what we really want*, and progressively generating shared visions that are also responsible (e.g., recognizing the physical limits of our resources).

(6) An inclusive conversation that gathers up everyone's heartfelt desires and does not leave anything or anyone behind, ensuring that the end result is truly reflective of every participant's vision—not a process of consensus, compromise or lowest common denominator.

(7) A story rather than a sentence, that details a rich picture of how we really want to experience the environment or the activity under consideration.

(8) Pictures or other art that help to bypass our habits of analysis may prompt and accompany the story.

Most of these characteristics are consistent with practice emerging within the discipline of *future search* since the 1990's [30].

In the case of forming *sustainable* communities or organizations, we would suggest that there is an additional reason for the importance of creating a shared vision. Envisioning *what we really want* consistently produces shared visions that appear to be inherently interconnected, integrated and "sustainable". It may be that these heart-felt stories reflect an innate capacity to respond systemically to a complex environment.

When we began our own journey of experimenting with groups of people and facilitating envisioning processes for sustainability, we anticipated that the act of envisioning would be "adaptive", as proposed by Heifetz [23], since people reprioritized values aligned with their current way of experiencing life to those required for a newer sustainable way in the future. But our observation of people engaging joyously, without hesitation or confusion and, on nearly every occasion, without serious disagreement, suggests that the work is more "technical" in nature—there appears, both through observation and interviewing participants after the envisioning, to be no reprioritization of values taking place, just a spontaneous and unselfconscious re-cognition of how people really want to experience their lives and work—a rediscovery of what they already know.

This notion that people have an innate understanding of how to act and live best in complex environments is consistent with Hämäläinen and Saarinen's notion of *systems intelligence* [32]. Systems Intelligence is the product of eons of human evolution. Humans are born with it and may develop it further as they live out their lives in complex adaptive systems. Viewed in this light, it makes sense that people already have a "feel" for how to engage with complex systems and indeed have "knowledge", at some level, of the conditions in which they are most likely to thrive. Through this innate understanding, the paradigm shift to a sustaining state is available to us, even if our dominant mental models reflect the existing or old paradigm ("Sustaining" is a term coined in the organizational literature by Dunphy *et al.* [33]. It describes an organization that has moved beyond reducing harm, to one that nourishes and nurtures the environmental and social ecologies in which it is embedded. It also reflects the paradigm shift). And so it is that *one way forward*'s envisioning process, appears to display the characteristics of "technical" work—at some level, we already "know" all that we need to know in regard to the new paradigm.

Although the process of envisioning does require careful introduction and framing to put some participants at ease in revealing and sharing "what I really want", within the *one way forward* model, envisioning presents as one of the easier activities.

4.1.2. Embedded in the Vision: Values Expressed as Core Messages

Because the vision is about the things we care most about, it is a values-rich story. Once the group has revealed its shared vision, it is possible to identify the values already embedded in the vision as core messages. As with the envisioning, this is a collaborative exercise.

Values are important because they direct our individual and collective actions and participating in a process that makes the shared values explicit provides a stronger foundation—both in awareness and social bonds—to undertake the tough decisions that a group will need to make. These values or core messages, once identified, can be used to build a bridge between the vision and actions on the ground that seek to bring the vision into being.

From a facilitative perspective, this process is gentle on both facilitators and participants. It is possible that this reflects prior participant experience of working with values—it is not unfamiliar territory in a "strategic planning process" or in "team building" work. What is worth noting in the *one way forward* model, however, is that the values are identified directly within the vision, not separate from it. This ensures that they are relevant to the future state—the values identified are "strategic" in themselves.

Our practical experience suggests that having the participants aggregate the core messages into a workable number, between five and seven, helps to crystallize and clarify their thinking, and to focus the efforts of the group in identifying the indicators of progress.

4.1.3. Indicators of Progress: A Concrete Reflection of the Core Messages of the Vision

The core messages extracted from the values-rich, co-created vision provide a springboard for identifying indicators of progress—what will we observe as we successfully bring our shared vision into being? ... "lovingly" into being, as Meadows describes it [18].

In undertaking any action, it is natural to seek to understand if what you have done has moved you towards your desired future or not. Traditionally, managers employ a range of quantitative measures—founded upon a received wisdom that "you can't manage what you can't measure". Measures *lag* outcomes. They are about what has already happened.

Indicators, on the other hand, monitor what is unfolding—they *lead* outcomes. They tell us how much progress we are making—whether we are on track. They focus on what we will observe in the tangible world as our vision is coming into being. As the vision is by its nature heart-felt and does not come with its own definitive pathway, complete with measurable milestones, the indicators of progress are also usually (although not necessarily) qualitative and unapologetically subjective, but they are observable, and the group is able to review whether they are seeing more of this particular indicator as they act to bring their vision into being.

By reflecting upon the presence or otherwise of specific indicators of progress as a group, there is some reassurance to those who are more comfortable with measures, that these subjective assessments do not reflect only one person's perspective. In all this work, "bringing the system together" in conversation is a fundamental principle [10] and in the context of identifying indicators of progress, the group provides a system wide and "responsible" perspective.

Of utmost importance is the recognition that the measures and indicators we choose may actually influence the system of interest and create potential for perverse outcomes—we must choose indicators wisely [34]. This is especially true if our indicator is, in fact, a measure—measures tend to measure the

Systems **2013**, *1*, 66–84

outputs in one or other *part* of the system, whereas qualitative or subjective indicators can attempt to capture the behaviour of the whole system, without submitting to the reductionist assumption that the whole is merely the sum of the parts. A numerical Key Performance *Indicator* (KPI) for example, may focus the energies of the organizational system on delivering that particular number in that particular part of the system, without regard to the "side"-effects on the system as a whole. The number—the measure—might be achieved, but there may be unexpected and unwelcome impacts in regard to creativity, collaboration, the success of the whole, and so on. A measure often constrains, rather than liberating, the self-organizing power of the system.

The lure of the measure is in great part a product of its accessibility and our collective, deeply socialized belief in the supremacy of "the objective" over "the subjective"—if something *can* be measured, it is tempting to convince ourselves that the measurement will be useful and important—like the driver who searches for his car keys under the street light, even though he dropped them somewhere else, because it is the only place with enough light to make searching easy! The forgoing is not to denigrate all measures—some are systemically useful, but measures should be "handled with care" because of the reductionist assumptions that often ignore their unseen systemic impacts.

Identifying indicators of progress appears to be *adaptive work* as there is "unlearning" and new learning to be grappled with [35]. This is the time when the group of stakeholders needs to identify what they might observe if the vision were being realised in the here and now. The identification of indicators can be seen as building a bridge between vision and action. These conversations are crucial and need careful facilitation to ensure the adaptive work is undertaken and not "avoided" by the group. It is tempting and easy to slip back into familiar "technical" solutions [23], such as existing approaches, or mechanical measures, that require no new learning ... and risk the health, or wholeness, of the system.

We should also expect the process of developing good and effective indicators to be one of continual adjustment and refinement ... learning which indicators are most effective to monitor progress in bringing the vision into being—indeed the vision, itself, may be refined as more is learned about the larger system and as the larger system itself evolves.

4.1.4. "Strategic Experiments": Indicators Prompt Concrete Action and Learning

In a complex environment, marked by "irreducible uncertainty" [18], where the shared vision orientates us, but the path only emerges as we tread it, we are dependent on a process of continuous learning, but the challenge is to decide on which pathways to try next. Indicators of progress based on the core messages of our shared vision help us to monitor our success in bringing the vision into being, but they are also, themselves, prompts to action. They provide another way to keep the vision alive, so that choices, decisions and actions remain informed by and connected to the vision. The indicators of progress prompt a group to experiment with different activities on a strategic basis to see what works and what does not—*what can we do that might give rise to the progress we are seeking?*—and to learn more about the complex system with which they are engaging. It is *strategic experimentation*, because these actions are taken to explore the most important and challenging facets of the vision—the core messages—as identified by the group.

Because we cannot predetermine or dictate outcomes, each *next step* is an experiment to learn what works within the context of our current experience of the complex system. The process is an iterative cycle of *action and learning*. The learning phase is a critical reflection upon what has eventuated as a result of the action, with reference to the shared vision, its core values and the indicators of progress (recognizing that long feedback loops may constrain a complete appreciation of the outcomes).

Importantly, the first phase is observing and learning—rather than action. Before rushing in to act, the initial learning involves gaining a collective understanding of, or feel for, the whole system and its possible leverage points, where interventions achieve the most impact for effort [35]. Meadows called this *getting the beat* of the system [18]—sensing, without analysing, the underlying dynamics and rhythms that are driving the behavior of the system. In the same way, the surfer sits on the beach and gets a feel for the surf, gets a sense of the frequency and shape and direction of the "system", before seeking to intervene. Organizationally it is not uncommon to hear managers talk about the quality of "energy" in their group—this is one example of "getting the beat" of the system.

The next steps are a continuous process of learning. In an ongoing iterative cycle, the action taken informs future strategic experiments, and is also likely to feed back into the vision, which evolves as more is learned—the model is dynamic and the vision is never final. The process of iteration is an important one as, in the non-linear world, it allows the system to fold back upon itself, amplifying novel ideas and unsettling the status quo. As Margaret Wheatley explains, "iteration helps small differences grow into powerful and unpredictable effects". ([10], p. 122). The process of iteration is not a "clean" one—it is a process that brings the system to the edge of chaos from which the new order emerges, and it will be experienced as "messy".

4.2. Loving the Messiness

The *one way forward* described above appears simple and easy to implement, but practice suggests that, like all change, it is not at all neat and is, indeed, messy. And that is a good thing, to be embraced. If the process is not experienced as messy and occasionally uncomfortable, we suggest that the adaptive work, the unlearning and learning, and reprioritization of values, is not taking place or that we are not "dancing" with the real complexity of living social systems. This involves exposing mental models to the air [7], letting go of, or "un-learning", past certainties, so that new possibilities can be explored and new learning undertaken. Those challenges confront everyone involved in the change, and it is no surprise that differences in the willingness to engage and in the rate of adaptive work, reflecting in part the self-preserving response of the established "system", will add to the experience of messiness.

The messiness requires, and is reflected in, our learning to surrender to the unknowable and to work deftly with events as they unfold—allowing "the answer" to emerge from people representing "the system" both at any one time and over time. As Meadows describes it, "It is to let go into Not Knowing" [36]. We suggest that one needs to surrender the desire for "neat" and "tidy" and "in control"—these are illusions anyway. If we are attempting to render everything nicely ordered and controlled, we have slipped back into the mechanistic paradigm whose inadequacies, in the context of change, were the starting point of this discussion. We need to learn to love the messiness! The journey, or process, is no less important than the deliverables in this case.

4.3. Joy and Leadership

Our research also suggests that the sense of joy is critically important. People need to be attracted to the process of change and if it is not one that is joyous, they will devote their time and energy elsewhere. Change agents then, become both provocateurs and nurturers of human spirit. Thinking about process and conditions that nourish the human spirit is perhaps one of their most important roles. One of *our* indicators of success as facilitators of *one way forward* is the amount of laughter we hear in the group along the way. The great tangible "payoff" of this way of being, which we recognize both conceptually and from experience, is that when we are able to catch the wave of change, when the timing is right and people are carried by the wave, systemic change is only a heartbeat away—we just cannot predict which heartbeat.

Time is important, as mentioned earlier, and so is patience; watching, influencing with a word of encouragement or challenge at the appropriate time and waiting for the wave of change. The power of "who" you are being in these circumstances can never be underestimated. This includes how you interact with people and how you continuously give the work back to those involved, how you self-regulate and let go of your own "solutions" so that they are free to emerge from the system.

And so we return to an underlying theme of this paper—personal and leadership development are critical for change agents and those working with them. Change agents need to learn not just about the system as an objective and disembodied thing, but about the system which includes themselves, their mental models and complexities as a person—and others within that "system"! This takes time—a progressive unfolding that may never seem complete.

4.4. Accountability

Practices such as "holding people accountable" by measuring their performance based upon delivery of outcomes, are neither fair nor practical when placed within the context of the principles underpinning a living system [37,38].

Accountability is best attached to the *process* that will influence the outcomes. This may be a "tougher" form of accountability, as it will include consideration of how people go about their work, the quality of their interactions with others, their commitment to learning and creativity and perhaps their influence on the indicators of progress. Members of the group committed to *influencing* outcomes in line with the indicators *hold themselves mutually accountable* for maintaining the integrity of the group *process*, always recognizing that direct cause and effect in relation to "performance" is an assumption of the machine metaphor, and will rarely be observed in the rich uncertainty of the living system. We view the accountability that we have started to explore here as a maturation of "performance management" as it has been practiced to date.

4.5. Time

In our modern, western, corporatized world, it seems there is no time for anything. We have become so attached to the idea of efficient, time-saving processes that we tend to baulk at the prospect of allowing a process to take the time it needs to take. Personal development and transformational change occur in their own time—not in accordance with our clocks, neat agendas, change management schedules or program funding milestones that demand deliverables by such and such a date. "Time is important, so a conversation may last a week or be continued over years rather than stay within the artificial constraint of an hour" ([20], Chapter 6, p. 7). We suggest that a major piece of adaptive work to be undertaken by those who wish to catalyze change for a sustaining future is to allow the processes to shape time, not the other way around—to allow enough time for the processes to get us to the future we really want. Maybe not days, but months, years and even decades... or maybe a heartbeat.

This involves the investment of sufficient time, not only for the initial iteration of envisioning and strategic experiment, but also for regular management processes that maintain the liveliness of the vision in the life of the organization, through its ongoing dialogue with indicators and action—"trying stuff". Without this continuing investment of perhaps an organization's most precious resource, the dynamic facilitated—midwifed—by envisioning can easily end up still born. This is at the heart of the adaptive challenge. *One way forward* is not a silver bullet, propelled by passion. It is a systemic response and requires a commitment beyond the first impulse. As all the "holistic", systemic traditions of healing proclaim, in one form of language or another, "Slow healing is good healing".

5. Conclusions

Implementing change systemically is not easy—otherwise we would see it done more often. But the traditional mechanistic approach to "change management" has proved itself inadequate and we suggest that the *one way forward* model may assist change agents who exhibit patience, humility, perseverance and a willingness to reconnect with their own wisdom, and the wisdom of the complex, living system.

Starik and Kanashiro have called for the development of management theory that addresses the practical demands of a shift to sustainability—"what theory of human management can account for (or otherwise address and/or advance) such an enormous change in human civilization?" ([1], p. 8). Responding to the challenge of shaping a truly sustaining organization with the capacity to influence the formation of a truly sustaining society and world requires us to unlearn much of what we thought we knew about "sustainability", "change" and how to facilitate it.

In this article we have explored the underlying assumptions made within the Newtonian paradigm about the nature and dynamic of change and we argue that this provides some insight into why 70–90% of all organizational change initiatives fail to deliver the intended results. Although many managers hold themselves (or their people) to blame for this poor track record, we suggest that it is the underlying assumptions being made about change and managing change that require review. When change is viewed and understood through the lens of complexity, a different way of catalyzing (rather than managing) change is revealed.

One way forward, has been developed employing an abductive methodology and the principles associated with the behavior of complex adaptive systems. We recognize it as just one way forward. But importantly, it is one way that is internally coherent and consistent in both its underlying conceptual framework and its application in practice. It does not succumb to the temptation to return to old and familiar ways of doing things which are more controlling and linear in nature. It challenges institutionalised understandings of how things are done (culture) at the level of mental models and deep unconscious assumptions, a level just below what Meadows refers to as the ultimate level of system intervention – transcending paradigms completely [36].

One way forward is an addition to the growing family of facilitated processes, such as Open Space Technology [39], Appreciative Inquiry [40] and World Café [41], that bring a whole system together and allow the future to emerge, influenced by a collective vision of possibilities. A distinguishing feature of *one way forward* is its theoretical foundation and its application as an alternative to existing "strategic planning" and "cultural change initiatives" within organizations (and communities) that face complex and adaptive challenges such as "planning" for whole system responses. Rather than a linear process that leaves "planning" or "consultation" behind in the wake of "implementation", *one way forward* shapes an ongoing dynamic of integrated engagement, planning, reviewing, experimenting and learning. It is a whole of system dynamic, reflecting and influencing the social ecology.

The major challenge presented by our global and individual state of unsustainability is to provide students of sustainability with the opportunity and the means to learn not just how to reduce harm, but to liberate and express a human capacity to nurture socio-ecological systems so that they flourish.

Conflicts of Interest: The authors declare no conflict of interest.

References

1. Starik, M.; Kanashiro, P. Toward a theory of sustainability management: Uncovering and integrating the nearly obvious. *Organ. Environ.* **2013**, *26*, 7–30. [CrossRef]
2. Beer, M.; Nohria, N. Cracking the code of change. *Harvard Bus. Rev.* **2000**, *78*, 133–141.
3. Higgs, M.; Rowland, D. All changes great and small: Exploring approaches to change and its leadership. *J. Change Manag.* **2005**, *5*, 121–151. [CrossRef]
4. Kotter, J.P. Leading change. *Harvard Bus. Rev.* **2007**, *85*, 96–103.
5. Kuhn, T. *The Structure of Scientific Revolutions*; Univeristy of Chicago Press: Chicago, IL, USA, 1962.
6. Marion, R. *The Edge of Organization: Chaos and Complexity Theories of Social Reform*; SAGE Publications: Thousand Oaks, CA, USA, 1999.
7. Senge, P. *The Fifth Discipline*; DoubleDay: New York, USA, 1994.
8. Stacey, R.D.; Griffin, D.; Shaw, P. *Complexity and Management: Fad or Radical Challenge to Systems Thinking?* Routledge: London, UK, 2000.
9. Uhl-Bien, M.; Marion, R.; McKelvey, B. Complexity leadership theory: Shifting leadership from the industrial age to the knowledge era. *Leadership Quart.* **2007**, *18*, 298–318. [CrossRef]
10. Wheatley, M.J. *Leadership and the New Science: Discovering Order in a Chaotic World*, 2nd ed.; Berrett-Koehler: San Francisco, CA, USA, 1999.
11. Beck, D. What is Spiral Dynamics Integral? Available online: http://www.sonic.net/ericskag/sris/IN-SDi%20Intro.pdf (accessed on 4 April 2013).
12. Meadows, D.; Meadows, D.; Randers, J.; Behrens, W.W., III. *The Limits to Growth*; Earth Island Ltd.: London, UK, 1972.

13. Meadows, D.; Randers, J.; Meadows, D. *Limits to Growth: The 30-Year Update*; Chelsea Green Publishing Company: White River Junction, VT, USA, 2004.
14. Richardson, K.; Cilliers, P.; Lissack, M. Complexity Science: A Grey Science for the "Stuff in between". In Proceedings of the 1st International Conference on Systems Thinking in Management, Geelong, Australia, 8–10 November 2000.
15. Hilborn, R.C. Sea gulls, butterflies, and grasshoppers: A brief history of the butterfly effect in nonlinear dynamics. *Am. J. Phys.* **2004**, *72*, 425–427. [CrossRef]
16. Kotter, J. Leading change: Why transformation efforts fail. *Harvard Bus. Rev.* **1995**, *73*, 59–67.
17. Kotter, J. Accelerate! *Harvard Bus. Rev.* **2012**, *90*, 45–58.
18. Meadows, D. Dancing with systems. *Syst. Think.* **2002**, *13*, 2–6.
19. Meadows, D. Envisioning a Sustainable World. In Proceedings of the 3rd Biennial Meeting of the International Society for Ecological Economics, San Jose, Costa Rica, 24–28 October 1994.
20. Banathy, B.; Rowland, G. *Creating Our Future: If We Don't Do It, Who Will?* Available online: http://www.ithaca.edu/rowland/ctf/chapters.htm (accessed on 6 September 2013).
21. Maturana, H.R.; Varela, F.G.; Uribe, R. Autopiesis: The organization of living systems, its characterization and a model. *Biosystems* **1974**, *5*, 187–196. [CrossRef]
22. Heifetz, R.; Linsky, M. *Leadership on the Line: Staying Alive through the Dangers of Leading*; Harvard Business Press: Boston, MA, USA, 2002.
23. Heifetz, R.; Grashow, A.; Linsky, M. *The Pratice of Adpative Leadership: Tools and Tactics for Changing Your Organisation and the World*; Harvard Business Press: Boston, MA, USA, 2009.
24. Edwards, M.G. The integral holon: A holonomic approach to organisational change and transformation. *J. Organ. Change Manag.* **2005**, *18*, 269–288. [CrossRef]
25. Koestler, A. *The Ghost in the Machine*, 2nd ed.; Picador: London, UK, 1976.
26. Sahtouris, E. Earthdance: Living Systems in Evolution, 1999. Available online: http://citeseerx.ist.psu.edu/viewdoc/download;jsessionid=AA19D2CF61BC8C8E47AB724E47D2A7BE?doi=10.1.1.133.2192&rep=rep1&type=pdf (accessed on 11 September 2013).
27. Mowles, C.; Stacey, R.; Griffin, D. What contribution can insights from the complexity sciences make to the theory and practice of development management? *J. Int. Dev.* **2008**, *20*, 804–820. [CrossRef]
28. Farley, J.; Costanza, R. Envisioning shared goals for humanity: A detailed, shared vision of a sustainable and desirable USA in 2100. *Ecol. Econ.* **2001**, *43*, 245–259. [CrossRef]
29. Boulding, E. Image and action in peace building. *J. Soc. Issues* **1988**, *44*, 17–37. [CrossRef]
30. Van der Helm, R. The vision phenomenon: Towards a theoretical underpinning of visions of the future and the process of envisioning. *Futures* **2009**, *41*, 96–104. [CrossRef]
31. Jackson, M.C. The origins and nature of critical systems thinking. *Syst. Practice* **1991**, *4*, 131–149. [CrossRef]
32. Saarinen, E.; Hämäläinen, R.P. Systems Intelligence: Connecting Engineering Thinking with Human Sensitivity. In *Systems Intelligence—Discovering a Hidden Competence in Human Action and Organizational Life*; Research Reports A88; Hämäläinen, R.P., Saarinen, E., Eds.; Helsinki University of Technology, Systems Analysis Laboratory: Aalto, Finland, 2004.
33. Dunphy, D.; Griffiths, A.; Benn, S. *Organizational Change for Corporate Sustainability: A Guide for Leaders and Change Agents of the Future*, 2nd ed.; Routledge: London, UK, 2007.
34. Meadows, D. *Indicators and Information Systems for Sustainable Development: A Report to the Ballaton Group*; The Sustainability Institute: Hartland Four Corners, VT, USA, 1998.
35. Heifetz, R. *Leadership without Easy Answers*; Harvard University Press: Boston, MA, USA, 1994.
36. Meadows, D. Places to Intervene in a System, 1997. Available online: http://center.sustainability.duke.edu/sites/default/files/documents/system_intervention.pdf (accessed on 11 September 2013).
37. Scholtes, P.R. *An Elaboration of Deming's Teachings on Performance Appraisal*; Joiner Associates Inc.: Madison, WI, USA, 1987.
38. Wells, S. Setting People up for Success: Sustainable Performance Management. In *Readings in HRM and Sustainability*; Clarke, M., Ed.; Tilde University Press: Prahran, Australia, 2011; pp. 61–63.
39. Owen, H. *Open Space Technology: A Users Guide*, 2nd ed.; Berrett-Koehler: San Francisco, CA, USA, 1997.

Systems **2013**, *1*, 66–84

40. Cooperridder, D.L.; Whitney, D.; Stavros, J.M. *Appreciative Inquiry Handbook: For Leaders of Change*, 2nd ed.; Crown Custom Publishing: Brunswick, OH, USA, 2008.
41. Brown, J.; Isaacs, D. *The World Cafe: Shaping Our Futures through Conversations That Matter*, 1st ed.; Berrett-Koehler: San Francisco, CA, USA, 2005.

systems MDPI

Communication

Taking on the Big Issues and Climbing the Mountains Ahead: Challenges and Opportunities in Asia †

John Richardson

Lee Kuan Yew School of Public Policy, National University of Singapore, 469C Bukit Timah Road, Singapore 259772; jrich@american.edu; Tel.: +65-6691-3037; Fax: +65-6799-5397

† This paper builds on an opening plenary address to the inaugural Asia-Pacific System Dynamics Conference held on 22–24 February 2014 in Tokyo, Japan.

Received: 3 June 2014; in revised form: 2 August 2014; Accepted: 6 August 2014; Published: 11 August 2014

Abstract: At the 2007 International System Dynamics Society Conference, Professor Jay Forrester posed a challenge: "We need books addressed to the public that are understandable, relevant, important and dramatic". We need to overcome the "constraints of academe" that inhibit path-breaking work. We need to address "the big issues". We need to march "upward from the present aimless plateau and start climbing the mountains ahead". This was a message that was intended to inspire and empower, not to criticize. Responding to Professor Forrester's challenge, this paper first describes the work of three inspiring role models, Dennis Meadows, Junko Edahiro and John Sterman. They have demonstrated how books can have an impact on people's lives, how "big issues" can be addressed, how the constraints of academe can be overcome and how mountains can be scaled. Second, it offers grounds for optimism about the future of system dynamics modeling in Asia, gained from my sojourn at the National University of Singapore. Third, it describes three "mountains ahead" to be scaled and highlights the work of individuals who have already begun the journey.

Keywords: system dynamics; *The Limits to Growth*; *C-Roads Project*; sustainable development; human happiness

1. Introduction: A Message from Professor Jay Forrester: The "Zen Master" of System Dynamics Modeling

Had Professor Jay W. Forrester been with us on this special day, inaugurating the System Dynamics Society's new Asia-Pacific outreach, what message might he have brought us? It might have been similar to the "caning" of a Zen master; similar to the message he delivered to the International System Dynamics Society Conference in 2007. He told assembled participants that after a period of growth, our field "has stagnated on an aimless plateau". "We need to address the big issues". "We need books addressed to the public that, like *Urban Dynamics*, *World Dynamics* and *Limits to Growth* are understandable, relevant, important and dramatic. We must focus debate in newspapers, blogs, League of Women Voters' meetings and parent-teacher associations". The constraints of academia are stifling the work of junior faculty while "senior faculties have settled comfortably into writing for professional journals rather than on matters of public concern". Many are trying to "dumb down" system dynamics into systems thinking and causal loop diagrams. At the end of this verbal caning, he left delegates with a challenge: "to plan for marching upward from the present aimless plateau and start climbing the mountains ahead" [1].

The importance of his message, of course, was not the critique of what was wrong, but an envisioning of what could be. Perhaps he was suggesting, as Kim Warren did in his July 2013 International System Dynamics Society "Presidential Address", that we spend more time seeking out experiences and opportunities with the potential to empower and inspire [2].

Systems **2014**, *2*, 366–378

In a similar vein, but without the caning, this paper offers three points. The first is about personal role models who have inspired me. You may have heard of them, but may not know that much about them. They have shown how books can be made powerful. They have empowered the general public to engage with big issues in their daily lives. They have demonstrated that the constraints of academe can be overcome. Second, it offers grounds for optimism about the future of system dynamics modeling in Asia, gained from my sojourn at the National University of Singapore. Third, it describes three "mountains ahead" to be scaled and highlights the work of individuals who have already begun the journey.

2. Three Personal Role Models Who Have Inspired Me

2.1. Dennis Meadows

Why do I believe that my friend of more than 30 years, Dennis Meadows, can serve as an inspiring role model?

When Professor Forrester expressed concern about the need for a genre of books having an impact that changed people's lives, he mentioned *The Limits to Growth* [3], along with *Urban Dynamics* [4] and *World Dynamics* [5]. Perhaps he might have given more credit to the long-lasting impact of *The Limits to Growth* and its successor volumes, *Beyond the Limits* [6] and *Limits to Growth: the 30 Year Update* [7].

As is widely known, this project was a partnership between Dennis and Dana Meadows until Dana's tragic and untimely death on 20 February 2001. Dennis and Dana had many achievements as individuals. However, in partnership, they provided an object lesson in what is required for a book—or in this case a series of books—to become powerful.

After Dana's death, Dennis committed himself further to keeping the message of *The Limits to Growth* alive—by producing a third iteration [7]. He has been an eloquent, itinerant advocate for the issues raised in the three volumes, giving at least hundreds and perhaps thousands of presentations throughout the world.

A noteworthy example of Dennis and Dana's continuing engagement was their founding of the Balaton Group, a network of scholar practitioners concerned with sustainability, in 1982. Recently the Balaton Group celebrated its 30th anniversary. It is among the most notable examples of the institutions and public outreach activities that Dennis and Dana created and sustained, to help ensure that the message of *The Limits to Growth* and its successor volumes remained viable and powerful.

2.2. Junko Edahiro

I first had the privilege of meeting my second inspiring role model, Junko Edahiro, when she was invited to the 2002 meeting of The Balaton Group [8] as one of the first Donella Meadows Fellows. If you want to know how to focus on the big issues and raise them in public consciousness, consider Junko's remarkable career. By the time we met, she had already established herself as a respected environmental journalist, using skills developed as a simultaneous Japanese-English translator to make books and articles on environmental issues and sustainable development available to Japanese audiences. Her book in Japanese, with the English title, *If You Get Up At Two You Can Do Whatever You Want To Do* captures the essence of Junko's work-ethic and helps explain why she has been one of my most inspiring personal role models ever since our paths first crossed (Unfortunately the book is not available in English).

Junko's biography describes her as "Social Entrepreneur, Environmental Journalist and Translator" [9]. It lists her as affiliated with nine organizations, many in the position of founder and President. Admirers have named her as Japan's "First Lady of the Environment" [10].

In collaboration with her colleague, Rich Oda, she conducts systems thinking workshops and has brought leaders in systems thinking and system dynamics modeling, such as Dennis Meadows and Peter Senge, to Japan. The newsletter of the organization she founded in 2002, *Japan for Sustainability*, publishes monthly in both Japanese and English [11]. She has translated or overseen the translation

Systems **2014**, *2*, 366–378

of four system dynamics modeling and systems thinking classics, including John Sterman's *Business Dynamics* [12]. She has also written books, articles and instruction manuals on systems thinking in Japanese.

Most recently, she has founded the *Institute for Studies in Happiness, Economy and Society* about which I shall have more to say shortly. Junko may not devote much of her time to system dynamics modeling, but there are few individuals who have been more effective, in any country, at raising big issues, viewed from a system dynamics vantage point. With skill, creativity and passion, she has brought them to the attention of both national leaders and ordinary citizens.

2.3. John Sterman

Finally, if you are looking for a role model to convince you that academic cultures need not be constraints and that system dynamics need not be "dumbed down", consider the career of my third role model, John Sterman.

John Sterman exemplifies a commitment to tackling the big issues, engaging in public discourse, and, perhaps most notably, achieving long-term viability for the field of System Dynamics at MIT. He is an award-winning teacher and scholar. He is a demanding and empowering mentor of doctoral students.

John's classic, *Business Dynamics: Systems Thinking and Modeling for a Complex World* [12], convincingly refutes those who question the mathematical rigour and scientific foundations of system dynamics modeling. Economists and management science academics cannot dismiss his publications. He can speak their language and has published in their top ranked journals. He has made major contributions to the field of organizational learning. He has developed innovative games and made them widely accessible. And just when one might have thought that John had accomplished all that there was to be accomplished, he began climbing an entirely new mountain with the C-Roads Climate Interactive Project [13], to which I will return.

2.4. Common Threads

Having briefly chronicled the contributions of these three role-models, one might legitimately pose the question, as did one of this paper's referees, "are there qualities that they have in common, apart from serving as role models who have personally inspired me and many others?" Courageous engaging with "big issues" and raising the profile of those issues in the perceptions of general publics are the qualities that are most noteworthy. However the differences are as noteworthy as the similarities. This is good news, in my opinion. System dynamics modelers seeking role models need not feel bound to a single template as they seek out life paths that will provide personal fulfillment, create new knowledge and contribute to human well being. My three role-models do have much in common but have traversed very different paths to achieve their current level of eminence. Let me elaborate further, very briefly.

With an assist from the Club of Rome, Dennis Meadows (and Dana Meadows too) embarked on the turbulent, demanding path of the public intellectual, addressing highly controversial issues during a very early chapter of his professional life. Though his contributions in other areas have been noteworthy, refining and keeping *The Limits to Growth*'s message alive has remained a central focus.

John Sterman chose a more conventional path emphasizing teaching, research and institution building. He attended to a challenge that had not been given priority by his mentor, Jay Forrester, building bridges to other disciplines and securing the place of system dynamics at MIT. His tackling of a "big issue" and emergence as a public intellectual came later. However, as will be told below, he has now embarked on that path with passion, discipline and skilled leadership.

Like John Sterman, Junko Edahiro defined herself as a public intellectual, building on her translation skills, commitment to systems thinking, and an incredibly disciplined work ethic somewhat later in life. What is noteworthy about her career, as will be told below is how she has expanded the scope of her concerns from sustainability to encompass the larger issue of envisioning a human

Systems **2014**, *2*, 366–378

society in which motivations of self-interest are supplanted by more altruistic motivations emphasizing human happiness.

3. Grounds for Optimism about the Future of System Dynamics in Asia, Gained from my Sojourn in Singapore

Let me next turn to the subject of academic institutions and, in particular, to the Lee Kuan Yew School of Public Policy at the National University of Singapore, where I now hold an appointment as Visiting Professor.

3.1. The Lee Kuan Yew School of Public Policy

It would be disingenuous to claim that the criticisms directed towards academic institutions by Professor Forrester—assistant professors who are afraid of making waves, senior professors that have settled into comfortable lives, priority given to publishing in "high impact" journals with little policy relevance, are imaginings.

Donella Meadows provides one example of a highly regarded systems thinker and modeler who was acutely conscious of the issues to which Professor Forrester's critique pointed. These contributed to her decision to give up a half-time tenured professorship at Dartmouth College, though they were not the only considerations.

However many senior scholar-practitioners in our field, including Dennis Meadows and John Sterman have functioned quite successfully in academic environments. The State of University of New York at Albany has provided a home for the System Dynamics Society and for two of the most eminent scholars in the system dynamics modeling community, George Richardson and David Anderson. I should also note that *Industrial Dynamics* [14], *Urban Dynamics* [4] and *The Limits to Growth* [3] were all written by individuals who were formally affiliated with MIT.

The Lee Kuan Yew School and the National University of Singapore, while not immunized from the problems to which Professor Forrester directs our attention, do appear to offer some distinctive features from which useful lessons can, perhaps, be drawn.

In my "Lifetime Achievement Award" address, given at the June 2013 System Dynamics Society International Conference [15], I recounted the improbable tale that lead to my present affiliation. Our system dynamics modeling course was catalyzed by two faculty members, whose modeling skills were complemented by extensive experience in public discourse and public policy. One was taking leave from a career at the Asian Development Bank. The other was a former journalist. Though still an elective, the course is being offered for a fourth year and by the end this Spring semester, will have reached nearly 100 students, including some enrolled in the Faculty of Engineering, the Department of Geography, the University Honours Program for undergraduates and the Duke-National University of Singapore Medical School.

Most students at the Lee Kuan Yew School enroll with the intention of pursuing public policy careers. Many have already begun such careers and will return to them. Students who complete our course are required to complete original system dynamics modeling projects. They compare favorably with papers that I have refereed and recommended for presentation at System Dynamics Society International Conferences.

However, quality work is not enough. Solid presentation skills are required. Our students are required to present their results using the *Pecha Kucha* format first pioneered by a community of architects in Japan [16].

In 2013—this too I mentioned in my July 2013 address [15]—our course culminated in a public event where students presented 18 original modeling projects using a modified *Pecha Kucha* format. 29 guests from the wider Singapore community, including representatives from four government ministries, three research institutes, three other Singapore universities and two for-profit consulting groups attended. Most remained for the entire three hours of presentations.

3.2. "Professor in the Practice of Public Policy": Dean Kishore Mahbubani

What explains the supportive environment for public policy research on the part of both faculty and students at the Lee Kuan Yew School of Public Policy and at other institutions characterized by a similarly supportive climate? I believe the leadership on the part of a supportive, effective dean who is committed to public policy research is essential. It is not enough for such a dean to profess support for research that focuses on the big issues and makes results of that research widely available. More important, he or she must exemplify that commitment in his or her own research, providing a visible and influential role model for both students and faculty.

While I conducted no survey to validate this observation, I doubt there are many deans that exemplify such a commitment with greater visibility and effectiveness than the Lee Kuan Yew School's Dean, Kishore Mahbubani. A check of Kishore's website reveals categories for "Books", "Articles", "Interviews", and "Media." In addition to his latest book, *The Great Convergence—Asia, the West and the Logic of One World* [17] along with scores of articles, interviews and media appearances, he has already published widely in 2014, with all of his contributions addressing what might be legitimately termed "big issues". In April 2014, Jonathan Derbyshire, Editor of the British Public Affairs Journal, *Prospect*, announced that Dean Mahbubani had been named to its list of "Top 50 World Thinkers" [18]. In this regard, the title of Dean Mahbubani's academic appointment, *Professor in the Practice of Public Policy*, is revealing. It conveys an important message of which Professor Forrester would approve, I believe.

3.3. System Dynamics Modeling at the National University of Singapore

While system dynamics modeling now appears to have found a secure position among elective course offerings at the Lee Kuan Yew School of Public Policy, interest in the field has also become a matter of interest to the National University of Singapore's President and Central Administration.

In 2009, NUS President Tan Chorh Chuan formed an *ad hoc* "Core Group" to explore the possibility that system dynamics might serve as a core methodology for the University's newly created Global Asia Institute. The faculty member who had catalyzed the teaching of System Dynamics modeling at the Lee Kuan Yew School, Visiting Professor K.E. Seetharam, was named to head the Institute. Chairing the task force was one of Singapore's most respected retired civil servants, Professor Lui Pao Chuen, who was also a strong system dynamics advocate.

In a 29 October 2010 "White Paper," submitted to President Tan, the Core Group recommended system dynamics as a core research methodology for the Global Asia Institute. "As a conceptual framework and methodology", its report concluded, "system dynamics integrates the best thinking of multiple disciplines and provides a mature yet evolving methodology for conceptualizing new theory".

The goal of what we called the Global Asia Institute's *System Dynamics Initiative* was to evolve a group, combining research and teaching that was patterned after MIT's System Dynamics Group. However a university-wide research institute without teaching responsibilities proved not to be the most effective platform for a university wide program. Those of us involved in the System Dynamics Initiative were reminded that if the "mountain" of institutionalizing system dynamics in a new university setting is to be scaled, strong teaching, as well as high impact research must be part of the picture. Now, new initiatives have been envisioned that include a strong teaching component.

3.4. Why Singapore Seems a More Receptive Environment for Public Policy Applications of System Dynamics Modeling than the US and a Point of Leverage for China's Public Policy?

This paper is based on an address that was given to help inaugurate System Dynamics Society—Asia-Pacific Region focused initiatives. There can be no doubt of the region's intrinsic importance, but how receptive are Asia-Pacific public policy processes likely to be to such initiatives? Generalizing about such a diverse region as a whole would be unrealistic. However it seems appropriate to elaborate further on why I chose Singapore as the focus of my own work, why Singapore's public policy environment has proved to be receptive, and why this receptivity is

Systems **2014**, *2*, 366–378

relevant to the nation whose public policies, in my view, will be most influential in shaping the region's future development, China.

Why Singapore? An examination of public policies contributing to Singapore's post independence success story makes it clear that systems thinking played an important role. The systems-thinking-oriented views of Singapore's two most important post-independence leaders, Lee Kuan Yew [19] and Goh Keng Swee [20] were particularly influential. In two papers [21,22], Elizabeth Ong and I have noted close correspondences between Singapore's development trajectory and policy guidelines emphasized in *Urban Dynamics*. This does not, however, fully explain the continued receptivity to systems thinking and modeling that I have personally experienced and that has been experienced by others. Fully documenting this would require a separate paper. However examples with which I am personally familiar include training programs conducted by the Civil Service College, the Ministry of Defense, and the Population and Talent Division, Office of the Prime Minister. Programs at Singapore's flagship National University of Singapore have already been mentioned. Soon, these will also include an initiative being developed by the new Director of the NUS-Based Temasek Defense Systems Institute, in which I will be personally involved.

In my 2013 plenary address to the 31st International System Dynamics Society Conference [15], I sought to explain this phenomenon, which differs so greatly from my personal experience of the US Public Policy environment, beginning with President Ronald Reagan's administration. I pointed to three factors that appeared to be particularly consequential. "First is the degree to which Singapore's political-social economy has been shaped by the systems thinking of its founding political leaders … This has been carried forward by their successors. Systems thinking has been institutionalized through planning and regulatory schemes … that are uniquely Singaporean".

"Second is the typical profile of Singapore's top leaders, especially those who occupy all-important Ministerial and Permanent Secretary positions. Most have educations that combine degrees in science, technology, and engineering, and with additional graduate work in public administration and management. All of the men have military service in their background, with a number having risen to very senior positions in the army and navy". When system dynamics models are effectively presented, even by students just completing their first semester of work, these leaders quickly grasp their usefulness for aiding public policy systems design and decision making.

"Third is the strong emphasis on science and technology in Singapore's secondary schools". This makes Singapore an unusually receptive environment for achieving the late Barry Richmond's goal, shared by 2011 Lifetime Achievement Award recipient Diana Fisher and many others, of creating a society populated by "systems citizens" [23].

I have described considerations that make Singapore an intrinsically promising public policy venue for system dynamics modeling, however viewed from an Asian perspective, those considerations are not the most compelling. More compelling is Singapore's past and continuing role in shaping the practice and direction of public policy in China. Ever since Deng Xiaoping's iconic visit to Singapore and conversations with Lee Kuan Yew in 1978 [19,24], Singapore has served as a beacon light and model for Chinese leaders regarding matters of governance and economic development. It is not the only model to be sure, but it remains an important one. Though others may differ, I believe that at this juncture, the applications of systems thinking and system dynamics modeling now being catalyzed in Singapore may have an even greater impact on China and perhaps other Asian countries as well, than were one to attempt introduction of those applications locally. As it has been in the past, Singapore can be a high leverage launching pad for such applications.

4. Conclusions: "Climbing the Mountains Ahead"

What other "mountains" should attract the vision, energy and dedication of present and future system dynamics scholar-practitioner-promoter-activists? I should like to share three, of surpassing importance, that top my list.

4.1. Economic Dynamics

First is the one to which I called attention in my July 2013 address [15]. I named it the fourth pillar in Professor Forrester's Legacy, a legacy that now comprises the insights we have gained from *Industrial Dynamics* [14], *Urban Dynamics* [4] and *World Dynamics* [5]. I am referring to his long-promised transformational book on economic dynamics, a project to which many members of the system dynamics modeling community have contributed.

There must also be a popularized version of that work, exhibiting the qualities of *The Limits to Growth* and its successor volumes that Professor Forrester has described so eloquently. Professor Khalid Saeed has now embarked on work that points in this direction [25]. He needs our encouragement and support, as well as the companionship of some hardy mountain climbers to accompany his trek. There may be no more important contribution that could be made, not only to the practice of system dynamics modeling, but also to the well-being of the human species, at this time in history.

4.2. The C-Roads Climate Interactive Project

A journey up a second mountain, transforming public and political consciousness, regarding the relationship between industrial development and climate change, is well underway.

In a user-friendly website and many presentations, both to policy makers and general publics, John Sterman and colleagues have described the basic elements of this path-breaking project. It is designed to be *fast*, generating climate change scenarios in response to policy interventions in less than a second. It is designed to be **accessible**. Its flexible, intuitive interface can be used easily on a laptop by individuals with no modeling experience. The model assumptions are **transparent**. The assumptions are "open box" accessible and available for review. A causal tracing feature permits auditing of behaviour. Finally, it is **grounded in and consistent with accepted climate science**. It has been reviewed by a distinguished panel of scientists and tested against other well-regarded models and data. Its structure and interface enable rapid and flexible sensitivity analysis [26].

However to capture public attention, there needs to be more than good science and good software interfaces to make that science accessible. Passionate, visionary project leadership is also needed. John Sterman is providing that essential ingredient. When, as a member of a large audience, I first heard John speak about the C-Roads Project from a distant platform, I was reminded of the Prophet Jeremiah, exhorting the people of Israel to refrain from their wayward ways or face the consequences if they did not. John brings a passion to this work that I had not seen in his earlier endeavours, path breaking though they have been. Perhaps passion is another ingredient that is needed if one is to climb mountains.

4.3. Modeling a Stable, Sustainable, Economically Viable Human Society that Maximizes Human Well Being

My third "mountain" is a role for system dynamics modeling in creating economies and societies that seek to maximize human well being. What I envision is a model that incorporates elements of the models described in *Urban Dynamics* and *World Dynamics* and that falls somewhere between the two of them in size. It also draws from the examples of two other system dynamics models, to be cited below, that sought to capture relevant ideas of fundamental importance for which no "hard data" was available.

This envisioning was motivated by another Junko Edahiro initiative, The Institute for Studies in Happiness, Economy and Society (ISHES), which held its inaugural event on March 4, 2011. Here is the Institute's mission statement—the highlighting is my addition:

> *ISHES plans to develop activities such as conducting research and studies, disseminating study results, shaping public opinion, encouraging dialogue, building networks to respond to world trends, and squarely addressing important questions, including **How should we deal with the limits of the Earth to build a truly happy society without making society and the***

economy unstable? and *What indicators should we use to measure society's true progress and happiness?*. [27]

4.4. What Makes These Three Projects, and the Mountains They Seek to Climb, Important and Distinctive?

Those of us who first engaged in "global modeling" can remember the rage which greeted presentations of the idea that limiting growth in capital accumulation, population, food production, natural resource consumption and pollution might be necessary to ensure the survival of the human species on planet earth. In a highly accessible survey volume, *Life Beyond Growth* [28], "sustainable development" scholar-activist Alan Atkisson documents the deeply rooted attitudes, embedded in and reinforced by dominant social-political institutions, that evoked these emotional reactions. The "growth paradigm" and the inevitability that it would produce good outcomes for the human species was an accepted, indisputable fact of life. It remains so today, though as Atkisson's survey highlights, new paradigms are emerging. Among many examples, prestigious mainstream documents such as the *Report by the Commission on the Measurement of Economic Performance and Social Progress* [29], and the Royal Society's *People and the Planet* report [30], demonstrate this.

Each of three projects I have highlighted has the potential to further the process of paradigm change that Atkisson's survey catalogues. ISHES and C-Roads have already achieved success. What are the qualities that evoke my optimism?

First, each is being lead and catalyzed by highly regarded, action-oriented members of the system dynamics community.

Second, because of this, C-Roads and, the work of ISHES have demonstrated that creating compelling, accessible deliverables based on work of high scholarly quality will not be a problem. *Life Beyond Growth* is, in fact an ISHES deliverable. Output from the project to fundamentally reshape economic thought, based on Professor Forrester's seminal but as yet incomplete theories and models should be the most compelling and high profile of all. Professor Khalid Saeed's recent work demonstrates what is possible [25].

Third, each project recognizes that changing attitudes both within institutions and among the public whose attitudes both shape and are shaped by institutions must be the overarching goal. Both the C-Roads and the ISHES projects have made progress in developing technologies that will facilitate attitude change. The Landmark BBC Series, *Century of the Self*, showing how Freudian Psychologist and public relations guru, Edward Bernays, implemented programs that, in the post war era "transformed American consumers from frugal savers to hungry consumers" [28] illustrates what is possible. To cite another example, Singapore's government, too, has achieved landmark (albeit sometimes controversial) results with programs intended to build patriotism, mutual respect, a "clean and green Singapore", and communal harmony among its citizens.

Fourth, each project questions attitudes emphasizing that maximizing economic growth combined with unconstrained functioning of the profit motive represent the surest paths to universal human well-being and the survival of our species. However powerful compelling demonstrations that maximizing human happiness through attitudes that emphasize altruistic compassion will produce better results remain to be demonstrated. Since producing such demonstrations is *my mountain*, this observation leads me to a concluding postscript.

4.5. Postcript

No one could doubt that the question defining the ISHES mission is an important one. But "What does this have to do with challenges and opportunities for system dynamics in Asia?" one might ask.

Here are my answers.

First, when, as a young faculty member, in 1972, I was told that Professor Jay Forrester was building a computer model of the world, I thought it was a joke. Two years later, I had helped develop such a model [31] and ten years later, I had co-authored a book about seven of them [32].

Systems **2014**, 2, 366–378

In 1978, Jack Homer, one of the most creative members of the system dynamics modeling profession created and described a system dynamics model, in a paper titled "Civilization as Enterprise" [33] that encompassed major theories describing the rise and fall of human civilizations.

In 1981–1982, John Sterman built and described a system dynamics model in several papers, beginning with "The Growth of Knowledge: Testing a Theory of Scientific Revolutions with a Formal Model" [34–36] that represented the dynamic described by Thomas Kuhn in his classic, *The Structure of Scientific Revolutions* [37].

The task of building system dynamics models that seek to answer the question "how should we deal with the limits of the earth to build a truly happy society, without making that society and the economy unstable" may be a difficult one. However, these examples, chosen from among many more, demonstrate that such a task is not impossible.

It is simply another mountain that is worth climbing.

I look forward to welcoming the companions who will join with me on this journey.

Acknowledgments: As noted above, an earlier version of this paper was given as an opening plenary address to the inaugural Asia-Pacific Conference of the System Dynamics Society. The organizational efforts of the conference chair, Akira Uchino, and the program chair, Bob Cavana, are gratefully acknowledged. My colleagues at the Lee Kuan Yew School of Public Policy, Elizabeth Ong Ling Lee and Kwan Chang Yee, also offered ideas, support and patient listening, as did my partner in many system dynamics modeling endeavors, Global Asia Institute staff member, Rehan Ali. The offering of a module in system dynamics modeling and other initiatives described in my paper would not have been possible without the support of Dean Kishore Mahbubani, who despite many commitments as a leader and public intellectual, is also welcoming to visitors and open to proposals for innovative public policy research and teaching initiatives.

Conflicts of Interest: The author declares no conflict of interest.

References

1. Forrester, J.W. System dynamics—The next fifty years. *Syst. Dynam. Rev.* **2007**, *23*, 359–370. [CrossRef]
2. Warren, K. Taking the Opportunity. 2013 Presidential Address. In Proceedings of the 31st International System Dynamics Society Conference, Cambridge, MA, USA, 21–25 July 2013.
3. Meadows, D.H.; Meadows, D.L.; Randers, J.; Behrens, W.W., III. *The Limits to Growth*; Universe Books: New York, NY, USA, 1972.
4. Forrester, J.W. *Urban Dynamics*; MIT Press: Cambridge, MA, USA, 1969.
5. Forrester, J.W. *World Dynamics*; Pegasus: Waltham, MA, USA, 1971.
6. Meadows, D.H.; Meadows, D.L.; Randers, J. *Beyond the Limits: Confronting Global Collapse, Envisioning a Sustainable Future*; Chelsea Green Publishing: White River Junction, VT, USA, 1992.
7. Meadows, D.H.; Meadows, D.L.; Randers, J. *Limits to Growth: The 30-Year Update*; Chelsea Green Publishing: White River Junction, VT, USA, 2004.
8. The Balaton Group. Available online: http://www.balatongroup.org (accessed on 3 June 2014).
9. Junko Edahiro Biography: About Us—Institute for Studies in Happiness, Economy and Society. Available online: http://ishes.org/en/aboutus/biography.html (accessed on 11 February 2014).
10. The Japan Times, Life, Asia's First Lady of the Environment. Available online: http://www.japantimes.co.jp/life/2008/11/26/environment/asias-first-lady-of-the-environment/#.U1zHEq2SxEN (accessed on 11 February 2014).
11. JFS. Japan for Sustainability (in English). Available online: http://www.japanfs.org (accessed on 3 June 2014).
12. Sterman, J. *Business Dynamics: Systems Thinking and Modeling for a Complex World*; Irwin McGraw Hill: Boston, MA, USA, 2000.
13. C-ROADS. Available online: http://www.climateinteractive.org/tools/c-roads/ (accessed on 3 June 2014).
14. Forrester, J.W. *Industrial Dynamics*; Pegasus: Waltham, MA, USA, 1961.
15. Richardson, J. The past is prologue: Reflections on forty-plus years of system dynamics modeling practice. *Syst. Dynam. Rev.* **2013**, *28*, 172–187. [CrossRef]
16. PechaKucha 20X20: Frequently Asked Questions. Available online: http://www.pechakucha.org/faq (accessed on 11 February 2014).

Systems **2014**, *2*, 366–378

17. Mahbubani, K. *The Great Convergence—Asia, the West and the Logic of One World*; Public Affairs: New York, NY, USA, 2013.

18. Kishore Mahbubani in Top 50 List of World Thinkers. Available online: http://news.nus.edu.sg/press-releases/7535-kishore-mahbubani-in-top-50-list-of-world-thinkers (accessed on 2 April 2014).

19. Yew, L.K. *From Third World to First: The Singapore Story: 1965-2000*; Marshall Cavendish Editions: Singapore, 2000.

20. Sun, T.S. *Goh Keng Swee: A Portrait*; Editions Didier Millet: Singapore, 2007.

21. Richardson, J.; Ong, E. The Relevance of Urban Dynamics to Singapore's Success Story: Lessons for Moving Beyond the Crisis. In Proceedings of the 28th International System Dynamics Society Conference, Seoul, Korea, 25–29 July 2010.

22. Richardson, J.; Ong, E. The improbable resilience of Singapore. *Solutions* **2012**, *5*, 63–71.

23. Fisher, D.M. Everybody thinking differently: K-12 is a leverage point. *Syst. Dynam. Rev.* **2011**, *27*, 394–411. [CrossRef]

24. Vogel, E.F. *Deng Xiaoping and the Transformation of China*; The Belknap Press of Harvard University Press: Cambridge, MA, USA, 2011.

25. Saeed, K. *Three Slices of Jay Forrester's General Theory of Economic Behaviour*; Working Paper, SPSS dept. WPI R-1; Worcester Polytechnic Institute: Worcester, MA, USA, 2013.

26. Climate Interactive: Tools for a Thriving Future. Available online: http://www.climateinteractive.org/tools/c-roads (accessed on 11 February 2014).

27. Institute for Studies in Happiness, Economy and Society. Available online: http://ishes.org/en/news/2011/inws_id000138.html (accessed on 11 February 2014).

28. Atkisson, A. *Life beyond Growth: Alternatives and Complements to GDP-Measured Growth as a Framing Concept for Social Progress*; Institute for Studies in Happiness, Economy and Society: Tokyo, Japan, 2012.

29. *Report by the Commission on the Measurement of Economic Performance and Social Progress.* (Professor Joseph E. Stiglitz, Chair). Available online: http://www.stiglitz-sen-fitoussi.fr (accessed on 8 July 2014).

30. *People and the Planet*; The Royal Society Policy Centre Report 01/12; The Royal Society: London, UK, 2012.

31. Mesarovic, M.D.; Pestel, E. *Mankind at the Turning Point*; Dutton: New York, NY, USA, 1974.

32. Meadows, D.H.; Richardson, J.; Bruckmann, G. *Groping in the Dark: The First Decade of Global Modeling*; John Wiley & Sons: Chichester, UK, 1983.

33. Homer, J.B. *Civilization as Enterprise: The Life Cycle of Cultural Production*; D-2951; System Dynamics Group, MIT: Cambridge, MA, USA, 1978.

34. Sterman, J. *The Growth of Knowledge: Testing a Theory of Scientific Revolutions with a Formal Model*; D-2909-3; System Dynamics Group, MIT: Cambridge, MA, USA, 1982.

35. Sterman, J. The Growth of Knowledge: Testing a theory of scientific revolutions with a formal model. *Technol. Forecast. Soc. Change* **1985**, *28*, 93–122. [CrossRef]

36. Sterman, J.; Wittenberg, J. Path dependence, competition and succession in the dynamics of scientific revolution. *Organ. Sci.* **1999**, *10*, 322–341. [CrossRef]

37. Kuhn, T.S. *The Structure of Scientific Revolutions*; The University of Chicago Press: Chicago, IL, USA, 1962.

MDPI AG

St. Alban-Anlage 66

4052 Basel, Switzerland

Tel. +41 61 683 77 34

Fax +41 61 302 89 18

http://www.mdpi.com

Systems Editorial Office

E-mail: systems@mdpi.com

http://www.mdpi.com/journal/systems